Guardians
of the Flutes

Guardians of the Flutes

IDIOMS OF MASCULINITY

Gilbert H. Herdt

NEW YORK   COLUMBIA UNIVERSITY PRESS

Columbia University Press Morningside Edition   1987
Columbia University Press
New York   Guildford, Surrey

Library of Congress Cataloging-in-Publication Data

Herdt, Gilbert H., 1949–
Guardians of the flutes.

Reprint. Originally published: New York : McGraw-Hill, 1981.
Bibliography: p.
Includes index.
1. Sambia (Papua New Guinea people)   2. Sambia
(Papua New Guinea people)—Sexual behavior.
3. Initiation rites—Papua New Guinea.   4. Homosexuality,
Male—Papua New Guinea.   5. Masculinity (Psychology)—
Papua New Guinea.   I. Title.
[DU740.42.H44 1987]   392'.14'09953   87-13244
ISBN 0-231-06631-7 (pbk)

This edition by arrangement with McGraw-Hill Book Company.

To Ted, Jesse, Cindy, and Thom

Contents

A Note on Language

There are no written materials available for the Sambia language. I have thus tended to follow the conventions adopted by Lloyd (1973) in his representations of the related Anga languages, employing conventionalized English spellings of Sambia words. The following values, then, apply to the text:

a	as	*a*	in	*father*
aa	as	*a*	in	*cat*
ai	as	*i*	in	*kite*
au	as	*ou*	in	*out*
e	as	*i*	in	*hit*
er	as	*ur*	in	*curb*
ei	as	*ei*	in	*veil*
i	as	*ee*	in	*seen*
o	as	*o*	in	*for*
oo	as	*oo*	in	*roof*
u	as	*u*	in	*sun*
j	as	*g*	in	*germ*
sh	as	*sh*	in	*shine*
ch	as	*ch*	in	*church*

but

Glottal stops are usually indicated by ' and tones are not rendered.

Foreword

Once in a great while, a study of one society profoundly challenges existing conceptions of human development and forces a reevaluation of basic assumptions concerning the range of normality for all humans. One thinks of Margaret Mead's *Coming of Age in Samoa* (1928) and the Kinsey reports (1948, 1953) as examples of research conducted in a single cultural setting that compelled revision of generalizations about adolescence and sexual development for the species as a whole. *Guardians of the Flutes* is such a study. In it, Gilbert Herdt reports on the customs of the Sambia people in the Highlands of New Guinea, but the implications for theories of sexual development and gender identity pertain to all humanity. For psychoanalytic and psychosocial theories, the evidence presented herein is of central significance. No future discussion of gender identity and its development as a human phenomenon will be able to ignore the contents of this book.

Dr. Herdt shows us a people who believe that the oral insemination of boys is necessary for them to grow into men, and he describes the cultural beliefs and rituals that encourage homosexual practices for all men before marriage. The ethnographic evidence, based on intensive and prolonged fieldwork, is rich and detailed. It contains no real surprises for those familiar with the anthropological literature on New Guinea, but Dr. Herdt is the first to conduct fieldwork among a people who had not yet abandoned these indigenous practices. The intact patterns of culture and experience he describes are not anticipated by current developmental models of sexuality and gender. Indeed, from a Western perspective it may seem almost unimaginable that any society would risk universal homosexuality among young males without endangering its survival. The fact that the Sambia do so and have created a symbolic environment in which it seems natural, normal, and necessary is convincingly demonstrated in this book. This fact poses a fundamental challenge to developmental theories of gender identity, which will have to be rewritten to encompass it.

It may surprise some readers that novel anthropological data are still coming in from other parts of the world. Hasn't cultural variation shrunk while our sophistication about it has expanded? The answers are instructive. First, the advance notices on the cultural homogenization of the world were grossly exaggerated. While it is both true and tragic that many hunting and gathering peoples have been exterminated or are currently threatened, this fact does not mean that the rest of the world is a melting pot. On the contrary, despite a superficial homogeneity imposed by bureaucracies and consumer goods, the larger and more isolated non-Western populations are proving to be more resilient in their cultural adaptations and more resistant to simple Westernization than had been imagined. Second, sophistication about cultural variation is still not widespread in developmental psychology or psychoanalysis, and one reason is that there have been few anthropological studies in these areas thorough enough to compel theoretical attention and explanation. This is particularly true of sexual behavior, on which anthropological documentation is thin and growing at a slow pace. Psychobiological investigators of sexual behavior and development will not take ethnographic reports seriously if they are superficial and impressionistic.

New Guinea is a case in point. As Dr. Herdt points out, homosexual practices in New Guinea rituals of manhood have been reported for more than half a century; they were offered by Ruth Benedict as illustrations of "discontinuity in cultural conditioning" in a well-known article published in 1938. Without the detailed documentation that Dr. Herdt has finally achieved, however, the problem posed by New Guinea ethnography to developmental psychology and psychiatry has not been seriously confronted. His book marks the beginning of a scientific confrontation that is long overdue.

Dr. Herdt devotes a great deal of this book to explicating the cultural terms in which the Sambia conceptualize and experience masculinity and femininity, the development of children and adolescents, and sexual behavior and relationships. He examines the symbols by which these categories and processes are represented in folklore and ritual. His analysis is cultural, but he also pursues the psychological significance of the symbols. As someone who has never visited New Guinea but has long been interested in antagonism between males and females reported from the New Guinea Highlands, I found Dr. Herdt's account clarifying and empathic.

Unlike many of his colleagues in social anthropology, Dr. Herdt is not content to place customs in their ecological, organizational, and ideological contexts without exploring what they mean to the individuals who practice them. His goal is to understand the subjective experience of Sambia men, and to that end he focuses on their verbal reports of that experience in the most salient contexts of their lives. This is what I call "person-centered ethnography": though psychological in aim, it begins with the premise that better ethnographic description of customs, as they are used and experienced by individuals, is prerequisite to an understanding of their unconscious significance. This book shows how much psychosocial understanding is made possible by this kind of ethnography. It gives us a vivid and convincing portrait of how Sambia men experience their sexual development and reveals the meanings with which they endow the rituals, relationships, and natural objects in their environment. Without heavy-handed Freudian interpretation, Dr. Herdt has permitted his material to describe much that is directly relevant to psychoanalytic theory.

Theories of gender identity and male initiation ceremonies are comprehensively reviewed in the concluding chapter, but Dr. Herdt does not claim to have arrived at a final theoretical interpretation of the Sambia material. On the contrary, committed to empirical research, he promises further studies focused on individual cases and developmental observations. But with this book he has thrown a great deal of light on an area of darkness and has confronted the study of personality development with an important anthropological problem.

ROBERT A. LeVINE

Roy E. Larsen Professor
of Education and Human Development
Chairman, Laboratory of Human
Development, Reading, and Counseling

Harvard University

References

Benedict, R. 1938. Continuities and discontinuities in cultural conditioning. *Psychiatry* 1:161–167.

Kinsey, A. C., W. B. Pomeroy, and C. E. Martin. 1948. *Sexual Behavior in the Human Male.* Philadelphia: Saunders.

Kinsey, A. C., W. B. Pomeroy, E. W. Martin, and P. H. Gebhard. 1953. *Sexual Behavior in the Human Female.* Philadelphia: Saunders.

Mead, M. 1928. *Coming of Age in Samoa.* New York: Morrow.

Preface to the
Morningside Edition

Sometimes life holds out to us the opportunity to encounter something radically new, an alternative reality. We are grateful for this. Yet such encounters exact a cost: a challenge to conventional wisdom, a sacrifice of perceptions dear to the self, and the uneasiness of constructing new models with which to chart an unknown frontier. In the anthropological experience, this encounter with an alternative reality, with the "Other" (as it is being called in some circles), is the source of new claims for change not only in ourselves but in our science and culture too. It is thus an enterprise in which a good deal is at stake. So we can scarcely help but doubt ourselves in the process and question the validity of finding in the strange something familiar enough for others to understand. We must, however, render due respect to how doubt tempers insight here; for in anthropology we are so terribly dependent upon the written word to interpret our experiences in another world, with all of its conscious and unconscious meanings and hidden texts; for as Freud once quipped, the lion springs once and once only. We sense that we cannot know enough to complete the interpretation and fear even more that what is missing can never be known. This same delicate struggle is present in my own encounter with the Sambia of Papua New Guinea as constructed in *Guardians of the Flutes,* wherein it is frozen in time.

For all of these reasons it is a pleasure to see *Guardians* republished. It is gratifying because this was my first book; it conveyed my account of, and affection for, the Sambia and remains the foundation of my work on culture and sexuality. It was also my first effort to show that cultural conventions cannot be studied apart from the individuals who experience them, a point which emphasizes the extraordinary interdependence of culture and subjective experience, a theme so much at the forefront of new work in interpretive social science.

At the same time it is a temptation to revise the book in the light of subsequent work and theoretical shifts in anthropology and gender studies, a temptation I have declined. Moreover, there have been critics of *Guardians,* as well as those who have applauded it. Since the book was drafted in 1978, my additional fieldwork among the Sambia, in 1979, 1981, 1983, and 1985, has added much new material to our understanding of them and, more broadly, their place in the human record (Herdt ed. 1982, 1984, 1987). This subsequent research has, however, confirmed my feeling that the interpretations in *Guardians* are robust, so that the later work has rounded out and filled in missing pieces, rather than overturned the earlier findings. For example, in the book I could only guess that the Sambian pattern of ritualized homosexual behavior between younger and older males was more pervasive elsewhere than we might have thought, because no systematic work had been done on the problem. We now know that such ritualized homosexuality occurs in at least 30 different societies of Melanesia, or between 10 and 20 percent of all of its groups (Herdt 1984), and that variants of the same sexual pattern occur in many places around the world (Adam 1986). The meaning of this psychocultural practice cannot be divorced from the behavioral environment of warfare and sexual antagonism (Herdt and Poole 1983) or the development of gender identity at large (Stoller and Herdt 1982). There has also been an acceleration of scholarship on Melanesia and gender as instanced by the outstanding work of Michael Allen, Anna Meigs, Shirley Lindenbaum, Fitz John Poole, Marilyn Strathern, and Donald Tuzin, among others. *Guardians* incorporates many of these theoretical issues and it has served to make accessible to readers from many fields the anthropology of ritual, gender, and Melanesia.

Another powerful reason for not revising the book has to do with the kind of interpretative study it represents. What I did and did not know about the Sambia in my first fieldwork (1974–1976) was, as I said, problematical in relation to the object of the work—the men's secret society and its most secret myth as reflected in "the characteristic things men have in mind when doing ritual" (Herdt 1981:4). *Guardians* examines the surface of Sambia masculine life—the things that men do and say, feel and think—to uncover signs for understanding the deeper meanings of their great institutions, ritual and myth. The book takes as its essential text the men's most sacred myth of male parthenogenesis, which tells how all humans emerged from the androgynous bodies of pseudohermaphroditic ancestors. The myth is more than a "just-so" story. Why should men who so pride themselves on their superiority to women, whom they deride, see reflected in themselves ambiguity and residues of femaleness? The answer to the question is found in the signs of men's idioms, personal meanings, and cultural symbols. These reflect in turn upon the place of cultural practices in masculine development across the lifespan. It is concern with this deeper reality that lends itself to an interpretation of the Sambian world as one containing a dialectical relationship between what is visible and hidden, especially the inner strivings of male gender identity.

Guardians of the Flutes is, as much as anything, an exploration into what Malinowski called the "imponderabilia" of actual life, as linked to the traditions of the men's secret society and its material conditions. This is maddeningly difficult to capture in a written text, because, as Susan Sontag (1982:106) has said, "The sensibility of an era is not only its most decisive but also its most perishable aspect." These are the aesthetics which are often left out or even removed from the ethnographic account. And yet, Sontag continues, "We may capture the ideas (intellectual history) and the behavior (social history) of an epoch without ever touching upon the taste which informed those ideas, that behavior." Clifford Geertz (1983:75) has reminded us, however, that these sensibilities—common sense—"affirm that its tenets are immediate deliverances of experience, not deliberated reflections upon it." We falter at this thought. How much do cultural practices reflect personal sensibilities and how much do they deliver Sambia from their experience? The ambiguity of symbolic androgyny provides a clue here. If Stoller (1985:33) is even half right about the aesthetics of excitement, which concern us if we are to understand the men's experience of myth-telling in chapter 9, then we can understand why the secret myth must "take knowledge and render it uncertain, ambiguous," because it is out of the safeties and dangers of this mythological structure of experience that Sambia generate the ritual excitement that supports normative male gender behavior.

Kenneth Read (1986:131), the phenomenal pioneer in Highlands New Guinea anthropology, whose remarkable reports made it known to a generation of readers, has recently said that he found his informants not noticeably introspective: "They were like swimmers who remain among the flurry and the foam of breaking waves, seldom returning out beyond them to the deep waters from where you look back upon the inshore agitation" (1986:75). Sambia are not entirely accounted for in this image, as you will see. Individuals among them brave into deeper waters of reflection. Seldom, however, do they remain there very long; the sociocentric "pull" of their face-to-face world is too powerful to sustain them very long in solitary reflection. This is not surprising—much of their adult lives anticipated the action of battle, not the ruminations of philosophy. I found in Sambia originally, however, and I still find at present, an immense capacity to see around the edges of their cultural practices, a result of their being ever curious to understand how the people next door, or those in the neighboring valley, or even those unseen from my own world have handled the problems of life. And then there is their system of secrecy, which is generated from internal contradictions within their society and in the male's development, that creates subtle awareness of the difference between stories for public consumption and jealously guarded ritual secrets, between the truth and falsehoods of rhetoric, between the way the world might have been without secrecy and the way that it must be to support the power structure of their society. Gender hierarchy and controversies of sexual antagonism were forever wedded to these machinations of reflection and rationalization, which found in warfare the bedrock material reality upon which they were all constructed.

Sambia society has undergone striking social change since my first field work in 1974. Then there were no roads or airstrips. Now one can fly into the valley and see a tiny and rustic but nonetheless firm outpost of a larger world to which Sambia are more directly connected. The first local school for elementary grades was opened in 1985 and I was asked to make a speech before the crowd assembled from the villages. My amazement in witnessing the scene, with its politicians flown in to greet local folks, throngs of males dressed in traditional initiation attire, and refreshment stands and loud speakers blasting directions to the crowd in the Sambian tongue, made me not speechless but uncertain of what I could possibly say to them, beyond offering my congratulations for achieving their long-sought school and reminding them that things had changed quickly and that it would do well to hear the elders remind us of our origins. No more than the usual anthropological adage that the old and the new are of a piece. And one elder did muster himself to the task, though he seemed small and somehow out of place. Almost lost. Yes, the Sambia have changed.

Yet less than a month before this happy staged event, representative of a new civilization, the Sambia had performed still another ritual cycle, much as before. Initiates were taken into the men's house. The main rites were performed, albeit truncated and with less grandeur than in olden days. *Plus ça change, plus c'est la même chose.* But how long their ritual cult will remain is uncertain. In adopting new social forms they have not simply traded in the old. Warfare is gone and Sambia are glad of it, for it made them ever vigilant and aggressive, and uneasy of being attacked, which exacted a great psychological cost from them. And verily, as I had suggested in *Guardians* years ago, sexual antagonism—the distance between men and women—has diminished but not disappeared. The technological changes have not wrought havoc; they have improved life in many blessed ways. Still, the old tensions of work and love under the hegemony of the men's secret society have not entirely disappeared, nor can we expect that the new era will be entirely free of its own dissatisfactions, for these, in the form of certain violences and petty thefts of a kind never before seen, are now evident. Here the problem of life is no different for Sambia than for ourselves: How shall we build "a culture that will ever better justify the price of uneasiness which we pay for the advantages it confers on us" (Bettelheim 1984:110)? This is an anthropological and, more, a human problem that is the most far-reaching point of *Guardians of the Flutes*.

GILBERT HERDT
April 1987

References for the Morningside Preface

Adam, Barry D. 1986. "Age, structure, and sexuality: Reflections on the anthropological evidence on homosexual relations," in *Anthropology and Homosexual Behavior*. Edited by E. Blackwood, pp. 19–34. New York: Haworth Press.

Bettelheim, Bruno. 1984. *Freud and Man's Soul*. New York: Vintage Books.

Geertz, Clifford. 1983. *Local Knowledge*. New York: Basic Books.

Herdt, Gilbert. 1984. "Ritualized homosexual behavior in the male cults of Melanesia, 1862–1983: An introduction," in G. Herdt, *Ritualized Homosexuality in Melanesia*, pp. 1–82.

——. 1987. *The Sambia: Ritual and Gender in New Guinea*. New York: Holt, Rinehart and Winston.

Herdt, Gilbert and Fitz John P. Poole. 1982. "Sexual Antagonism: The Intellectual History of a Concept in the Anthropology of New Guinea," in F. J. P. Poole and G. Herdt, eds., *Sexual Antagonism, Gender, and Social Change in Papua New Guinea, Social Analysis* (Special Issue), no. 12, pp. 3–28.

Herdt, Gilbert. Editor. 1982. *Rituals of Manhood: Male Initiation in Papua New Guinea*. Berkeley: University of California Press.

——. 1984. *Ritualized Homosexuality in Melanesia*. Berkeley: University of California Press.

Read, Kenneth E. 1986. *Return to the High Valley*. Berkeley: University of California Press.

Sontag, Susan. 1982. *A Susan Sontag Reader*. New York: Penguin Books.

Stoller, Robert J. 1985. *Observing the Erotic Imagination*. New Haven: Yale University Press.

Stoller, Robert J. and Gilbert Herdt. 1982. "The development of masculinity: a cross-cultural contribution," *Journal of the American Psychoanalytic Association* 30:29–59.

Introduction

> We know that Numboolyu's [fictitious ancestor] penis
> was sucked by his age-mate who himself became
> pregnant. His fellator's breasts swelled; he changed into a
> woman. This "woman" then gave birth—but only after
> Numboolyu created her vulva by slitting open the
> pregnant pubic area. A girl was the firstborn, and so now,
> girls grow faster than boys. . . . A boy must be initiated
> and [orally] inseminated, otherwise the girl betrothed to
> him will outgrow him and run away to another man.
> . . . If a boy doesn't "eat" semen, he remains small and
> weak.
>
> —TALI, a Sambia ritual expert

Why should a secret society of manly warriors believe that a boy must be orally inseminated to become masculine? What happens when this conviction is implemented through prolonged ritualized homosexuality? It is with the origins of this male developmental cycle that I will be concerned; with its behavioral manifestations that constantly polarize masculinity and femininity in idioms and myth; and with exploring ways in which we can set about studying that gender symbolism.

This book is my first step toward understanding these problems in the culture, behavior, and thought of Sambia. Here I have an immediate goal: to describe men's verbal knowledge, sayings, and a special myth of male parthenogenesis. This is thus an ethnographic study of a masculine subculture: how men view themselves as male persons, their ritual traditions, their females, and the cosmos, a small and still isolated corner of the great

Eastern Highlands. By its anthropological focus this study is, therefore, more than an account of the sexual ideology of a New Guinea people. So we cannot avoid drawing on comparative data or the anthropological theories sparked by them among Melanesianists,[1] as well as assessing the practice of ethnography—what anthropologists do in collecting data, and why we do it.

Moreover, my eventual aim has a trajectory extending beyond the choice of this narrower focus on oral traditions into a wider investigation. This I think of as the *behavioral* study of the Sambia initiatory cult. In this work, that begins with the description of verbal behavior, idioms pertaining to the maleness and femaleness of things, whose outlook finds its way into ritual and secular speech alike. In later works this approach will thus incorporate observations of organization and the institution of the male cult and its various ritual behaviors; plus the corresponding subjectivity through which that cult is also experienced by individuals; and lastly its psychodynamic aspects in masculine character structure. These complementary dimensions anticipate a broader study: namely, the origins of erotic excitement and the development of masculinity and femininity among Sambia.

Why should an anthropologist select this focus on sex and gender? What warrants this interest when so many other aspects of a ritual cult want attention? The reasons follow from the form of Sambia gender identity formation, a pattern that raises a number of problems for all the behavioral sciences.

My anthropological task is this: to explain a puzzling pattern of culturally constituted development in which Sambia heterosexual manhood emerges only after years of normatively prescribed and prolonged homosexual activities.

This is, by the conventions of Western society, a perplexing outcome. Seven-to-ten-year-old Sambia boys are taken from their mothers when first initiated into the male cult, and thereafter experience the most powerful and seductive homosexual fellatio activities. For some ten to fifteen years, they engage in these practices on a daily basis, first as fellator, and then as fellated. Elders teach that semen is absolutely vital: it should be consumed daily since the creation of biological maleness and the maintenance of masculinity depend on it. Hence, from middle childhood until puberty, boys should perform fellatio on older youths.

Near puberty the same initiates become dominant youths. Ritual helps remake their social and erotic identity, the bachelors becoming the fellated partners for a new crop of ritual novices. And at the same time, youths

---

1. Melanesia is a geographic area embracing Papua New Guinea, Irian Jaya, and their offshore islands, including the Solomon Islands, New Hebrides, New Caledonia, and many more.

and boys alike must absolutely avoid women, on pain of punishment. For not only must secret homoeroticism be hidden from women but females are also believed to be contaminating—their menstrual blood polluting, and worse, lethal. This dual pattern—prescribed homosexual activities and avoidance of women—persists until marriage. So all heterosexual relationships, intrigues, and even casual conversations among boys and girls are blocked, and forbidden.

Whereas homosexual practices begin with initiation, they become far more than a ceremony. All boys are forcibly initiated. They scarcely have choice. For long afterwards, ritualized homosexuality becomes the center of their existence. Born from the deepest trauma of maternal separation and ritual threats, homosexual fellatio is dangerous and enticing, powerful and cruel. And from such experiences is born a boy's sense of masculinity. Masculinity is thus a product of a regime of ritualized homosexuality leading into manhood.

Such findings are unsettling to Western theories of masculine development. Even so, what has this practice to do with the meaning of masculinity among Westerners? Just this: Although homosexual practices emerge from ritual trauma, abundant evidence indicates that most youths also experience them as pleasurable and erotically exciting. Yet, in spite of this formidable background, the final outcome is exclusive heterosexuality—of a particular form. Youths eventually become sexually attracted to women. At marriage (c. sixteen to twenty-five years of age), they may even act as true bisexuals, for a time. With fatherhood, however, homosexuality should cease; thereafter men should engage only in heterosexual activities. Soon enough, the cycle starts over as men steer their young sons, too, along the traditional way into the cult. My research has shown, furthermore, that nearly all men actually conform to this erotic pattern.

In short, Sambia boys undergo profound social conditioning through early, exciting homosexual experiences that continue for years. Yet they emerge as competent, exclusively heterosexual adults, not homosexuals.[2] Contrary to Western belief, transitional homoeroticism is the royal road to Sambia manliness.

---

2. It is crucial that we distinguish from the start between homosexual *identity* and *behavior*. All Sambia males undergo the experience of ritually introduced, secret, socially sanctioned homosexual behaviors of only one sort—fellatio: oral sex, stimulating the (fellated's) penis with the (fellator's) mouth, usually leading to the older male's ejaculating into the younger male's mouth. Strict rules govern this erotic relationship: younger initiates may act only as fellators, and the opposite almost never (in three cases out of a hundred reported) occurs: older males cannot suck younger boys, and they evince no interest in doing so. (The reasons for this rigid dichotomy are described later.) I thus describe these activities as ritualized homosexual behaviors, or fellatio activities, and do not use the loaded term pederasty (see Rossman 1973), which implies sodomy, or anal intercourse (see Pierson and D'Antonio 1974:83), an erotic act that Sambia do not engage in. (Note also that, within homosexual

We shall be concerned with the meaning of this ritualized erotic pattern, and with the various ways the cult influences the growth of masculine conduct. And, behind that, we shall examine the cult's growing impact on male identity: boys' subjective sense of themselves and what that means for their capacity to be erotically excited by both women and boys. In this and subsequent volumes I hope to examine piecemeal the details of this pattern and its context in the lives of some individuals.

Obviously I cannot take up all these problems here. In this book I wish, rather, to provide essential information about the cultural background of male initiation. Not the rituals themselves but why men feel they must be performed. This purpose means considering the characteristic things men have in mind when they set out to organize their collective rites every three or four years. Men's guiding fiction of the virile warrior plays a big part in this organization, as we shall see. So does their more extravagant myth of men begetting humanity. These are powerful political weapons. Hence, although this book is primarily concerned with male ideology, we will touch on the process through which ritual idioms are projected into interpersonal behavior; the relationship of beliefs, sayings, and myth to men's personal scripts; and the capacity of these cultural factors to influence ordinary perception and social behavior. To show the need of a behavioral approach in tackling them I had best make clear my research stance.

Anthropology has long held a place among the behavioral sciences for its studies of ritual symbolism in tribal societies. Its achievements are many. Yet we have proceeded as if it were possible to understand the processes and content of symbolic behavior while staying removed from the study of individual experience. This has led field-workers systematically to exclude events—the informational contents of mind and behavior—from their accounts. Our approach has thus limited the range of data we have collected and thereby colored our interpretations of it.

Since Durkheim (1965), anthropologists have known of the tremendous influence that society (social institutions, relationships, and values)

---

relationships, there is no transvestitism or fetishistic cross-dressing, and I have never observed any.) Fellatio activities are institutionalized and transitional, then, for 95 percent or more of the male population. At either end of the behavioral distribution of individuals, however, there are a very small number of deviants: a few who are known to have had a low interest in homosexual activities and who are extremely heterosexual; and a few who have a high interest in homosexual fellatio, persisting in its practice past the appropriate transitional period. These persons are ignored in the following report; I consider them elsewhere. These relationships thus do not make Sambia into homosexuals (which is a statement about one's sense of self: see Stoller 1977:205) in our meaning of that term: Sambia do not think of themselves as attracted only to males during the stage of homosexual activity; they are also excited by women's bodies; and in most cases, men leave behind homosexual behavior following marriage. Throughout the text I have tried to adhere to these distinctions.

has on the particular forms of ritual behavior in tribal societies. It was Durkheim who shaped modern sociology by teaching us how individual action results from social constraints. His contemporary, Freud, argued for a parallel influence of unconscious forces on individual behavior. For reasons still sadly present in the intellectual history of the behavioral sciences, these two approaches came to be opposed, not complementary. Unfortunately, this antithesis of individual and society affected anthropology, too, and it still pervades our research. (For a discussion of these problems, see Appendix A.[3]) What mainly interests me is how anthropologists have generally come to view traditions of ritual symbolism apart from the individuals who embody them. There is no doubt that traditions constrain individuals; the problem is our lack of interest in describing their effects on individual subjectivity and behavior with the result that we have bypassed the effects of personal experience on tradition.

The Durkheimian model was defensible in its own day. Anthropology and the other behavioral sciences were still struggling infants. The concept of culture was only beginning to come into its own as a "good thing" (Sapir 1949:401) in itself. The early anthropologists were intensely aware of battling against simple-minded evolutionism, racist bigotry, and psychobiological reductionism (see Freeman 1970; Harris 1968; Mead 1962; Stocking 1968). Modern ethnography was only emerging as a scientific form of research whereas before it lacked a theoretical discipline. Durkheim (1965) and Freud (1955a) alike drew from the meager ethnographic reports of the times, and rather uncritically at that (see Evans-Pritchard 1962:176); there was little attempt to distinguish bad reports from good, even in old-fashioned ethnographic writings where a knowledgeable missionary who lived among tribesmen simply recorded his impressions of things. Malinowski, who, during the same period, was still conducting his New Guinea research on the Trobriand Islands, almost single-handedly changed this state of affairs (see Evans-Pritchard 1965:9). Malinowski (1922) was followed by Evans-Pritchard (1937), Firth (1967), Radcliffe-Brown (1922), Richards (1956), Turner (1957, 1962, 1967, 1968a), and Wilson (1957), to name but a few workers who helped pioneer the study of ritual symbolism.

A delimited sociological paradigm is no longer warranted today. The earlier studies were absolutely essential in the circumscription of a field of problems; their contribution was substantial in building theory; their

3. For this reason, and because most studies of tribal initiation in Africa, Australia, and Melanesia have been conducted by social anthropologists (see Allen 1967; Evans-Pritchard 1965; Skorupski 1976; Turner 1975), my comments will mainly concern that theoretical school.

perspectives also helped lessen the unenviable complexities of studying symbolic behavior; and all research, of course, must adhere to conventions of disciplinary interest. These earlier studies were thereby restricted, in scope and selection of data, to mainly sociological considerations. The result has been, nonetheless, a virtual omission of attention to cultural and psychological factors in the study of male cults and ritual symbolism, particularly in New Guinea (Langness 1976:102ff.). We now need an expanded paradigm for research that encompasses subjective meanings, and one that can enrich the sociocultural studies already in hand.

Anthropology can thus no longer afford to turn its back on the psychological dimension of cultural symbolism. As earlier writers recognized long ago (see Bateson 1958; Hallowell 1967; Mead 1962; Sapir 1949: 569–577), there are sound reasons for exploring that phenomenon in building a better theory of culture. A generation ago social anthropology may have gotten some mileage from its complete rejection of psychological variables, models, and theories. That situation has changed, as noted in the writings of those, such as LeVine (1973:251ff.), who emphasize the subjective meanings of cultural symbols for individuals within societies (see also Beidelman 1964, 1966a, 1966b; Crapanzano 1973; Geertz 1966a; Keesing 1976; Langness 1976:102ff.; Munn 1973:216; Sperber 1975; Spiro 1964, 1966, 1969; Tuzin 1972, 1977). Now, it is less productive to claim that such research problems are beyond our competence (Turner 1964). The increasing integration of the behavioral sciences better favors a creative enterprise and verifiable observations and results, irrespective of the feeble boundaries that are more a product of academic history than of scientific progress (Becker 1971). Durkheim, Freud, and our predecessors knew little of human paleontology, genetics, or neuroscience. They had no recourse to experimental animal studies or field studies of higher primates; and what we know of human phylogeny and its behavioral concomitants in childhood cognitive development, and of consciousness and identity, would have astounded them. Some of those elements, along with culture and institutions, we might consider as elements in an overall system of cybernetic feedback (Bateson 1972). This has subsequently led some workers to consider the relationship between ritual symbols and their meaning for individual identity as undertaken here (Cohen 1964a, 1964b; Newman 1964; Murphy 1959; Poole 1980; Tuzin 1980). And Turner (1978), a leader in the field, has also come to consider this perspective. Even so, our methodology still remains tied to the older paradigm.

Our present methodological stance is mainly an outmoded product of Durkheim's writing. It commands us to concentrate on the normative patterns of ritual action, i.e., as custom or institutionalized social relationships. Or it impels us to attend to its "symbolic structure," its normative pattern of expressive "symbols," "contexts," and "categories" (with wide disagreement about the definition of these concepts). By this approach we avoid the actual observations of ritual (or secular) behavior. Moreover, the scope of investigation is given a deceptively wide latitude—the entire social universe filtered through the ethnographer's mind.

Here I must confess some skepticism. Unlike experimental biology or physics, anthropology is fond of studying great human events among the people of a tribe; controls, experimental conditions, or sample procedures are virtually impossible to implement, nor would it be ethical to implement them. But the social anthropological approach, more in the terms of Radcliffe-Brown (1952) than of Malinowski (1922, 1929), is still based on the perspectives of philosophical positivism in studying a complex phenomenon like a ritual cult. Our research stance is, I think, among the less useful of several alternative methodological orientations available to us and better suited to our endeavors.

The Durkheimian imperative, if accepted at face value, would require the ethnographer somehow to survey and take into account the sweep of social action and collective symbolization for all segments of a populace. Rarely, if ever, is this monumental goal actually attempted or attained. To name but one example: the normative action of women has largely been omitted, and their ideological positions have been conveyed through the eyes of men (see E. Ardener 1975). At the very least, this oversight resulted in the neglect of investigations concerning the existence of countervailing mythological and symbolic systems (male or female) in reference to ritual. This omission is, however, an expectable artifact of a nonbehavioral approach that postulates sociocultural tradition as a phenomenon removed from the individuals who embody it.

Only a normative bias could accommodate the philosophical position that we study Durkheim's postulated society *sui generis* on its own global terms. A single ethnographer cannot study everything, and yet many students are still expected to provide a detailed, objective, and potentially replicable description of an entire social universe. This descriptive aim is manageable, however, because workers are seldom required to demonstrate the observations from which the custom or culture of ritual is presumably abstracted. The Durkheimian doctrines of social solidarity and experiential unity (see below) made this demonstration, after all, unnecessary. Obviously if the speech and action, beliefs and motives of a whole society of individuals are alike, the observer can safely ignore the nuances of what is done, said, or thought. This affords an ethnographer the luxury of lumping together casual observations of individual behavior with abstracted summaries of group expressions and activities. In short, one worker succeeds where an army would fail since he or she can remain aloof from the messy business of citing actual behavior.

But by so doing we must admit of sacrificing science for art and the anthropologist's subjectivity for that of the natives. Seldom in modern studies, for instance, are readers ever forced to consider how an ethnographer's assessments of ritual meaning and behavior approximate those of individual natives. Yet I believe that this problem is fundamental to the study of meaning in any human science: without available observations (or statements about the conditions under which they were made) we cannot confirm or falsify the adequacy of a symbolic interpretation (see Taylor 1971; Harré and Secord 1972). Our studies have therefore fostered a bias that has resulted in three serious shortcomings. First, we know practically nothing of the general psychological processes involved in ritual symbolism. Second, we have neglected a study of developmental behavior and subjectivity in favor of typology or classification, with the result that our models are needlessly static. Third, the Durkheimian approach has failed to stimulate the creation of a cross-cultural theory of symbolism, something urgently needed by ethnography and anthropology alike, and a task our discipline is uniquely qualified to undertake. All these interests and problems will concern us, for the Sambia ritual cult involves all of them. This leads to the present problem of my perspective in studying the meaning of Sambia ritualized homoerotic development.

The Sambia developmental pattern obviously confounds a strictly biological or learning theory explanation of homosexual behavior. On the one hand, there are the genetic determinists who hold that innate biological dispositions precipitate adult homosexuality (see Diamond 1968; Kallmar 1952; Kolodny et al. 1971). At the other end of the theoretical spectrum are the behaviorists who draw on social learning theory and its experimental settings. These writers (Bandura and Walters 1963; Money and Ehrhardt 1972:227–235; Sears et al. 1957) suggest that only the rewards and punishments of critical learning experiences create or sustain sexual excitement and behavior. Neither of these viewpoints is entirely adequate to account for the phenomenon of ritualized homosexuality among Sambia (and other Melanesian tribes: see Chapter 9). All Sambia males experience extraordinary and prolonged homosexual activities, but they still become exclusively heterosexual. There are, however, two alternative approaches to the problem, and they both entail methodologies different from those mentioned above.

Between behaviorist and biologizer stand two old antagonists—anthropology and psychoanalysis.[4] Despite their differences they share an

---

4. Psychoanalysis has its roots in the writings of Freud just as anthropology is historically derived from Malinowski, Boas, and Radcliffe-Brown. Our ancestors, however, knew far less

insider's interest in the complex alchemy of human meaning. I say antagonists, since Turner's (1964:51) friendly poke at the analyst, for example, reveals the kinder side of a long-standing tension in the relationship between the two disciplines. Born of the same intellectual period, with concern for human existence and not just fragments of it, the two fields have nonetheless distinct histories, training grounds, and, presumably, contrary data, methods, and theories. They are antagonists because of approach: the analyst spends years with a single troubled person, attempting to recapture the meanings of past experience through the exigencies of present words, acts, and associations. All this work occurs confidentially, and trustingly, behind closed doors. By contrast, of course, the anthropologist belongs to what Turner called the "light of social day": a tribal society or culture is our ostensible quest. So the ethnographer belongs to palm-shrouded villages, or the crowds of a ceremonial feast or marketplace. These comfortable stereotypes no doubt contain much truth. Yet they also belie a fundamental premise that unites anthropologist and psychoanalyst. Both share the conviction that each is more than simply a tourist in the lives of those with whom they work (see Lévi-Strauss 1969: 54–64).

This is the key difference that separates us from the biologist or behaviorist. Unlike them we possess no experimental laboratories under controlled conditions. And we disdain as "superficial" the feckless questionnaires of the sociologist. Like the analyst, then, we claim access to privileged knowledge: the intimate workings of peoples' "genuine," that is, "true," naturalistic thoughts, actions, and meanings. But even though our observations derive from a human investigator and interpersonal communications, we largely ignore these powerful conditions in assessing ethnographic information. This is not, therefore, science as it pertains to our phenomena (Colby 1978; Harré and Secord 1972; LeVine 1973: 43–59, 185–202; Popper and Eccles 1977). For science requires objective observations for which we are, as researchers, accountable. It also wants a statement of the conditions under which the observations were collected and detailed instances to assess the generality of results. Our studies of ritual symbolism are far removed from this enviable position (LeVine 1973:249ff.). But they are attainable if we better define the scope of our observations and shift methodology to accommodate them.

In other words, our methods quite simply require the field-worker to attend to everything "objectively," as if he or she were a microscope

---

than we do today; and, I think this is true of modern psychoanalysis and psychiatry too. I am not referring, then, to the theory-laden writings of a Roheim (1974), but have in mind, for example, the clinical ethnography of a Stoller (1973).

through which a strain of bacteria is made visible. Our individual personalities and motives count as nothing in the research. By remaining "objective" observers we simply "absorb" the impressions of our senses, as if they were sterile staining materials; our reports are thus held up as the undistorted results. Never mind that we may filter observations by way of human error, inadequate understanding, personal projection, or theoretical bias. This leads to the unsurprising Durkheimian viewpoint: an observer, any observer, simply by watching a ritual, is able to infer the shared norms and meanings of its participants (Leach 1964b:14–15). Likewise, the readers of such reports can seldom glimpse the individuals whose realities and behavior bring a ritual into being. This approach is possible only because, as Leach (1961:297) concedes:

> The ethnographer is content to record "custom," that is to say the facts which are generally true of society in a broad sense; the individual appears only as a stereotype, a creature who conforms to custom unthinkingly and without motive. In contrast, the social anthropologist stresses that custom is synthetic and quite distinct from the behavior of individuals.

Nowhere as in the study of symbolism and powerful emotive ritual could this anachronistic methodology be more harmful. The feelings and precise flow of utterances and acts slip through our waiting fingertips when we take this stance. Coming generations may lament that our contemporary anthropology gave us grand and clever reports of exotic (and extinct) human events but never bothered to understand their meanings in the behavior of individuals. How else are we to know what is anthropological fiction or fact in deciphering the sensuous surface of ritual and meaning in tribal societies?

Lévi-Strauss (1968:351) anticipated this problem by asking: "What is really truth in anthropology? What is proved?" He countered himself by questioning principally our own awareness of ourselves in the data.

> When we are told that fifty-year-old facts (which cannot be re-studied) are not exactly like those observed by the present-day observer, we are led to wonder whether it is the anthropological objects which have changed or whether it is anthropology itself which has changed . . .

Ethnographers collect their data, of whatever sort, by respect of their particular relationship to particular people. This medium is our mother lode, but it may also be our downfall. We lack the experimentalists' controlled conditions, routinized procedures, and precise vocabulary. Nor do ethnographers possess a special Rosetta stone for understanding meaning. We, like those we study, are human beings; our data represent the communications that arise from that *inter*subjectivity. If we desire to know what others really do, say, and think—and our present methodology can tell us little about the first category and nothing about the last—we must form the most reflective interpersonal relationships based on trust. We would be arrogant, and worse still, self-deceptive, were we to believe that tribal people communicate information unhampered to just anybody, under just any conditions. Certainly not simply because we are Europeans. "Is anthropological truth factual evidence of the same kind as that sought by the exact sciences, or does it consist in a special kind of relationship between the observed and observer?" (Lévi-Strauss 1968:351). The answer to this question is plain enough, only we have failed to consider its implications.

To collect data on Sambia ritual, with its core of secret behaviors and their powerful effects in the lives of individuals, required that I stop being a tourist; that I live with them; and that people trust me. I lived with Sambia for two years; nevertheless, even though I resided in a men's house for a few weeks, and then lived in quite close proximity to them, I could not, for instance, confirm the existence of secret homosexuality until some weeks after I arrived. It is kept that closely guarded and hidden. (Even then I learned only through the confidences of my two best informants.) Several months later I became the first European to observe the rituals through which homosexual fellatio, its associated beliefs and practices, are taught to boys. From this point onward I began to work with particular boys and men. I attempted to recount the subjectivity of ritual itself; what a boy had felt and thought. I then turned to life history. This exploration led to the vicissitudes of relationships with parents; dreams and fantasy, erotic experience and excitement; and, by this roundabout course, back to the marriage of ritual symbols and gender identity.

To recapture these observations I must try to depict some of the qualities of my relationships with informants and the communications that enabled them to trust me. I must be careful to label a ritual expert's viewpoints as such, and not confuse these with other individuals' feelings, opinions, or simply statements made to me or others, and to record whether my informant was in an expansive mood, or sullen, sad, or reflective: those contextual data condition observations too (see Appendix A). And somehow I must also assess how believable or authentic I felt a person's communications were. What is it, for example, that a youth reveals as interesting and exciting about copulating with a particular eight-year-old boy, and how authentic are these communications? What experiences, in the development of a Sambia youth, characteristically lead him to the excitement of that erection in his fellatio relationship? In short, this book, and those to follow, are concerned not just with social action but with intimate communications: what particular men, in particular circumstances, have said to me in particular.

I submit that, now, our most urgent and significant questions about the anthropological phenomena of ritual symbolism involve the mind (subjective processes) and behavioral development. No longer can we ignore the unspoken number one research issue underlying symbolic studies: What is in the black box? A generation has passed since Sapir, our early genius, foresaw this dimension of research:

> If the ultimate criterion of value interpretation, and even "existence," in the world of socialized behavior is nothing more than consensus of opinion, it is difficult to see how cultural anthropology can escape the ultimate necessity of testing out its analysis of patterns called "social" or "cultural" in terms of individual realities. [1949:572]

How to set about doing this is in no way mysterious. Sapir knew:

> We shall have to operate as though we knew nothing about culture but were interested in analyzing as well as we could what a given number of human beings accustomed to live with each other actually think and do in their day to day relationships. We shall then find that we are driven, willy-nilly, to the recognition of certain permanencies . . . in these relationships . . . [1949:574]

To know what is in the black box does not mean that we may ignore behavior, culture, or social structure. But we have often done the reverse. To test individual realities we must collect the data of nonverbal behavior, and the individual's precise feelings, intentions, and thoughts about his or her verbal behavior. Only in this way are we able to describe the precise meanings an individual attaches to experience. Ethnographers have remained curiously ambivalent toward the black box, but its subjectivity has now become of central interest. And indeed, that great palace, the mind, also belongs to anthropology—only we have feared assuming our rightful title to it.

The ethnographer of a ritual cult has, therefore, not one but several complementary jobs to do. Let me now sketch these to define the aims of this book and those that are to follow it.

dioms of Masculinity. Perhaps the first task, certainly the most conventional one, is a description of the *cultural context* of ritual. This includes some attention to the ecological setting and social traditions of the people whose ritual symbolism is the focus of observation.

In close conjunction to this task is the *culture* of Sambia, the cognitive system of values, norms, and rules influencing perception and behavior. An individual's perceptual set is strongly influenced by this body of "knowledge." Here, however, the questions of "participation" and "knowledge" are crucial. What do we mean when we unequivocally state that people "share" in a culture; that this culture posits firm "beliefs," or that its myths encode meanings which constrain behavior? How does such a hypothetical tradition of encyclopedic knowledge and belief differ within the segments of a population, thereby taking somewhat different forms in what various individuals do, say, and think? And if, as we find among Sambia and other New Guinea peoples, secret traditions of knowledge and belief (reinforced by social taboos) create differing developmental histories, phenomenology, and behavior between the sexes, we are then justified in speaking of disjunctive *subcultures,* i.e., masculine and feminine. The way these differences filter through men's idioms of maleness and femaleness in natural species and humans is the topic of this book.

Ritual Behavior.   Second, there is the *social organization* of ritual: its organizing social principles, relationships, and alliances that integrate individuals as persons into inclusive male associations. Ritual is the bedrock of this social contract among Sambia. And, typically, it is a contract of and for men's interests, as elsewhere in New Guinea societies. So initiation likewise separates (and sometimes excludes) women and children as a class. This exclusion has major implications for our assessment of social action and power relationships. Ritual reproduces the status quo social order. It must be performed in the same sense that the social contract among men is based on political alliance, warrior roles, and common military defense. A ritual cult is thus a defensive measure to nourish and sustain men's social contract.

  This involves another ethnographic task. A description of the normative features of the men's cult, i.e., its *customs,* is only the beginning. In traditional ethnographies, as I noted, the individual appeared only as a stereotype, a convenient summary of observations. Our ethnographic reports have told us little about the actual behavior of ritual: what individuals say and do and what emotions they feel; and the mood and attachments through which a ritual gets done. This I will call the *behavioral system* of Sambia ritual. There, I shall try to understand the concomitants of ritual in individual affects, mood states, and identification, as well as culturally constituted fantasy and interpersonal relationships.

Ritualized Gender Identity.   Yet these perspectives do not exhaust the anthropological significance of ritual behavior and symbolism. We are still left wondering about the individual's *meanings* associated with ritual experience, and his conscious and subliminal attachments to myth, symbol, and rite. These data, I take it, can only be had through the detailed investigation of individual behavior and psychodynamic functioning.

  Here I acknowledge another research goal that will separate me from conventional sociocultural anthropology. Elsewhere I shall try to describe the influence of these traditional rites, and subsequent homosexual associations, on the developing boy's sense of himself and his maleness—what psychiatrists call *gender identity* (Stoller 1968). This clinical ethnography will entail the subjectivity of ritual and secular experience that leads to adolescent masculinity and eroticism.

Manhood and Heterosexuality.   And finally, I shall attempt to define and assess the role of the *symbolic system* (beliefs, myth, and ritual) and its behavioral concomitants in the psychodynamic functioning of adult masculine character. Where in the transitional period the boy's sense of maleness stems from the effects of maternal bonding and early family life, we must needs be concerned with the ontogeny of meanings, attachments, and *psychodynamic motives.* In the latter case of manhood, clinical ethnography must also portray the continuing role of ritual experience in character structure —the subjective orientations, attitudes, moods, fantasy, dreams, sexual excitement, and especially interpersonal relationships that constitute adult heterosexuality. These psychosocial dimensions can be measured in various ways; I shall rely primarily on longitudinal clinical interviewing and naturalistic observations of men in subsequent studies.

This book represents the first part of that wider study of the Sambia secret cult, and it aims to sketch the background and male belief system concerning collective initiation. By belief system I mean the ordinary sense of a coordinated body of motivating ideas and concepts about human life and the cosmos. Verbal idioms will especially concern us since I think of them as a primary expressive channel linking individuals with their ritual traditions. By idioms I mean characteristic expressions having peculiarities of cognitive and emotional meaning and style established in the ordinary interpersonal communications of Sambia. An individual's choice of idioms is constrained by situational and personal history, knowledge, and intention. This implies that pragmatic knowledge, together with tacit premises about the nature of things, contributes to the unique sense of idioms through which Sambia convey their understanding of natural species and themselves.

Like those of other Highlanders, Sambia masculine beliefs are based on rampant sexual polarity and secret ritual. Ritual initiation inculcates men's convictions about the nature of maleness and femaleness. Men posit a need to separate boys from their mothers and other women, thereafter ritually treating them so that the boys may make a competent adjustment to the masculine role modeled on the ideal aggressive warrior. Yet unlike most other Highlands tribes, Sambia also institutionalize homosexual fellatio as an urgent means toward this end. Why have Sambia developed this particular developmental cycle cloaked in sexual idioms and homoerotic behaviors? It almost certainly concerns the creation of a particular kind of phallic masculine subjectivity, identity, and behavior.

Male cults have been known from Melanesia for decades, and neither the form nor the content of Sambia ritual is altogether unique to this setting. A close cultural parallel is the Keraki Trans-Fly River peoples (Williams 1936b) of Papua. Their emphasis on an aggressive warriorhood and ritualized homosexuality (sodomy, not fellatio) is strikingly similar to that of Sambia. The general form of Sambia beliefs and practices, further-more, strongly resembles what Read (1952) first reported of the Eastern Highlands *nama* ritual cult. This resemblance holds despite the absence of ritualized homosexuality among Read's Gahuku-Gama or other High-lands tribes and the lack of ceremonial pig feasts among Sambia (see Berndt 1962; Langness 1967, 1974; Newman 1965; Salisbury 1965; Watson 1973). These similarities and differences in ritual beliefs and erotic behavior I shall examine below. Here let us concentrate on Read's (1951) basic insight into New Guinea sexual polarity, which has, for the most part, been neglected by later workers.

Early on, Read (1951) recognized an essential contradiction within the ritual cult of Gahuku-Gama. "Sexual antagonism" seemed to permeate all facets of social life. The difference between male and female was, Read noted, "strongly marked"; and it was more "than the simple assignment of different roles and respective spheres of interest to men and women."

> Men like to see themselves as superior both physically and intellectually. . . . Such, briefly, is the *ideal pattern* of the relationships between the sexes. But in actuality men, for their own security, are continually compelled to reaffirm their supremacy in ritual. [1951:162; emphasis mine]

> In the final analysis, the idea which men hold of themselves is based primarily on what men do rather than what they have at birth. They recognize, indeed, that in physiological endowment men are inferior to women, and, characteristi-cally, they have recourse to elaborate artificial means to redress the contradic-tion and demonstrate its opposite. [1952:14]

Here Read captured a stupendous dilemma present within the difference between male dogma and secret ritual behavior. It holds equally well for Sambia: men are, by birth, biologically unfinished compared to women. Only ritual can correct that imbalance.

This dilemma points to a pervasive discrepancy between what men feel and say in everyday life and what they do in ritual. If men feel themselves superior to women, why must they perform rituals to assure that? Nor is it clear why men make these rituals secret and thereby hide them from those whom they seek to master. It is these common elements—sexual polarity, male biological incompleteness, and ritual secrecy—that link the male cults of Melanesia around a common theme. Let us consider that theme.

Each society becomes preoccupied with only a handful of myths. Men's and women's capacities to project their myths into cultural idiom, to nurture them, to deny their personal doubts about them or sanctify them imperiously in ritual, at whatever price (while sustaining the consequences of so doing), presage the quality of life and the eventual successes and failures of that society.

Such a guiding myth nearly always exists in tension. There is that which it affirms: the way the world came to be; the need of that; the right of enjoying its privileges; and a warning of disaster if this pattern is violated. Yet it implies its inverse. A myth hints at other possibilities, and denies them, by its sheer existence. So the ethnographer learns that a myth is important not only for the experiences it embraces but for those it denies. In short, a myth represents a compelling choice of idioms, the guiding fiction of a people's design for living.

It is the tension between the glorified mythology of masculinity and these other possibilities that I pursue below. Drawing on myth and knowledge, Sambia men spin their idioms into a particular conception of manhood. Their belief in the idealized war leader (*aamooluku*) is the guiding fiction of the masculine gender role and manly behavior. The fight leader is, in every sense, strong, aggressive, and virile—the purest form of maleness. So Sambia are, consequently, preoccupied with a warrior's concept of masculinity. *Jerungdu,*[5] a Sambia concept meaning physical substance and masculine prowess, is the key concept in this ideal. Since its connotations imply biological maleness or strength, *jerungdu* is virtually synonymous with masculine comportment. Femininity is the very antithesis of strength. And yet neither strength nor masculinity is a natural achievement in Sambia eyes: both must be ritually simulated through long years of ritual treatment.

On top of this is men's most secret myth—the myth of male parthenogenesis. Here again men declare maleness and masculinity to be stronger since men, alone, created humanity through fellatio homosexuality. That cultural fantasy is a comforting thought, for it allows one the conviction that men, after all, first held a power akin to female parturition. And yet, homosexual practices and this myth, which Tali cited above, are secret and fundamentally hidden from women. In both instances, as we shall see, these secret activities also disguise aspects of men's identities, even from themselves.

---

5. Throughout the text the term *jerungdu* will be translated as "strength" or its masculine equivalents in appropriate contexts.

In men's ritual idioms and in myth, then, we must confront men's overriding concern with being fully male and masculine, inside and outside; with denying that any part of oneself arises from female contact or femininity in oneself; and with rigidly adhering to the ideals of masculine conduct. This dichotomy—being fully masculine, not being feminine—we shall encounter redundantly in men's idioms. What men do in ritual and say about themselves supports their ordinary inclinations to be fully masculine. Such are the idioms that men want to live by.

But there is another side to men's idioms of natural species and humans that reveals something contrary. If one attends only to ritual dogmas, as I suggest many New Guinea workers have done, that something else is missed. Another principle is at work in how Sambia men perceive natural species, like pandanus trees or cassowaries. This perceptual pattern seems to regard things as female, fundamental, and, in most respects, more efficacious in life than is maleness. That principle gets exaggerated in men's views of femininity and masculinity. Men's idioms and associated thoughts ambivalently affirm that the capacity for reproductive competence is thus innate in females alone. The vitality of humans is thought to stem from a female aspect, and, finally, maleness itself emerges from femaleness. This is not the public dogma of men. It is not the social reality with which they wish to live. Nevertheless, that sense of maleness is transparently concealed in the myth of parthenogenesis, and that subjectivity is what I believe cements manhood.

These are the outlines of that contradiction in Sambia masculine life. Masculine dogma props up the guiding fiction of masculinity as all-powerful, and the rituals secretly reinforce that position. Quietly, nonetheless, men's mundane idioms tacitly assume that natural species, like women, are inherently powerful because of their very femaleness. The ordinary discourse of men sometimes glosses over or suspends this female principle; and since secrecy is institutionalized on a wide scale, we shall also need to examine some questions of subjective awareness and duplicity in Sambia culture. This culturally constituted contradiction is always present, therefore, be it dangerous, desired, or shameful. And men bear this mundane tension as men do: with noisy bravado or in quiet desperation. Ritual behavior is another matter. It is this very conflict which provides the dynamic force that lies at the heart of men's secret cult and their need to reenact its rituals, time after time.

I will try to confront these essential conflicts in men's views of themselves. Their idioms have reference to four central domains: warfare; masculinity and femininity; natural species and the cosmos; and the supernatural. We shall touch on all of these but focus on human gender and natural species. Starting in this way we will be forced to consider masculine idioms along with their subjective basis in actual interactions and expectations about behavior.

We shall consider, for example, the difference between mere survival and the mastery of masculine pride in war or the hunt; and the dramatic tension between men's stupendous dread of women and men's constant, disconcerting simulation of feminine powers. We need to consider these verbal idioms in their own right, for they will set the stage for understanding actual behavioral observations of ritual initiation elsewhere. Warfare is of such importance, however, that although I cannot consider its dark forms in the present volume, it is essential to underline how much it conditioned the state of Sambia life.

The real test of Sambia masculinity existed in almost constant war. War had been, after all, chronic, pervasive, and destructive. How is it really possible, now, even to attempt to recapture the sense in which a Sambia man lived life in the face of the day-to-day possibility that he could be snipered in his gardens, be cut down in battle and axed to death, or have his wife stolen by another man, physical strength and stamina his only steady insurance against such threats? How is it possible to forget past battles and brushes with death? And nothing can erase the memory of brutally massacred comrades and kinsmen and friends. War belonged to men. Women supplied food to their husbands and other warriors, and along with their children they suffered the ravages and horrors of war. They exerted negligible control over fighting or public affairs in general. Then, too, only men journeyed on arduous, danger-filled guerilla raids to enemy lands. On the raid, no less than in the battle, a man had to demonstrate his masculine "strength" or face destruction. This demonstration might mean a show of aggressive bravado, seeking thrills and quick-witted demonstrations of virility through physical action. This was the climate of Sambia life and the true test of masculinity—the only one that really counted. In what follows, we must remember that men's myths and idioms belong to that stark reality.

Sambia men hold that it is a matter of utmost urgency that a boy be initiated and masculinized to make him a warrior. This entails constant homosexual inseminations to transmit maleness. Later I will note the parallels to this ritualized pattern elsewhere in Melanesia. One thing should still be made clear. This pattern of masculine development is not unique; and Vanggaard (1972:32–35, 69–70) argues that its Greek forms were old even at the time of ancient Sparta. (Precisely what this form of erotic institution means and why anthropologists have neglected it I consider elsewhere.)

Unlike the ancient Spartans, of course, the inner workings of the Sambia secret cult can still be investigated. Myth, ritual, and everyday behavior all form the material from which this and subsequent observations are drawn. But how are the doings of what Malinowski (1922:18) called "the imponderabilia of actual life," its mundane routines and idioms and stream of subjectivity, linked to the great traditions of the men's secret cult?

This is, for me, the most important and interesting question of all. And this is, for good reason, precisely the information in short supply in the anthropological archives. It takes years to collect and understand such material. This book is a first attempt, and I forewarn the reader: what follows is not what Sambia culture or its people are like. I spent two years with them; that counts for collecting extensive observations and developing an empathic understanding of a very different way of life. But it counts as nothing when one tries to recapture the realities of individuals I know there; whole persons, warm and friendly and alive within me. Somehow, the printed word always fails to capture that richness. This monograph is only an approximation of that wholeness, a mimesis of a few particulars. I don't have enough information to examine these problems as well as I might like. More data, and other similar material from other Melanesian societies, are still needed and can be had. Much remains to be known. It is my hope, however, that despite its shortcomings this book allows a glimpse of a wider reality than we have hitherto succeeded in understanding.

CHAPTER ONE *People of the Mountain Forest*

Sambia are a mountain people and they are fond of saying that their home is the nest of the high-ranging eagle. They practice subsistence horticulture and extensive hunting in narrow river valleys of the remote Eastern Highlands. Their steep mountain hamlets, comely against the breathtaking panorama of Papuan mountains, nestle amid broken rain forest. It is a land of visual extremes and horrendous isolation, with heavy rains, at roughly 150 inches per year, that fall regularly for nine months (from September to May). With frequent low-lying fog, visibility is poor, and the melancholy rain dulls the senses, as Sambia assent. Sambia territory forms a roughly rectangular expanse near the Papuan border. The entire area constitutes a southern flank of the central eastern portion of New Guinea's great cordillera. Great mountain peaks surround each Sambia population settlement. Ranging from 4,000 to 10,000 feet, these mountains culminate in awesome Mt. Guinea (11,000 feet) in whose shadow lie Sambia communities.

Sambia number in all about 2,000 persons dispersed in six major population groupings in distinct river valleys. The traditional boundaries of these settlements encompass natural barriers such as mountains and watercourses. The entire Sambia tribal territory is surrounded by rugged precipices. Hence a road has yet to be pushed into Mountain Patrol Station, to the embarrassment of the provincial government.

My research was conducted primarily among the people of the Upper Sambia River Valley. (I have, moreover, visited all but one of the Sambia-speaking areas, and I have made a census of most of the population.) A thousand people inhabit eleven hamlets within this long and often vertical glen. The settlements generally follow the grain of the land from northwest to southeast. The Papuan-Vailala Divide geographically separates Sambia River Valley inhabitants from their more numerous Anga neighbors to the north. From that mountain range drains the Sambia River, physically dividing the upper reaches of the valley into two sides, territorial and kinship units, or phratries. On the eastern side of the Sambia River, four hamlets constitute the Seboolu phratry (with a population of 400 persons in 1976). Their hunting grounds extend to the mountain peaks overlooking them (this territory, then, adjoins the forest land of their ancestral phratry, the Seboolu-i, in the northwestern part of the Lower Green River Valley). Opposite the Seboola on the western side of the river are the several hamlets of the Wunyu-Sambia phratry (with a population of 500). Their hunting territory and gardens likewise extend to the top of the Blue Mountain peaks rising behind them. These people and their land are the subject of the following discussion.

Because of our late contact with them, nothing is known of Sambia before 1957. (Government patrol records date only from 1962.) Of Sambia origins, then, we have only their myths and legends to tell of their ancestral immigration, following an ancient war and dispersal, into their present-day area.

Sambia are on the fringes of the Highlands but they trace their descent to the Papuan hinterland. Their homeland they call "Kokona," and there are several legends telling how Sambia phratries came about. Those tales relate how diverse groups of ancestral pioneers generations ago originally settled within the Lower Green River Valley, the Sambia Valley, and the Yellow Valley. The Seboolu phratry origin myth is the clearest. Seboolu men believe their ancestors originally migrated from Menyamya, penetrating the Lower Green River Valley and there establishing an outpost hamlet. (Nilangu men claim their clan ancestors originated from this hamlet.) From there, four named, putative ancestral "brothers" immigrated into the Sambia River Valley, eventually warring with and overcoming the indigenous Yulami phratry,[1] thereby founding Seboolu clan hamlets. Sambia elders are vague about why their ancestors left the Green River Valley and settled over the ranges in the Sambia Valley. One myth relates that men followed the east-to-west movement of the sun, which bore them pandanus fruit and spears but neglected to provide stone axes or war clubs. Such weapons were eventually acquired from neighboring tribes, men say; at any rate, Sambia generally associate their origins with that primordial warfare and intertribal conflict in general. (The southeastern Yana tribe, moreover, holds a myth that explains the origins of all the Mountain Station area tribes, including Sambia. That myth tells of a great battle, a cannibalistic feast of the victims, and the immigration of two abandoned initiates from Menyama through the Yana area of the southeastern Sambia Mountains into the Lower Green Valley. The boys [age-mates] were also identified with the founders of Sambia hamlets: are they the central figures of the myth of parthenogenesis? See Chapter 8.) Sambia legends of neighboring tribes thus stress the historical ties of Sambia with lowland tribes of the coastal area.

Ecological Zones

The economic strategies of Sambia reflect their overall adaptation to the borderland ecological zones of their Highlands forest habitat. These strategies revolve around four basic economic pursuits. First, subsistence agriculture is directed toward the cultivation of sweet potatoes and taro. Second, hunting is the major subsistence activity of men, and it provides most meat protein. Third, intermittent gathering of wild foods is a valuable supplement, both for food intake and in providing needed raw materials. Fourth, pig husbandry provides quite small and irregular amounts of meat. In these respects, Sambia culture and economy thus reflect a mixture of influences from the Highlands and Papuan coastal region.

Their forest homeland and hunting interests clearly distinguish Sambia from other, more numerous and powerful grassland-dwelling societies of the Highlands (see Brookfield and Hart 1971; Watson 1964, 1967, 1973, 1977). Unlike vast stretches of the Central Highlands, the jagged Sambia mountain ranges contain little deforested grassland. Thick virgin rain forest blankets about 80 percent of the entire habitat. The more populous neighboring Baruya peoples, by contrast, inhabit far flatter and grassier country (I estimate that grassland covers more than half of their territories). And, for Sambia men, hunting remains a hallmark of manhood and

---

1. This phratry at present numbers 100 persons occupying two small hamlets.

of ceremonial life, the indigenous possum, tree kangaroo, and other marsupials still being the most important source of meat. Only the mysterious cassowary (which resembles an ostrich) holds as much interest for men because of its place in myth and ritual. Men seek the marsupials for all ceremonial feasts and exchanges, and much ritual lore also surrounds them (see Meigs 1976 for a similar emphasis).

Sambia have, moreover, very few pigs, and those they have are of scant social or ceremonial importance. Elders argue that they have never had many pigs and that they were introduced only within the last several generations. In 1976, for example, Nilangu hamlet (with its population of 140 persons) boasted a total pig population of only fifteen. Like their tribal neighbors, too, Sambia do not participate in ceremonial exchange activities, and there is, in sum, no wide-scale utilization of pig meat for social presentations as commonly occurs elsewhere in the Highlands (see Meggitt 1969:5–6; A. Strathern 1971).

Wungul-Kwaku (Habitation Area).   Our understanding of Sambia ecological zones ought to begin with the habitation area, for, in cultural terms, the hamlet is home, and all paths lead from it. The term *wungul-kwaku* refers to two distinct but contiguous spaces: the hamlet and its adjacent garden land Figure 1.

Hamlets perch on mountain spurs rising steeply from the valley floor.

FIGURE 1   *Nilangu Hamlet and the Sambia River Valley*

People live within the range of 3,500 to 5,500 feet. Thus the house sites and gardens are carved from lower montane rain forest (Brookfield 1964: 38*n*.; Robbins 1961). The sides of the ridges deteriorate rapidly into small streams draining from the mountains, so hamlets have a defensive advantage in being fortified by deep gullies and watercourses. Within the Sambia River Valley, as I noted, hamlets of opposite phratries are divided by the river, and during warfare, the single bridge traversing the river was always destroyed, further insurance against surprise attack. Settlements assume a line formation in which houses straddle the narrow inclining spurs, a pattern characteristic of the Eastern Highlands (Watson 1973: 227–229). In addition to their defensive location on ridges, hamlets were also fortified by tall concentric barricades of cordylines, wild sugarcane, and trees. Moreover, the gullies and streams below hamlets served as clan boundaries demarcating garden land and waterfront property.

Wunyu-Wulu (Riverine Land).   Riverine land refers to the banks and marshes of watercourses, whether mountain streams or rivers. The banks of lower-altitude streams provide fertile and moist soil for plantings of banana, taro, cane reeds, etc. Taro, and pandanus trees, appear particularly well suited to the silty mud flats of narrow flood zones alongside the rivers. Men[2] jealously guard trapping rights for eels and possum on this waterfront property (which is contained within clan territories). Clans own segments of this property. Traps set in the water provide an occasional freshwater eel, a greatly relished food. During the dry season, the rivers are dammed for catching local scavenger fish. These communal activities, however, occur only at the lowest ebb of the river, for Sambia morbidly fear drowning (they, like other Highlanders, did not traditionally swim). People also avoid water pools because of their association with malevolent ghosts and nature spirits.

Angoolendoowi (Edge-land Forest).   A narrow patchwork zone of grasses and secondary forest extends between riverine gardens and the edge-land rain forest. Most of this idle terrain derives from old abandoned gardens. In the Sambia River Valley, in addition, there are several small areas of stabilized short grassland between the gardens and the lower forest (see Brookfield 1964:32), a relatively rare feature of the local ecosystem. The secondary forest also surrounds gardens at somewhat higher elevations. Patches of these reforested areas descend to embroider groves of soft-wood trees and pandanus. Near the edges of the rain forest, on the upper

---

2. Throughout the text I shall adhere to these categorical distinctions for males: boys, preinitiates; initiates, first- and second-stage ritual novices; bachelors, third-stage ritual initiates; men, married, completed sixth-stage initiation, fatherhood; elders, gray-headed senior men.

slopes of the mountainsides, the thin tree cover provides shaded and moist spaces for small plots of taro and areca (betel) nut groves. Above the hamlet, in these areas, a small flat place is usually set aside for performing individual-focused (fourth-stage) initiation feast rituals. Closer to some hamlets a larger flat surface is periodically used as the men's ritual dance ground.

Larger gardens of either individual or communal cultivation exist on hillsides away from the hamlet, where land is more plentiful. On forested ridges above such gardens, occasional pig-herding houses or more common garden houses provide living quarters for people temporarily residing away from the hamlet. (Women tending pigs, especially if widowed, may spend long periods within these houses.) And even though the most distant gardens require no more than a three-hour walk from the hamlet, women and married couples often prefer living in the garden house during the long weeks of preparing new gardens.

Koonai-Wumdu (Pandanus-Nut Forest).   Above the edge-land forest the rising landscape changes greatly. One leaves behind the familiar clearings of habitation and passes into virgin rain forest. The flora alters, "the typical features of lowland rainforest such as buttresses and creepers disappear, and tree ferns take their place as the visible features of the lower storey" (Brookfield and Hart 1971:49). These mixed forests spawn an array of oak, pine, beech, and broad-leafed trees (see Brookfield and Hart 1971: 49), with bright orchids and overhanging parasitic vines and creepers. From 5,000 to 8,000 feet the pandanus nut—a local delicacy and important food supplement—grows well. Cultivated groves of pandanus, numerous but scattered, grow along rugged mountain expanses for a half mile or so, up until the colder cloud forest. These pandanus groves are tended by individual men (the groves were established by them or their fathers) whose clan owns the surrounding stand of forest. Well-built pandanus-nut collecting houses (*kunaal-angu*) further identify clan forest territories. During the pandanus-nut harvest season, such houses become a base camp from which the nuts are collected, stored, and smoked over the hearth. Pandanus houses also become homes for hunters who trap possum and cassowary in the rich surrounding forest.

Kai-Wumdu (High Forest Hunting Territory).   Vast stretches of the wild mountain rain forest slope upward above the pandanus zone. Brookfield and Hart (1971:49–51) refer to this area as the "high montane cloud forest" because of its mossy, damp undergrowth and perpetual cloud cover. The tree cover thins out to a single layer of gnarled and crooked trees whose branches are festooned with liverworts and other parasites. The trails become difficult to traverse since they weave around aerial roots, dense creepers, and limestone outcrops, often passing over slick tree bridges suspended above surging streams. Here, too, men avoid the stone out-crops and eerie cold swamps, which they believe are inhabited by evil nature spirits. Little wonder that Sambia joke among themselves that their homeland requires them to be like the wily tree possum.

Clans own various large tracts of high-altitude forest land. Natural features like ridges and streams mark their boundaries vis-à-vis the territo-ries of other clans. These forest territories are essential as the primary hunting ground of a clan. Hunting trails connect the lower-elevation pandanus houses with hunting lodges loosely constructed by clansmen. When a lodge falls into disrepair, a new one is usually built on the same spot. Hunting lodges provide cold and damp shelter, and they are infested with leeches during the greater part of the year; by any measure, they are thoroughly uncomfortable. Yet men can spend weeks hunting from them. Within the surrounding forest, clan hunting parties launch large-scale possum hunts in preparation for initiation, marriage, and funeral ceremo-nies.

Economy

Long-fallow cultivation of sweet potatoes is the single most intensive and important horticultural activity. Literally dozens of species are grown, and yet sweet potato production occupies a less prominent position among Sambia than in the agricultural regimes of most Central Highlands peoples (see Brookfield and Hart 1971:94–116). Impermanent clearings are planted and harvested; the plots are used for one to two years, after which they are allowed to lie fallow for some years. Gardens of tubers, such as sweet potatoes, tend to be mixed since a variety of other vegetable crops are planted alongside them in a "single undifferentiated swidden" (Wad-dell 1972:212–253). Usually the most intensive gardening occurs closer to hamlets (see also Godelier 1969).

Several clansmen may till gardens together working as a team. They may be aided by other clansmen and affines. Their wives follow them, clearing the gardens of brush and debris for eventual planting. The cleared section is then subdivided into smaller plots and staked off by flowers and sticks and cordylines. Traditionally, men used the stone axe and women the digging stick. The polarity between digging stick and stone axe, as a technological theme, underscores the unusually strong sexual division of labor, even by New Guinea standards. Until fifteen years ago the stone axe remained the only ready tool for clearing the land. Understandably, it made the felling of trees exhausting and tedious. The steel axe and machete have now completely replaced the stone axe. (Sambia also say that the steel axe has enabled them to prepare garden plots more easily and quicker than before; they also assert that they have more tubers and are "less hungry" than they used to be.) But the digging stick is still the women's key tool.

Garden cycles vary according to the crop under production. The land for sweet potato gardens is prepared and planted in cycles of six to nine months' duration. The largest sweet potato gardens are exhausted after five or six months of regular harvesting. Taro has a similar cyclical form. (I observed a taro garden planted and initially harvested ten months later.) Taro, however, must be used up quickly or else the corms rot. So it has a shorter period of availability and it must be frequently replanted. Yams are planted and harvested in cycles of six months (for blue-colored yams) and nine months (for red-colored yams). Edible pitpit is planted every six or seven months (beans, corn, and potatoes, which I observed planted in May, 1976, were being eaten by the following September). Unless they are unusually fertile, tiny taro patches are allowed to lie dormant for a few years before being reused. Sweet potatoes, on the other hand, have a much longer fallow cycle, varying from some five to twenty years, as judged by the stands of secondary forest within old garden sites.

By any economic measure, sweet potatoes are still the chief staple of life. Sambia favor taro over the sweet potato in their daily meals, but it represents a much smaller portion of the food consumed over the course of a year. The seasonal yam is even less valuable economically than sweet potato and taro, since it is abundant for only a few weeks a year. Nevertheless, taro and yams are crucial for ceremonial feasts, and they figure in most rituals. (Sambia share this emphasis with their neighbors as well as with many other Highlands peoples; see Barth 1975; Brookfield 1964; Godelier 1971:55; Watson 1967, 1977.) Other mundane crops such as edible greens, sugarcane, wing beans, and native squash also supplement the diet. And nowadays the Sambia menu is enriched by European-introduced cucumbers, corn, pumpkin, and green crops, which are also sold occasionally to local missionaries or the odd traveling patrol officer on his yearly inspections.

A sharp sexual polarity underlies agricultural routines and most economic pursuits. New Guinea specialists have tended to regard that division of labor as "complementary rather than cooperative," to use the words of Brown and Buchbinder (1976:4). Sambia economic activities are likewise fiercely focused—compartmentalized—by the norms and taboos of gender-role behavior. Men, of course, regard this situation as the natural and essential order of things. Men are consigned to the domain of warfare, hunting, and the initial stages of garden preparation. Women bear children, plant and harvest tubers, or tend what few pigs their kinsmen acquire.

In cultivating gardens, for instance, men first fell trees and then chop away the undergrowth, an arduous job. Women follow, cutting off grass and lower vegetation. Henceforth, however, the burden of gardening sweet potatoes falls upon a woman and she is responsible for the lot: burning off vegetation, breaking the surface turf, followed by the eventual planting, weeding, and harvesting of tubers. Individual taro plantings can be cultivated and harvested by both men and women. Clearing land for large taro or yam feast crops is a community endeavor, a healthy sign of sociality. Nearly everyone, including children and initiates, may participate (although males do not harvest the tubers until they have married), but most of the weeding still falls upon women. Green vegetables, too, belong solely to women. Only heavy, intermittent construction of fences, and the placing of support poles for cane and banana, fall especially to men.

Social Units

Sambia viewed the hamlet as a precarious haven amid multitudes of enemy groups and devouring spirits. Beyond its boundaries all groups were potentially hostile and distrusted. The possibility of attack remained a focal point in men's activities and plans. The hamlet was, then, a fortress prone to isolation, its walls containing siblings and other kin who were more trustworthy than any other persons. Without the protection of the hamlet the family could not have survived, and life would have been unbearably chaotic. Earlier I suggested how economic activities radiate from the hamlet. Hunting and gardening forays are essential, and like occasional trading expeditions, they provide a welcome relief from the confines of the hamlet. But in the past they were safely undertaken only during peacetime. In such small worlds Sambia spend much of their lives.

Before examining the institutions of the hamlet in more detail, it will be helpful to identify the major units of Sambia society, some of which link the hamlet with other social groupings.

The Family.   A man, his wife, and their children cohabit within a single household. This makes of the nuclear family (or polygynous family, since men may have multiple wives) a true residential unit, an institution virtually unknown to the New Guinea Highlands (see Meggitt 1964; Read 1954). (I wish to emphasize that this is a traditional pattern, not an introduced one, that initiates still live in the men's house and avoid women, and that the same patterns are to be found among most of the Mountain District tribes.) Sambia know of no other household arrangement either in living memory, legend, or myth. After a few months of marriage a man builds a house for himself and his wife. He leaves the men's house behind. Cohabitation by the couple is thereafter interrupted only by the woman's menstrual periods, childbirth, and the man's activities, whereupon one or both of the spouses temporarily resides elsewhere. Their children are reared in the house with them. The first-stage initiation removes the boy and places him in the men's house around the age of seven to ten years. Girls, however, reside with their parents till marriage.

There are two types of family households, and they are related to the practice of polygyny among Sambia. In a "compound household" (see Hogbin and Wedgwood 1953:272–274), a man resides with one or more of his wives and their children. Later, if his wives argue, a separate "simple household" is built for the second wife and her children. The former pattern is still the more common.

The Patriclan.   The men of a patriclan (*iku,* hereafter shortened to "clan") trace patrilineal descent from a named ancestor who is usually believed to have died nearby on clan soil. The clan is exogamous; its members should not intermarry, and this is consistent with their behavior as classificatory, sentimentally close siblings.[3] The clan is a localized descent group, all members of which ideally reside together in a single hamlet. Clansmen act as a corporate group in matters of the ownership, inheritance, and use of property, marriage transactions, and ritual. They should and usually do support one another in fights with others.

The Clan Segment.   Less commonly, a clan may be dispersed, some of its clansmen residing in other hamlets. These men still continue, however, to retain jural rights and duties in respect of their natal clan and hamlet. They also retain their identity as members of the parent clan, and this applies to their participation in marriage transactions, ritual, and warfare.

The Great Clan.   Two or more clans form a larger corporate grouping that I shall call the great-clan hamlet (hereafter referred to as "hamlet" [*aanjemi*], for convenience). Its members claim descent from a common, putative, named ancestor. (The genealogical depth between living clansmen and hamlet ancestors varies from two to five generations.) A great clan normally resides together in a single hamlet, and, in most instances, hamlet history and identity are socially synonymous with those of its founding great clan (which may be prefixed to the term *aanjemi* when referring to the hamlet: e.g., Nilangu-*aanjemi* is also Wokwor-*aanjemi,* after the founding great clan, Wokworu). The great clan may number as many as a few dozen men (see Table 1). The component clans of a great clan may

---

3. See Godelier (1971), who refers to a similar unit as the "lineage" and to what I call a great clan as a "clan." I prefer to stress the exogamous principle; therefore I describe these minimal exogamous units as clans that may intermarry with others inside or outside a hamlet.

TABLE 1 *Population of the Clans and Great Clans in Nilangu Hamlet (1976)*[1]

Name of Great Clan	Name of Clan							Total
	Yalushi	Wokworu	Woogetnchi	Kiloo	Kworu	Bagu	Googupi	
Wokworu	10	27	11	25	35			108
Googupi							23	23
Bagu							19	19
Other								8
Total								158

[1]In-marrying wives are included with their husbands' clan.

intermarry, forging strong ties on which the needed hamlet unity is based. The hamlet also acts as an independent unit in sponsoring initiation rituals and ceremonies. Patriclansmen hold rights in riverine property and hunting territories ranging up and down the mountainsides of the hamlet. In marriage transactions within the hamlet, the exogamous clans of a great clan tend to act interdependently, whereas in transactions with other great clans, or hamlets, they are more autonomous. In disputes, great-clansmen should support one another, although in practice this varies according to the individuals involved, their intentions, and the context of the conflict.

The Hamlet. The hamlet is a residential and political unit organized as a fortified house group. Hamlets vary in size, and within the Sambia River Valley they range from 40 persons to the 158 persons of Nilangu hamlet.[4] A hamlet, as noted, tends to form a single economic unit for communal gardening and hunting associated with ceremonies. In ritual and warfare the hamlet has a local identity centered on its clubhouse and leaders. Hamlets act as political and ritual units, then, in collective initiations with neighboring hamlets. They also possess clearly defined territories since the tracts of their component clans are usually contiguous along the site of their mountain settlement.

There are two types of hamlet, and their modes of recruitment influence residence patterns. A "simple hamlet"—by far the most common type—I define as one in which the men of a single great clan reside together. A "conglomerate hamlet" is more complex, being composed of members of two (more rarely three) great clans. Except in unusual cases, the clans or great-clan groups of conglomerate hamlets still derive from the same phratry. A conglomerate hamlet is founded by a "core" great clan (the group after which the hamlet is titled). They are joined by a few men of one or two other distinct great clans, and these "refugee" clan remnants are usually of the same phratry.[5]

The Phratry. The men of propinquant hamlets are also identified in matters of ritual and warfare, an association I refer to as a phratry. They claim descent from ancestors believed to have been "brothers" or "age-mates," and thus they may regard one another as kinsmen. These men, too, hold

---

4. This figure, and subsequent statistical material, derive from my own census work and sociological surveys conducted in 1975–1976.

5. Nilangu hamlet is an example of this pattern. Around 1971, Nilangu consolidated with its neighboring hamlet, Moonumkwambi, both of which belong to Seboola phratry and frequently intermarry. Elders assert that a visiting patrol officer urged the Moonumkwambi people to abandon their own hamlet and join Nilangu, although I could find no mention of this in patrol records. Consequently, Nilangu is composed of its founding great clan, Wokworu, and the people of the two great clans formerly residing in Moonunkwambi. This fact also helps account for Nilangu's large size.

an origin myth that asserts their common geographic origin. Their ritual customs are similar, as is their grass sporran—a mark of unchangeable ritual identity—and they tend to perform collective ritual initiations together on the same dance ground. In times of war the hamlets of a phratry called upon each other for support. Phratries vary considerably in numerical size, but within the Upper Sambia Valley, for instance, they are fairly evenly numbered (e.g., the Seboola phratry numbers some 400 people, while the Wunyu-Sambia, their traditional opponents, number 500).

The Dance-Ground Confederacy. A propinquant cluster of aligned hamlets form what I call a dance-ground confederacy, a political unit. They jointly organize the grand initiatory cycle every three or four years. But they also fight and intermarry. The sponsoring men are usually age-mates themselves or contemporaries.

There are two types of confederacies. One form is roughly synonymous with the phratry.[6] These initiation associations occur in three population settlements: the Yellow River, Papuan River, and Lower Green River phratries. Individual men and, more rarely, clans, could choose to initiate their sons outside the confederacy. But this is not a standard practice: a man would be foolish to risk cruel ritual treatment toward his son in initiation at an alien dance ground where he lacked the presence of reliable supporters.

The second type of confederacy is more complex and rests on the tenuous association of hamlets of different phratries. This makes of the initiates age-mates, politically linked as members of an age-set, which fact complicates their phratry commitments. Interphratry confederacies at present exist in the Upper Green River Valley and the Sambia River Valley. While collective initiations can be performed on the smaller dance-ground sites of any member hamlet of a confederacy, they are usually held on the same collective dance ground. It is, in short, the regional political association, rather than the actual dance-ground site itself, which is most important for understanding the prevailing organization of initiations.

Hamlet Organization

The men's clubhouse holds dominion in every Sambia hamlet, being the nucleus of its military and ritual existence. A defensive fortress, the hamlet was dependent on its corps of warriors residing in its clubhouse. Even today men's common interests and communal activities center on it. Ini-

---

6. Read (1952:3) calls a unit akin to my phratry the "subtribe," and it is exclusively identified with the "men's organization" and initiation. Apparently, then, Gahuku initiation is associated with a "phratry confederacy" of this sort.

tiated bachelors live a spartan life in the clubhouse, sharing food and sometimes intimacies. Together with senior men, initiates constitute a warriorhood, the community's fighting strength. Weapons of war, like ceremonial decorations, are stored in the back reaches of the house. And although married men cohabit with their wives, elders still admonish younger men to sleep frequently in the clubhouse. This is some insurance against the debilitating effects of female contact, for the clubhouse, men say, regenerates the tone and "heat" of the bodies of warriors. Women may not approach the men's house, and children must avoid it after nightfall. Concerns about female pollution and the superiority of their domain prompt men to enforce these restrictions. But another hidden motive is far more powerful: this is men's smug and fervent complicity as secret sharers in a tradition of institutionalized homosexuality. Of these arrangements I shall have more to say later.

Men are reared within the hamlet and reside there as adults. Even the abandonment of a hamlet does not markedly alter this pattern since new communities are raised on nearby soil. Children are reared as classificatory siblings or cousins (a pattern that unifies, but complicates intrahamlet marriage). All adults tend to become caretakers and authorities over children. They are consequently addressed as mother or grandmother and father or grandfather according to their relative age (see Figure 2). (The Sambia kin terminological system is thus an "Omaha" type with marked generational skewing.) These kin ties can be warm and strong despite the absence of actual genealogical links. Small boys and girls form play groups with relative freedom, their associations becoming a source of lifelong amity among them. Soon, however, boys play only with boys, both from choice and parental guidance, the lads taking to roaming together in the gardens and forests; after initiation they become ritual age-mates. Because clansmen share a mystical body "substance" (see below) and are reared together, marriage within the hamlet is permissible only so long as the men and women belong to different clans. Most men profess to dislike intrahamlet marriage, and they abhor intraclan marriage; and although there are a few marriages culturally regarded as "incestuous,"[7] these norms are rarely violated. After male initiation, boys strictly avoid girls. The bonds between classificatory siblings remain strong since classificatory brothers and sisters ought to be mutually supportive and protective. Age is a fundamental principle of hamlet organization, for socialization creates divisions between elder and younger siblings, senior and junior genera-

---

7. About 4 percent of all marriages in the northern Sambia Valley hamlets are "incestuous" in these terms, e.g., men are marrying their first cousins, nieces, and more rarely, classificatory sisters. The reasons for such marriages are complex, but the scarcity of women, and personality, are chief among them.

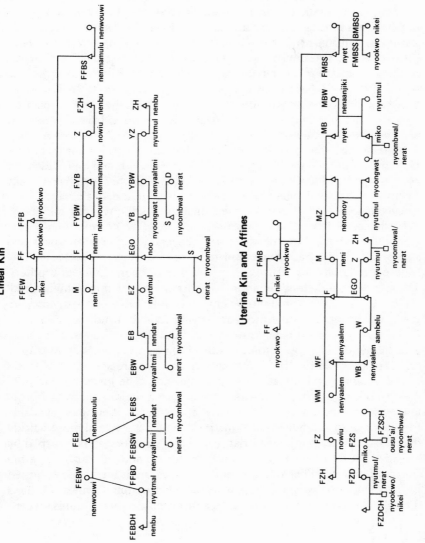

FIGURE 2 *Kin Terminology: Lineal, Uterine, and Affinal*

tions. So the children of a hamlet become the core of siblings within their natal hamlets, and men share a common residence and corporate estate founded on such sibling sets.

The military defense and political needs of hamlets gave rise to men residing in the hamlets of their fathers. Men doggedly express this norm in patrilineal idioms such as "a man should take his father's place," "he should remain on his father's land," i.e., "his land" (*gami kwaku-tei*).[8] (This norm is strongly borne out in practice: of a total of 131 males residing in the four hamlets of the Upper Sambia River Valley, for instance, 126, or 96 percent, reside patrilocally; see Table 2). Ideally, then, clansmen live together as a sibling group who assert their common ancestry and claim a bounded territory. A man who departs from this norm is somewhat stigmatized as *bomwalyu,* "an uprooted man," i.e., one residing away from his father's land. This is a derogatory classification that arises from men's attitude that the hamlet has lost a warrior and a provider. By contrast, the incidence of uxorilocal residence is thus correspondingly low. Residence with one's wife's people (outside a man's natal hamlet) usually arises from fights that drive a man to seek shelter with his affines.

In the management and possession of property no less than in the struggle to find a wife, brothers are one another's greatest rivals and supporters. Mutual assistance and defense is an ideal norm governing fraternal relationships. This is especially true of consanguinean brothers. There are, nonetheless, situational factors present within Sambia childhood that make boys prone to be envious rivals. Boys are, first, competitors for their mother's attentions and food and love. Later they seek their father's support in all manner of things, but especially in their marriage arrangements. The troublesome character of marriage transactions is a key aspect of fraternal rivalries. Marriage transactions are specific, and rights to a woman are individualized so that she should be given by clan X to clan Y. But in practice such rights often raise large organizational problems. For instance, a man's son may die, leaving his betrothed available for marriage to another man; or the girl may have matured more quickly than a lad marked for her marriage; or a boy's rights may be usurped by an elder brother. In short, men vie for wives, and this struggle is the source of much conflict among them. The situation is further complicated in that levirate marriage raises suspicions and doubts about a brother's intentions toward one's wives—a fact that men can never quite forget.

---

8. By the same token, Sambia assert that a "girl should take her mother's place" and return to the clan group that bestowed her mother to the hamlet in a delayed-exchange marriage.

TABLE 2 *Male Residence in Four Northern Sambia Valley Hamlets (1976)*

Hamlet	Male Residence[1]			Total Residing Patrilocally	Total Males per Hamlet	Percentage of Males Residing Patrilocally
	Married Men Patrilocal-Virilocal	Uxorilocal	Initiates			
Kwoli	12	1	7	19	20	95
Wunjeptu	21	2	8	29	31	94
Pundei	23	1	7	30	31	97
Nilangu	34	1	14	48	49	98
Total	90	5	36	126	131	96

[1]This sample includes men absent from hamlets; they have been represented on the basis of residence at the time of departure.

Idioms of Filiation and Descent

Sambia beliefs condition the reckoning of descent and filiation in precise ways, but men do not adhere to these beliefs absolutely nor to the same extent in all instances. Perhaps that is because land is plentiful, and men have no great need at present to be concerned about genealogical connections (see also Kelly 1968). For instance, cultivation rights are sometimes extended to an out-marrying female clanswoman and her husband as well as to incorporated kin or affines (see Lawrence 1971:10). Sambia were, moreover, inclined to recruit warriors to their clan hamlets to bolster their fighting strength. This is indeed such a strong preoccupation that when men cast their arguments in persuading a youth to join their hamlet, they still use idioms of fighting strength and solidarity (see Lawrence 1971:10–11). In contexts of initiation and political rhetoric, men stress the fact that their hamlets have but "one name," and they are "sons of one father" (see A. Strathern 1972). Yet, within the hamlet, clan and great-clan divisions are scrupulously kept distinct, mainly because of property inheritance issues and marriage.

Men's views of the making of a child furnish the outstanding idioms through which Sambia discuss filiation and descent. Two polar principles are fundamental: womb and *moyu.* The womb is primarily associated with the mother's heritage and the infant's blood. Identification with one's mother and her clan comes to be reckoned as a function of the uterine womb. So blood relationship to one's mother's clansmen is reckoned by reference to "my womb" (*mi ketu*) and "my mother's people." Contrarily, *moyu,* a mystical notion referring to male substance, is linked to semen. (These beliefs are described in greater detail in Chapters 7 and 8.)

The inheritance of *moyu* substance (see also Wagner 1967) is crucial for understanding patrilineal descent and masculine social identity. *Moyu* has several distinct, complementary referents. Chief among them is "male genitals."[9] It is the father's semen that creates and nourishes the embryo. When men speak of *moyu* as a concept, they invariably have in mind the idea of "penis/stick." This sense of *moyu* refers to the spring-loaded stick of snares for hunting cassowary, pig, and possum. Men can thus extend the meaning of *moyu* to the possession of male genitals, hunting, and hunting tracts. Each of these aspects separates the male from the female descendants of a man, since women are, through marriage, incorporated into their husbands' hamlets, and men inherit the land. A man's children are identified with his *moyu* (which is also a gloss for clan). *Moyu* substance is inherited only from one's father; one's semen and maleness are therefore unchangeable; and the descendants of an ancestor share "one *moyu*

9. Penis is *laakelu;* testes are *koot'ngoolu,* "old man's net-string bag."

and one semen substance" (see also A. Strathern 1972:10–11).

Moyu substance also establishes discrete identities for the component groups (clans) residing within a hamlet. The men of a hamlet assert that they are descendants of one ancestor, and they thus share one "father" and one "substance." But they do not then make the further leap in asserting that their *moyu* substance is the same. Hence clan identities remain separate; clans never merge, they only become extinct. The kinship divisions thus created by different lines of *moyu* substance sociologically separate clans within the hamlet, ensuring the perpetuation of clan property and centrifugal possibilities for intermarriage among them.

Marriage

A man may marry any woman of similar or younger age outside his clan. Clans are thus exogamous but hamlets are not (see Lloyd 1974:109 on the related Baruya). Men ideally prefer wives from other hamlets, asserting that women of their own hamlet are less exciting sexually; and although this predilection is borne out in case studies, it does not prevent some men from getting intrahamlet wives. (Since women are drawn from hostile hamlets, we shall later need to consider what role this fact plays in erotic behavior.) Before pacification, marriage used to be strongly influenced by warfare and politics, which often compelled marriage transactions from within the hamlet. Marriage today is largely a pragmatic matter, as it was in the past, and there is little personal choice of spouse. Infant betrothal (*ichenyu*) is the culturally preferred ("delayed-exchange") marriage contract. Some such marriage transactions occur within the hamlet, again, for mostly political reasons. This custom involves ceremonial gift-giving, feasting, and pomp, things that Sambia enjoy in themselves. Sister exchange ("direct-exchange") is, by contrast, a colorless matter devoid of much ceremony. And this less risky, more sensible type of marriage transaction occurs outside the hamlet more frequently. Perhaps for this and other reasons, sister-exchange marriages appear to be gaining in popularity.[10]

Bride service is a rarer, residual means of obtaining a wife. Marriage transactions are arranged by elders; bachelors have little voice in them; women have almost none. Much as women dislike leaving their natal hamlets for marriage, and much as their parents express reluctance to send them away, that is still common practice. Perhaps 95 percent of all mar-

---

10. This is no doubt mostly an effect of pacification and labor migration. Sambia still do not have bride purchase, but this could well come with the weakening of the "ceremonial aspect of marriage" (see Reay 1966:168; see also Cook 1969:104).

riages occur either within one's hamlet or with those visible from one's house. Further, hamlets usually have long-standing marriage-exchange relationships with one (or sometimes two) neighboring hamlets. The affinally allied hamlets are referred to as *nenbu-nenyaalum,* "sister's husband, my affines." Wives are rarely obtained outside the Sambia Valley; intertribal marriage is all but unknown. Marriages are thus normally contracted within the dance-ground confederacy, a fact that bluntly conditions the meaning of marriage and masculinity. Let me now briefly describe the customary arrangements surrounding these different types of marriage.

Delayed exchange is based on the institution of infant betrothal. There is one norm: if a woman is bestowed by A upon B, another woman must be returned to A in the following generation. (This rule applies to bride-service transactions and some instances of widow marriage too.) The usual arrangement is for a woman to be given with the expectation that her daughter (or an acceptable substitute) will be returned to the bestowers. Hence women are ideally "circulated" among the men of clans in affinal "alliance." A man arranges to bestow a woman on another man who may or may not marry her. In the latter case, she will be utilized by him in a further transaction with a third party. Marriage obligations to return a wife to an individual or clan can be met, therefore, by multiple givers, not simply one category, i.e., the original recipient of a wife.[11] In other words, there are multiple givers and takers of a wife.

There is no preference or rule, however, specifying that particular men must marry particular women (see Needham 1962 on patrilateral prescriptive alliance; see also Cook 1969; Meggitt 1969:11–14; Reay 1959: 57; Salisbury 1956). Moreover, not only do clans effect delayed-exchange marriages with other clans inside their hamlet, contrary to other areas of New Guinea (see, for example, Gell 1975:80–81; Schwimmer 1977:29–33; Williams 1936b:166–169), but they do so more often than with clans of other hamlets. This was, men say, largely a result of war. When hamlets battled on for long periods, marriage negotiations were difficult, if not impossible. Nowadays, intrahamlet marriages constitute as few as 14 percent (in Kwoli hamlet) or as many as 50 percent (in Wunjeptu hamlet) of all marriages in the Upper Sambia Valley communities. And of 127 marriages in that area, 53 (or 42 percent) were contracted on the basis of infant betrothal or bride service (see Table 3). Men do not express a preference for marriage within the hamlet; they see it as a matter of necessity. (The same is sometimes feebly asserted about incestuous mar-

---

11. A common instance of this is a boy whose assigned wife (by infant betrothal) is both his father's sister's daughter (FZD) and mother's brother's daughter (MBD). Whereas marriage to FZD is reluctantly accepted, men do not like MBD marriage. The girl may therefore be exchanged to a third party to obtain a different wife for him.

riages, i.e., those within the clan.) "He searched but could not find a wife," his sympathizers say. Nonetheless, most persons condemn such marriages as bad, no better than the animal impulses of "dogs or pigs" (see Lloyd 1974:109).

A delayed-exchange transaction is instituted at a girl's birth (see Wagner 1967:68). Custom prescribes that the birth ceremony (*moondangu*, new pain) be celebrated with a presentation of possum meat, hunted by the father, his brothers, and age-mates. This catch is presented to the new mother, who redistributes it. That gift is also referred to as *ichenyu*, after the term for infant betrothal.[12] But other ambitious hunters, who wish to make a marriage claim on the infant for their sons, may also present a meat gift. Eventually, discussions are held about the proposed transaction, and acceptance of the possum gift implies a contractual agreement. (Note, however, that the donor must be of another clan than that of the infant's father.)

That initial possum gift is only the start: the first donor must render continuous gifts (possum or pig or vegetal salt) to the girl's parents over the years to cement the contract. These later gifts are referred to as *doowangulu*, meaning both "sweat of labor" and "heat of shame" (shame is *wungulu; doo* denotes heat). Like other Sambia idioms, this one graphically describes the manly troubles of securing a wife for one's son. The prospective groom's father must toil and achieve a friendly posture of sufferance toward the infant's parents. When the girl matures and the marriage is consummated, her clansmen await the birth of a child. Her first female child normally becomes the return female to the donor group.[13] A small possum gift should be given (but is not always) to the mother to reassert the jural claim of marriage over the infant girl. (That gift is called *muloonju*.) Men proverbially refer to a wife returned to her mother's natal group as *ganiangu-ravu aitn'dookwanj dolumwaluno*, "She returns to her mother's place [and resides there]." More usually they simply refer to the process as *aitn'dookwanj*, a metaphorical reference to gray pockets of fertile ash (vivid against the black garden soil) left over from burning away a garden. Men assert that where there once grew a healthy plant only ash remains. But if new, healthy shoots are replanted in those spots—if a daughter is returned to her mother's group to bear healthy children—the garden (i.e., a clan) will again flourish (see also Rappaport cited in Cook 1969:107–108).

The *ichenyu* custom makes a man's marriage to his FZD a conventional

---

12. Menstrual blood is, generically, *chenchi;* a carnivorous possum commonly trapped is *chenyu.*

13. A male child may have an *ichenyu* gift of possum donated to the mother too. This establishes the (remunerated) right to act as the boy's ritual sponsor in first-stage initiation and subsequent initiations.

TABLE 3 *Contracted Marriages in Four Northern Sambia Hamlets (1976)*

Hamlet of Male	Provenance of Wife					Total No. Wives
	Nilangu	Pundei	Wunjeptu	Kwoli	Other Sambia Hamlets	
Nilangu	19 (41%)	12 (26%)	2 (4%)	5 (11%)	8 (17%)	46
Pundei	12 (32%)	10 (27%)	2 (5%)	6 (16%)	7 (19%)	37
Wunjeptu	2 (6%)	7 (23%)	15 (50%)	4 (13%)	2 (7%)	30
Kwoli	6 (43%)	2 (14%)	2 (14%)	2 (14%)	2 (14%)	14
Total No. Males	39	31	21	17	19	127 / 127

possibility. There are several instances of actual FZD marriage; classificatory FZD marriages are common. When these marriages involve a woman born outside the hamlet, they are unproblematic. But some intrahamlet instances are known.[14]

Sister-exchange marriage is more frequently contracted outside the hamlet. The incidence of sister-exchange marriages thus tends to be less common than that of infant-betrothal marriages within hamlets. And of 127 existing marriages within the northern Sambia Valley, only 34 percent (42 marriages) are the product of sister exchanges. Direct exchange is based on the possibilities of equivalent ages in prospective spouses. (Equivalence, in this context, implies a peculiar formula for linking the ages of the boy and girl despite the fact that the boy may be ten years older than his fiancée; see below.) An older sister may be bestowed on a man in marriage with the expectation that her younger brother will, at maturity, be returned a wife by this brother-in-law.[15] Sometimes this is an actual consanguineal sister exchange. These exchanges do not entail gift-giving or the transfer of valuables to the wife's group. However, the marriage ceremony, the wife's menarche, as well as the birth of her first four children all call for the husband's conventional prestations of possum meat distributed to the woman's cognatic, especially matrilateral, kin (who may include some of her husband's people). A man always tries to remain on good terms with his affines, particularly his parents-in-law, frequently providing them with food and other gifts.

Exchange of sisters by men of different clans also effects close ties among their children. A child's mother's brother is also his FZHu; his father's sister is his MBWi. This accounts for the terminological duality Sambia express toward the category of FZHu. It also creates a conceptual equation between FZch and MBch, which is expressed in kin terminology as male cross-cousin, *miko,* and female cross-cousin, *nyutmul,* or "sister." Ties to one's mother's brother are close and nurturant. This is one factor in men's distaste for marriage to their mother's brother's daughter, which some men describe as a "bad choice" (but such marriages still occur; this

---

14. This is illustrated by the dual terminology related to FZD. She may be called either *nerat* (daughter) or *nyutmul* (sister). Marriage to daughter is forbidden, while marriage to women of other clans within the hamlet (who are referred to as classificatory sister, *hap sista* in Neo-Melanesian) is acceptable. Boys grow up referring to their MZD as their "daughter." Parents try to hide marriage arrangements from children, and it is considered morally improper for the lad to ask about them. But eventually he knows of his fiancée's identity (usually around the time of his third-stage initiation, when he hears the ceremonial naming of his mother-in-law). His elders tell him that he shall marry his "sister"; and at this time, one supposes, her identity is transformed from "daughter" to "woman." Nonetheless, he must never call her name and refers to the girl as "her." When they are married, he calls this woman "wife."

15. Who may serve as his homosexual fellated, too; see below.

pattern results from kinship, political, and personality factors described elsewhere). The general effect, however, is to minimize actual marriage to MBD. When a man receives such a girl, she is likely to be used by the recipient man to obtain an alternative wife. He can hold that his MBD is "like my true sister" and dislike marrying her.

Most bride-service marriages involve persons of the same hamlet. A man lacking sisters or others to assist him in arranging a marriage can ingratiate himself with the father of a girl. Their relationship begins in friendly terms of mutual assistance and support in fights. The bachelor helps his senior in building fences and gardens, and in giving him meat or bartered items, such as vegetal salt. Eventually, Sambia say, the older man may feel "sorry" for him and bestow his real or clan daughter on him. Such marriages are referred to as *yashwotwi* (freely given). A wife must be returned to the donor group in the following generation; this person would normally be the woman's daughter.

Bride capture is a highly prestigious and phallic means of acquiring a wife, but it is more of a masculine fantasy than a practical reality. Several captured brides are, however, living in the northern Sambia Valley hamlets. These women (old widows now) reside in other hamlets, and one lives in Nilangu. Normally, no return was made for such wives. The single exception was a woman stolen from a nearby hamlet in past generations. A return is made (of her daughter to her natal group) to prevent animosity and further possible claims leading to war.

Leadership and Social Control

Sambia is an acephalous society in which leadership demands assertive strength no matter what the field of competence is. Traditionally, power was achieved, and shared, by the war leader, elders, and the shaman.

The hamlet of historical Sambia owed much to the war leader (*aamooluku*), and he was inclined to remind his fellow clansmen of it. Esteem and military power derived from demonstrations of strength by lines of warriors. Men were judged to be virile and successful by their exploits in warfare as well as hunting. Nor must we forget the popular belief among Sambia men, even today, that the strong and masculine man has women wanting him as a lover or husband. In such ways the war leader should excel and strive to surpass his age-mates and siblings. Otherwise he was not an authentic, widely feared warrior "with a name." Above all, prowess in war was critical. A renowned war leader (and many are still living) became an irreplaceable asset (see Watson 1964:7) to his hamlet and those of his affines elsewhere who relied on his support. He led attacks on other hamlets and stimulated enthusiasm and morale among his peers. He in-

structed initiates in battle techniques, and in his exploits he created a
reputation as a marksman and fearless fighter. In time this reputation, as
much as his presence, became a deterrent against unprovoked or feeble
raids.

Aatmangootu, a Sambia term of respect signifying "senior important
man," comes closest to being a political functionary. The name means
"man with a big mouth." "Big mouth" does not, incidentally, allude to
his prolixity as a talker, which is nonetheless undeniable. Rather, it signifies his stirring leadership at songfests or of dance groups that chant war
songs on the dance ground during initiation. It especially recalls his authority as a speaker at ritual teachings and his capacity as a yodeler.[16]
Aatmangootu connotes age and accumulated knowledge of all things,
particularly ritual. Elders unfailingly allude to one of their distinctive traits
as inherent confirmation of "wisdom": their balding heads. (We shall
learn more of the implications of this notion later, but it signifies strength
and lifelong adherence to ritual custom held to ensure longevity.[17]) The
aatmangootu is then a senior authority figure who can be addressed and
spoken of as "our father" or "old one" by all younger members of a
hamlet irrespective of their kinship.

Age dignifies these men. Sambia elders have a presence about them that
is deliberate and no doubt disciplined with age. They believe in themselves: their standing is based on accumulated knowledge, their speech,
and the support of their younger affines and sons, not on a pig or two they
might possess or some feather decorations in their huts. This comportment
distinguishes them from the ruthless warriors they once were. Elders hold
ritual secrets too. (I elsewhere discuss the enormous power of this knowledge as a system of symbolic tokens constraining the actions of the younger men.) But their influence, unlike that of the brazen war leader, is
persuasive and not blustering. It is measured by their ability to coax men
and push them into acceptance of particular compromises, a balance of age
and blustering strength (see Read 1959:433).

Shamans (*kwooluku*) were also critical in warfare, and much of the
reason was once succinctly put to me by a renowned war leader. In doing
routine census-taking and genealogy-collecting at a distant hamlet, a borderland village near the most hated Sambia enemies, I discovered an

---

16. Senior men, as I can well testify, have the invincible habit of emitting a great series of
yodeling bellows at dusk and, unfortunately, at dawn when arising; this is an assertion of
manliness no initiate would dare, from shame and fear of being mocked.

17. In Nilangu there are five such elders, ranging in age from forty-nine to about seventy; and
they are an especially rich source of information and also, I think, of the pride in Sambia
custom that is undeniably greater than in communities lacking grandfatherly figures who
have the time and determination to caution constantly against too much change too fast.

inordinate number of shamans (deceased and living) compared to Sambia society at large. In answer to my question as to why this might be, a war leader (then about fifty years old) said this of his community:

> We live near the Idma [Anga-speaking tribe]—our enemies. They raid us. Who can foresee their attacks? Who could help us? Shamans' dreams foretell raids. . . . If they see [dream] particular enemy warriors, we know those men will die before us.

The shaman was an oracle, then, whose allegedly infallible advice no doubt foretold as well as stimulated military activities. From their divinations and dreams (and those of war leaders and elders) shamans foretold the success of a battle, a stealthy raid, or an impending attack. Shamans offered supernatural protection for warriors by performing healing ceremonies in the clubhouse (where such ceremonies still take place). Each warrior received protection, and this must have given some comfort to men who faced an early morning battle. Their persons and weapons needed expurgation of residues of female pollution too. Such traces made warriors weak and vulnerable, for Sambia men believe that the "smell of women" attracts arrows like a magnet.

But shamans did even more. They are also believed capable of cleansing warriors of blood stains following battles. After battles, shamanistic ceremonies expurgated the blood of slain enemies from the weapons and bodies of warriors. This purge lessened the possibility of reprisal attacks by the ghosts of their victims. In sum, a shaman could heal, oraculate, and was also crucial for the magical strengthening and cleansing of warriors.

Discussion of leadership in New Guinea societies evokes images of the entrepreneurial "big man" (see Sahlins 1963), but figures of this sort are not found among Sambia. We might expect this since they lack ceremonial exchange systems with which big men have been elsewhere so well identified (Oliver 1955; Salisbury 1966; A. Strathern 1971).[18] Only now, with the government's belated introduction of a cash economy, coffee production, and the council system, is the notion of *bik man* (from Neo-Melanesian) gaining any acceptance. Younger fight leaders, as we might expect, have stepped into the contemporary political arena. Their initial election (virtually by block vote of their hamlets) illustrated that political expectations and alignments were focused on hamlet war leaders as a

---

18. Critics have increasingly disputed the significance of the concept "big man" (see Hau'ofa 1975; Keesing 1976:354), and my data support this view in Sambia and surrounding societies. I suspect that the term *bikpela man* is gaining acceptance as a cover term for elder (*aatmangootu*) in response to the perceived corruption of the power brokerage of senior men, which is a result of the introduction of the government.

power in interhamlet relationships.[19]

Fights within hamlets had to be muted lest individual and clan rivalries disrupt military solidarity. The *mulu,* a fight using sticks and fists, was a common disruption during my stay. Fighting within a hamlet traditionally weakened the ideal of warriors' solidarity and offered enemies an opportunity to attack. But no matter how sharply individual or clan differences divided the hamlet, clansmen still usually fought for the hamlet. They quarreled and brawled over matters such as a pig spoiling a garden or accusations of adultery. But marital infidelities still occur, and abundant speculations about them circulate as idle gossip; as so often happens in isolated communities, people are easily embroiled in such bickering or petty misunderstandings, which create their own tensions. War leaders found it difficult to avoid becoming entangled in these contentious situations. And Sambia always recognize that intrahamlet fights are potentially disastrous. Kinsmen, moreover, tend to take sides, brother helping father or sister, increasing the potential for violence to occur. An injury escalated the conflict so that the original source of the dispute was all but forgotten (see also Koch 1974b). The necessity of blood revenge was ever-present, and thus elders, women, or cross-cousins tried to step into arguments to calm and soothe. Shamans, moreover, still use their healing ceremonies as a therapeutic means of helping people, and this therapy tends to help others forget their differences. Nowadays, with war abolished, people make an effort to quell fights quickly and restore peace. (No doubt they did so in the past, too, but the patrol officer and his policemen are an immediate force that can jail and punish, and this modern political threat remains uppermost in men's thought.)

Today the most important traditional means through which men constrain conflict is the moot, a masculine institution that serves to check potential violence in the hamlet. The moot is a busy, noisy meeting that spontaneously emerges whenever arguments occur over destructive pigs, marital squabbles, and marriage-exchange negotiations. Although women intervene occasionally—and they may indeed be the subject of the rhetoric—men do most of the talking, and it is men who must reach accord. A moot can drag on for hours and days. I have observed plaintiffs holding back in pained restraint when listening to others speak. There is implied in this patience a message that, as long as opponents vent their spleen and

---

19. The government unwittingly reinforced this perception by appointing a notorious war leader, in 1964, as the first *luluai.* Men saw in his position a potential for reclaiming some focused power. But this came to nothing. The *kaunsalman*'s power is too diffused, his rewards too meager, his prestige uncertain; hence the role is still regarded with ambivalence. This also creates difficulties for the mediation of disputes between rival groups who see in the *kaunsalman* either a friend or a foe, not a neutral (see A. Strathern 1971; M. Strathern 1972a).

express their thoughts, a peaceful compromise remains possible. Silence forebodes disaster. If a man walks away from a disagreement, that indicates a grudge, with its vindictive potential. An impetuous counterstroke, at a later time, may then plunge the hamlet into chaos, people screaming and men brandishing sticks and knives, completely beside themselves. (I have observed this, too, on a few occasions.) Among combative clansmen in a hamlet the moot becomes a fight with words. After hours of such arguing, men become hoarse and drained, their testiness played out: this is precisely the unspoken goal. Still, a matter may smoulder for days, and men will avail themselves of opportunities to rekindle it. Moots tend to take on a sense of timelessness, therefore, no matter what their protracted outcome. In the past they were often the corollary of fighting and warfare; nowadays they turn into issues involving locally elected officials (*kaunsalman*).

Elsewhere I try to show how Sambia masculine values and interpersonal relationships tended to precipitate forceful assertions, local disputes, and, beyond the hamlet, warfare. In what follows, however, I briefly sketch how pacification came about and how it has changed some of these arrangements; and, in addition, what peace has done to alter the tempo of Sambia life.

Pacification and Change (1956–1976)

Sambia were the last Eastern Highlands people to be pacified. But the end to warfare and subsequent social changes should be viewed as but a minor episode in the larger drama of the pacification and colonialization of New Guinea by Australia (see, e.g., Nelson 1972 and Rowley 1970). Contact with lowland coastal peoples of Papua began around the turn of the century (see Chinnery 1934; Murray 1912). In the late 1920s, the discovery of gold near Bulolo on the Lower Watut River placed pressures on the administration to provide protection for the miners. A local patrol station was established around 1930, precipitating further social changes in the surrounding populations (see Blackwood, 1939a, 1939b, 1950:9–10). In the early 1930s the Menyamya Patrol Station was founded further inland (see Simpson 1953). Expeditions into the mountainous interior were stepped up. Menyamya patrol officers reached the Yana tribe, bordering the Sambia, in the late 1950s. Sinclair (1966), in search of the tribe of Baruya "salt makers," mounted a well-known patrol from Menyamya, which resulted in the first contact of Baruya speakers in 1951 (see also Godelier 1971). Meanwhile, the Highlands were being opened up in the 1920s and early 1930s. Patrols from Kainantu penetrated into the Fore area, partly as a response to medical investigations of the disease *kuru*

(Gajdusek and Zigas 1961). One such patrol, in the late 1950s, established the first European contact with a Sambia group.

The people of Nilangu first encountered Europeans on an administration patrol in 1956 that penetrated into the drainage area of the neighboring phratry hamlets by crossing the Papuan River. (That expedition, by two Australian patrol officers, originated from the Kainantu station.) The strange-colored skins of the Europeans, as well as their guns and other equipment, frightened the local Sambia, who fled and sought refuge in their forest houses.

A year later the next patrol advanced beyond the Yellow River hamlets over the Blue Mountains into the Sambia Valley. The visitors noted some general features of social organization and behavior, such as initiated boys' avoidance of women, hamlet localities, and the caution with which Sambia approached the party. The patrol, however, remained for only a few days within the valley before returning to their patrol station.

The administrative history of Sambia dates from 1960 with the establishment of the Mountain Patrol Post. The Baruya tribes, because of their closer proximity to the patrol post, experienced very strong pressures from patrol officers. The administration chose the airstrip as the seat of the newly formed district. The airlifts of materials provided the basis of the government's lifeline. Then, as now, the transport of supplies and personnel between Goroka (the provincial capital) and the patrol post was entirely by light aircraft.

Within the ensuing year the administration had subjugated Baruya communities near the patrol post, leaving Sambia unaffected. All that was known of Sambia was their warring reputation. Their troublesomeness for administrators persisted until the late 1960s. Beyond the acquisition of more steel axes and trade items (which filtered through the hands of Baruya into Sambia), there were no major consequences of the administration's presence for Sambia society. Nor did leaders then appreciate the great power that patrol officers would soon exercise over their lives, as they have retrospectively assessed the events of recent years in our conversations.

The intermittence of initial contacts postponed effective confrontation between the administration and Sambia communities until the early 1960s. Then, in 1963, Patrol Officer D. K. Gordon undertook a series of surveillance and pacification patrols of great importance for Sambia history. Gordon attempted to quash several indigenous battles in the Sambia River Valley. He established a government rest house and appointed the first *luluai* figurehead in 1964. (The government had appointed tribal "chiefs" under the former Australian administration.) He engaged Sambia warriors in chase at least twice, and eventually managed to implement pacification by massive jailings of the warriors. This intervention

(1964–1965) completed the total "derestriction" of the subdistrict in 1968.

As a strategy toward the achievement of pacification, the mass jailing was completely successful. No widespread fighting has occurred since that time. The Upper Sambia River hamlets, regarded by the administration as the most troublesome and volatile of the district, had been pacified. This pacification eliminated the convention of resorting to violence for territorial expansion, ostentatious male display, and the resolution of disputes. (Those instances of rife intratribal fighting within the Sambia River Valley, recorded by patrol officers, substantiate my own reconstruction of past warfare.) Chronic and pervasive fighting among Sambia as well as their neighbors came to an end. The pacification had been bloodless, and it wrought only minor changes in other social institutions. Sambia elders, furthermore, remain proud of their aggressive warring reputations despite the fact that they rarely mourn the passing of warfare violence (see also Watson 1964:9).

This rough sketch of warfare, Australia-enforced pacification, and its subsequent effects on Sambia helps set the stage for appreciating the overall pattern of their traditional and contemporary life. Warfare, its masculine values, and what it demanded of men and women are keys to understanding Sambian adaptation. Elsewhere I will examine those factors in detail. Without those finer data, male ritual is less meaningful. But for the moment it is enough to add that, despite the end of war, the recent and occasional preaching of missionaries, and the intermittent government patrol, Sambia life rolls on, its men's society and supporting value system much intact. This conservatism is not simply a product of isolation; it runs deep in masculine character, as we shall see.

Initiation and the Male Cult

Before turning to idioms, we need to find a place for them in the broader context of the male secret cult and its initiatory cycle. This is not to suggest that either the structure of the men's cult or its ideology ought to come analytically before the other.[20] My reasons—for organizational clarity— are much more mundane than that: it is simply easier to describe a course

---

20. The Sambia, like human beings everywhere, not only believe and think and occupy roles in an economic and social system, but also participate in a male secret cult whose traditions are based on an ideology and social institutions and a psychodynamic character structure. All these aspects are parts of a wider cybernetic system also constrained by the environment. In my view, it is spurious to argue that one factor "causes" the other variables to operate, although the variables are weighted differently in producing measurable consequences. The heuristic value of this study of idioms and ideology is largely in providing a semantic context for the more complex ritual behaviors and social action arising within it.

of ontogenetic development that, in idiom, follows closely the ladder of male initiation ceremonies if we have a framework to refer to. I wish to present here my own observer's model of the entire system instead of detailing idioms. Sambia, too, could do this, although not in as analytic or streamlined a manner.[21]

In simplest terms Sambia values and beliefs convey a warrior's conception of manhood. This plainly follows all I have hitherto said. Men should be strong, brave, and unyielding in the pursuit of all tasks; and most of all in facing the enemy.

"Strength" (*jerungdu*) is the pivotal idea in this outlook. Strength is a male trait. Indeed, strength could be aptly translated as both maleness and manliness. Strength has come to be virtually synonymous with idealized conformity to ritual routine. Before conquest and pacification by the Australians, "strength" had its primary significance in the battlefield. Strength had come to mean toughness on arduous, danger-filled guerilla raids to distant enemy lands. Strength meant that if cornered and ambushed by an enemy group, one stood alone, creating havoc and taking as many warriors as possible with oneself to the grave. Ritualized bowfights[22] were led by fight leaders. They could still be deadly, as many a wartale sadly bemoans. So even in the vicinity of one's own hamlet, warfare made men demonstrate their strength by means of aggressive bravado.

Yet for all its consuming importance, ritual, not nature, is the provider of strength. *Jerungdu* is the fundamental consequence of achieving biological maturity through initiations, male associations, and erotic interactions. The physical referents of strength—semen and bone—are the embodiments of biological maleness and the sense of all that is essentially masculine. The vitality of this notion men project into the fighting arena.

Men's values bind their idioms to hardened stereotypes of manhood. Sambia constantly measure masculine achievements against the twin poles of the splendid warrior and unmanly weakling. The polar categories war

---

21. Individual Sambia do hold their own mental models of the male cult, of course; otherwise how should they be able to articulate the interplay between homosexuality and semen and masculine growth, for example? (See Chapters 6 and 7.) They do that among themselves in ritual teachings: they do it also for me. Theirs is less analysis-oriented since they have little use for such a perspective. Nor could they provide it without a Western education, the lack of which would also prevent Westerners from similarly conceptualizing their own cultures. This point of Barth's (1975:225f.) is well taken. But to go further (and Barth believes he must since Baktaman lack an "exegetic system") would discount the native system and what Sambia can and cannot teach us about themselves.

22. Most intratribal warfare uses only bow and arrows. Intertribal warfare required war clubs and axes, too, and it aimed for murder and destruction, not just routinized displays of male solidarity. Warfare is the authentic background of male initiation and, along with the concept *jerungdu,* gets fuller treatment elsewhere.

leader (*aamooluku*) and rubbish man (*wusaatu,* soft person; literally, sweet potato man) pinpoint the purist forms of such stereotypy, even today. Beyond providing the daring lead in battle, war leaders represent the phallic traits expected of males in all walks of life. Men's attitudes leave no doubt as to their vaulting ambitions. Nor can they: a man's actions establish him from youth as a virile warrior or the dejected rubbish man.[23] Such reputations, without doubt, so overshadowed the lives of some men that brilliant prowess or awful tragedy were surely created by them.

The war leader personifies the model of the physically aggressive man of action. Initiation makes all males warriors. Yet the aspiring youth is shown again and again that the gist of the warrior's strength derives from his imitation of the *aamooluku.* This means, first, that the war leader is *primus inter pares.* True, Sambia is a classless state, and men fiercely defend their masculine autonomy. Yet here, as elsewhere in New Guinea (see Watson 1972), equality is undermined by ritual status, individual constitutional factors, and personal history. Ritual places elders first; warfare promoted fight leaders first. A people of simple technology, Sambia have few material means through which men achieve control over others.[24] Men may gradually surpass others since they may outperform them in war and hunting, leadership, or fathering children. To repeat, every hamlet boasts at least one or two war leaders, even today, on whose fighting skills, no less than their presence, survival depended. Their loss was catastrophic.

And next, the hypermasculine warleader is no friend of women nor of weakness in men. True men loathe frailty in others. So it is against the roaring prowess of the *aamooluku* that males get measured throughout their lives, in fighting, hunting, ritual, and even in erotic conquests. Of course individual differences matter; of course physique and health and character are noticed; of course they can block the attainment of the *aamooluku* ideal; Sambia note all this, of course. Never mind: whatever lip service is paid these facts counts as nothing in men's hearts. Even if few men get the permanent recognition due an *aamooluku,* all of them unfailingly shrink from being cast into the effeminate mold of the useless rubbish man. This is a message never lost on youths aspiring to be men.

Manhood has its roots in the long first-stage initiation (*kwulai'u-moku* or simply *moku*) that severs boys from childhood freedom and maternal

---

23. The shaman excepted. But some shamans were also war leaders, though they still held prestige if they were not. This is an idealized picture: a fuller description would show that ambiguity one obtains from observations.

24. Without a ceremonial exchange system, the odd pig or a few shell valuables are less important than elsewhere, especially, say, among the Hagen (see A. Strathern 1971).

love and demands conscription into the rough standards of a spartan men's society. Mother and playmates are left behind. In becoming first-stage initiates (*choowinuku*), boys pay the price of needing always to respect their elders and obey their instructions. This initiation combines the care of paternal love and the bite of cold-hearted military education. The lads hold the lowest status in the clubhouse and are subjected to the authority, hazing, and abuse of its older occupants. This is necessary; out of the soft and undisciplined boys must be created men, and not just any men, but warriors. Boys are thus expected to show allegiance to the warriors of their own hamlet and by so doing to disclaim all other loyalties.

From initiation a lad learns the ways of a warrior. He becomes a member of a lifelong age-set that includes his brothers and playmates and rivals, and sometimes even his enemies. His primary bonds—of identification, comparison, friendship—must always be with men. So in a single stroke initiation decisively separates him from the women in his life: mother, sisters, and especially his prospective wife. Men deem it good and necessary that senior men should dominate their juniors, just as men control women and children. After all, men rationalize, it is men who know best what course to steer for the community.

Their motives for attacking foes were less lofty. Warriors sought to defeat their neighboring opponents by brilliant, showy displays of marksmanship from afar, atop their opposite mountain stockades. Initiates joined in. Yet when the battle thickened, following woundings and death, boys were sent to safety: ambush and heavy assaults were men's work, demanding strength and disciplined skill. When a ceremonialized bowfight led to a killing, finally, nothing short of blood revenge sufficed to restore the political balance.

No evenhanded balance prevailed in raids on enemy tribes. Those stealthy attacks inflicted death and wide-scale destruction. A whole hamlet would be besieged at dawn: all men (and usually women and children too) were killed; valuables were looted; sometimes a few desired women were abducted for wives; and then the entire hamlet was literally burnt to the ground. Sambia hamlets were likewise pillaged and destroyed.

Yet it was precisely this act of destruction that contained the seeds of achieving Sambia manhood. Such raids were an integral part of the old initiatory process confirming puberty. They were sometimes launched expressly by and for new third-stage initiates, allowing them to confirm their warrior status in the act of the killing itself. And these raids earned Sambia the deep and unremitting hatred of their tribal enemies. Such raiding is gone, but Sambia men remain as proud of the fearfulness they instilled and the glory they earned from war as of their warrior regalia and their status in a military order into which boys are still inducted.

Initiation rests solely in the hands of the men's secret society. It is this organization that brings to life the collective initiatory cycle (called *iku mokeiyu; iku,* tree/man; *mo/moo,* food, breastfood; *moku,* first-stage rites; *mokeiyu,* collective dance-ground ceremony). The collective happenings are usually held jointly by neighboring hamlets every three or four years as allowed by their own chronic bickering and bowfighting. The large feast-crop gardens (taro and yams), leadership, and ritual knowledge they require dictate that a handful of elders, war leaders, and ritual experts are in full command of the actual staging of the event. All else is secondary.

There are six intermittent initiations from the age of seven to ten years onward. They are, however, constituted and conceptualized as two distinct cultural systems. First-stage (*moku*), second-stage (*imbutu*), and third-stage (*ipmangwi*) initiations—bachelorhood rites—are collectively performed for a group of boys as age-mates. Each initiation is held consecutively, as part of a sequence, over a few months. The ritual residence and nerve center of each initiation, in turn, is a great cult house (*moo-angu*), constructed anew on a traditional dance ground. It is the ceremonial building of this structure that inaugurates the whole cycle.

Fourth-stage (*nuposha*),[25] fifth-stage (*taiketnyi*), and sixth-stage (*moon-dangu*) initiations are, conversely, individual-centered events not associated with the confederacy of hamlets, cult house, or dance ground. Each of these initiations, like all the preceding ones, does have its own ritual status, role, and title (see Table 4). Yet the triggering event for each, unlike the collective rites, is not a cult-house raising or political agreement to act collectively, but is instead the growing femininity and life crises in the women assigned in marriage to the youths who become novices.

Fourth-stage initiation, therefore, is a semipublic activity organized by the youth's clansmen (and sometimes his male affines). Its secret purifications and other rites are followed by the formal marriage ceremony in the hamlet. The fifth-stage initiation follows later with the assigned woman's menarche, when her husband is introduced to essential purificatory and erotic techniques. Sixth-stage initiation issues from the birth of a man's first child and constitutes *de jure* the attainment of near manhood. The first birth is elaborately celebrated. The next three births are likewise celebrated in similar but truncated fashion; they bestow complete manhood. Two children provide the social basis for full personhood (*aatmwunu*) in husband and wife alike. Birth ceremonies are suspended after the fourth birth: no reason to belabor what is obvious: a man is fully competent in reproduction.

---

25. Fourth-stage initiation has some features of a collective ritual: thus at least two or more youths should be simultaneously married, and wide-scale preparations are entailed. But otherwise it, too, assumes the appearance of an initiation performed by and for individuals whose secret rites are attended mostly by hamlet clansmen and invited affines.

TABLE 4 *Male Initiation System: Ritual and Sexual Status*

Initiation Grade	Age (years)	Social Status	Residential/Marital Status	Sexual Activity	
Individually focused					
6th stage	20–30	Adult (*aatmwunu*)	Married—cohabiting with wife	Heterosexual	
5th stage	17+	Newlywed (*aatmwul chenchorai*)	Married—not co-habiting with wife	Bisexual	Fellated
4th stage	16+			Bisexual	
Collective					
3rd stage	14–16	Bachelor (*moongenyu*)	Unmarried, living in men's clubhouse	Homosexual	
2nd stage	10–13	Initiate (*kuwatni'u*)		Homosexual	Fellator
1st stage	7–10		Unmarried, living in men's clubhouse	Homosexual	

My major concern, in this book, is to provide a background for the collective rites leading to puberty (the subject of subsequent writings). Let us glance at the overall integration of those three initiations as a backdrop to men's idioms.

The initiatory cycle begins with the construction of the cult house and is followed quickly by third-stage initiation. Two principles dictate why third-stage rites take precedence. Once initiated, the bachelors are expected to help organize the ensuing ritual activities: they assist in hunting possum and in setting up the paraphernalia required as props in staging various rites—ones they themselves have undergone—and ones that, incidentally, they should memorize for the time when they become full-fledged initiators and fathers. The second principle is one loaded with the ambivalence of their new status. The bachelors get soundly thrashed and nose-bled, and they otherwise suffer much. This is how it should be, elders assert, for the youths must become "strong" and "angry" because of what has been done to them. But they can "pay back" that anger by doing to younger initiates what was done to them: beating and otherwise traumatizing them. In addition, they can do something equally laden with power: they are urged to channel that anger and relax their tight penises, by serving as dominant fellateds (for the first time) of younger initiates who are also encouraged to ingest the youths' semen.

That act of ritualized fellatio confirms the respective statuses of bachelor and initiate alike, and it establishes a definite pattern of eroticism, dominance, and subordination in their interactions for years to come.

Third-stage puberty rites come when most youths are in the throes of adolescence. Most of them have actually attained puberty; most of them already have girls assigned for their eventual marriages; and most of them are age-mates. (Occasionally a precocious youth, often against his protests, will be initiated ahead of his mates, or an older youth will be included if circumstances—e.g., past sickness—so require.) The third-stage initiation lasts a few weeks. It is then followed by second-stage initiation, elevating initiates from their previous first-stage status. This leaves the first-stage age grade vacant; men attest that this is "wrong and it must be quickly filled." So lastly, *moku* rites are performed on a new crop of uninitiated boys. *Moku* is, therefore, the last, the grandest, and the most festive initiation of all, and rightly so. For it anticipates a new string of warriors for the hamlet and confederacy, firmly cementing the male cult traditions in another generation of men.

To sum up: male initiation and the warriorhood are thought to be the only means for stimulating masculinity in boys. Ritual orders the whole texture of their personal and erotic attachments years before their wives are chosen for them. That is men's vantage point; let us now proceed to investigate why it is considered so vital.

CHAPTER TWO *Idioms*

and Verbal Behavior

When they gaze out into their forests or talk with others, what do Sambia sense? By "sensing" I mean: what do they perceive; what are the subjectivities of those percepts; why are certain perceptions absorbing while others are avoided; and how are these individual experiences related to men's cultural idioms? Do their sayings simply mirror culture or social structure or the ecology of their tropical surroundings?

Sambia are close to their fellows and equally close to the natural forces of life, death, and reproduction. In this chapter I wish to orient readers to the issues and methods of investigating men's tacit knowledge of these matters in mundane life. My interest primarily concerns verbal idioms, the characteristic ways men express the *Sambia* scheme of things. So this, and subsequent material, hinges on verbal behavior, its context and significance. At this point I have only a tangential concern with the wholeness of individual minds, since we must understand some sources of cultural knowledge to describe how individuals may experience idioms. Still, this task in itself requires illustrative sampling of individual behavior. Indeed, such sampling is entailed by all anthropological attempts at conveying information about belief and myth, and the particular verbal behaviors through which they are expressed. In most ethnographic reports this goes without saying. Why should this be so?

This book stems from a premise that anthropologists usually ignore individual verbal behavior and experience for understanding identity, communicative acts, and ritual symbolism. Social anthropologists have made symbolic representations the handmaiden of social structure. The significance (often equated with the "meaning") of these representations is "located" in group collective rituals. "Location," in this sense, implies both time and space, thought and action. Ritual is taken as the paramount scenario orienting all social action. Ritual is a propellant of "social constraint," a fabric of institutions engendering conformity to a system of "sentiments" (i.e., a "logic" of affects), institutionalized relationships, and group alignments (i.e., an action system). Other occasions of social behavior outside ritual are normally considered reflections of, or at the very least contingencies of, the collective representations (see Gell 1975; Moore and Myerhoff 1977) expressed through the rituals of "a society," when considered at all. Individual verbal behavior usually, but not always, has been ignored, although Turner's (1978) recent work illustrates a new trend.[1] If cited at all, speech behavior is often typified through "apt examples" that demonstrate the unavoidable tautology that individual acts reflect the equilibrium and shifting disequilibrium of social structure (Gluckman 1967; 1969:109–136).

This conventional model usually obscures our understanding of how individuals make sense of their world and day-to-day experiences in thought and speech. And its perspective hinders investigation of the relationship between everyday thinking and speaking and their subjective forms in ritual. The prevailing *modus operandi* allows the observer to

1. "Some of the notions I have just advanced have been influenced by fairly recent anthropological thought (Gregory Bateson, Clifford Geertz, Erving Goffman, Roberto da Matta, Barbara Babcock, Terence Turner, etc.) stressing that ritual language is often a language 'about' nonritual social processes rather than a direct expression or reflection of it, as the functionalists supposed it to be. It is a metalanguage with its own special grammar and vocabulary for scrutinizing the assumptions and principles which in nonritual (mundane, secular, everyday, or profane) contexts are apparently axiomatic. This critical function of ritual is still incompletely recognized by investigators who continue to see ritual either as a distorted reflection of 'reality' (i.e., 'empirical' or 'pragmatic' reality) or as an obsessional defense mechanism of culture against culturally defined illicit impulses and emotions" (Turner 1978:578).

move much too quickly, through summaries of observations concerning mundane verbal and nonverbal action, to the grand abstractions of collective representations evinced from rituals. Let us examine this model more carefully.

I wish to begin by distinguishing between the forms, the contents, and the meanings of idioms that individuals communicate through ordinary verbal behavior—usually indexed by casual references to ritual knowledge—and their designata within the collective representations of ritual. This is based on a model of idiomatic speech as a communication medium and as a psychological frame (Bateson 1972:184–193) that differs from the usual anthropological model. One of the virtues of this approach is in how it allows us to describe and understand how knowledge and experience in secular life impinge on all cultural behavior. Next, we could add how those same secular factors are also directed toward ritual idioms and behavior, the totality of which is subsumed within an individual's experience of ritual. This is, of course, an interactional process. For eventually we should be led back to describe how ritual experience influences an individual's thinking processes and thought contents in everyday speech and action. This book is mostly concerned with the first problem, the use of ritual and nonritual idioms in secular behavior.

Interfacing an individual's subjectivity and symbolic representations in rituals, then, is an intermediate behavioral form: the interpersonal communications of everyday life. To converse or comment, individuals draw on the information of *idios,* traditional and idiosyncratic sayings, similes, and analogies that subsume personal experience.

Idioms are natural vehicles for transmitting personal and encyclopedic knowledge. Their expressive dimensions derive from lexical signification, "an arbitrary, tautologous relationship between signifier and signified" (significata) (Wagner 1972:5; see also Fernandez 1965, 1974; Leach 1976:9ff.; and Sperber 1975:12–16). Yet idioms also take metaphoric significance stemming from the nonarbitrary (subjective) meanings they evoke within individual speakers and listeners. Wagner (1972:5), for one, suggests that the key to the difference between lexical and metaphoric significance is "the fact of the relationship itself": a metaphor brings an element into a relationship with the "system of meanings in a culture," whereas "lexical signification merely registers its conventions of labelling." This view differs from my own.

Wagner's approach to cultural meaning tends to isolate, and mechanize, the observer's abstracted system of normative constructs. In the above passage, for instance, the normative significance of verbal behavior is reified through Wagner's use of the term "its" (conventions of labeling), implying that in tribal societies at least, lexical, and especially metaphoric, signification has reference to some external code—which is alleged to be inferred from (and sometimes transcend) individuals' communications.[2] Or, as Sperber has criticized it, "each symbol corresponds to a fixed set of interpretations" (1975:15). What is the source of these "conventions of labeling" in a preliterate society without dictionary, encyclopedia, or a formal academy? What is the codifier of the metaphoric "system of meanings"? Wagner (1972:145–167) implies that it is ritual. This perspective, as later ethnographic material suggests, is inadequate in several respects. Not only does it mechanize metaphoric and lexical signification, it also attributes frozen, transcendent "meanings" to cultural forms—like idioms—that may or may not arouse such meanings in individuals responding to the words and acts of other individuals.

In contrast, I argue that the metaphoric and lexical significance of verbal behavior draws from ritual, social relationships, personal knowledge, and fantasy (see also Barth 1975:206–207). This viewpoint, to be useful, must also be empirically demonstrable.

Idiomatic expressions are a channel of communication. Through them, individuals give voice to crucial information, manifest and latent, which may be used in understanding the significance of interpersonal communications. The idioms, and their personal and ritual content, constitute a system of information. This information is distinctive to a form of thought: perceptual patterns that underlie pragmatic references to the significata of the idioms, i.e., their perceived entities in the real world; or the indexical uses of this information in mundane and ritual contexts. So it is individual verbal behavior, with its idioms and associated knowledge, that interfaces individual thought and collective representations—including those of ritual. Idioms, like myth and folktales, all belong to a cultural matrix; what Lévi-Strauss (1966:1–35) calls the "science of the concrete."[3] This belonging we take for granted. But how are these crystallized cultural products related to the thought contents and processes of those who experience them? We need observations of actual communications to assess the symbolic or pragmatic aspects of related verbal behavior, based on the view that verbal behavior is a golden gateway for describing the idiomatic modes of individual thought. Furthermore, naturalistic speech behavior draws on idiomatic reality and culturally constituted fantasy alike (see Devereux 1975; La Barre 1970; LeVine 1973:237–240; Parsons

---

2. Wagner's (1975, 1978) recent work has somewhat modified this viewpoint, but his treatment of cultural meaning appears to be substantially unchanged. See also Clay (1975), for another presentation of this approach in New Guinea studies.

3. I shall have occasion later (see Chapter 9) to mention Lévi-Strauss's (1966:16–36) commentary on the stereotyped "bricoleur," a subject of obvious intellectual concern to specialists. I omit it here mainly by objection to its normative bias and its author's disregard of individual behavior and diachronic processes (see Tuzin 1976:xxv–xxx, 327f.).

1969; Spiro 1968a; Tuzin 1977) in all cultures—but especially those of preliterate tribal societies.

Let us conceptualize the verbal behavior of idiomatic statements as being based on psychological frames and premises which encircle the information of both reality and fantasy. The idioms of communication acts impart understanding to listeners based on a shorthand for experience. Idioms amplify manifest references to a point of focus, the foreground "figure" (designata) of intentionality and of speech, set in contrast to its "field" of tacit background significance (see LeVine 1973:216–218; Lewin 1949). For example, Hamlet's figurative question, "To be or not to be," draws its force metaphorically against a wider field of sayings such as "to be alive," "to be a man," or "to be dead." Shakespeare's soliloquy draws on the eloquent possibilities of life and manhood and suicide. But to understand the meaning more precisely, we would need to ask Hamlet and his peers what he intended; and what the devil Shakespeare was about in choosing that particular expression.

Men seldom bother to make this information explicit since it is seldom necessary for communication. Speech, like conversation, as Wagner (1972:5–6) has noted, entertains as well as informs. But that is not all. Some of these background data are bound to remain "tacit knowledge" (Polanyi 1966), information that is embedded within one's experience of, or the communicative context of, the idiom. To wit: "I know more than I can tell," Polanyi (1966:4) has written; and that simple idea challenges a whole dimension of ethnographic research. How much of the background information of our speech behavior is immediately available to us, and at what levels of consciousness? (This question raises many momentous problems about human consciousness [see Colby 1978, 1979; Sartre 1956; Tart 1975] that lead away from my line of inquiry. I shall later return to them again, however, since their implications link anthropology with other behavioral sciences.) What needs emphasis here is another facet of Polanyi's problem: one that is of direct interest for describing the communicative properties of idioms and their background knowledge as a shorthand for experience.

Let me extend Polanyi: "I know more than I need to tell." Here is an illustration. I am traveling with a group of Sambia through the village of a nearby tribe. A great hulk of a middle-aged war leader is telling us of a battle, fifteen years ago, in which he participated. Neighboring Baruya tribesmen ambushed a related neighboring Sambia hamlet, killing many of its people, while others managed to escape. He and some comrades then retaliated by attacking the enemy village; they slew several men and captured a few women and children. They were to be killed. But a young woman among the captives grabbed hold of him. This is what he recounted of her words to him: "Take me. I will help you clean out your nose."

As he said the word "nose," he instantly pointed to my genitals. He and my fellow travelers and those around us all laughed. He had made his point well and I was absorbed. But nothing more, directly or indirectly, then or later, was said about his choice of idioms in communicating his point.

This example is commonplace both in form and lascivious content. Why did he (and his female captive) substitute the nose as a "verbal bridge"[4] to the penis? Why select the action of "cleaning the nose" as an equivalent for sexual intercourse? Why was the finale humorous? All this background knowledge is familiar and transparent to any Sambia adult. None of it needs elaboration. Indeed, to elaborate would be the perfect way to ruin a good joke, as any comedian knows. While this is true, it is of little solace to ethnographers, either in their research or in their personal capacities. How many ethnographers can tell a good joke in the company of their informants? Why should this be so? Does that issue shed light on the lack of humor in our ethnographic reports (see Young 1977)?

The trouble is that our informants share a lifetime of similar developmental experiences that we do not (see Cole 1975; Guthrie 1975): a lifetime of familiarity with a small geography and its natural species and elements; a lifetime of acquaintance with a closed community of persons known since birth; a lifetime of experience with Sambia sayings and conversations; and a lifetime of participating in traditions of cultural knowledge whose fantasies and realities literally take as many years "to learn." (Consider the years it would require to absorb only a part of the average American's manifest and latent knowledge, itself only partially encoded in the *Encyclopedia Americana*.) All that information is *not* needed, of course, to interact and communicate with others who share similar experiences.

There lies the trouble. "I know more than I need to tell" in competently interacting with other natives. The alien ethnographer knows far less. Added to which is a factor too often ignored in intersubjective communication with those known intimately: our every word or act may resonate meanings in the other because of the wealth of our intersubjective repertoire of experiences constructed between us over years of intercommunication. An act, a word, or an idiom carries a load of information deriving from such an interpersonal history.

---

4. Nose is *chembootu;* glans penis is *laakelu chembootu* (penis-nose), sometimes shortened simply to *chembootu* in puns or jokes like this one. The concept of "verbal bridge" is taken from Freud (1953:376n., 401), who was especially interested in how unconscious elements intercede in one's choice of words and manner of expression. On the earliest "symbolic analysis" of jokes, see, of course, *Jokes and Their Relation to the Unconscious* (Freud 1960: 181–236, especially 191). In this work I have almost ignored unconscious factors.

The writings of contemporary cultural anthropologists, like Geertz (1966b, 1973), have not so much ignored as avoided the crux of this problem since they allow the ethnographer such a wide interpretive license. Geertz's ethnographic notion of "thick description," for instance, entails information about all sorts of "symbolic forms"—categories, institutions, ceremonies—and the terms of which, in each place, "people actually represented themselves to themselves and to one another" (1976:225). This hodgepodge of phenomena labeled "symbolic forms" is indeed vast and somewhat familiar, echoing the normative, sociocultural constructs of a Benedict (1946) or Mauss (1967). No individuals, no "actually represented" communications or behaviors. In support of his approach, Geertz argues that "seeing things from the native's point of view," Malinowski style, does not mean "putting oneself into someone else's skin."

> The trick is not to get yourself into some inner correspondence of spirit with your informants. . . . The trick is to figure out what the devil they think they are up to. [Thus:] The ethnographer does not, and, in my opinion, largely cannot, perceive what his informants perceive. What he perceives, and that uncertainly enough, is what they perceive "with"—or "by means of," or "through" . . . or whatever the word should be. In the country of the blind, who are not as unobservant as they look, the one-eyed is not king, he is spectator. [Geertz 1976:224]

With such a conclusion I agree precisely: one remains only a spectator by taking this approach. A sophisticated spectator, to be sure; a chronicler of acts and words—the cultural disguises of the visible. But I am skeptical that artful documentaries of "symbolic forms" are all that can be known of the "native's point of view." This is certainly not what Malinowski (1922) showed or Sapir (1949) believed. Here, of course, I am not suggesting that the ethnographer "merge" with the natives, since a thin membrane of separateness is always required for even the thickest empathetic research. But is it true, as Oscar Wilde said, that "only shallow people do not judge by appearances"? That "the mystery of the world is the visible, not the invisible" (Sontag 1966:3)? This is what much of contemporary cultural analysis implies. I think this perspective is mistaken. The mystery of the world is the relationship between the visible and invisible, of cultural disguises and underlying subjectivity. And of that we anthropologists still have much to learn.

To understand the Sambia war leader's meanings about the use of "nose-cleaning" in our anecdote, one would need to assess the load of information surrounding his idioms, their designata, e.g., human nose and sexual coitus, and his meanings and experience of those things. How others responded to his communication revolves around equivalent, *but not identical,* personal and interpersonal knowledge and experience. We need not assume identical developmental experiences or meanings, supporting knowledge or behavior, as suggested by Douglas (1975), Lévi-Strauss (1963), and Leach (1964a), in communicating with others.

Wallace (1969:19–38) has argued persuasively in formal terms why this is so. Communication rests on what he calls cognitive "equivalence structures," similar life experiences, values, and goals. Further, Wallace has concluded that available empirical studies point toward a certain heterogeneity, not homogeneity, of measurable cultural content relative to various indices among people participating in tribal traditions (see also Honigmann 1978; Pelto 1970:30–44; Pelto and Pelto 1975).

For one Sambia, the nose may simply be a human facial appendage with orifices; for another, the nose may be like a phallus, and phalluses may be present in his perception of many different phenomena. The point is that humans, in general, may tend to experience qualities of the nose as a phallus in some manner (see Leach 1973), and why this is so remains unclear. Yet surely not all of them do; nor do they do so in identical ways. To investigate the why and how of such a subjective problem requires sampling individual behavior in its intersubjective communication context. With this sample we may then begin to correlate individual subjective orientations with naturalistic behavior. And, eventually, we will be led to link verbal behavior with the designata of idioms and knowledge naturally encountered in everyday life and more rarely observed in ritual behavior.

To grasp the encyclopedic knowledge underlying cultural idioms we must confront the problem of belief systems, as Geertz (1964), Needham (1973), and Wagner (1972) have argued. A compelling system of inter-related ideas and convictions guiding social action, a belief system is an integument that constrains much of what Sambia say and how they say it—especially regarding masculinity and secret ritual. (For example, men's steadfast view that nose-bleeding eliminates female contaminants.) Like other Melanesian peoples, however, there is no simple correlation between belief and behavior. For elements of belief stem from both public knowledge, i.e., male and female interaction, and secret ritual knowledge. This ideological bifurcation poses a special challenge to the spectator's documentary of the visible, creating theoretical and methodological problems not easily accommodated within its paradigm. Such problems we have only begun to consider.

Consider one of the most outstanding: the Sambia system of beliefs about masculinity itself. Masculinity derives its *public force,* idioms, behavioral traits, and mythology from its rampant misogyny. Masculinity is deceptively powerful by virtue of its negativity: the suppression of women in public affairs, and the stylized castigation of feminine qualities in men's private conversation or activities. Secret ritual, the *private force* lying behind masculine behavior, is altogether another matter. The logical paradox of Sambia thought and speech is that secret male ritual takes some of its most powerful symbolic imagery from the supremely feminine. For example, menstruation: men simulate in themselves nose-bleeding, which they culturally and consciously relate to menstruation, as the very wellspring of masculine vitality and strength.

This symbolic action is not, incidentally, regarded as a paradox by Sambia men. Quite the contrary: the beliefs and affects of nose-bleeding rituals are the "right and natural" order of things, in men's eyes. This does not, however, mean that Sambia public masculine behavior and secret ritual coexist in blissful harmony. Sambia society is disjunctive; so interpersonal tensions and psychological conflict, as well as political suppression, seem necessary to ensure the persistence of these male institutions. Of course. Sambia ritual advises that we are dealing with more than merely cultural belief or surface behavior in trying to understand how different sorts of knowledge and experience get worked into men's idioms. To describe that topography of public and subjective forces we must study what Sambia study in their world—and through their own terms as far as possible. But cultural forms are not all that will be necessary in analyzing the informational content of men's idioms.

We must also attend to the actual behavior through which the idioms are conveyed. This includes the tacit knowledge in which idioms are suspended, the "mood-signs" (Bateson 1972:189) conveying the idioms (including paralinguistic information), and their sequential order as a train of messages espoused in verbal behavior. None of this work is simple, and I am not a linguist. So I am unable to do the phonetic, semantic, and proxemic analysis that should also be done. Yet such analyses would take me too far beyond my primary goal—to describe the relevant behavioral properties of masculine idioms, especially their experiential and cultural knowledge contents. (The mood-signs and sequential order of verbalizations will simply be noted and elucidated, where relevant, in the following chapters.)

It is to the first aspect of the idioms, their tacit knowledge, that I wish to direct the most attention. First, because this topic has been a longstanding subject of interest in discussions of ritual symbolism (see Barth 1975; Douglas 1970; Leach 1961, 1964a; Sperber 1975; Turner 1964). And second, because workers have neglected a psychosocial dimension that seems to me so striking about Sambia communicative acts: namely, that idioms are sustained by modes of reasoning constituted through "fantasy" elements and "magical" (sympathetic and contagious) thought processes (see also Tambiah 1973).

To grasp the tacit knowledge of tribal communicative acts is as difficult and elusive as describing the report of another person's dream. Why this

analogy? Because the thought processes and contents of a dream are alien
to us, not to mention the dreamer himself, in terms of conscious waking
life. Yet only the dreamer's report and verbal associations, honestly communicated, can enable another person to comprehend the meanings of the
dream (see also LeVine 1973:251). The dream content, whether manifest
or latent, remains otherwise meaningless or else falls victim to clever
parlor-game interpretations among spectators.[5] Sambia speech, which incorporates verbal idioms, and especially ritual designata,[6] has precisely
this intersubjective quality. Here I am in agreement with Geertz:[7] the
idiom system, its underlying thought processes, and tacit experience are
so omnipresent, so plausible, and so familiar to Sambia that they are taken
for granted in most intersubjective communications with others.

Where does this leave the alien observer, the spectator of their verbal
behavior and rituals? In a sense, ethnographers, although they observe
these intersubjective communications, are in a far worse position than are
archaeologists with their shards. For we are missing a Rosetta stone with
its cryptic iconic code to crack. Even worse, we are prone to project our
own meaning into such communications since we are so humanly comfort-

---

5. We would do well to recall Freud's (1953) insights on this point, and indeed, in the
following passage the analogy between idioms and dreams holds well if one simply substitutes "idioms" for "dreams" in each instance: "We are thus obliged, in dealing with those
elements of the dream content which must be recognized as symbolic, to adopt a combined
technique, which on the one hand rests on the dreamer's associations and on the other hand
fills the gaps from the interpreter's knowledge of symbols. We must combine a critical
caution in resolving symbols with a careful study of them in dreams which afford particularly
clear instances of their use, in order to disarm any charge of arbitrariness in dream-interpretation. The uncertainties which still attach to our activities as interpreters of dreams spring in
part from our incomplete knowledge, which can be progressively improved as we advance
further, but in part from certain characteristics of dream-symbols themselves. They frequently have more than one or even several meanings, and, as with Chinese script, the correct
interpretation can only be arrived at on *each occasion from the context*' (p. 388). "At the
same time, however, I should like to utter an express warning against over-estimating the
importance of symbols in dream-interpretation, against restricting the work of translating
dreams merely to translating symbols and against abandoning the technique of making use
of the dreamer's association. The two techniques of dream-interpretation must be complementary to each other; *but both in practice and in theory the first place continues to be held
by the procedure which I began by describing and which attributes the decisive significance to
the comments made by the dreamer . . .*" (p. 395, my emphasis).

6. Here we are in obvious need of a finer vocabulary including fantasy, images, varieties of
"belief" experiences, and symbolic equations (see later chapters).

7. Geertz (1976:224) has stated similarly: "People use experience-near concepts spontaneously, unselfconsciously, as it were colloquially; they do not, except fleetingly and on occasion,
recognize that there are any 'concepts' involved at all. This is what experience-near means—
that ideas and the realities they inform are naturally and indissolubly bound up together."
Oddly enough, Sambia tend to make finer distinctions in their dream reports and interpretations (which are gleaned from omens) than in other interpersonal communications (see
Chapter 5).

able (or uncomfortable!) with pieces of them. Ritual cannot be such a Rosetta stone. That analogy implies that the communications within ritual intrinsically contain the information needed to comprehend the meaning of "their symbol code" (Barth 1975:226f.). This is wrongheaded: foreign ethnographers do not participate in ritual (at least consciously) in this manner; nor does the observer share in the same idiom or fantasy system, "magical" thought processes, or tacit knowledge as do the natives. In short, through the conventional methodology we are prone to treat alien rituals as much too familiar.

Here as nowhere else the term "participant-observer" is a misleading and fraudulent concept. It is true that we may observe a ritual, unlike a dream. It is also true that as humans we share the same psychoneurological machinery with which to scan the information of dream and ritual (see Leach 1964b:14–15; 1976:41f.). But we are attempting to decipher alchemy, and for this job our tools are poor, our concepts inept. I observe—I have not taken in all the parts of—the sense of perceptions, experience, and identifications Sambia "know" within ritual. (Here again I am in agreement with Geertz [1976:224].) Obviously we do not share a Sambia developmental pattern with its prolonged years of breast-feeding, open and sometimes brutal hostility between the sexes, omnipotence of fantastic myth in everyday life, or its long wars with political uncertainties and chaos. I participate vicariously in these events through my own subjective experience and understanding of Sambia behavior. But that observer involvement is seldom utilized directly in ethnographic reports, and indeed, it is usually concealed to lend a greater semblance of "objectivity" (see Devereux 1967). Consequently, all that can be said empirically about participant observation is this: the richness of our levels of intersubjective participation is measured in how much we are able better to describe, from various observations, what individuals actually do, say, and think regarding the "meaning" of symbolic representations in collective ritual.[8] How else can we hope to explain the significance of the unfamiliar equivalence between nose-bleeding and menstruation? The problem is even greater for individual verbal behavior, i.e., in explaining our war leader's meaning regarding noses and penises, snot and semen, nose-cleaning and sexual intercourse.

Or take the cassowary, for another instance; an odd creature figuring prominently in Sambia verbal idioms and ritual. It is not just a bird, a wingless biped or a powerful prey for the Sambia hunter. Cassowaries are also anomalously aggressive "females"; and the Sambia liken them to

---

8. This pertains to individual meaning. As Turner's (1964, 1967) work has shown, moreover, there are other dimensions of meaning in "multivocal" symbols, i.e., the exegetical, operational, and positional levels, which link symbols to group ritual.

women. Yet they are thought to give birth through their anuses, and are, on top of all that, spiritual powers. (See Chapter 5.)

The Sambia world, to sum up, is animated; Sambia are animists. What does this fact add to what has been said? It establishes a methodological point, and a crucial one for symbolic analysis. Western anthropologists have been prone to interpret the form and content of tribal speech behavior and symbolic representations through the lens of their own intellectualized logical systems. Sambia statements and thinking are usually, although not always, rational, coherent, and plausible; but they can also be illogical in the everyday sense of that term or its scientific applications (Spiro 1964).[9] In analyzing Sambia meaning, whose "logic" does one take: theirs or ours? My approach is to utilize both: observations of verbal behavior—idioms, ideas, associations—that are also measured against the element of intersubjective communications in which I took a part. My analysis tries to remain faithful to that behavior, even when it later rises above it. Here the analogy of the dream report is again useful. Just as a psychiatric investigator makes a dream report, I have described idioms *within the medium* of the naturalistic remarks associated with their occurrence; and I have thus interpreted them according to the speaker's (dreamer's) acts, meanings, and thinking processes.

In this way, the ethnographer can describe instances of verbal idioms, along with their manifest and tacit content, as parts of a wider communicative system. This may require years of sustained research on a single people. Nevertheless, unless we sample verbal behavior and longitudinal sequences of individual behavior, and unless we systematically ask questions about that behavior at appropriate points, as noted below, we may remain only spectators of the significance of symbolic behavior among the tribal peoples with whom we work.

Readers seeking a more detailed examination of this methodology, and how the conditions of field research among Sambia led to its adoption, should refer to Appendix A, "Tali Says," where I also provide a sketch of the interpersonal relationships that have facilitated the collection of these data on individuals.

My task, in this report, is to attempt to show that verifiable perceptions of cultural knowledge and fantasy should be included as components of what Sambia experience about themselves and their world. These elements constitute the fabric of Sambia idioms, linking individuals and culture at a level of anthropological understanding. To repeat, idioms are

---

9. As Sperber has put it: "I note then as symbolic all activity where the means put into play seem to me clearly disproportionate to the explicit or implicit end, whether this end be knowledge, communication or production—that is to say, all activity whose rationale escapes me. In short, the criterion I use in the field is in fact one of irrationality" (1975:3–4).

embedded in particular states of cultural significance experienced by particular individuals in particular contexts. It is their alchemy and its subjectivity that will be the fluid of this study.

CHAPTER THREE *The*

Inward Cosmos

A tribal people like Sambia look outward from a historical time and space with minds that assimilate experience by way of personal knowledge and their traditions of idiom, myth, and ritual. Their history and geography may appear changeless; the traditions are not. Idioms, like the rest of a culture, have human origins: they are fashioned by particular speakers, particular communications, and the circumstances in which they emerge. If compelling, or at least apt, idioms may be assimilated by others. Like myths, sayings are no doubt transformed or "edited" (see La Barre 1970: 7) in the process of being articulated and transmitted to others.

An idiom's trajectory of significance, then, be it lexical or metaphoric, extends from that point in the individual speaker's past, when it was first adopted, to its present moment of contextual use. For example, "women

have vaginas," men like to say, "so they produce abundant tubers within
the earth." In this saying men touch on a wealth of prior interpersonal
experiences idiomized throughout everyday routines. What springs afresh
to the mind often, though not always, finds its way into familiar expressions like this one. Our knowledge, our beliefs, our identities get tied to
them—and not always by conscious design (see Chapter 2, *n.* 4 and 5).
Idioms, in this viewpoint, provide the luminescent cultural solution in
which the residues of past thoughts and experiences are suspended.

The everyday life of Sambia encompasses the narrow sweep of their
mountain forests. Tleirs is a land of breathtaking topographic extremes;
of great craggy peaks and desolate garden patches set in deep ravines; of
frequent earth tremors and astonishing fluctuations in daily climate. It is
a brooding and restless land. Shades of this landscape filter through men's
speech in sayings that impinge on its "natural" flora and fauna, and in
other idioms that embrace the "supernatural" beings with which Sambia
have also populated this terrain. The sum of these natural and supernatural
entities constitutes the cultural fabric of the Sambia cosmos.

Since men's idioms embody supernatural forces and beings, they clearly
transcend the phenomenal world, disclosing the inward cosmos of Sambia.
By this I mean a choice of perceptual pattern and tone, inherent in native
idioms that are contingent on reality but not isomorphic with it. The
inward cosmos of a Sambia individual thus represents a guiding image of
the morally *right order of things*. This projective system is socially plausible
because all Sambia share in a pattern of behavioral development that
precipitates similar life experiences and life goals. The right order of the
cosmos takes shape from this particular, nonrandom filter of perceptions
and expectations about what ought to be. The cosmos ought to be familiar
and morally regular; and, perhaps most of all, we should feel that it is
under control. (This sense of one's inward cosmos is close to being a
philosophical creed, what anthropologists term a "world view" or
"ethos.")

It comes as something of a surprise to discover, then, the dramatic
dissimulation running throughout the gamut of Sambia men's choice of
idioms. What men conceal pertains mainly to ritual secrets and is thus only
marginally visible to women. Indeed, it will become clear that men are
only partly conscious of their dissimulation in the sense of its being a
subject of their everyday discourse. The core of men's idioms and associated knowledge suggests that natural species, like all humans, are propelled
by a "female" principle that represents their natal or resting state.[1] This

---

1. The presentation of this idea and related material here, and especially in Chapters 7 and 8,
was greatly enriched by conversations with Dr. Robert J. Stoller, to whom I am much
indebted.

masculine notion is partially secret; and it is coupled with a pronounced inclination of Sambia not only to anthropomorphize but to sexualize—or, more precisely, genderize—animate and inanimate things, especially by projecting into them the imagery of human reproductive organs.

How shall we account for men's perceptions of pandanus aerial roots, for instance, as the latent form of a phallus or female breast? This question is fundamental to masculine culture since similar perceptions influence a man's sense of mastery and control over the right order of things in nature and himself (see A. Strathern and M. Strathern 1968:180–181). Why men should stress a male and female polarity in living things and why a female principle is believed to be the more fundamental—these broader questions I take up later (see Chapters 6 and 7). The present chapter lays the foundation for those data too, by exploring the polarity of men's idioms as they reveal the difference between an individual's inner cosmos and its outward expressions in verbal behavior. This exploration will help demonstrate how idioms redundantly play on the latent femaleness of natural species, as we shall see. But first a general note about masculine attitudes toward the environment.

Sambia are not a people who look much to their past, though their custom is tied to it. Men have scant interest in long-dead ancestors or bygone ages. The constant challenges of their mountain homeland are a prime cause, for they tax one's vitality and give but meager rewards. Survival in warfare demanded raw courage; scaling tall trees and chopping them down calls for enduring stamina and strength; and a successful hunt requires fearless, cunning technique. In these ways men must strive for mastery in their land—and it is this task that fosters a materialism now foreign to most Westerners. Sambia live in the present, then, because they must do so to eke out a living. This disposition is itself a profound source of their ability to tolerate the malevolent forces of war and sickness and hostile spirits. So when elders sometimes speak wistfully of a mythic past when all manner of riches were enviably those of their ancestors, even the goods of Europeans, such fantasies never gain much acceptance. (This is a prime reason why there have been no cargo cults in the area.) For there is a pragmatism about Sambia that belies fantastic notions too distant from mundane concerns. Men are, instead, caught up in the business of masculine life: the doings of hunting and war, the interlude of occasional ritual.

Sambia are thus necessary materialists of a special kind: their culture is based on limitation, the undersupply of valuable resources and a shortage of manpower. This does not mean than Sambia starve or that their society is waning, though famine occurs and malnutrition is prevalent.[2] Yet malaria, tuberculosis, and pneumonia are common; infant mortality is also

---

2. In 1976 I noted two cases of extreme malnutrition in Sambia newborn, but this same area

high. These deadly facts must never be forgotten. Death is never far away from Sambia, nor can they afford to forget it. Sambia face constantly the knife edge of nature. Daily they experience rain, cold, and hunger. Pain and disease prey on them; and they have little contact with modern medicine or hospitals. In the past, those who could not survive these conditions ordinarily succumbed to them. All this is true enough; consequently Sambia are for the most part healthy and robust people who have little time for glancing backwards or forwards.

Of telling importance for us, then, is the masculine attitude addressing these hostile conditions. Through their idioms men cope with both gentle and harsh circumstances. Unlike ourselves, Sambia do not have the comforts of electronic technology. Their sharp edges have not been so dulled that they require the violent excitement of secondhand television fantasies to stir them. Sambia have no need to sharpen their firsthand sensual experience; the raw miracles of death and birth constantly besiege them. They are not wont to exalt sensuality: rather they attempt to insulate it or filter it, thereby mastering what they experience constantly in their striving for the valuable resources of the cosmos. This we can trace, beginning with their handling of the division between habitation zones and the forest.

Spatial Rhythms

The cosmological separation of three different zones seems "natural and essential" to Sambia: hamlet, garden, and forest. Their division is fundamental. Men's values, beliefs, and attitudes define their perceptions of appropriate activities and relationships associated with these zones. So gender ideology is at work. The forest is a masculine realm of hunting and ritual. The garden is, to a great extent, a feminine zone. Clearing away trees is men's work; but the bulk of digging, planting, tending, and harvesting belongs to women. The hamlet is a residence for both men and women, but because of the ever-present danger of female pollution and secret penetration, certain activities, like male ritual, are therein prohibited. These spatial rhythms are of course correlated with the economic division of labor and with kinship organization too. Social routines and relationships, and the patterning of day and nighttime events, reflect those socioeconomic factors. Taken alone, however, they are inadequate for understanding how Sambia conceptualize their spatial movements. We need also to consider sexual polarity for describing who does what, how

---

suffered a mild famine. Protein deficiency is common among children, as is the case elsewhere in Melanesia. Sambia see their own population as small and vulnerable to attack by others, though they also believe that their numbers are growing (see Kelly 1977).

and where they do it, and with whom it gets done.

We should recall the physical setting of the hamlet: a narrow stockade containing a few houses encircling a modest plaza on a narrow mountain terrace. Hamlets embody a human tidiness which sets them apart from the encroaching forest. The houses are built in a line formation, the men's house being situated at the higher end of the sloping ridge. This formation afforded the widest surveillance during wartime, it is true. But by placing the clubhouse at the top of the residential zone, nearest the forest, men also reduce the possibilities of female pollution. Women are constrained from walking "above" the clubhouse, thereby contaminating its younger initiates, war weapons, and ritual paraphernalia. "Women belong down below, men on top," Weiyu told me. This pat statement, whose idioms stigmatize women because of their polluting vaginas, rationalizes residential arrangements. On this basis, sexual segregation goes even further. Let me briefly diverge to mention its effects on social organization in the hamlet.

A cultural mosaic of spatial taboos and architectural designs separate women from men inside the hamlet. Its narrow confines are sexually segregated into men's spaces and women's spaces. Zones of female movement become polluted, according to male dogma, and since no area is immune to this contagion, persons must be restricted by taboos. A startling assortment of such taboos and avoidance rules curtail the movements of women, initiates, and men. No part of the hamlet is perceived as being unrestricted by sex-related taboos save the central plaza (and even this is nonneutral during some ceremonies). Interpersonal heterosexual behavior is therefore rigidly structured. Women are not at all free to move about as they wish; nor are the initiates. Men hold that women may pollute them by simply "stepping over" (*pulungatnyi*), above, or beside them, or by touching persons, food, or possessions. During their menstrual periods women leave their houses and retire to the menstrual hut, which is situated slightly below the hamlet. Men and initiates completely avoid the area of the hut. Likewise, women must not walk near the men's clubhouse or look inside.[3]

Men's fear of pollution also extends to the living arrangements within the family domicile. The coresidence of men and women does not reduce their separateness, it only exacerbates it. Family houses are small enclosures (about 8 × 10 feet). Generally, male and female movements inside

---

3. As far as I was able to observe, women never violated these rules. No woman, men assert, has ever been inside the men's house. I once suggested that perhaps men might admit old (postmenopausal) women in their house, as do men of other Highland cultures. But Tali and several friends rejected this idea as impossible since old women are still females who "have a vagina, not a penis."

are severely limited by strict rules, and in such closely confined quarters this limitation is remarkable. Hard and fast taboos are particularly demanding of women, who must, for instance, immediately squat to the floor on entering the doorway of the house. By such obeisance a woman is believed to reduce the possibility of transferring her polluting fluids to others. A man, as head of the house, occupies the innermost "male" living space opposite the door (see Figure 3). "Female" spaces are nearest the door. The men's and women's spaces are physically outlined by crudely hewn planks laid across the floor. The men's space takes up about two-fifths of the total living area, the remaining portion being used by women and children. The planks are a visual reminder of "cosmic" taboo: women may never step up or over the hearth or enter the male space. These taboos remain effective throughout life, and they do not alter as a person ages. Only small children, as befits their sexual immaturity and gregariousness, sometimes confound the rigor of these rules.

The footpaths that span the hamlet are likewise sexually segregated. Two main paths extend along the ridge top, a "male" path for use only by initiates and men, and a "female" path for women and girls. The main footpath entering the hamlet gate from the lower river area forks just inside the gate. The lower path is used by women, while the slightly higher path traversing the top of the ridge is the men's. A breach of the rules results in chastisement or punishment of both initiates and women by men.[4]

This brief aside illustrates plainly, I hope, men's all too visible concern with feminine pollution, and the institutionalized precautions taken to control women inside the hamlet. Sambia ideas about female contamination conform to the Frazerian principle of contagious magic—whatever women are in contact with is polluted. Even more, female contagion obeys, in Western (not Sambian) terms, the law of gravity, since it is believed to infect only things situated at the same or lower elevations. Simple Western hygiene concerning water is analogous: we are taught not to drink water running below the homes (and especially toilets) of humans. (Sambia implicitly recognize this principle by preferring to drink water from streams at higher elevations.) Sambia conceptualize *pulungatnyi* similarly, but it applies exclusively to women's menstrual and vaginal fluids. Both men *and* women are vulnerable to female pollution, but men are far more easily and mortally affected, in men's eyes (see Chapter 7). It is, ironically enough, these feminine fluids that bestow on women their life-giving fecundity.

---

4. I have never observed a woman being punished for breaking this rule, but I have seen them reprimanded. I have seen boys shamed and physically punished, however, for violating these taboos.

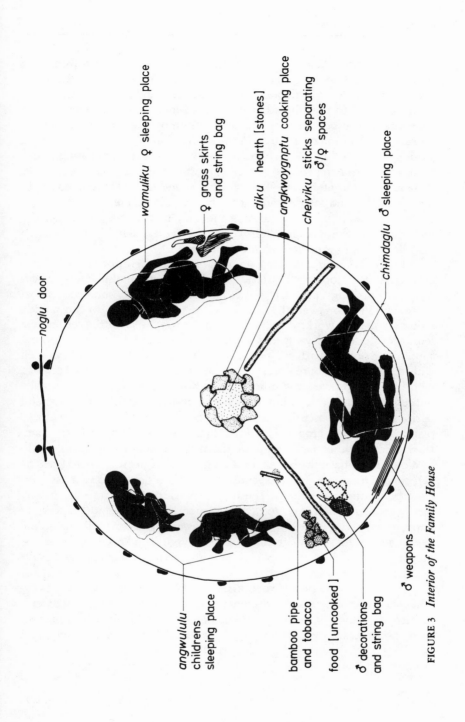

noglu door

wamuliku ♀ sleeping place

♀ grass skirts and string bag

diku hearth [stones]

angkwoygnptu cooking place

cheiviku sticks separating ♂/♀ spaces

chimdaglu ♂ sleeping place

angwululu childrens sleeping place

bamboo pipe and tobacco

food [uncooked]

♂ decorations and string bag

♂ weapons

FIGURE 3 Interior of the Family House

Now I wish to sketch how women's powers separate them from men in domestic and economic activities. After glancing at agricultural work and its idioms, we will then consider the forest and its animal species.

Earlier I noted that the strict division of labor burdens women with heavy garden responsibilities, allowing men more time to hunt. Men, to be sure, play an important part in the cultivation cycle. The painstaking garden chores of initially chopping away trees and eliminating brush belong to men. After this, to reiterate, most of the work—and it requires daily and tedious attention—falls to women and girls. There is no doubt that females spend longer and harder hours than do men in the cycle of seasonal gardening. Nor do hunting and gathering, nowadays, altogether make up the difference. In other words, the average Sambia middle-aged man has more leisure time than does his wife.[5]

Cultural idioms support the role of the sexes in their distinctive subsist- ence tasks. Men look with distaste on the earthy work of planting, weed- ing, and digging, preferring the challenge of the hunt, occasional house-building, or even the heavy toil of clearing trees to the muddy tedium of garden work. What planting they carry out is for the ceremonial feast crops, taro and yams and sugarcane (for which men must also cut supporting poles). Earlier I noted how men explicitly associate women with the earth: both are cold, damp, and ever so steadfast. By contrast, men liken themselves to the fiery sun, whose dramatic bursts seasonally impregnate living things but which is nonetheless destined to wasteful periods of cloudy obscurity. Men say women have the knack for regularly planting almost any crop and getting it to flourish. Sweet potato, taro, yam, leafy greens, and bananas: all these foods thrive under a woman's touch.

Women also have the benefit of their garden magic; such spells (*belaap- tu*), simple incantations said secretly to promote staple crops, a girl gets from her mother or father. (The magic spells for feast crops are mostly men's concern.) Men say, too, that women have other hidden ways of implanting special leaves or flowers, cassowary bone or shell, inside the garden turf to magically "fertilize" it. Although men know similar tricks, they are convinced that there is something innate in women that results in the fecundity of their gardens.

"Women have vaginas," men assert: "They produce abundant sweet potatoes." This saying pinpoints female anatomy as the source of women's success in cultivating sweet potatoes, the staple of Sambia life. Indeed, sweet potatoes are the "female crop" par excellence. Of her sweet potato

---

5. Though I conducted only random observations in reaching this conclusion, the pattern is consistent with other aspects of Sambia society, and, historically, we need not look beyond warfare and male chauvinism to understand it; see Brown and Buchbinder (1976:3–10).

patches, men say that a woman cultivator is "the mother of her garden." This analogy refers to a wide range of lexical contexts pressing on the same metaphoric link. For instance, a woman is "the mother of a pig," its caretaker; or a "good" woman who freely feeds the boys in a hamlet is "identical to their mother."[6] But more than nurturance or metaphoric kinship is at issue (see Chapter 6).

Men extend these analogies with women's procreative functions into statements about tuber growth. A woman is not only the garden's "mother," she also tends "her many children, the tubers inside of the earth," Weiyu has said. Here we see a latent (analogical) association linking different domains of idioms: women's vaginas make them fertile; the earth is like a woman; and the tubers inside the ground are akin to her children. The runners of a sweet potato plant are characterized as a plethora of the woman's "umbilical cords" (*nbwut-oolu*) extending from her root plantings to their maturing tubers growing hidden in the earth. (Similar idioms are used in reference to the growth of cucumbers on vines, and to wild squash.) Ritual idioms make special use of such imagery. Hence, in first-stage initiation rites, women rhetorically scold boy initiates for "stealing" their "children" (sweet potatoes and cucumbers) and for severing their "umbilical cords." Boys are also lectured on their manly gardening responsibilities and on how they should act differently from females.

The sexes differ greatly in what is perceived to be an appropriate agricultural routine. Women have virtually unlimited leeway to plant, tend, and harvest all crops. No tuber or leafy vegetable is off limits to them, though men share in planting taro and yam gardens. Even banana trees and sugarcane plantings women will take on if they so desire or need. Not so with men. Males are restricted in their horticultural activities by what we might call the gender taboos of a crop, i.e., whether a plant's culturally defined "disposition" of growth is "feminine" or "masculine" (see Tuzin 1972:232f.). It is simply unmanly for a male to fuss with certain crops.

In a war-dominated society we should expect a gender-role dichotomy that restricts men's attention, and use of weapons, to vigorous jobs like chopping down trees or hunting. By the same token, women ought to assume nurturant tasks like childrearing and gardening. This sociological schedule is certainly true of other New Guinea peoples. But for Sambia there is something else too: call it encyclopedic knowledge that implicit-

---

6. Compare an alternate saying for a man: "He is the father of that pandanus fruit" (its owner); or, "We need to ask his permission to use his hunting tract since he is its father" (both owner and caretaker).

ly—*symbolically*[7]—supports the gender-role constraints in gardening and other activities.

Hard and Soft Foods

The significance of this Sambia knowledge takes two complementary forms. First, cross-cutting the Sambia menu is an idiomatic opposition between "hard" (*jerungdu*) crops versus "soft" (*imenyu*) crops. (This semantic dichotomy is also examined in subsequent chapters.) Sweet potatoes are especially soft and taboo; men may neither plant, weed, nor dig them. When cooked, they become moist and mushy; so those tubers are "only stomach food," men repeat; they become "only feces." Taro and yams, however, are "hard" foods; they are firm and they stick to one's gullet, supporting tough skin and firm bones. These "hard" tubers thus sustain "strength" and endurance on long-distance guerilla raids—endurance tests simulated for initiates during initiation ordeals. Leafy greens (and pitpit) are likewise "soft" crops since they boil into tender pliancy. Greens are "identical to the noses of women," idiom states, owing to both their softness and how much women savor them. Only a stiff woody-stemmed shrub (called *inumdu,* showing dark leaves) is considered a hard vegetal green that men can also cultivate. But women may also tend it. Sugarcane is decidedly strong, with its hard tall stalks and bristly leaves, even though its inner pulp is sweet and watery. In general, then, greens and sweet potato are soft feminine foods; women ought rightfully to plant them since women are also soft and cold, like the earth. Men, however, should tend hard foods, the firm taro and yam, the tall inflexible sugarcane and *inumdu* plant, and trees such as bananas, for these are masculine crops (see Clarke 1971:124; Poole 1980).

The second form of tacit knowledge supporting this role polarity in agriculture is more obscure, and, unfortunately, I can only mention it here.[8] That information concerns men's perceptions of the actual growth patterns of plants, especially tubers.[9] Yam and taro grow vertically inside the earth, a pattern that contrasts with what sweet potatoes do: they grow horizontally. Yams "go downwards" (*kwakukwol-mulaiyo*) into the earth,

---

7. This tacit sense of symbolic information is what some anthropologists have in mind when writing of "sexual symbolism" in the New Guinea Highlands. See, for example, the essay by Buchbinder and Rappaport (1976).

8. No Sambia ever summarized or even outlined the preceding data for me, and I doubt that they could give the following information readily; however, I also lack the data to be certain about that here.

9. The perceived *rate of growth* of trees and plants is an important feature of their use and efficacy as vehicles for sympathetic magical identification in masculine ritual. See again Tuzin's (1972:234f.) interesting data on this subject.

while their luxuriant leafy vines grow upwards, supported by the tall yam poles (*muluptu-iku,* literally, yam tree) that men erect. Taro grows in reverse, as every gardener knows; its tubers "go upwards" (*teku chelaam-mwalyu*). And so does wild taro (*peigatwei*) and wild tapioca (*i-wusu,* literally, tree sweet potato). This latter root, incidentally (like wild yam with which it forms a cultural category), is a food prohibited to initiates until they reach third-stage bachelorhood (i.e., are pubescent), or until they have proved themselves adept possum hunters. The ostensible reason: "The wild tapioca is the very same as the possum tail" (in appearance), Weiyu said when I asked. Possum tail is taboo to those initiates and so, too, is the tuber. Contrast this perceptual correspondence again with what is said of sweet potatoes: men can eat them but not grow them. They grow sideways, the tubers "lie down" (*kwaku-kwutcho*), expanding horizontally within the earth. Men refer to the maturing sweet potato (while it remains in the soil) as *wusa-ketu,* "food net-bag/womb." In short, Sambia idioms of horticultural growth here parallel the "hard/soft" polarity of foods: "hard" taro and yam grow vertically erect; "soft" sweet potatoes horizontally creep.[10]

This material, thin though it is, implies that Sambia draw on (are motivated by) the imagery of phallus and vaginal penetration as a psychological frame orienting their idioms and cultural domains pertaining to horticultural activities. But what model of consciousness and culture is taken in the treatment of such data? Do we utilize conscious intentionality and fantasy, or pragmatic behaviors that apparently motivate speech without much intentional awareness? Such problems are fundamental, and we have only begun to consider them. Since I lack much solid data on this topic, I, too, am able to offer little but speculation.

With this caution, however, consider one possibility. Could the imagery of phallic erection, a seemingly panhuman theme (see Vanggaard 1972), somehow inform men's "interest" in the tacit use of knowledge underlying gender-role idioms? For instance, does that "interest" help explain why men deride the homely sweet potato, the staff of life, since, like a woman,[11] the tuber lies down (in the process of "reproduction") as it matures, and is also soft inside? And have men chosen taro, by contrast, as a manly food that ritually purifies the insides because of its tough whiteness, grainy textured roundness, and its "reproduction" pattern that sprouts it upwards through the soil, phalluslike?

(Part of the information needed to understand such sensitive semantic

---

10. Sweet potatoes grow faster and are usually more prolific, say Sambia, than the feast crops of men. Watson (1967) notes generally that taro (and yam) are ritual crops of men.

11. Sambia practice only the "missionary position" in coitus, men universally attest; or else they engage in fellatio, the woman acting as fellator.

questions is embedded in the normative description of food and sex taboos, as anthropologists have long known [see Barth 1975:162–171; Keesing 1979; Lévi-Strauss 1963:22–23, 28–29]. But we would also like to have data on what individuals actually do and say about these taboos—their psychological reality [see Spiro 1979:6f.]. This objective has been omitted from the work of Leach [1964a:30f.], for example, who cites summaries of observations about taboos that are held to reflect normative meanings for entire tribal populations. Neither quantitative data nor individual behavioral studies are provided in detail.)

Many tribal peoples tend to associate food with gender distinctions and eating with eroticism. Sambia do this in various ways. They hold, moreover, a staggering array of food taboos, sex taboos, and what is equally important, psychological frames in regard to them. Those frames draw significance, among Sambia, from the *relationships* of individual speech behavior to: (1) the *erotic and reproductive status* of ego and alter (e.g., pubescent bachelor, postmenopausal woman), (2) *gender identity,* and (3) the *situational context* (e.g., secret ritual, coitus, or mundane eating).[12] Whereas individual speech behavior is frequently attuned to (1) as a conscious factor influencing social action, (2) and (3) can be experienced both as subjective states *and* as others' expectations or directives. Viewed through the dualism of figure/background relationships, (1) and (3) stand out in sharp relief as consciously influencing the actor's purposive behavior; whereas (2), gender identity, which I believe to be vital, may be so omnipresent and diffuse that our feelings of self and sense of maleness or femaleness are background information, implicitly influencing much of what we do, say, and think.[13] To illustrate: Sambia masculine dogma dictates the following: one should not enter yam or taro gardens after coitus or the crops will be spoiled; it is forbidden to cook meat (pig, cassowary, and possum) inside of gardens; one must not engage in sexual intercourse at the base of pandanus trees or eat red foods following coitus. This is only a tiny fraction of the Sambia labyrinth of ritual taboos, as we shall see.

This note on taboo leads to a final point concerning horticultural idioms. So far I have concentrated on relatively unambiguous, seemingly *rational* idioms focused on gardening activities. Let me go a step further to consid-

---

12. Keesing (1972; 1979:29f.) has insightfully considered similar factors for understanding what he has labeled highly complex "pragmatic grammars" of cultural knowledge.

13. Even this formulation, however, is grossly inadequate for understanding how we *compartmentalize* aspects of our sense of self. For example, I experience my sense of maleness differently when playing tennis aggressively, delivering scholarly papers, or vicariously sensing a director's fantasies in movies. Likewise, I suspect that Sambia compartmentalize certain feelings, impulses, and fantasies by way of myth, ritual, and food or sex taboos, as we shall see.

er the "causation" imputed by idioms (and framed as analogies) that link action in horticultural contexts to other masculine activities. Only rarely do men need to spell out why gender-role activities in gardening take their customary form. From the time they are small, boys have this drummed into them in rituals; and by the time they reach adolescence, it goes unspoken since it is accepted as tacit knowledge. Weiyu told me spontaneously, when speaking of maleness and femaleness: "Women can cultivate sweet potatoes so well because they have no 'stick' [penis]; they can't climb trees because they have a cunt,[14] and a big arse." Elsewhere (and independently), Tali told me why he felt men cannot plant sweet potatoes and "soft" greens. If men did that, "They will not catch possum, cassowary, or eels in traps or snares. Your *moyu-stick*[15] will not get sprung." (The latter is a common idiom.) And he continued that a man who planted sweet potatoes "would not be able to climb trees to catch them [possums]" by hand. Here is a use of idiom (and verbal association) to stress what for Tali is obvious: a man who engages in female routines will be ineffective in all forms of hunting and impotent in that most masculine pursuit.

This stream of thought, while plausible and rational for Sambia, is obviously not logical. A general principle is at work: inappropriate action by an agent (men) in one context (gardening) has a negative sympathetic effect on him (the same agent) in another context (hunting). The negative consequences are disastrous, since hunting is so vital to being a virile, manly male. For example, men believe that a wife will leave her husband for another man who is a better hunter.[16]

The negativity of masculine idioms supports the economic status quo and defends men against the need or desire to compete with women gardeners. So be it; but why do men then mock themselves with envious irony?

Men say that precisely because they possess penises they are unable to produce sweet potatoes. This is not said boastfully; and indeed, idioms tend to play down the affects associated with what might be labeled a sensitive spot in men's perceptions of the women whom they so often deride. Men state that if they planted their own sweet potatoes, the yield would be only stunted, "stringy" tubers matted with hairlike feeder roots,

---

14. Sambia have two terms for vagina but prefer to use various circumlocutions for it, and one of them is this Pidgin term they have conveniently imported, for women speak little Neo-Melanesian, as I have noted.

15. *Moyu* is a cover term for male genitals and is related to patrilineality; *moyu-stick* is the spring-loaded sapling that triggers a snare trap, as I said.

16. This notion is analogous to the American saying that a man "brings home the bacon"; a male who fails in this role is not effectively functioning, which sometimes has a latent erotic association: a husband is not manly or virile toward wife and family, or may feel subjectively compelled to demonstrate his virility elsewhere, through compensatory behavior.

akin to "our penises," Weiyu told me rather glibly. Here is Tali once more:

> You and me—we men—have penises, so it [sweet potato vine] would not grow well for us. It will only produce root hairs; it will come up like a penis—long, with thin roots. The woman is its [the sweet potato's] age-mate; her plantings grow properly within the earth.

This little comment idiomizes the relationship between the genitals and sweet potato fecundity. Tubers are metaphoric extensions of anatomy: long stringy penis versus the earlier analogies of umbilical cord (vine) and "net bag/womb" (tubers in situ). Men are impotent sweet potato gardeners for the same reason that they are good hunters: they have penises. So here, Tali's latent association ("we men have penises, so it would not grow well for us") supports his choice of idioms ("it will only produce root hairs, it will come up like a penis," and "the woman is its age-mate").

With these last data we begin to glimpse the edges of masculine projection and how it influences men's words and thoughts, ostensibly about horticulture. A partial understanding of the content of these idioms hinges on knowledge of the culturally constituted fantasy system and not just cultural dogma. Men are manly warriors and hunters; but, in fantasy, if they planted sweet potatoes, they would fail miserably by producing only stringy, inedible, narrow roots. In this imagined script there is something missing in men; they are incomplete. The fantasy system supplies the missing pieces in the perceptual images we have already examined: vines like umbilical cords; horizontally maturing tubers; tubers referred to as womb and vagina. Through such metaphors, then, men seem to perceive in women's procreative capacities the vital ("magical") fecundity needed to master garden crops.

Where Imagination Blows

To trace men's forest idioms is to abandon hamlet domesticity and ascend into a wilderness where men stalk game at the risk of being themselves hunted by forest spirits. Here, in the high mountains, Sambia are near the roof of their world. Men journey there to hunt and enact intermittent ritual. Women seldom trespass. This is, then, an especially masculine realm, and one where solitary, sometimes lonely groups and individuals perceive all manner of things in the lush greenery of endless rain forest.

Women have, as I noted, virtually unlimited access to the river valley lowlands, gardens, and hamlet. So these zones are felt to be contaminated by women's constant comings and goings. Nor can men ever quite forget this: their well-being hinges on being mindful of it. Just as this lower countryside is assumed to be "unclean," so too the forest is thought to be virtually free of women's influence. The forest has its dangers, but feminine pollution is not among them.

It is young boys in play groups who first take to exploring the woods near their hamlets. I suspect that this occurs earlier and more often nowadays than before pacification, when people constantly feared surprise attack. Even so, children are still made to stay near their mothers, sisters, and playmates most of the time. For Sambia fear that ghosts or hamlet spirits may jealously steal their children away to untimely death if they are left unwatched. Boys thus grow up in the security of the garden-ringed village, assisting or accompanying women in their domestic chores. Occasionally, a man's family will accompany him to the forest for hunting or pandanus-nut collecting, and then children may reside away from hamlets for weeks. (This varies greatly among families and depends in large measure on how much of a hunter is the man of the house.[17]) Gradually a boy is shown the property (its plots and boundary marks) of his father and clan; and most fathers, I think, do this job with the pride born of ownership hard-earned in their rugged country. It is these boys and their play group, in sum, who experience their habitat together, who eventually become ritual age-mates, who constitute the inheritors of their clan's corporate estate, and who will, one day, replace their fathers as managers of its forest territories.

This carefree childhood is soon followed by the warriorhood established by the lads' first initiation. Its rituals require boys to take the difficult step of joining men in their forest activities, like long possum hunts. It is therefore expectable that the most secret of these rites first occur in the forest, not the village or ritual culthouse. The novices are first shown the sacred bamboo flutes there. Boys are coopted into similar ritual dramas, played out again and again within the forest, as they grow older. The forest, indeed, provides the needed props for ritual settings, like pandanus and palm trees, or forest streams for nose-bleeding. It also contributes much ritual paraphernalia—leaves, flowers, and vines chosen precisely for perceptual qualities like color, texture, or a plant's perceived pattern of growth. There is embedded in this tradition, then, something fundamental to the drawn-out process of masculine development: experiencing solemn rituals away from childhood surroundings high in the mountain forests.

---

17. Here is where an individual history fills in the ideals of a culture. Although all men should be great warriors and hunters, few really are, since men differ in interests, dispositions, and skills. The man who is an avid hunter actually prefers to be in the forest or hunting lodge, hunting instead of gardening. If he is accompanied frequently by his wife and children, these boys and girls will experience somewhat different childhood histories, such as in sleeping arrangements, than they would have in the staid hamlet.

Following their first rituals, boys begin encountering directly the wonders of this luxuriant wild treasure, there for the taking if only they are men enough. Elders encourage them to hunt its rainbow of birds, so by an early age, Sambia boys are good marksmen. On moonlit nights, too, boys venture out in groups to hunt nocturnal possums, propping up each other's courage against the darkness. Bands of boisterous age-mates now begin to wander about the forest alone, leaving behind the sheltered play of before.

A new world opens up to them, and their elders charge them with mastering it. They must master—and rather quickly at that—how to cross slick moss-covered tree bridges suspended high over glassy, gushing streams. They also learn how to set possum snares over such logs and how to rig hanging snares in nearby trees and rock crevices. They learn the techniques for constructing duck blinds from which to shoot birds at ponds, and how to dig and camouflage pit snares for wild boar, a creature dangerous enough to gore men and kill their dogs. Boys have to get the trick of laying snares on the borders of stagnant pools, and they must have drawn out of them a dread of the evil nature spirits that animate these eerie cold bogs. They also learn of the various caves and limestone outcrops in the region, each stone monument possessing a name and folk history.

Still higher in the mountains they are shown how to climb lofty pandanus trees, scaling the tall slippery trunks without benefit of rope. This gargantuan tree, its spiny leaves sprouting from every side like an exploding windmill, must be mastered (see Chapter 4). For one must overcome the fear of falling from it, or of being cut by its sharp needles, to sever and harvest its nuts or to root out the possums that dwell at its crown. Likewise, boys must tackle climbing the great pine, cedar, and oak nearby to trap by hand the possums day-sleeping in their tree holes. The leaves and other edible parts of these trees, shrubs, and plants can be also ritually consumed. By adulthood, males ceremonially consume over 150 different species of plants, and they master the names and forest niches of hundreds more. A boy is shown the habits of animal species, too, both in ritual teachings and, more casually, by his father and kinsmen. This domain he must not only fit into but seek to rule.

It is also shared with other beings. First there are the forest spirits (*ikeiaru*), souls of deceased "big men" ancestors said to stand guard over the woodland. Men believe them to be only of the male gender and to be dangerous to everyone, especially unwary foreigners. The spirits are armed with a spray of great war weapons enabling them, like witches, to soar through the skies. Forest spirits are sometimes said to take the pugnacious cassowaries as their "wives"; at other times men claim that it is the female hamlet spirits (*aatmogwambu*) who cohabit with these spirits, and whose offspring are really the cassowaries. Sambia also say that the tree kangaroo is the forest spirits' "hunting dog," and this special status makes men cautious about trapping the animals. Besides these spirits there are nature spirits, such as those I alluded to above, haunting caves and swamps and deep river pools.

To sum up, men must adapt to forest life, mastering its natural species, while vying for preeminence against supernatural beings of their own making. This suggests that in these lofty stamping grounds men are closer to where the imagination blows them, the roof of the sky.

Possums

Men prize three sorts of animals—all of which they associate with the high trees of the forest. Possum, cuscus, and other furry marsupials are lumped into the category *yaamwi*. Birds of all kinds are categorized as *duk'a*. The exception is the cassowary, which men classify alone in its own category, *kaiouwugu*. These three categorical distinctions hold for most classifications and metaphoric references too, but they also conceal some ambiguity, which I will touch on. What matters is that in hunting lore, folktales, and dream augury, men's knowledge centers on these categories. The animal sorts of spirit familiars (*numelyu*), too, cluster around these categories.

All three of these types of animal are used in ritual, and of this fact we should not lose sight. Plumes from birds, pelts and fur from possum, bones, feathers, and feces of cassowary all have a place in the doings of male initiation. In addition, the habits of species are also imitated. For instance, the pugnacious habits of possums are actually mimed, and the cassowary's mating display simulated, in ritual drama. Men, in short, impersonate the actions of the animals.

(What data I present here are inadequate for understanding the larger role of these animal categories in masculine culture. We lack behavioral observations showing how men actually use and refer to animals in ritual, and without the benefit of those data it is impossible to give animal categories full treatment. Instead, I shall sketch certain idioms and knowledge relevant to birds and possums. The remaining animal category, the cassowary, requires more extensive treatment for reasons described below, and we shall return to it in Chapter 5.)

Climbing through the dense vegetation of their forests, men like to repeat, "We follow the tree path of the lofty possum, we share the same home." This saying embraces men's forest haunts and fixes a certain identification with possums that pervades the rites and ideology of masculine culture.

The category *yaamwi* covers possum, dogs, and pigs, but it is really only the forest's furry marsupials that are ceremonially emphasized. In contrast to Hua (Meigs 1976) or Baktaman (Barth 1975:180f.), Sambia classify together the flesh of most mammals, including domesticated species. Idiomatic reference seems to stress two distinctive features: all *yaamwi* walk on all fours, and such animals are edible flesh. All pigs, both wild and domesticated, are eaten.[18] Wild dogs are eaten on the rare occasions when they are (unintentionally) trapped, and while men say they are not very tasty, Sambia still relish any animal meat they acquire. (Snakes, eels, and grubs are eaten, but they are not classified *yaamwi*.) It is, then, possum, moomoot, tree kangaroo (two species), spiny anteater, and forest rats to which men readily turn when discussing *yaamwi*. And marsupial *yaamwi* thus subsumes some nineteen subtypes. Some of these subtypes have two or three different names, and their polysemy is a general indicator of the cultural ambience of such species.

The ceremonial life of Sambia is inextricably linked with the use of possum (and birds), and this reliance is impressive. Pigs are few, as I said; so unlike other regions of New Guinea, Sambia *must hunt* to acquire marsupials for the meat to celebrate marriages, funerals, and, especially, male initiations. This in itself would be enough to ensure possum a prominent place in Sambia culture. Men come to associate the pungent taste of its flesh with grand occasions, and to link the peculiar smell of its singed fur with collective hunts, feasts, and the numerous ceremonies in which fur-burning provides a means of "cleansing" individuals of female pollution.

Then, too, men associate possum with spirits, as I mentioned above. Many are the folktales telling of how lonely hunters have been tricked, set upon, and killed by forest spirits or ghosts disguised as possums; once captured, the prey transforms itself back into a spirit, overtaking the unsuspecting trapper. Spirits thus use the guise of marsupials to inflict their damage on men. Men, in turn, hunt and eat possum: this is the course of things as Sambia see it. So men mock themselves, saying dolefully, "We are the pig, the possum, the helpless meat of our ghosts."[19]

This material establishes two trends. Possum are near enough men to be identified with their ghosts. And possums have some special power, intrinsic to their fur and flesh, that can dispel the contagion of women's fluids (see also A. Strathern and M. Strathern 1968:197).[20] The same

---

18. Domesticated male pigs are castrated; females are permitted to forage in the bush and to mate with feral boars, which men fear, despise, and hunt.

19. Ghosts are believed literally to consume one's innards, or to roast whole the humans they strike or unearth, to feast on them. This image men sometimes reveal in dreams.

20. Even so, puzzles exist. For example, the *aamungenyu* possum is believed to be "stronger" because of its smell, and men say it "smells just like a woman." Hence first-stage initiates are not allowed to eat the possum for fear that it will "stunt their growth."

potency is associated with its pungent flesh, the smell of the burning fur, and its ample blood that men compare to their own. The meat is indeed too powerful, since possums are "like ghosts," or "they are the children of ghosts." So one's intake of possum meat must be controlled, and various *yaamwi* species are surrounded with innumerable food and sex taboos.

These semihuman traits, and their use in masculine ritual, condition what men say about possum gender. *Yaamwi* are clearly divided into males and females. Captive male piglets are castrated. The penis and testes of possum, dog, and pigs are all referred to by the cover term *moyu*, as is also true of humans. In possums, especially, it is the testes (which in certain species are bright-colored and visible from a long distance) that distinguish the male from the female. Men say that male *yaamwi* have a "little semen," but not much, whereas female *yaamwi* have a menstrual blood organ (*tingu*) like women (see below). This *yaamwi-tingu* is, incidentally, not eaten, but dried and smoked and hung as an amulet around the necks of women.

Yet despite these clear assignations, men still refer to the immature young of possum as *tai*, "girls, immature female," *yaamwi-tai*. This categorical lumping of its young into a *tai* category does not apply to humans. Girls are *tai*, and boys are *kwulai'u;* generically, individuals may refer to a group of boys and girls as *kwulai-tai*, or sometimes, *yangu*, "grandparent/old person, grandchild." But in pigs and dogs and possum the young are only *tai;* not until animals reach reproductive age are they classified separately as *aambelu* (female) or *aatmwul* (male).

Perceptions of gender play an important part in how male ritual makes special use of possums and their natural habits. The niche of a species is important in what men say of it. Whether a species is ground-dwelling or tree-dwelling influences what can be done with it, since here the arboreal animal is generally believed to be "cleaner" and safer food (for initiated males). Cave dwellers, like the spiny anteater, and ground-nesting (hole-nesting) rats are hemmed in by more taboos, especially for immature ritual initiates. The diet of an animal also matters. Leaf eaters are handled differently from the omnivorous *chenyu*, with its doglike teeth and snout and its black tail. Its flesh is also "stronger," so boys cannot eat it until they reach bachelorhood. Anatomy is significant: men use the female *tingu* and male fur-covered scrotum, as I said. Certain marsupial anatomical traits are selected as being "masculine," for example, the girth of the tree kangaroo's chest, which is especially masculine; or, negatively, especially long tails, snouts, or the absence of a tail (the spiny anteater) distinguish one species from others. These qualities are used in ritual.

The *numunyu* (it also has three other names) marsupial deserves mention for what it does that fascinates men: "It nose-bleeds itself." The animal allegedly scratches inside its nostrils with leaves and grasses, making them (sometimes? always?) bleed. "The *numunyu* imitates us in nose-bleeding," men say secretly. And occasionally men have come upon an animal that is said to have accidentally killed itself in this way. (Such animals are cooked and eaten, men say, but I have never actually observed such an occurrence.) "The male nose-bleeds itself as its wife looks on, teaching her," Tali has said; "then she imitates him." Precisely why this is done is unclear. But the belief is certain enough, and this species, its snout and nasal cartilage, is taboo to boys until they are older. Both the long-nosed spiny anteater and the nose-bleeding *numunyu* are completely taboo to women. They are the only *yaamwi* species, incidentally, that women *cannot* eat. (One other major animal food source is also off limits to women, namely the cassowary, as we shall see.)

The marsupial's fur color and its use as a male decoration are the two most important factors influencing men's food taboos. Of these fur-color "motivated" taboos, three predominate: white, black, and orange-red. White furry *yaamwi* species—five of them—are most prohibited; one of them, the *aweiawei* possum, whose scrotum is mounted on the headdress of newlywed (fourth-stage) initiates, is taboo for life. That is because men say they wear the animal's skin and cannot, therefore, eat it. The *ikambi* possum is taboo until old age because Sambia fear that by eating its white fur-covered flesh boys may hasten their decline into "white-haired old age." Black and black-and-white species (seven in all) are taboo too, most of them until adulthood. Three orange-red species are also prohibited. Other factors intervene; the *maambootu* species is white but lives in a ground hole, and both of these attributes draw concern. The *aalyuwuntu* species is black and white but is also water-loving like a beaver.

These ambiguities make it difficult to account logically for food taboos on their own. Elsewhere I shall detail more of a spectrum of such data to show the interrelationship of ritual life-cycle changes and corresponding food and sex taboos.

Birds

We need initially to take note of the fact that men also compare birds to humans. Birds are like (*havalt-nunta*) men.

> They sleep at night; in the morning they get up. At early morning, they search for food. In the late afternoon they eat. You and me, men, we eat possums; birds hunt insects. [Weiyu]

Of more telling importance, for Moondi, is a bird's morphology: "Birds walk on two legs as we do, but possums and pigs walk on all fours." This remark shows that on birds men tend to project positive attributes. Birds are "pure" because they dwell in trees and can fly and soar. Once again, idiomatic contrasts are not based on a metaphysical principle of neat cosmic oppositions but simply on the "cleanliness" of trees and the sky versus the soiled, damp, cool undergrowth of things on the ground.

The habits of particular bird species become the focus of ritual emphasis. A case in point is the *nungetnyu* (the crested bird of paradise?), an orange-red bird that actually constructs a round platform (of straw and twigs) on which it performs mating displays.[21] The bird, men assert, builds its own "dance ground" (*korumundiku*) during mating season as men do in their initiations. It collects brush. The bird flies off in search of food. "The *nungetnyu* has a mind [*koontu,* thought or awareness]; it gets food and stores it near its dance ground so it doesn't need to search for it later." Then it "stands up to sing," as do groups of men who ceremonially perform on the dance ground. Young, brightly plumed birds take center stage on their "dance ground"; they "sing their songs." Meanwhile, the elder birds "fly and sit in nearby trees," watching the bright-plumed young birds.

But here is the rub: *nungetnyu* are said to be only of the female gender. Tali told me this:

> The old female birds [*yangu,* old woman] come and sit around the *nungetnyu* "dance ground" to watch. The *nungetnyu* has no men; there are only females. The *yangu*—their old women—come to sit and watch the young *nungetnyu-aambelu* [women-birds] dance.

The lexical and metaphoric significance of this statement took me almost two years to appreciate. Now it seems simple.

The *nungetnyu* species, with habits that remind men of their own initiation customs, is the focus of idiom and belief, only there is a total inversion of gender: the all-female-bird group mating ceremony is projected (and thereby substituted) in place of men's all-male dance-ground initiation rites. (I need to add one more fact. The *nungetnyu*'s platform materials, e.g., straw, are crucial ingredients for making a powerful ceremonial leaf wreath [called *aamunandu,* literally, without mother's breast] ushering in the initiatory cycle of ritual-cult-house-raising festivities. Men believe that the wreath, by being hung inside the house from its ceiling, bestows a kind of magnetism that lures spirit familiars into the cult house.[22]) All these aspects—the *nungetnyu* display, its singing and food-collecting, the "elder birds" watching on in approval, and its dancing—men note and compare

---

21. High in the mountains I have seen these platforms near trails. They are made of matted straw, some 15 inches in diameter, and perhaps 3 to 6 inches deep. I have even seen a stick protruding out of the center of the platform, which men liken to their firewood pillars in dance grounds. But I have not observed the bird's display itself.

22. In addition, an identical wreath is placed inside every new men's clubhouse at its building, which is celebrated by performing a shaman's initiation and songfest for attracting familiars (see also Herdt 1977:157).

to their great initiation proceedings on dance grounds. And yet, amazingly, *nungetnyu* are only of the female sex.

So let us examine the gender of other bird species, contrasting them with this striking set of male perceptions. On this score, men are unflinchingly clear and dogmatic.

Newly hatched bird chicks are again called only *duk'a-tai,* "bird-girls." Here, language certainly restricts classification, since no other category, except *tai* (i.e., girl), is applicable to immature birds.

But in mature birds of all species known to me (and all that I could elicit from my informants), full, bright-colored plumage unambiguously identifies only male birds. Indeed, it is these brilliant male plumes that men hunt, celebrate, and take for themselves for their feather headdresses. Dull-colored birds, or birds of the same species without tail plumes, are handled in two ways. Either they are said to be "old birds," *yangu* (old man or woman), or they are called "females" (again, *duk'a-aambelu,* bird-woman).[23]

"Old birds" are therefore implicitly female. Age is ascertained by the size of the body, dull plumage, nesting habits, and by a lack of bright tail plumes. Only "old birds lay eggs," men say. This idiom also implies its converse: reproductively mature birds lack bright plumes; and bright-plumed birds do not lay eggs. Finally, this contrast is reinforced by native classification: young birds are generically *moongenyu,* the term for post-pubescent bachelors and one which contrasts with old *yangu,* as we saw.

Two additional observations are in order. First, Sambia implicitly associate the generic changes in birds with sex-gender changes. The predominant tendency is to assign birds to the female sex, first as chicks, and then as egg-laying old females; "male bright plumage" is but a brief florescence, a transition along the way. The shift of metaphoric and lexical significance in the associated idioms depends on age: colorful, youthful, and male characteristics appear to give way to dull, mature, and female traits. Sambia, of course, recognize that some birds lay eggs while others do not. They also know that in certain birds, like the kalanga, plumage color does not change with age. But these discrepancies are avoided. What counts is the tacit categorical association between cocky maleness and bright plumage; and dull reproductive competence with femaleness.[24]

---

23. Here is yet another case in which the ethnographer asks silly questions, which no Sambia asks, or else he goes ignorant. The second category, *aambelu,* is rarely used by Sambia except in reference to cassowaries or *nungetnyu,* as we saw. This is because ideological emphasis is on "male" bright-plumed birds, or old females who lay eggs. I had to elicit the contrasts carefully.

24. Precisely how egg-laying birds (and eels) reproduce is a mystery to Sambia. For instance, Weiyu, in telling me about such matters, once mused to himself: "What sex is the eel, the cassowary, or birds? How do they have coitus that they can produce eggs?"

Second, bright plumes, worn in headdresses, are lexically labeled "arse-tail" (*elutnjoomwi'u: elut* = arse; *joomwi'u* = transfix, [*joo*]-*choowi'u* = tail, as in *yaamwi-choowi'u,* possum tail). No matter where the feathers are plucked from (wing, tail, or headcrest, though most derive from tail plumes), they are classified as "arse feathers," as are all cassowary feathers. This lexical information contains two clues for understanding bird idioms. First, like possum tails and genitals, bird feathers are stood up, vertically erect, atop a man's head. The feathers are especially vulnerable to a women's touch and pollution, i.e., they are said to "go limp and dull."[25] Second, male dogma classifies all headdress feathers as deriving either from the wing or tail of birds. The crowned pigeon is the only bird whose *headcrest* feathers are ceremonially used (see Table 5), but this fact is hidden from women and children, who are deceivingly told that such feathers come from the bird's tail.[26]

This chapter has opened up the several issues that pertain substantively to the two following chapters. I began by specifying some of men's views of their cosmos: hamlet rules, gardening idioms, and forest lore. I related the basis of these data to Sambia knowledge about their cosmos. Then I recounted how idioms are normally bound up in a communicational medium that transmits, to Sambia, both manifest and latent information. Verbal statements often do different things, and what they communicate depends on the speaker, topic, and context. A speaker's statement links an idiom with related surface thoughts; if need be (or if asked), individuals often verbally associate such thoughts to other tacit knowledge within themselves. This investigatory procedure seems as easy as retracing a friend's footsteps along a familiar path while blindfolded. Only here, the path is unknown. The problem is that so far little has been said about the commonness or rarity of the idioms cited. I have also avoided the hoary issue of what "surface thoughts," "verbal associations," or "latent knowledge" mean. *Mean* to whom?

In the following chapters, I try to confront this issue by providing more detailed information about particular natural species. In Chapter 4, "Genderizing the Pandanus Tree," we shall consider more of Sambia botanical knowledge. (The material on pandanus trees also affords me an opportuni-

---

25. See Read (1955:270), who makes a similar observation, also noting that Gahuku men strictly forbid women to touch their hair or head; Sambia share in this implicit rule too.

26. The crowned pigeon is secretly called *mindu,* "head." This refers to the fact that men hide the knowledge that they take its feathers not from its tail (or wing) but from its crest. Men are careful to conceal the natural facts, they say. In hunting they quickly tear out crest feathers and tail feathers simultaneously, telling children or women that they have already removed its "tail plumes."

TABLE 5   *Bird Plumes Hunted and Worn in Ritual*

Name of Species[1]	Valued Color of Plume	Ritual Status of Male Initiate	Plumes of Bird Never Worn	Plume Taken from
Raggiana bird of paradise (male) (*banu*)	Orange-red	2nd	Brown	Wing
Male brown sicklebill (*wanboogu*)	Deep-blue (tail feather)	4th	Short feathers	Tail
Kalanga (Eclectus female parrot) (*nowi'u*)	Red (green)	3rd		Tail
Black-capped and purple-bellied lory (*woolyu*)	Yellow-red (red-yellow-green)	3rd		Tail
Sulphur-crested cockatoo (*wiaaku*)	White	4th-6th	Short feathers	Wing
Crowned pigeon (*gonjumdu*)[2]	White	4th	Tail feathers	Headcrest
Kokomo (great hornbill) (*mesagu*)	Black (blue-green)	4th-6th		Tail

[1]See Peckover and Filewood (1976).
[2]Secret name, *mindu,* "head."

ty to speak with anthropologist readers on methodological problems.) In Chapter 5, "The Phantom Cassowary," I shall take up a more striking mixture of Sambia fantasy and reality surrounding the cassowary. This animal is its own unique cultural category for Sambia, and it is of great ritual and secular interest. Data on the cassowary are also richer (and therefore more complicated) than my data on the disparate topics I have examined in this chapter. These chapters, taken together, will thus enable us to establish a general approach for tackling the more controversial topics of human sexuality and parthenogenesis that follow them. What men have said about their cosmos, therefore, anticipates my larger contention: namely, that Sambia are fascinated with the gender of things; that their idioms focus on mastering the morally right order of things as they wish to perceive them; and that the significance of natural species in masculine ritual depends precisely on their perceived attributes as innately female, innately fertile things in nature.

CHAPTER FOUR *Genderizing the Pandanus Tree*

Sambia perceive in pandanus trees a reproductive cycle comparable to their own. Masculine idioms hypothesize even more than this: "Female pandanus are identical to our women: they give birth to nuts." Men also liken the tree's long aerial roots to "women's breasts." Its white fleshy nut meats are equated to "mother's breast milk." But the crimson juice of red pandanus fruit,[1] men say, is "identical to menstrual blood." So the ingestion taboos associated with menstruation apply to it. And then, men have

---

1. There are two broad families of pandanus species in New Guinea: pandanus trees that bear nuts with coconutlike meat (Sambia call them *kunaalu*), and pandanus fruit trees (Sambia call them *ishoyu*), which produce long red seed-filled bodies. Both nuts and fruit are eaten; see Paijmans (1976:132).

this secret: they tap pandanus aerial roots for their "milk sap," which is drunk to replenish lost semen.

These idioms voice cultural belief, but they also carry the stamp of personal conviction. How can this be studied? We need interpersonal communications: conversations, casual remarks or spontaneous associations, and the statements we ethnographers not only observe but provoke. Metaphor abounds; so does personal knowledge, and behind that, fantasy. For instance, precise sexual identifications and "symbolic" substitutions occur: tree sap *is* mother's milk. The overall projection of human gender attributes into a taxon of trees is another example. What such communications mean for individuals is the focus of this and subsequent chapters.

So far my verbal material on the environment has been discursive. Garden crops and food are constant topics of conversation. Their idioms provide convenient props for communicating other tacit information; some of that information is drawn from interpersonal and social relationships, and some stems from subjective orientations. The psychological frame encompassing garden work, as we saw, is visibly polarized around the opposition between male and female. Perhaps because garden references are so familiar and immediate, my comprehension of how idioms fitted into personal knowledge came slowly. Still, it was not so difficult to grasp men's association between garden tubers and feminine procreative powers since women were the chief gardeners. Warfare made this understandable. It is even easier to anthropomorphize animals with humanlike traits; and it is, likewise, reasonable that men impersonate those species in their rites, and identify birds—their decorative plumes—with the ritual emblems that make men masculine. Men's idioms provided that information, and I tried in piecemeal ways to assimilate it to the right order of things as men characterize their perceptions of the world. Now, in greater detail, let us examine a more troublesome topic.

Pandanus trees differ from these domains in many respects. They are trees. The nut-bearing trees, *kunaalu* (which I shall concentrate on), grow only in the high forest. They are exclusively the business of men—their ownership, care, and harvest. They are personalized: each tree is individually owned, and a man, "its father," gives it a name and takes pride in its nut harvest. Beyond this personalization, pandanus are, indeed, quite extraordinary. Unlike most trees, they bear edible nuts (or fruits, *isho-yu*) seasonally. They are exotic; and their tallness and growth in murky groves in overcast mountains add to their wildness. (See Figure 4.)

Most of all, there is nothing soft about pandanus: they possess hard, rough trunks and are vertical and unbending. They have protruding, knotted aerial roots that jut out unpredictably medusoid; and they wear a crown of sharp, unfriendly leaves. Men must scale the tree to get at its nut pods, and they do so without benefit of protective padding, ropes, or supports. It is men who do the work of clearing away debris and brush from their bases, and who otherwise tend them. Women are uninvolved, except that all Sambia love the delicious coconutlike meat of the nuts. (Likewise the pungent taste of red pandanus fruit that one comes to crave.) These trees are removed from hamlet life; they also lack the animation of birds or possums. Sambia men have, nonetheless, fixed on the pandanus as a compelling image for projecting themselves into this piece of their cosmos. The trees, as designata, provide a contrast, a pseudocontrol, for the tendency of men to genderize their beliefs and personal knowledge about floral species.

Classifications

Before examining the pandanus, we need to understand a bit more about the general significance of trees in masculine culture and, especially, ritual.

Sambia distinguish two types of trees, both of which concern us. All kinds of deciduous, evergreen, and pine are classified into a major taxon, *iku. Iku* is, then, generic for tree, and its Neo-Melanesian cover term is

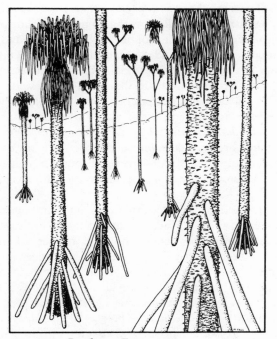

FIGURE 4   *Pandanus Forest*

diwai. The only other major category encompasses both palms and pandanus trees. It lacks a single categorical gloss, however, so for convenience I shall refer to it as *kunaalu,* the name of cultivated pandanus trees and nuts. (Sambia do not do this; this major taxon is an unmarked linguistic category.) When Sambia speak on such global levels (which is seldom), they refer to *iku,* in the first case, or to the minor taxonomic name of particular palm or pandanus species. *Iku* is also a prefix marker for persons, particularly (but not exclusively) men; and it is also generic for "clan," as noted above, such as in the expression *gami ikutuvu,* "his clan" (cf. *gami ikutuvo,* her clan).

Sambia also tend to dichotomize *iku* and *kunaalu* on the basis of moisture, i.e., "moist" (*wunyu-tei,* water-bearing) versus "dry" (*yaalkoogu*) tree species. These attributes are not unique to trees, but they are essential for understanding how men utilize them and what they say and think about them. (The same contrast between "dry" and "wet" applies to humans too; see below.) *Iku* trees are said to be moist to the touch, since their bark and leaves are easily permeable, and because they can naturally exude tree sap. *Kunaalu,* on the other hand, have tough skins dry to the touch, nor do they naturally exude sap. To clarify this distinction further I should mention what men say about tree sap.

There are two kinds of tree sap. Most *iku* species exude seasonally their own crystalline syrup (*wakooglu-nambelu,* also the name for "shadow"), usually tinted like maple syrup. This kind of sap (to my knowledge) is seldom utilized by Sambia, except for crudely (as distinct from carefully) binding parcels together in the forest. Now, certain trees, if cut (tapped) also exude a milky latexlike sap, as does the rubber tree (which randomly grows in Sambia forests). Their leaves, if torn, or twigs, if broken, exude a similar "milk sap" (I hereafter refer to it this way). All such milk saps Sambia lump together as *i-aamoonaalyu* (*i,* tree or man; *aamoo,* breast milk; *aalyu,* water; mother's breast milk is *aamoonaalyu*). These milk saps Sambia make use of in various ways. A mundane practice: the *ngoolu* tree sap (which is highly sticky) is collected as a glue, and is then used to bind arrowheads to shafts.

Yet by far the most spectacular "job" of this white milk sap begins in secret male ritual: it is eaten. Not all saps are ingested. Of the several dozen tree species that Sambia know to contain milk sap, thirteen different *iku* species have white-colored sap (two of them are, however, tinted yellow) and are ceremonially utilized by men. These white fluids are thought to be the "lifeblood" of trees; they are all ingested constantly. Indeed, crystalline syrup and the various milk saps alike are indexed by the cover term "tree blood," *iku-menjaaka* (*menjaaku* is "blood" in animals and humans). So here we see how "wet" *iku* are also linked to animals and humans. *Kunaalu* species, on the other hand, do not exude syrup, and only one species, *kambeilaako* (wild pandanus trees), is sometimes tapped for its milk sap.

Men believe these fluids are vital to the life support of trees, primarily *iku*. So "tree blood" is, I think, an apt translation of this concept. This does not imply, however, that Sambia fully comprehend the physiology of human or plant circulatory systems. For instance, there is no notion of what one's heartbeat or heartrate implies; and there is no concept of a blood circulatory system connected to respiration or body heat. The pulse is noted, but its meaning is not understood. Nor do Sambia recognize the function of the lymphatic system or the lungs. I say this to dispel the hint of Sambia sophistication in the area of anatomy and physiology (see Chapters 7 and 8) so as to make more meaningful what follows (see also Glick 1964; Meigs 1976:394–395). What matters for Sambia is the viability and growth of an organism, be it animal, plant, or human.

In this sense blood is absolutely vital. The "free flow" of blood, or bloodlike fluids (i.e., "tree blood"), is necessary for both growth and life. Loss of blood is dangerous; it signals a life threat and, if left unchecked, imminent death. Men recognize that by superficially "ringing" a tree trunk with a circular cut (this is also the means for killing garden trees left standing for later use as firewood) they can hasten its growth. Tree fluids, then, like human blood, are endowed with a life-giving force, and this principle leads to the issue of Sambia perceptions of gender classification.

All trees are classified as either male or female, and this sex contrast underlies their ritual significance. *Iku* are said to be either male (*iku-kwolu*) or female (*iku-aambelu*) largely on the basis of which trees produce fruit (*iku-chelu; chelu* is also "stone" and "heart"). "Female *iku* have fruit, males do not," men assert. Alternatively, male trees are generally identified by producing flowers (*powuptu*). Tree flowers and fruit are not eaten by men; they are the "food of birds and possums." Milk sap, which is only a human food, and a masculine one at that, is the product of only female *iku*. "Only female *iku* have *iaamoonaalyu,* male trees have none," men say (but see below). Conversely, men say, "Trees without milk are male trees." *Kunaalu* trees are defined as male (*kunaal-kwolu*) or female (*kunaal-aambelu*) or, occasionally, hermaphrodite (*kwol-aatmwol;* this term also applies to human hermaphrodites). Generally, as well, flower-bearing pandanus are classified as male and nut-bearing pandanus as female; but tree anatomy is also taken into account, so I shall describe the finer points later. Before proceeding further, I need to mention an anatomical part of plants and trees that Sambia axiomatically associate with the femaleness of living things.

Men call this appendage the *tingu.* We have already seen reference to the *tingu* reproductive organ in female animals. The *tingu* of possums (like that of pigs and dogs) is tannish red on the outside (when dried). In living mammals, men believe, it is filled with blood. Now, the same concept is extended to the base (tree trunk or stalk, *kablu*) of trees, out of which grow shoots or saplings of the plant. This attribute of *tingu* men compare to the *yaamwi-tingu* of mammals and an organ in women (also called *tingu*). Weiyu says this: "Of other things—banana trees, native ginger— we men, look at them; they're the same [as *yaamwi-tingu*]; so we mark them *tingu* [too]." The new, inner stalk of the black palm tree (*yooglanyu*, classed with *kunaalu*), for instance, is *yooglanyu-tingu;* like the possum *tingu* it is reddish brown (as opposed to the white palm heart). Likewise, various tree shoots are labeled *nagi-tingu* (banana), *aamboogu-tingu* (a scarce wild palm from which bows are carved), and *kunaalu-tingu*. "The *tingu* is not food, nothing [no animal] eats it"; and Weiyu says that men never eat it. Men do, however, eat palm hearts (especially the cabbage palm, which is commonly collected), all except that of the black palm, which is taboo until one is aged.

On being asked how the *tingu* actually worked, Weiyu replied un- equivocally: "It grows [*perulyapi*, produces] the new stalks [of the tree]. But it is not for eating." Here, then, is a clear notion that trees are stimulated and grown by virtue of a reproduction-related appendage dubbed the *tingu*. Perceptions of whether a plant is either female or male are a secondary manifestation of something else. It is rather the *tingu* appendage present within the plant that somehow "grows" it. In Chapters 7 and 8 we shall see how men link this concept with ritual and nonritual idioms of human sexuality. Anticipating that discussion and the present focus, I wish here to glance at the contextual significance of forest trees in initiation rites.

Trees in Ritual

This book is a preface to initiation idioms among Sambia, men so wedded to their rituals that human existence and compulsive observance are one and the same. Sambia know no other way. Surely the absolute, all-encom- passing power of such a reality has been lost on us Westerners, for whom ritual has become pigeonholed into the stylized handshake, the tedious factory assembly line, or the social hour of Sunday church attendance. We are the captives of rational industrialization. Sambia are consumed with their rituals. By noting this I am not, of course, lamenting the loss of some kind of Rousseauesque paradise (Sontag 1966:69–81). But there remains a superordinate quality of Sambia existence that distinguishes them, and their long experience in rituals, from us: shared passion.[2] Why have

---

2. The distinction between "hot" and "cold" societies suggested by Lévi-Strauss (1966) indeed

ethnographers usually failed to communicate the passion of ritual, and what difference does it make?

Ethnographers are required to describe and classify what they see. Yet this practice has normally meant recording only the customs of ritual. In the ethnographic archives there are numerous records of ritual routines involving plants and animals. Here is a Sambia illustration.

Third-stage initiation is nearing an end. Men go to the high forest. They select a wild pandanus-nut tree. A ritual "bridge" (*ngatu*) is built around its base. The initiates are led up onto the structure facing the tree. The youths are told to remove a pubic hair; the hair is handed to an elder who then inserts it into the trunk of the living tree. The boys are next shown the Jew's harp in a ritual teaching. They are told what it means to play the harp: that they are pubescent, sexually mature bachelors; and that the Jew's harp is like their wife's vagina in that they soon will penetrate it. They are implored not to engage in promiscuous heterosexuality and threatened with the sanction of death for breaking this taboo. They then are given some sugarcane and special leaves and flowers, which are masticated and actually spit outwards and up, toward the tree trunk.[3] Men refer to the tree as the youths' age-mate. The novices are then told to grab hold of the trunk, and together they shake the tree while collectively emitting a sharp sound (associated with being stung with nettles), an odd, vigorous signal. Now men know the youths are more disciplined and linked as an age-set.

This account tells us a lot. The setting and the actors are established. The ritual paraphernalia are sketched: pandanus tree, a special bridge, leaves, and Jew's harp. While more detail would widen our understanding, we know enough to construct an image of what happened. I said just enough to disclose how crucial is the pandanus tree for carrying out the routine (and this procedure exists in four of six male initiations that justify the label "routine"). We sense, too, how this rite aims at creating subjective feelings of interest, or an "identification," among the boys, toward this tree in which they have deposited pubic hair and saliva, both vital substances. The tree is their age-mate: every sensory channel—the vision of the soaring tree, vocalizing together, tasting and spitting, and touching the trunk—is placed in the service of establishing a bond with the tree. All this

---

implies the opposite: tribal societies are hopelessly cold because experience and behavior are stymied by ritual routine; Western society is intellectually hot since we can technologically adjust to constant and rapid change unshackled by ritual (see Geertz 1967; Wagner 1972:4). I quite doubt the value of those ideal types: tribesmen also innovate; their societies no doubt change; and civilizations have been known to collapse with or without ritual.

3. An act referred to generically as *koomdu oovutu; koomdu,* "sugarcane" (which is masticated); and *oovutu,* "to spit outwards" (not down).

is true enough. But it is still inadequate for understanding what Sambia experienced, and what we, as readers, want to know about what they experienced. The proof of this inadequacy is contained in this very recapitulation of the ritual.

My ritual data were inadequate because they did not reveal the passions men expressed. Now passion is an old-fashioned word; but so is ritual. My *eyewitness* ethnography (Sontag 1966:75) was straightforward, yet it lacked animation: there was no accounting of its emotions. So in the seductive summary of it I was forced to compensate: in that regard the preceding paragraph makes use of words completely absent from the ethnographic description: image, feelings, identification, sensory channel, and bond. These constructs appear to have been established on the basis of inferences drawn from the data. Not so: by omitting qualitative details of the affective behavior, I deprived the constructs of any authentic heuristic value. To compensate, I dressed up the summary of the technical routine with human feelings. It was essential to have done that. Sambia rituals are more than routines: men also experience stirring emotions, desires, and even lust, which can come about either in the gravest silence or in outbursts of great excitement.

So now I must affectively qualify the description. The old men stood back, and some were even distracted; it was really the younger adults who grew zealous. It was their enthusiasm that got the "bridge" up. One of the initiates (Moondi) did not surrender a pubic hair. (I later learned he had only pretended to; afterwards he told me that this was because he felt "ashamed of having other men know I had pubic hair," so he didn't want to do it.) When the boys were lectured on adultery, two of them grinned and had to look down to avoid being reprimanded for doing so. And last, when those youths clung to the tree, several of them—the oldest, the most serious—spat with a grim and determined vengeance that had to be seen to be believed. I knew them, and my heart sank: Would they eventually redirect that hardness toward their wives and children and fellows?

Men need no other reminder of the passion of their marriage to ritual than the very trees that surround them. All kinds of trees, shrubs, and plants get worked in. Different sorts of secret ritual make use of them. Here, I want to establish certain relationships between trees and ritual, and between pandanus trees and humans. What matters is that men commune secretly with plants and trees. They constantly consume tree products, and they also insert their own body substances into trees and plants. For a people like Sambia—who are so cautious and alert about what they eat, fearing sorcery or pollution, and who are so careful about the disposal of food leavings for the same reasons—such intimate communions reveal a lot. Men obviously trust the "cleanliness" of trees since they eat them. They trust the security of their own forest haunts and specially chosen trees for depositing their body fluids.

This leads to a final word about the wider role of *kunaalu* trees in masculine initiation. Every one of the six grades of initiation draws heavily on wild pandanus and black palm species. First initiation begins with a black-palm purificatory ceremony (*akovanyu*) and is performed when boys are seven to ten years old; and the last initiation (some fifteen or twenty years later) begins again with a black-palm (or alternatively a wild pandanus) spitting ritual. That first ceremony requires that the boy's old (childhood) noseplug be taken from him and actually inserted into the palm tree; thereafter, the tree is said to be his age-mate. The final ritual of first initiation, furthermore, centers on the domesticated pandanus and the ingestion of its nuts. Second-stage initiation, by contrast, is organized around the collection, ceremonial parading, and final consumption of red pandanus fruits, long, brilliant red offspring of that weird tree. And from the fronds covering the (cultivated) pandanus flower only men can weave warrior armbands (*aatmwonandu*), paramount emblems of manhood that are mounted in the puberty rites. In third-stage initiation, too, and in the three initiations that follow, the most powerful teaching again centers on wild pandanus at the time of the spitting rituals. Those rites, then, simple though they are, constitute a highlight of third-, fourth-, fifth-, and sixth-stage initiations leading to manhood. From this aside we can begin to fathom the outward manifestations of a deeply felt association between ritualized masculinity and pandanus. What are its ramifications in idioms?

The Reproductive Cycle

Sexual intercourse nearly always involves procreation—"making babies" —for Sambia, men and women alike. Initiation thus turns boys into men. And to achieve full manhood means that one must be married (fourth-stage initiation); celebrate and defend oneself against one's (assigned) wife's menarche (fifth-stage initiation); and then father a child by her, appropriately ritualizing the birth event (sixth-stage initiation). Other considerations, however, still bear on the subject of reproduction for Sambia, particularly in discussions of humans, lower mammals, and pandanus trees.

There is, first of all, the determination of sex at birth. Sex assignment commonly crops up in such questions as "Is it male or female?" and "Does it have a penis and testes?"

Next there is an associated question about the choice of sexual intercourse: What form did it take? Sambia recognize only two possibilities or techniques, coitus and fellatio.[4] The possibilities are also limited by custom. Men and women engage in both types of erotic intercourse; but among bachelors and initiates, homosexual contacts are confined to asymmetrical fellatio. In both cases, one's choice of erotic technique *always* suggests this: a man lusts for his partner; his semen enters the body of his partner; and the semen goes to "strengthen" the body of his partner and, in women, also to create a child.[5]

Finally, and in addition to these cultural and experiential "universals" that apply to most Sambia men, there are specific erotic attributes that individuals are excited by and may act on in the particular circumstances of a situation. It is not enough to say simply that a man lusts after another person: we also need to know what erotic desire means for him, i.e., what is exciting about that particular person at that particular moment. (See Chapter 8.)

The same particularities apply to most of the other facets of reproduction and sexual intercourse. Consider now how men draw on these factors in what they say of pandanus.

Sex assignment in pandanus is fixed concretely by perceptions of the physical attributes of trees. This is true in how men's idioms characterize tree morphology, leaf coloration, and seasonal changes as sex-related attributes.

Two morphological traits dominate all others: nuts and flowers. Idiomatically, pandanus trees bearing nut pods (like the above-mentioned tree fruit) are "female," since the pods are its "children," created through a "pregnancy," and, like humans and lower mammals, "only females procreate." Some pandanus produce nuts, others do not. Therefore, nut-bearing trees are categorically "female," while the other trees are believed to be nonfemale. (This statement constitutes, incidentally, a close facsimile of how Sambia think about humans and trees. A barren woman is *kwol-iku*, "a malelike person/tree," a female who possesses a vagina but does not procreate. Conversely, male pandanus trees flower the way men develop mature glans penises.) Men associate *iku* tree fruit with "female" trees, but they do not so closely associate *iku* flowers with "maleness" in trees. Male pandanus trees, on the other hand, bear long white flowers (*koonai-kwolu; koonai,* noun stem denoting *kunaalu; kwolu* = male), which are likened to penises. These classifications draw some metaphoric support from gender-related idioms describing animal categories and *iku* trees too. Yet here men go further, encompassing other of the trees' perceptual attributes that uphold their views about pandanus dimorphism.

---

4. Hereafter I shall mean by coitus heterosexual genital-to-genital intercourse, the "missionary" position, as distinct from fellatio.

5. Other factors are also relevant; see Chapters 7 and 8.

One of these species-specific traits is clearly paramount in the ritual classification and treatment of the entire taxon of *kunaalu:* the fact that certain *kunaalu* species produce what men call a "grass skirt" (*koonaikoogu*).[6] This morphological feature is so important that it deserves to be labeled a global attribute[7] in men's perceptions of *kunaalu* species. Pandanus trees sporting a grass skirt are usually lexically (not just metaphorically) categorized as female; those lacking that trait are classed as male. So this creates two related but distinct types of sex assignment complicating what was noted above regarding flowers and nuts. *Kunaalu* trees (and whole species) are said to be either male or female by virtue of producing nuts. But pandanus trees *without* grass skirts (even wild species that produce nuts) are semantically indexed toward, and are exclusively utilized in, ritual, because they are "male" trees. Sambia perceive the trees this way, and yet they do not oppose—they entertain—one mode of classification over another. This apparent contradiction requires explanation.

What men call a grass skirt is a hanging cluster of dried, matted palm branches and fronds. The dead fronds droop from but remain attached to the trunk, hanging some 2 to 3 feet below the crown of living green palm leaves. As leaves die, the old fronds are replaced by new fronds (also called *kwolu*) at the crest of the tree. The old dried fronds tend to stay affixed to the trunk in certain species like domesticated pandanus. In other species, like black palm and wild pandanus, the fronds simply fall out, giving the trunk a "naked sweep" to the eye, from its base to its leaf cluster. These morphological differences among pandanus species men compare explicitly to Sambia attire in men versus women. The *kunaalu* (domesticated species) "grass skirt" is the "same as the *kanyelu* [round] grass skirt of women," men say. Sambia women do indeed clothe themselves in a grass-fiber skirt (which they weave from reeds) that entirely encircles the waist and covers the buttocks (below the knees). By contrast, men and all initiates wear only a frontal grass sporran, shielding the abdomen and pubic area, to just above the knees, thus exposing the back and buttocks (which are protected by bark capes).

On the basis of this constant, nonseasonal characteristic, then, whole species of *kunaalu* are sex-typed. For example, the domesticated pandanus, Tali said, "is identically the same as women, its grass skirt is the same as the women's." But the absence of a grass skirt, i.e., as in the long naked trunk of the black palm, "is the same as we men, identically the

---

6. Recall that *koogu* is the "soul." Elsewhere I show how men utilize this designata in idioms and ritual imagery.

7. By global I mean the sense that such a perceptual feature is subjectively prior to others and seems to be measured across all *kunaalu* species.

same as ours [men's sporran]." Men's rituals draw on this distinctive polarity in various ways.

One example: the wild pandanus tree (*kambeilaako*), as we saw above, is selected for the spitting ritual in fifth- and sixth-stage ceremonies expressly because its naked trunk is "male." I asked Tali why, and he stated flatly: "When its [*kambeilaako*] leaves are dry, they fall away . . . fall out, unlike the trunk of the *kunaalu* [domesticated pandanus], which is just like a woman's grass skirt. It [*kambeilaako*] has a clean, smooth trunk."

This is what masculine idiom alleges: it establishes a bifocal classification. One type is based on seasonal reproductive traits—like nuts and flowers—which are dogmatically associated with sex and sex assignment in particular trees. The other classification stems from a different morphological attribute, the dried-frond grass skirt, one that is permanent and nonseasonal, but that men metaphorically extend by globally indexing whole species, not just individual trees, as either male or female (by virtue of the presence or absence of that trait). These perceptual attributes not only distinguish sex type, they also imply things about the functional role of such traits in the reproductive cycle.

To clarify what such sex distinctions assume about the reproductive cycle of pandanus we need to consider other details of tree morphology. It is apparent that men link gross morphology to the sex assignment of individual trees and entire species. It also seems plausible that idioms indexically point toward—are contingent on, not caused by—ritual.

Now we can go further. If masculine idioms genderize pandanus morphology in this way, splitting up the wholeness of the tree into pieces labeled "male" or "female," perhaps I am simply showing isolated examples of a much larger superorganic process at work: the machine workings of the human mind, which polarizes and codes percepts binarily, by opposition, into subtypes, two of which, male and female, are focal categories in Sambia culture.

This Lévi-Straussian (1963, 1966) argument is attractive; it has its adherents (see Douglas 1966; Leach 1976); and it has been recently applied to similar New Guinea materials by Alfred Gell (1975, especially pp. 123–155). Yet its difficulties are formidable: first, because we are given so few observations with which to understand how individual action, speech, and thought are related to these structural categories; second, because we are offered summaries of what appear to be inferences from custom and behavior, inferences that are then binarily constructed (without a sample) so as to suggest that the analysis represents, at some level of meaning, the experience of individuals. The methodology of these procedures is still unknown. And please note of Sambia: on what basis should we assume that a culturally constituted suit of armor so ironclad as the dos and don'ts of gender taboos and roles "reflects" the inner subjectivity of individuals? Why should we not question whether these normative classifications and idioms do not *also* belie, distort, or screen other knowledge or thoughts? Naturalistic verbal material should help to clarify: it will enable us to examine both if and how individual perceptions and knowledge are genderized in speech in line with cultural idioms. And last, the Lévi-Straussian approach, as others have said (see Nutini 1965), ignores context, the functionalist shibboleth. We should be wary of assuming that these cultural polarities apply always, invariably, since any number of contextual attributes—like person, time, and conduct—may also influence their permutations (Geertz 1966b). Are individual projection, and the circumstances of particular situations, plus the ethnographers' own presence, also involved? I think that they are; and to illustrate, I shall describe how pieces of disparate information on pandanus morphology fit together into a larger whole: individual Sambia perceptions of pandanus reproduction.

Men genderize five attributes of pandanus morphology in their understanding of the tree's reproductive cycle. Nuts and flowers, the two most significant traits, I have already mentioned, but I need to add more detail. The remaining attributes—pandanus aerial roots, the fronds covering flowers, and the large sprays of new leaf buds—I shall also describe in that order of significance.

Sambia men are convinced that, like "female" *iku* that exude tree milk sap, only "female" pandanus produce nuts. All pandanus are usually referred to as *kunaalu*, and yet casual comments often suggest finer distinctions. "True *kunaalu* has got food [nuts; *nu-tokeno*, food] belonging to it," Weiyu said. Weiyu's comment shifts his emphasis from the tree to its nuts, its "food," which male trees absolutely lack. The female tree, "with nuts, has its own milk" (*kunaal-aamoonaalyu*, pandanus "mother's milk"). This, too, male trees lack. The nuts emerge from a large seedpod (*koonai-pweiyu; pweiyu* is "to bind or wrap," and is also the noun for ritual) as large as 2 feet in diameter. The pod grows suspended from a "feeder rope" (*koonai-soolu*) just below the level of the grass skirt. The nut pod is explicitly conceptualized as a *kunaalu* pregnancy; and the same term, *kwulai'u-mutnyi* (male-child stomach), is applied to women and pandanus alike.

Kunaalu, unlike *iku*, have "dry" (lacking sap) tree skins. This state of "dryness" has another form too: the capacity to bear nuts. "Dryness" pertains to reproductive capacity; for example, immature trees and those dying are completely "dry," since they do not bear nuts. Male trees without nuts are also described as "dry." (Here is a first indication that the categories "dryness" and "wetness" involve tacit procreative principles.)

Now we can go further and note how pandanus nuts are said to be the "same" (*havaltnu*) as mother's milk. To be more precise, the "equation" concerns white "milk-looking" substances treated as food (*nu*), i.e., milk food solids (*aamoonaalyu nu-tokeno*). Both *iku* "milk saps" (*i-aamoonaa-lyu*) and pandanus nuts (*kunaal-aamoonaalyu*) are treated culturally,[8] in ritual *and* secular contexts, as mother's milk (*aamoonaalyu*) equivalents (and, in some cases, as its substitutes). In terms of this cultural category only one other substance—semen—is treated as a precise equivalent or classed together with mother's milk (see Chapters 7 and 8).[9] Nonetheless, the "sameness" of these milklike substances is problematic. (Here abound many difficult problems of symbolic analysis: What is really implied by Sambia connotations of "sameness," similarity, or equation? The fine details are needed to reach a finer understanding of "symbolic" behavior, its meaning and context.) What seems clear, however, is this: it is given in the femaleness of living things that they can produce "milk food." Male trees and men cannot do so.

Only male trees boast pandanus flowers, as I said. The flower is spectacular: long (6 to 15 inches) and creamy white, with thick fleshy petals. Toward the end of the gloomy monsoon the flowers emerge and unfold, hanging from a thick stem just below the grass skirt of the treetop. The feeder stem men sometimes jokingly call the tree's "penis" (*laakelu*), the flower petals its "testes" (*kootngoolu*). When I first heard a man refer to the flower as a penis, he was talking with another Sambia. I listened in disbelief: after doing research for a few months I still knew only that men were fond of referring to *kunaalu* as being "much like women." The former comment, however, opened up another dimension: either all cultural idioms among Sambia were pervasively genderized, or else *pandanus* idioms were, for some unknown reason, especially polarized around a gender theme. Whereas I often heard men refer to "female pandanus trees" and discuss their nuts, only rarely—perhaps two or three times at most—did I ever hear men spontaneously genderize pandanus flowers. So I took to probing carefully about the flowers, too, in the *same context* as men's discursive comments about the trees and nuts. I noted the individuals and the situations, and much later began to elicit material on the pandanus myself, by asking individual men, or groups of them, to say

8. The question of the psychological reality of these cultural equations is complex; and here, when confronted with the precise details of individual studies, we become aware of the dangers of too quickly moving from cultural constructs to individual experience (see Chapter 8).

9. This assertion is not quite correct. Another substance, cassowary grease (*kaiouwugu moonugu*), is sometimes, rather weakly, classed together with milklike substances; see Chapter 5. (I might add that this substance is "biologically" much less important to masculinity than the others.)

more. Finally, I reached a viewpoint that both possibilities were tenable: cultural idioms *are* pervasively genderized; while men's knowledge and thinking pertaining to pandanus idioms appear to be focused on its gender and sexual reproduction.

Next came information about the aerial roots (*koonai-pooliku,* or *pooli-ku-aamdu,* root/hand breast). The aerial roots are a primary distinguishing trait separating *kunaalu* from other *iku* trees. Three aspects of the roots find their way into idioms. Domesticated *kunaalu* trees are occasionally tapped for milk sap in a manner similar to what is done to deciduous trees, with this difference: only the tips of the aerial roots (not the trunk) are sliced open for tapping. The sap is then drunk directly from the root tip by placing one's mouth against it. This men do with a particular thought in mind. Here is Tali.

> The newer *pooliku,* before they enter the earth, are tapped for milk. . . . These *pooliku* are called *aamdu* [women's breast]. . . . It [the root] is the same as the breast of a woman, *identically* [emphatic]; the very tip [of the root] is its "nose," *aam-chembootu* [female breast nipple],[10] from which milk is taken. The tip is cut, the milk is drunk. I drank it when I was a bachelor to replace my semen, what I lost from "playing" [copulating] with boys.

Bachelors learn this procedure in third-stage initiation (and utilize it until better milk-sap practices are later learned). The milk sap is an elixir believed to replenish semen "lost" through their fellatio inseminations of younger boys. Notice, too, how Tali not only links women's breasts and aerial roots but emphatically describes them as "identical."

Not only is the pandanus utilized in various male secret spitting rituals, but its aerial roots are the focus during the most dramatic teachings. The first of these sequential initiation rites began as I described above, although third-stage initiation does not use the aerial roots. In fourth-stage initiation this begins, however: during its spitting ceremony the roots are referred to and represented as women's breasts. The upper, shorter roots, for example, which are newer sprouts, are compared to the breasts of young women assigned in marriage to the fourth-stage initiates. The bride's nubile breasts are said to be "small and uplifting," like the short aerial roots growing at the upper extremities of the pandanus trunk.[11]

---

10. Note these distinctions: female breast is *aamdu;* the entire darker colored nipple is *aamdetn-jilu;* the nipple point is *aamdu-chembootu* (*chembootu* is nose); male breast nipple is *aamjiku.*
11. A secret practice related to this knowledge: a youth, betrothed to a girl, may cut off the new tip of a *kunaalu* root ("a breast root"), mash it up, and mix it illicitly with some food, which he will have given to her—all to stimulate the rapid growth of her breasts, and marriage.

They are immature compared to the older, longer roots that grow nearer the earth, limbs that are likened to older females, the wives of senior and elder men with "flat, fallen breasts." Youths, in this ceremony, are enjoined to be faithful and felicitous to "their women" (those "given to them by elders"). They are warned against adultery, and threatened with death if they break this taboo. In short, the longer roots (older women, reproductively competent) are identified with older men, and vice versa.

As if to confound this identification, the smallest aerial roots at the top of the trees are likened, in the midst of ritual rhetoric, to "penises." The youths are said to have smaller, shorter penises, whereas their elders are supposed to have bigger, maturer penises: the (longer) roots growing beneath those. (I wish to emphasize, here, that while men often refer to aerial roots as *aamdu*—and they mean by that women's breasts—*only in ritual* do men make use of this other substitution, describing small roots as penises. Like the "reproductive" difference I noted earlier between nuts and flowers, one rarely hears men, in secular conversations, talk about aerial roots as penises, which comments are treated as a joke.) On this point Weiyu added: "We men, among ourselves, call the smaller roots [on top] the same as the penis [*laakelu*] [3- to 8-inch-long roots]. We say the shorter roots atop the tree are like penises attached to *kunaalu* and *kambeilaako.*"

Here is, then, a clear instance of what I shall call a *focal projection:* a piece (aerial roots) of a larger entity (pandanus trees, the whole designata) serves as a focus for externalizing and representing subjective thoughts, feelings, and fantasy. Typically, as in this case, the designata chosen from nature bear a perceptual correspondence to the designatum, often a human organ. And typically, these focal projections concern the separation and fusion of sex traits and gender qualities. This secret ritual, for instance, uses pandanus aerial roots both as penises and female breasts (although we should take notice that men are careful never to confuse the same root as *both* penis and breast). The character of this perceptual "attitude" (the quotation marks here indicate that this concept is used metaphorically; it is unclear how much conscious intentionality is involved) is also important. The psychological and cultural process involved I shall call *genderizing:* projecting qualities of femininity and masculinity into an entity that has (for reasons still unclear) created in men a subjective response along the lines of its perceptual correspondence to something else (breast and penis).

Now to the next trait. The leaf fronds from which the pandanus flowers (*kwolu*) emerge are the substance from which are woven masculine armbands. These fronds are tough and fibrous. The material is cut from the tree (while still alive); it is dried and flattened and shredded into rattanlike fibers. (A wild rattan species is also used as a substitute on occasion, but men favor pandanus.) Men make very fine matted arm bracelets (*aatm-wonandu,* literally, without/lacking male), the key insignia of manhood placed on youths, as new warriors, at third-stage initiation. The flower fronds are also interwoven with yellow orchid fiber (*mooniglu*) in making male warrior bandoliers, headbands, and waistbands, put on boys in first- and second-stage rituals. On this score, pandanus flowers are closely linked to masculinity.

No Sambia has ever commented to me on the significance of this material except to state the inobvious: warrior armbands are "woven from flowers." Sambia tend to lump together the flower and its frond as material substances. On occasion the fronds are called the "children" of the flowers. And, in the black palm, the long fruit pods (akin to betel nut pods but smaller and not as clustered) are shielded by a frond, called *yooglanyu-tai*[12] (black-palm girl), or sometimes, *depmowi'u* (bark-cape buttock cover of males). Of this, men remark: "The black palm likes to decorate its child [fruit pods] with a *depmowi'u* [frond], covering its flower." This allusion to "immature female" reminds us again of the earlier reference to the *tingu* in black palm: the palm bears no nuts; it is the object of first-stage initiation purificatory ceremonies; and it is globally only "male" (see Table 6). But its semantics still play on femaleness. Men say the black palm is "identical to men" because it lacks a (woman's) "grass skirt," and because its trunk is tall, strong, and smooth, unfettered by leaves or branches, "like men." Here again *kunaalu* is being genderized, but both masculine and feminine qualities are involved.

The last perceptual attribute of *kunaalu* is the spray of leafy buds emerging from its thorny crest of topmost leaves. The spray (*kwolu,* too, like the flower) will eventually precipitate new aerial roots as the tree ages; and it will produce leaves. The leafy spray is large, as much as a foot across, rounded or domed, until it sprouts. It is "just like our face," men say, and it is referred to as such in ritual. More precisely, men tend to think of the *kambeilaako* spray as resembling a man's head.

We say they [spray of buds] are *kamdal-kulatnuku,* a man with a high hairline, like Y [a Nilangu village man]. The "bark-cape" fronds of the buds fall away from the head, making it look like you and me, our hairline, especially that [kind of] man [e.g., Y] with a high hairline [*mindu-koogu*].[13] [Weiyu]

This trait, itself, conditions the attribution of masculinity to the *kam-beilaako* species of wild pandanus: "It's like our face, so we hide it,"

---

12. An alternate name is *tai'ukwi,* "girl-thing."
13. Sambia distinguish between a high male hairline, *mindu-kooglu,* and a lower female hairline, which has no categorical name.

TABLE 6 *Gender Traits and Ritual Uses of Pandanus Trees*

Name of Species	Has "Grass Skirt"	Global "Metaphoric" Gender	Individual Sex Assignment Based on Perceptual Attributes		Tree Uses in Initiation Rites		Special Food Taboos
			Male	Female	*Akovanyu* Purificatory Ceremonies	Spitting Ceremonies	
Domesticated pandanus (*kunaalu*)	Yes	Female	Flowers	Nuts	1st stage		Nuts taboo till 2nd-stage initiation
Lower altitude wild pandanus (*kambeilaako*)	No	Male	Flowers	Nuts		3rd stage	
High altitude wild pandanus (*itnandu*)	No	Male	Flowers	Nuts	3rd stage	4th stage 5th stage 6th stage	Nuts taboo to women; palm heart is secret male food

					1st stage	...th stage 5th stage 6th stage	
Black palm (yooglanyu)	No	Male	Flowers		1st stage		taboo to younger men
Bow palm (aamboogu)	Yes	Male					Taboo: used for making bow and arrows and bull roarers
Areca (betel nut) palm (nungooglu)		Female	Flowers	Betel nuts	1st stage		Betel nut taboo till 2nd-stage initiation
Pandanus fruit (ishoyu)	No	Female	(Does not flower)	Fruits	2nd stage		Pandanus fruit taboo till 2nd-stage initiation
Forest trees (iku)			Flowers	Fruits	1st stage through 6th stage	optional: 4th stage 5th stage 6th stage	Milk saps hidden from women

Weiyu said. "So we perform *akovanyu* purifications with it, and spitting ceremonies."

The heart of the wild pandanus, its fleshy insides white and watery, is, like palm hearts, also eaten. It also constitutes a ritual food of newly married men, since its whiteness, like taro, makes it one of the few foods considered safe for youths to consume at the period of their wives' menarche.

For this reason, too, women are forbidden to eat the nuts or palm heart of wild pandanus. "We wouldn't [then] look good [i.e., manly] at the *iku-mokeiyu* [initiation rites]," Tali told me. Here is sympathetic and contagious thought at work again. Men identify leaf pods of the wild pandanus as "being like" a masculine head; they utilize the tree in rites; so if women ate any part of the tree men would be spoiled in their ritual appearance and attire.

These concrete perceptual traits—nuts and flowers, aerial roots, fronds and leaf buds—are the basis of gender distinctions concerning pandanus. They also have a definite time dimension. Men note that domesticated *kunaalu* seasonally bear nuts twice a year; initially in April, toward the end of the dry season, and then again at the advent of the light monsoon (*koololu*). "That first time, *kunaalu* likes to carry its new offspring [nuts] in the rainy season," Moondi said. "Later, during the sunny period, the nuts grow a little stronger [maturer]." This is associated with the sun's heat: "The sun cooks it, the leaf completely dries, and so it [nut pod] can ripen quickly," said Moondi. The dry season brings other changes too; not only pandanus, but yam, taro, and banana ripen, and the leaves yellow and wither. The cassowary (and possum) is trapped more frequently, the sun having brought it out of its hiding place. These things enable men to perform the *kwulai'u-moku* collective initiatory cycle.

The last event of first-stage initiation, and thus of the whole cycle, is the pandanus-nut ritual (*koonai-pweiyu*), performed with cultivated nuts. The last nuts harvested in the following season (several months after the rituals are over) are collected for the purpose. This important confirmatory ceremony is the final initiation ritual boys undergo until their second initiation some three or four years later.

Now let us consider how men understand the overall reproductive cycle of cultivated pandanus. What needs saying, first, is that men invariably speak of the dimorphic reproductive role of trees as if it were isomorphic with that of humans. There are thus "male trees" with flowers and "female trees" bearing nuts. This dichotomy permeates both conversations and global generalizations.

In the rainy season, as I said, male trees produce white flowers. Both sexes of trees are vigorously healthy with nice (*singundu*) bright green leaves. Then the male tree "copulates with" the female tree, an act somehow accomplished with its "flower penis." As the flower begins to wilt, the male tree's "wife" (a nearby female tree) begins to "carry a child," Nilutwo said. The male flower then dries and yellows (several weeks later), whereafter men refer to it as *koonai-kwolu nugenjiku* (our male breast flower).[14] Elsewhere Tali remarked, "The *kweikoonbooku* (semen) of the male [pandanus] tree, it turns into a *boongu*;[15] it wants to make a child." He added, "That is true of *kunaalu* and humans too." Weiyu said (elsewhere, independently), "As female trees with nuts, pandanus have milk [nuts]; as a male tree the flower only dries up; it has no milk." When *kunaalu* male trees produce flowers, its "female trees [start to] bear nuts." When the male flower rots, "the female tree has nuts."

Thereafter, men assert, perceptible changes begin to occur in the appearance of both sexes. Here is Tali's account.

> The female tree carries nuts; both male and female trees turn yellow-colored [*woogetnchu*]. She [female tree] can develop slack skin [*cherep'nji*], for she is sick.[16] *Kunaalu* wants to carry a child [*cheruptu-aamandumaiyo;* nearing parturition]; her breasts can blacken [*belaak' aandumaiyo; belaaku* is ashes; lactating breasts].[17] Her skin is then completely yellow. The nut pod has matured and is felled. . . . Their skin is not nice; it becomes black or red-colored, the leaves dull and dry yellow [*koonai-cherooptu*]. . . . [After the nut pod is cut off] the tree leaves turn back to green; they [leaves] are nice again.

Here the comparison between "female" pandanus and women is precise: impregnation causes visible changes in both: parturition stimulates physical debilitation and a sickly appearance that clears up after a birth.[18]

Reference to this reproductive trait occurs in ritual contexts too. For example: following the first-stage initiation, boys cannot eat pandanus nuts till after the ritual. Here is Tali again: "When *kunaalu* first carries nuts its leaves are yellow. We ceremonially beat the initiates at *moku* [initiation]; they cannot eat *kunaalu:* not good that the boys should turn yellow, like *kunaalu*." Later we shall see further references to the color yellow and its ritual significance. What matters here is that Tali also described the

---

14. Recall that female breast is *aamdu,* male breast *jiku.* Also, an old person of either sex can be called *jiku;* and *chatniku* (*n/-jiku*) denotes "he/she has no water of his/her own," where "water" glosses sexual fluids.

15. *Boongu,* cold swamp bog; metaphorically used, too, in reference to embryonic fluids; see Chapter 6.

16. Pregnant women are also described as *cherep'nji.*

17. Identical terms describe women.

18. The emphasis on sickness is illuminating, for *cherooptu* is noted especially during pregnancy and is compared to jaundice or extreme malnutrition. "If a man is sick, his skin comes up yellow. His mouth turns yellow," said Tali.

process of bearing nuts and babies as parallel. Men thus extend *cheruptu aamandumaiyo*—the idea that the "pandanus carries children" as its leaves yellow—to how "women carry children" as their skins yellow and their breasts darken. And, to what happens to those foolish initiates who too early ingest pandanus nuts.

These comparisons are made: fervently, with a seriousness that betokens the straitlaced men who (in ritual) grimly forbid young initiates to eat nuts; snidely, with grins and jokes, scoffing privately at how pregnant women and female pandanus are so weak and vulnerable and unmanly; and with puzzlement, by the same men who only partially comprehend how these reproductive processes create the prized nuts harvested as regularly as clockwork.

On the basis of these procreative processes, then, men further classify pandanus trees into subtypes. Reproductive history seems to be the key. I describe them in order from the youngest to oldest: (1) *beikulyu*:[19] definitely a female *kunaalu,* but one without aerial roots yet; (2) *koonai-tulu*:[20] a new *kunaalu,* still without aerial roots, but which has produced nuts once; (3) *aambei-walu*:[21] a tree with short roots that has carried nuts one or more times; (4) *kunaalu-aamooluku*:[22] either male or female trees whose long, snub-nosed roots are said to resemble hammerhead arrows; (5) *yangu-kunaalu*:[23] an old "female" who bears nuts many times, has very long roots, and "is close to dying"; (6) *looverupi:* an old tree that dies.

One other subtype should be added, although its status, in this typology, is as uncertain as its "sex." This is *kwei-kunaalu,* which men speak of as a "hermaphroditic" tree.[24] I have never actually observed what men claim: that the odd tree sometimes sprouts flowers and at other times bears nuts. Men assert that "when initially you see it, it bears a nut pod"; and then again, at another season, the same tree (which before produced nuts) now bears only a flower. Therefore, this anomalous tree is "like a *kwol-aatmwol,*" a hermaphrodite who displays both male and female characteristics. *Kwei-kunaalu* confounds the rigid certainty of Sambia classification, though men do not understand it nor can they explain it. Once again sex

---

19. Also a woman's proper name.
20. Elsewhere *tulu* seems to suggest the connotation "gender unclear."
21. *Aambei-walu,* being *aambei, aambelu* = women; *aam/-imbei, imbei* = cassowary.
22. *Aamooluku:* the name of the hammerhead arrow and also "fight leader."
23. *Yangu,* as I noted, is the generic term for old person or grandchild.
24. On hermaphrodites, see Chapters 7 and 8. The prefix *kwei,* however, always denotes masculine gender or attire; for example, *kwei-aalyuwaku* is a category name for male ritual paraphernalia, such as feathers; *kwei-mutnyi* is one name of the red ritual sacred objects used in initiation and described in Chapter 7.

classification in pandanus turns back on the production of nuts. How do the nuts then fit into this reproductive scheme?

Few topics absorb Sambia as much as the edible nuts themselves. For men, of course, there is war and hunting, matters that spark lively discussion; but there is an added element in what is said of the nuts. Unlike the retelling of old war tales, there is a pleasant expectation in this banter: anticipation of the nuts' delicious taste. And unlike the hunt, one feels certainty in the talk, for the trees produce faithfully; the nuts emerge simply for the taking. So when men discuss pandanus—when they roast the nuts, eat them, or compare their taste—there is something of a connoisseur's zeal in judging their sizes, textures, and flavors. To state only that Sambia eat pandanus nuts, then, is like saying that Frenchmen savor just any old wine. Three things are involved in men's zealous knowledge of pandanus: perceptions of the nut pod and its relationship to the reproductive cycle; beliefs about the source of pandanus "milk"; and sayings about the maturation of nuts. I shall touch on each point.

Knowledge of the nut pod impinges on its perceptual correspondence to a woman's pregnancy, an association that merits close examination. The nut pod, *koonai-pweiyu,* is referred to as a "pregnancy," a child, the female tree's offspring. This fused image of mother/infant is indeed apparent in how men speak and think of the tree, for they invariably select human procreative metaphors and analogies in depicting the growth of a seedpod. (In fact, one wonders if the lexical term *kúnaalu* is not linguistically "motivated" by a very close referential pronoun, *kánaalu,* denoting a "mother and child" pair.[25]) The nut pod, described above, has a feeder stem that men compare to a human umbilical cord (*kwulai'u-oolu*). The pod, as a whole, is also referred to as both *chemulku* (stomach) and pregnancy; and the place at which the feeder stem joins the top of the pod is called *kanyu-mangu,* "mouth" (*kanyelu* = grass skirt; *mangu* = mouth), while the bottom of the pod is termed *mindu* or "head."

As the seedpod emerges from the tree and grows, its changes are charted and classified by men. First the "pod appears, but isn't swollen" (*chembenju*). After a few weeks the "nut pod hangs heavy, resting down a little swollen" (*yolat'nji*). Then, after the monsoon, the outer fronds that originally shield the pod wither and dry from the sun. The nuts inside become "a little firm and can be eaten" (*dumbu lut'nji*). Another few sunny weeks dry out the pod's external shell, hastening the nut harvest: the skin of the nut pod becomes "completely hard," while inside "its nuts are still not firm" (*dachoowi'u,* firm nuts, where *choowi'u* is tail). Finally,

---

25. Compare similar objective case pronouns: *kámdaal,* a "father and child," or *kánutu,* a "mother and her [three or four] children."

at harvest time, the nuts become edible: *wusaam-judai,* the "outer fronds are rotten, the inner nuts are nearly ripe." (Note how in most pandanus these visible changes in the nut pod generally correspond to the seasonal cycle of sunny weather.) This leads to the changes said to occur inside the nut pod, where the nuts are gestating.

Pandanus nuts grow like kernels of corn around a corncob, only the seedpod is round, large, and heavy. (The pods vary in size according to tree size and age; pods can range between 1 and 2 feet in diameter, weighing perhaps 10 to 50 pounds depending on maturity.) The nuts grow symmetrically from an inner fleshy core in only a single layer. The outer tips of the nuts grow tightly together, with small bristlelike protrusions; the inner base is blunt and smooth-shelled. The pod has two spongy inner linings: the nucleus of corncob material (called simply *wusu,* food or sweet potato), if consumed early enough, while still fleshy, provides a good supplement to the diet; the outer fleshy lining (called *liku* or feces), however, is discarded as rubbery and tasteless. The nuts, when examined within a broken pod, take various names. The bristlelike tip (or "tail") of a nutshell is commonly called *chelu,* "stone or seed"; the sides of the shell are usually called *chemulku,* "stomach or pregnancy"; and the inner base of the shell is called *chembootu,* or "nose." Men recognize that the "nose" of the seed can produce a new seedling if it is planted. But what concerns us are the nuts that are eaten.

There are essentially seven stages through which the nuts pass and by which Sambia classify their degree of edibility. These grades parallel the growth of the nut pods sketched above. First come "new" nuts (*aiyu,* daughter-in-law; or *kwulai'u-aiyu,* a newborn baby); men metaphorically refer to them as *chenamdu,* "snot," because they are watery and milky-looking, "identical to snot."[26] When the nuts are a little firmer but still soft white (like coconut meat), they are called *kool-úku* or *kool-léku.* They are still not solid and are mushy and runny, "like semen," men say. Next, the fleshy nuts take on a slightly orange (*katmuntu*) cast, so that they are called *katmuntu* or *dachoowi'u.* Here, men metaphorically compare this stage of the nuts to first- and second-stage (prepubertal) initiates, who likewise are still "soft." The pod is "close to [making] mature nuts," implying that until the nuts firm up (inside their shells) they remain immature "offspring." When the nuts begin hardening, after a few weeks, they become *choowi'u* (tail), "firm but not ripe"; and older men compare their qualities to those of fourth- and fifth-stage initiates, who are close to manliness but not yet full men. The next stage comes in the dry season

---

26. Two other names also apply: *keriku-keriku,* a homonym for the male semen organ, for which men say "it [pod] wants to start a child but has none yet"; and *chembenju,* a watery condition, like breast milk.

when the nuts approach ripeness (*wusaam-moonjai*), being white, *moonyu* or "new food." And then, as the pod dries, its weight bearing down on the tree, its outer shell dark now, the nuts are called *miku* (*mikei ouleiup-maiyo,* "it [pod] has itself weighted down"; *miko* is the term for male cross-cousin). These nuts have become ripe and hard: they can withstand exposure to the elements and are, in this respect, compared with adult men, *aatmwunu,* who are *bwi-nutnuku,* "impervious to even heavy rain drenching them." There is, following the harvest, a final, man-made stage in the cycle: the smoking of nuts over a hearth to cure them for flavoring and temporary (as long as three months) storage. Sambia love smoked nuts, so some of the harvest is usually set aside for that purpose. Smoked nuts are termed *yalkoogu,* "completely dry" and lacking in watery juices, "as dry as an old person."

Different things emerge about these idioms of ripeness. Tangible references to body fluids, milk and semen, often underlie the perception of the nuts. Particularly when fleshy, the nuts are equated to "mother's milk" (as their name denotes). The softness cum firmness of nut meats is also a general classificatory principle. Analogies link types of nuts (their degree of hardness) with types of masculinity, as in the case of *choowi'u* nuts being likened to quasi-manly newlyweds. The nomenclature of nuts also plays on the category names of males and females (as was also true of the nomenclature for whole pandanus trees). This again reveals: identification processes; the projection of gender traits into nuts and trees; and the outlines of men's tacit psychological frames for understanding human sexual and procreative fluids. This leads to a last point about the source of pandanus nut milk.

About this matter men are emphatic: the nut milk derives from a species of large worm inhabiting pandanus trees. The worm, called *koonai-tuleit-woglu* or *kaiumbwash* (*kai,* pandanus forest; *bwash,* to teach), has pronounced blue and tan stripes and exudes a milky fluid. (I have seen the worm's skin actually squirt this fluid when touched.) The worm allegedly "eats lots of earth," as does the earthworm, both of which have a "lot of milk." This white fluid is called *koonai tuleitwoglu aamoonaalyu.* Somehow, men believe, the worm distributes this milky fluid within a pandanus tree, hence the fluid concentrates in its nuts.[27] The worm's head is *hable-chembootu,* a "nose," "since it has no teeth," Weiyu told me; its tail is *hablepootu,* "anus." Men, like Tali, state that the *kunaalu* "has its own

---

27. Inge Riebe, speaking of her long research among the Karam tribe of Highlands New Guinea, tells me that her informants expressed an identical belief. Among Sambia, the worm's fluid is labeled *aamoonaalyu,* the category name for mother's milk; but this substance is rarely mentioned with semen, milk, or tree milk saps; and indeed, as noted below, it is less that fluid than the worm's feces that initiates are fed.

milk" because the *kaiumbwash* has "milk." He said this emphatically on more than one occasion.[28]

When men get around to performing the pandanus-nut ritual (the final event of first-stage initiation), the nuts and the worm both figure in what is ceremonially eaten. First, the nut pods are harvested. They are then broken into pieces and, inside the cult house, are scraped against the boy's skin: the bristly ends of the nuts (still attached to pieces of the pod) are scrubbed against their bodies long enough to draw blood. The forehead and upper arms are scraped. The ostensible aim of the rite is to desensitize the lads, who must learn not to fear climbing pandanus trees to harvest their nut pods. Boys learn that it is a masculine prerogative to scale the trees and harvest the nuts, despite their great heights and sharp leaves. Otherwise, women and their peers will mock them. Second, the scraping removes the fine down from a lad's body; this is said to leave traces of *kunaalu* "water" (*wunyu*) and "seed bristles" (*chelu*) on his skin, enabling him to climb trees better. The process also aids his growth—actually "changes his skin"—so boys mature faster. Afterwards, the novice is fed a substance whose contents are a secret to him, but which includes shelled nuts, special tree leaves, and the worm's feces with bits of its milky fluid. These substances are believed to be especially vital in triggering a spurt of growth in the novice. And so it comes about that masculine ritual makes the pandanus nut (and its milk provider, the worm) a part of a boy, inside and outside, the beginning of a lifetime union.

Where does this prolonged, intimate ritual synchrony between boys and pandanus lead? Take one example, men's nosy attachment to their nut harvest.

Pandanus nuts are metaphorical "noses," as we saw, but this identification seems to be experienced more deeply than as mere metaphor. Men are prone to associate nuts and noses verbally in casual conversation. Here is Tali: "If the nose of the *kunaalu* is long, then it is good; if it's not long, it's no good." Let me clarify this. Both wild (*itnandu*) and domesticated pandanus have nuts that, if long enough, men commonly and explicitly refer to as *chembootu,* the primary denotata of which is nose. Short nuts, however, are never labeled *chembootu.* ("Short" nuts men describe as from ½ to 1 inch long; "long" nuts are an inch or larger, up to 3 inches or so in length.) Neither *kambeilaako* nor *nboolu* wild pandanus is called *chembootu,* by contrast, because they are not eaten.

In short, only long, edible pandanus nuts are called "noses." Here is Tali once again:

---

28. Weiyu once told me he thought the worm's fluid and a fluid-exuding species of frog (*goolungatnyi,* strictly taboo for men to eat) were both sources of nut milk, but no other man ever told me this.

> *Kunaalu* is the same as a man or a woman; if [its nuts are] long, it is good.
> . . . We feel sorry [*kalu*] for nice nuts if they are long. If [the tree has] long
> nuts, we give them names. . . . It gives food [nuts] quickly all the time
> . . . [but] if [its nuts are] short, we don't give it a name.

So long nuts, "noses," come from trees that are accordingly named by, and
identified with, their owner, the "father" of a tree. Such trees provide
food regularly (nut milk), for which, Tali says, men are *kalu*, sorrowfully
mindful.[29] Long nuts may be called both *yangu-nalu* (old ones) and
kunaalu-iku (in the sense of a tree's tallness). Short nuts are disparagingly
referred to as *yaal-kunaalu*, (dry ones), or worse, *nyoot* (the *nyoot* is a
small sugar glider that people consider ugly owing to its short snout; it is
a provocative insult to call a man a *nyoot*). The very longest nuts are
dut-mangu—gloriously long, "like the spiny anteater's nose." I scarcely
need add what is now apparent about humans too: as Tali says, "A short
nose is bad, a long nose is nice [*singundu*]." Apart from skin tone and the
mouth, no other feature gets as much attention as the nose in Sambia
notions of beauty.

It follows from these comparisons that Sambia not only admire the nose,
but that they also direct a certain kind of verbal abuse, *berulu*, at nuts and
noses, amounting to the redirection of feelings from a man's pandanus to
his person (i.e., nose) and self-esteem. Sambia laud the long, well-shaped
nose of a child or adult. They favor the elongated, or aquiline nose over
the upturned, short, or flared nose and nostrils. So to abuse a man's
pandanus nuts is like derogating his very nose and person.

> Suppose a man says bad things about your *kunaalu*. You can retort to him: "You
> are not bad-mouthing my *kunaalu* [nuts], you are criticizing my very *nose*
> [emphasis]! So you say my nose is small!" So now, that cursing provokes a fight.
> [Tali]

Manly pride is at stake: a man angry or indignant has a "red nose"
(*cheruntu*): he can either fight or stand coldly silent, "his nose in the air."
If you want to insult a man, then criticize his pandanus, for that is tantamount to assaulting his masculinity.

A final comment on the pandanus fruit. I have avoided mentioning the
fruits since they and the nuts differ in nature and in seasonal cycle. Men
note this, and they treat the fruit accordingly. For example, different food
and sex taboos surround the fruits. When a woman menstruates, it is taboo
for her or her husband and his age-mates to eat the blood-red fruit.

---

29. The verb *kalu* has a range of connotations including longing and being sorrowful in the sense
of missing someone's presence, as well as being beholden and mindful of someone who has
cared for one.

Moreover, pandanus-fruit trees bear no flowers, men say, so they are therefore only of the female sex.

What matters most is that the oily red juices of the fruit are explicitly equated with menstrual blood. Weiyu said:

> The grease [*ishoyu-munugu;* vaginal and penile fluids are also *munugu*] is the same as women's blood. You can see it; it's the very same kind. . . . So if you eat *ishoyu*, it's the same as copulating with a woman. Women have lots of blood. Not good that you eat *ishoyu* and you become ill.

The implications of this thought we shall consider more in Chapter 6. I mention it here to indicate how genderizing and focal projection involve both pandanus nut and fruit trees.

It should now be apparent that Sambia men tend to polarize pandanus phenomena into dimorphic types according to associated gender traits. Not content merely to classify pandanus trees into male and female types, men evaluate the trees and nuts as "dryly" masculine or "wetly" procreative and feminine. Focal projection links the perceptually correlated features of aerial roots with long womanly breasts and shorter manly penises, and the nuts with noses. Thoughts and feelings are projected out and then redirected from one's pandanus nuts to one's person. Likewise, men identify milky fluids as nutritive and procreative and feminine; and although semen is remarkable in its life-giving properties, we shall later see that, unlike female fluids, it is not a natural body product. (A weak exception to this principle, men's rationalizations about mother's milk, is examined in Chapter 6.) White fluids are, however, associated with mother's milk, just as pandanus-fruit grease is likened to menstrual blood. (This polarization of white and red fluids is pervasive in Sambia culture.) These elements recur in idioms and verbal behavior. Some are veiled in secrecy; some are matters of men's private clubhouse talk; and others are matters of public (heterosexual) discourse. I'll tell why later.

These characteristics, then, point toward the cumulative experience of men's repeated, intimate exchanges with pandanus and other plants: eating and handling them, inserting one's substance into them. This trend adds up to the viewpoint that Sambia men can merge their sense of themselves with these substances and entities in the course of masculine development.

Flowers and Feathers: Elicited Associations

Unlike other contemporary ethnographers, I have drawn mostly from individuals for fragments of sayings and other verbal behavior on the theme of pandanus trees. What has been established so far?

All these pandanus idioms concern knowledge and experience. They suggest *meaning:* by weaving together observations I confer a core of related meaning on all Sambia men. This is done somewhat surreptitiously, by omitting the ambiguous and redundant and by not identifying in detail my informants, the context of their expressions, or how their behavior and its mood-signs vary. But why allege only one code of *Meaning* instead of multiple meanings among individuals? This requires that we consider a sample of meanings for particular individuals. Even though this book concerns cultural idioms, I cannot avoid this issue in conceptualizing a theory of Sambia culture or ritual symbolism. Here is why: individual meanings contain information essential for determining both the forms and contents of idiomatic messages in all interpersonal (including symbolic) behavior. Without a sample of *individuals'* precise meanings, the systematic infrastructure of lexical, metaphoric, and personal meanings of cultural idioms in communication escapes us. One example for many.

With Weiyu and Tali, once again, I have been discussing pandanus. We are near my house in Nilangu hamlet. It is morning; we have been talking for a while now, and I have begun to ask questions. I have been in the hamlet now for eighteen months; both men see me daily; I know their interests, personalities, backgrounds fairly well. I was present at Weiyu's marriage; his wife is now pregnant. Over the months they have mentioned pandanus perhaps scores of times. Again they start discussing the sex of the trees. Again they state that only female trees bear nuts. Again they come around to retelling what I have seen: how wild pandanus are used in secret ritual. And again I am struck by the fact that only "skirtless," "male" wild pandanus are utilized in secret ritual. I have listened and heard tell of the trees and their nuts.

But this time, for a moment, I choose to question Weiyu about the pandanus flowers: not just a description of them, for I have heard that too, but rather his personal thoughts about the flowers in contrast to what he has said about the female nuts of trees. "What are the flowers like?" I ask. His immediate, unreflected response is: "The same as bird feathers." And cheerfully: "The flowers of the tree are like bird feathers." This remark came so quickly, without hesitation, and so astonished me that I then said, "Why is that?" Weiyu smiled and remarked, bright-eyed:

It's the *ilaiyu* [joy or pride] period for trees—the tree has flowers; it is close to the period when his woman wants to carry a child [bear nuts]. We men, too, learn to mount bird feathers atop our heads [enthusiastic] when it is the period of our *ilaiyu* at songfests, or when we initiate. The male tree produces white flower [sic] when it comes time for the woman [tree] to have offspring [nuts].

When *kunaalu* bear flowers, it's the same *identically* as the *koomdu-oovutu* [spitting ceremony] of us men.

This naturalistic communication contains a wealth of information, and for Weiyu, I think, it genuinely condenses a lifetime of experiences into a certain funnel of thought.

The male pandanus is captured in the image of its phallic flower. The flower itself is associated with a feeling close to what we call joy, but also having connotations of strutting masculine pride. Men mount feathers "just as" trees produce their flowers: this concrete association explicitly reveals sympathetic "magical" identification. The thought implies that the "reproductive aim" of pandanus flowers and men's feathers is one. Men wear feathers at initiation rituals, a custom also associated with the same mood state, *ilaiyu*. Is the "same" pseudoprocreative "aim" therefore present in men's reasoning about what they do to boys—ritually treat and inseminate them—in initiation rites? That is my hunch; but to investigate one needs more than this fragment of data. (More follows in later chapters.) Male pandanus trees produce flowers that determine how and when female trees bear nuts. Hence, Weiyu postulates, men wear feathers in the same way that male trees spawn flowers (their phalluses); male flowers impregnate nearby female trees, while men, in their spitting ceremonies, celebrate reproductive changes in the lives of their women by actually spitting onto the trees (also using the trees as physical "props").

If we glance back for a moment (see pp. 103–104), Weiyu's comment unlocks the treasure of what those youths, like himself, may actually have felt and thought when they stood on the ritual ladder of the wild tree, tasting, feeling, and touching it, temporarily suppressing the boundary between themselves and the great pandanus.

This clinical technique may be our only way of penetrating the meaning of such passionate experiences (cf. Geertz 1968:107–114). The ethnographer can proceed, step by step, through present behavior into past experience, working back from acts, words, or thoughts. Unfortunately, the subjectivity of that ritual behavior—its psychological frames and mood-signs as experienced by individuals—cannot yet be objectively measured or described except in this way. And despite the great difficulties posed by this kind of research, we surely cannot ignore these qualitative data; they refuse to disappear. If we dispose of their subtle indications in observable behavior, like Weiyu's insight, we then diminish what our descriptive reports authoritatively say about another people's subjectivity.

In a single moment Weiyu tacitly communicated as much as a hundred pages about pandanus customs. His statement identified himself psychologically, too, since I believe that he authentically disclosed some of what he actually thought and felt. The data contained in his train of thought mean virtually nothing, of course, unless we already know about pandanus-related idioms and Sambia culture in general. This is the stupendous methodological problem besetting most ethnographic, especially symbolic, analyses: so much background information is needed to evaluate contextually fragments of individual behavior.

How can I be certain that my own presence and interpersonal relationship with Weiyu did not distort this communication? How can we ascertain not if but how, in particular ways, these elicitation techniques and that situational interest (communicated consciously and subliminally) influenced and predisposed Weiyu to say what was described?

This has been the understandable worry of ethnographers like Barth (1975:223–231) and Gell (1975:210–213), who were confronted with similar problems in field research among other isolated New Guinea tribes. Barth explicates his transactional approach in unusual and welcome detail and provides a reconsideration of the sensitive issues involved in the use of native comments or interpretations of ritual (i.e., "exegesis": Turner 1962, 1967). Like Barth (1975:226), as noted above, I recorded "spontaneous, unelicited word and act." But unlike him, in my second year of fieldwork, I needed to go further to investigate individual knowledge and experience. Those two types of data—unelicited and elicited— are related but distinct, and they are presented as such. Sambia also have a native interpretational system in ritual, unlike the Baktaman whom Barth studied; nonetheless, one must here agree with Barth (1975:225f.) and others (Sperber 1975:18–23; Tuzin 1975:564–565) that those data, too, must be explained as "symbolic" elements, in the observer's analysis, which must refer to them as parts of the greater behavioral system. (See Appendix A for a closer examination of this problem.) It is in this regard that my approach breaks with that of Barth (1975:225), who argues that native "insights can *not* be used as data on the content of their cultural tradition" (original emphasis).

While Barth's concern not to "adulterize" his data is certainly warranted, other ethnographers would probably agree that his position is too extreme. Most of us who utilize "participant observation" not only value but eventually seek native insights that can extend an analysis of cultural life. And yet, despite that ad hoc acceptance of individual verbal material, symbolic methodology and theory has scarcely taken note of this procedure. This raises a general issue. In the *practice* of field research, ethnographers acquire and employ native individuals' comments, insights, and interpretations. In *theory*, however, we still accord almost no function systematically to that level of information—the individual as innovator, storehouse, or transmitter of meanings—in the constitution of models.

This implicit bias against deploying observations of individual behavior has seriously hindered our attempts at constructing a better theory of

symbolism. A generation ago, in a place like New Guinea, this was probably justified, since little was known of the ethnically complex configura-
tions of the island (see Read 1954). Surely this is no longer as true:
linguistic, historical, and cultural studies have crisscrossed the whole island; indeed, one wonders if the continued emphasis on lonely groups as
isolated cultural pockets has not helped thwart comparative studies in an
area so much in need of them. When, however, certain workers go further
in substituting their own cultural or linguistic naïveté for that purportedly
held by the natives, there is a certain danger that we shall misrepresent
the individual and political complexities of these undefended exotic communities. If that criticism is justified, then why should we not appropriately
use individuals' insights in understanding and assessing their cultural traditions?

   This standard we should also apply to ourselves. Would we permit a
foreigner of uncertain acquaintance with our language and customs—not
to mention our interpersonal relationships—to reject our insights about
why Mass is celebrated, why individuals wear gold rings on their left
hands, or why a man's home is his castle? Of course not. And if it is
impossible to distinguish these elements of individual behavior from the
norm or the actually observed, then most ethnography is untenable, for
all conventional fieldwork requires that we make judgments and decisions
of this sort all the time.

   The more deeply we commit ourselves to studying a people, the more
impossible it becomes to ignore what they say and think, including their
insights.[30] This fact does not absolve the ethnographer from making clear
his or her methodology, as precisely as possible; and if we put words in
the mouths of our informants, or thoughts in their minds, we are of course
distorting their behavior. But most ethnographers know that, or can at
least become aware of it. When describing verbal data it is particularly
urgent that we define the techniques, interpersonal relationships, and
context through which our observations came about. And whether we
choose to recognize it or not, removing oneself, physically or psychologically, from individuals and groups is as much a *methodological stance* as
is close interpersonal involvement (see Barth 1975:226–228; Gell 1975:
215). In either case, the data reflect both what we are told and what we
are not told, and the methodology must be explicated—in sentences, or
pages of sentences, accompanying the report.

   Verbal associations and insights can be used. They will assist us in
moving closer to understanding a symbolic tradition and the behaviors
through which it is experienced inside by those we study—and whose

---

30. See F. E. Williams's (1936b:ixff.) remarkably insightful comments regarding this point in
his Papuan researches, which extended over a period of some twenty years.

realities we have chosen to report. When statements about reality openly incorporate fantasy, our ethnographic task becomes even harder, and this symbolic methodology, I believe, is even more useful. These problems are taken up in the next chapter, on the cassowary.

CHAPTER FIVE *The*
Phantom Cassowary

Phantom of the forest: this image opens up men's curious idioms surrounding the obstreperous cassowary, the focus of this chapter. The data, I hope, will round out my thumbnail sketch of men's beliefs and sayings about their forest habitat and show something more: a pervasive trend in their fantasy that depicts the cassowary as a masculinized female. That thought reveals more about men's inward cosmos, and it anticipates what is said below about human masculinity and femininity. What follows is both more and less than what one usually expects to find in an anthropological report. Like the two preceding chapters, this one describes verbal idioms and here, their bearing on the meaning of gender traits in cassowaries. So again I usually ignore social action. (Ritual and institutionalized social relationships pertaining to cassowary representations are examined elsewhere.)

This chapter explores a theme of Sambia masculine fantasy in verbal behavior, cultural knowledge, and expressions of individual subjectivity. Sambia men persistently genderize the cassowary. Into that forest creature they project fantastic origins, procreative powers, and gender attributes. I try to tell how this projection is done. This will fall short, however, of offering an adequate model of Sambia fantasy, or a general theory of fantasy, for that would require more observations, especially detailed studies of individual behavior, and a different kind of presentation. With this constraint in mind, then, we shall examine patterns of cassowary-related fantasy, idioms, and mundane knowledge.

Myth and spirits anthropology has easily, perhaps too quickly, ascribed to "supernaturalism," "political dogma," "ideology," and the like. (See Leach 1964b, 1969; Lawrence and Meggitt 1965; Spiro 1966, 1968a.) We still do not understand how actual verbal behavior fits into or reflects reality or fantasy (Devereux 1975). Fantasy (let us call it that) is at play when everyday comments, encircling belief and folktales, clearly transcend the ethnographer's descriptions of perceptible reality, and when the natives' expectations fail to be restrained by perceptual information but instead refer, not to the sensations of a phenomenon, but to its imagined character.

Phantom of the Forest

Try to imagine a most imposing creature of mysterious anatomy with origins and habits unlike any other, a seldom-seen, alien being. This phantom is the cassowary (*kaiouwugu*).[1] Its relationship to men is quite special.

An odd, flightless bird resembling an ostrich, the cassowary roams the wildest reaches of Sambia forest. Its appearance is disturbing (see Figure 5). A powerful, swift runner, the cassowary has a reputation for being unruly and aggressive. It defies domestication. (Unlike other New Guineans, Sambia do not raise cassowaries from chicks.[2]) Too fast and keen to be hunted by bow and arrow, the bird must be trapped. Trapping them requires powerful magic and a gift for experiencing a certain kind of

---

1. This term is the most general category noun Sambia use in reference to cassowaries. *Imbei,* "adolescent" cassowary (and a metaphoric term for women), is also common.

2. But compare Salisbury (1962:91) on the Siane people of the Eastern Highlands: "Cassowaries were few in number, being difficult and dangerous to keep, and in 1953 there were three [domesticated] in an area whose human population was 3,000."

dream. So cassowary hunters are few, and good cassowary hunters are rare. The animal's flesh is so inherently powerful that special taboos restrict its use as food. Perhaps this fact, too, is related to its appearance. For despite its solitary, cantankerous habits, the cassowary is oddly manlike. The hunter knows that it peers at him with large, soft eyes of ashen violet. In addition to its near human size is the fact that it is a biped, the only large creature besides man that inhabits the Sambia cosmos walking upright on two legs, its head aloft.

This makes the metaphor of the phantom especially apt. The cassowary is rarely sighted alive, and when men encounter it trespassing on their forest domain, it startles and vanishes in the brush. More often the cassowary is identified by its comings and goings and its prolific fecal droppings.

Its calling card is an extraordinary trumpet bark.[3] Nothing in the timberland is as challenging to men as the booming, warlike cries (*deiku*) of a cassowary invisible in nearby trees. The barks interrupt the forest silence long enough to remind one that another presence is at large. This is where the cassowary runs; amid pandanus and luxuriant undergrowth, the creatures assume a presence akin to man's. Yet they are believed to mingle with evil forest spirits, even to be taken as their "wives." And like the spirits, cassowaries are ascribed the ruggedness of masculinity needed to

FIGURE 5 *Adult Cassowary*

3. "When confronted by another cassowary or an animal such as man, a dog, or a cow, a display (stretch display) is performed. . . . In this display the body and neck are stretched vertically, the feathers from the rump forward are raised at the same time so that the bird appears larger, and a rumbling call is given. This is the form of the display when males meet" (Crome 1975:8). See also Roheim (1974:224 n.7), who mentions similar reports on the cassowary's cousin, the Australian emu.

survive in the wild. We must recall that this is the top of the world: there is no room for the alleged weakness of women here.

Nonetheless, the cassowary is fundamentally "female," and to this perplexing thought I will return shortly.

The habits of the cassowary are reason enough to ensure it a prominent place in the forest. There is, first, the creature's threatening size. Hunting tales warn of how men have been gored, their dogs killed, while cornering the fierce-clawed bird. Since the cassowary cannot fly, it forages the ground for fallen tree fruit, seeds, and leaves. And so, second, the cassowary is not classed as a bird, even though it has but two legs; rather, it is uniquely classified as a terrestrial creature different from mammals (see also Bulmer 1967). Indeed, the cassowary feeds on almost anything, greedily swallowing whole whatever it uncovers in the underbrush. Its oversized anus emits abundant droppings, revealing (to trappers) a bird's forage route. Men note that the droppings sometimes contain whole seeds, like pandanus nuts, from which spring new seedlings, a fact having ritual significance.

Next there is its homelessness. Unlike bush hens or turkeys, men say, cassowaries do not construct nests, nor do they permanently roost. In addition, it seems to be a solitary creature, preferring to travel alone (see Crome 1975:14). Last, added to these traits, there is the pattern of its predictable (seasonal) migrations. In their annual forays, cassowaries appear and disappear as regularly as clockwork, following, en masse, some inner drive that leads them all to vanish simultaneously, even though they are solitary. Such movements are a mystery to Sambia, although men know that they are concerned with the availability of wild tree fruit. The bird's migrations do, however, provide a visible focus for Sambia perceptions about local cycles of climatic change. This last point deserves to be elaborated on.

Men's comments about cassowary migrations shed light on its mystical origins. At the dullest ebb of the long monsoon (December–April) men argue that cassowaries simply vanish. (See also Crome 1975:12.) Precisely how or why is uncertain. Hunters recognize, of course, that birds and animals that feed off particular forest trees also disappear or make themselves scarce. They also know that the sun of the dry season draws game back in greater numbers. And as the monsoon progresses, forest tree fruit grows scarce, as does the garden produce of men. All this Sambia know. Yet unlike other species, cassowaries disappear completely and quickly—en masse—and later they seem to reappear just as inexplicably. Not until the close of the dry season (around August) do they return. This perplexes men.

From signs of the bird's return—barks and droppings—sightings follow from the zenith of the dry season. Hunters begin to set snares for it. In conversations men advise, "The sun is here, and so is the cassowary." At the same time, the ritual feast crops are nearing harvest, and the pandanus nuts begin maturing. During this period of a few weeks before the new rainy season begins, thunder (*koololu*) booms and lightning (*mulaamuptu*) streaks the skies, and these electrical storms, too, are linked to the doings of cassowary. For instance, I sat talking in my house one afternoon late in August with my informant, Nilutwo, a cassowary hunter. He was recounting some of his life history when a bolt of lightning cracked across the sky. He immediately halted, interrupted himself, and said to me, "The cassowary is back." There was a gleam on his face. This mental association gains support from cultural beliefs. Before going further, however, we need to understand how men classify cassowaries into subtypes.

Belief helps explain the different types of cassowary. There are two subgroups (or species) and the key trait demarcating them is the "length of their legs." One type we may term "sky dwellers" (*moonyu kwooluaambwotu; moonyu* = sky, or elevated place; *kwoolu/kwolu* = masculine prefix [e.g., *kwooluku*, shaman]; *aam*, generic for breast; *nbwutu*, navel). The others are "earth dwellers" (*chelaambu-mokeno; chelu* = stone or seed; *aambu/du* = female breast; *mokeno* = is being). Sky dwellers are short-legged whereas earth dwellers are long-legged.[4] With their longer limbs, Sambia say, earth dwellers are more adept runners, even harder to catch. Sky dwellers are the more commonly trapped. (This difference may reflect the greater scarcity of the lowlands *C. casuarius* species in the Sambia Mountains.)

Earth dwellers are the larger species, nearer a man's size. The legs are important in two ways: first for locomotion—the longer-legged creatures are alleged to get around better; and second for self-protection or attacking. Its legs are the bird's primary weapon; a powerful charge is coupled with treacherous claws, used to slash and gore.[5] An animal's leg length and relative strength go together, then, and the leg size is a measure of its dangerousness.[6]

---

4. These classifications seem to parallel the two species that occur throughout New Guinea: a dwarf cassowary (*Casuarius bennettii*), the common highlands type, up to a range of 7,000 feet; and the larger, double-wattled species (*Casuarius casuarius*) of the lowlands. Apparently both species range in Sambia forests.

5. Gilliard (1953:332) reports this observed attack on an unsuspecting woman: "It [cassowary] leaped with its great feet forward and struck the woman resoundingly with both of its weapon-feet. . . . The native went down as though shot, then began screaming. I found that her abdomen had been punctured to a depth of about an inch by the left foot and that her right upper arm had been cut to the bone by the stilettolike inner nail of the right foot." With massive medication, the woman barely survived the attack; but the same animal had previously attacked and killed an old man in the Kubor Mountains (Gilliard 1953:484).

6. See Gilliard (1953:332), who states that of the two species penned together, "The wattled bird was the more aggressive."

This leads to Sambia ideas about the sex assignment of cassowaries, ideas that are related to the anatomical differences between sky dwellers and earth dwellers. Two physical traits are associated with biological sex in cassowaries: color markings on the neck and the length of the legs. But these traits crosscut the two species, and they are evaluated differently.

By public dogma men always metaphorically classify the short-legged sky dwellers as male and the longer-legged earth dwellers as female. This metaphoric classification is, furthermore, correlated with gender according to different-colored neck stripes that occur in the two species. In a quieter way, then, the red-necked (*ipmoogu*) cassowary is implicitly acknowledged to be also "male"; the "female" is, by contrast, also denoted by its cobalt-blue neck rings (*kai-kwaku*).[7] Neither genitals nor any other anatomical trait figure in. There is, in general, both a metaphoric and gender association between the long-legged creatures with blue necks, and red-necked cassowaries having shorter legs. This association is true despite the fact that the color markings also divide each species up (into males and females), and Sambia recognize this crosscutting sex distinction. But I must raise a caution: although these traits are actually ascribed to the birds (they have been pointed out to me on the carcasses of snared cassowaries), they are infrequently mentioned in casual conversation: it is the long-legged femaleness of cassowaries that counts. There is obvious ambiguity here, but men ignore it. Yes, the species-specific and sex traits are important; yet, like the multivalent attributes of the pandanus flower, they are seldom discussed, except by allusion, and almost never at length.[8]

Yet cassowaries are genderized as females constantly, with certainty, and in precise ways far outweighing the tacit ambiguity of perceptual traits indexed in men's thought and speech. Cassowaries are "identical to women," and men sometimes metaphorically refer to women as cassowaries. To understand how, we must return to the origins of the birds; why they are not only associated with but believed to command thunder and lightning.

Men say that all cassowaries except one disappear at the rainy season. A solitary old "female" cassowary, they believe, the "mother of all cassowaries," stays behind. Sambia call her *Yowusiku,* the category name of all older, black-feathered birds. (I capitalize that name to represent this be-

---

7. The *ipmoogu* is the red (dyed tree bark) headband of initiates. Shamans make use of the red headband in ritual and healing ceremonies. There is some association here between the red neck rings and headcloth and shamans who, alone, wear cassowary headdresses. *Kai-kwaku* is blue-gray-colored mud used by women as a beauty aid, and by shamans to "cool the body."

8. I should not care to press these distinctions any further. Ambiguity in shared perceptions is clearly present in what men say; we should not try to cover up that divided opinion. To say more would require individual statements, and those I cannot present here.

ing, whom men refer to in the singular form.) It is she who directs the movements of all cassowaries. Most men, and especially cassowary hunters, refer to Yowusiku as the "great mother," i.e., protector, of cassowaries.[9] During the monsoon (as the forest tree fruit thins out), their food gone, Yowusiku scatters her flock, "dividing them up" into groups, sending them away. The "old mother" stays behind in the forest as a "boss"— the guardian of her forest preserve. She also holds a special "power" (*jerungdu*) that enables her to elude hunters, so neither can she be snared nor does she die. "She is steadfast like the earth itself," men grudgingly acknowledge. During the months of dreary monsoon, then, men gradually stop setting snares since no cassowaries can be caught: Yowusiku is indefatigable, and she has her "children" in hiding.

Yowusiku is believed to distribute one group into the heavens and the other into the bowels of the earth. The female earth dwellers, because of their elongated legs, are thought actually to penetrate the earth and "hide" inside it. The male sky dwellers do exactly what their name implies: they escape the forest into the clouds and heavens. How such fantastic transmigrations occur is unknown, but they are not a subject of much interest. If men are questioned, they state simply that cassowaries "have that power," and they do not claim to understand how Yowusiku arranges it. It is a mystery. Here is a clue, however: cassowaries are like the female hamlet spirits, men have told me. Those spirits live close at hand, inside bamboo clusters, or the hamlet earth, or at the base of great trees; and although they are seldom seen, one still sees the signs of their works and senses that presence.

It is Yowusiku, the immortal caretaker, who finally signals the cassowaries to return from their hiding places at the dry-season harvest. Using the stiletto nail of her inner right foot (men are precise), she repeatedly gores (*nulumberei*) the trunk of wild fruit and pandanus trees.[10] The tree's produce tumbles down whole into her waiting mouth. Other produce she scatters for future use. Then she trumpet-barks, beckoning her female brood to return to her from inside the earth. Her shrieks become the sound of thunder, the sound Nilutwo instantly associated with cassowary. Last, she commands lightning, "the pathway of the sky dwellers," sending thunderbolts that brighten a luminescent way for the male creatures who descend from the sky into the forest. From underneath the earth and

---

9. The hunters make use of the Neo-Melanesian term, *bik meri,* a term Sambia seldom say. One older man, Konu, a cassowary hunter, said he knows Yowusiku's secret name, *Iglewo Mandekatnyi,* but he offered no other meaning for this name, and no other informants knew of it.

10. Such idioms may refer to male cassowary courtship displays (see Crome 1975:8–9).

above the heavens, the migrants are thus compelled to reappear, almost overnight, in the forests where they can be trapped once more.

The Hunter's Predilections

Let us turn now, briefly, from the hunted to the hunter, not just to catalogue custom or the techniques of a livelihood, though those things are important, but to peer inside the mind of a particular hunter to examine his predilection for stalking cassowary, and what he suffers and enjoys by doing that.

Enough has been said to show the zest and seriousness men bring to the hunt. Hunting is a social necessity. It provides Sambia with their only ready supply of meat; it provides the gifts of game that custom demands as a marriage payment to secure a wife; it provides meat for the ceremonial ritual feasts, glamorous occasions when the hunter rightly earns praise for his work; and it provides feather decorations and pelts, festive attire that signals one's prowess in the hunt.

As much as these desirable trappings, however, hunting also provides a personal perspective for achieving and measuring masculinity: positive ways of changing the wish for mastery into the accomplishment of a kill.

There is an emotional investment in hunting as certain as masculinity itself. I want to survey the most general features of this trend; seven aspects are especially relevant. They provide clues, indicators of a fit between the psychodynamics of a certain masculine character structure and the cultural pattern of Sambia hunting. The data are inadequate: one would need more observations to generalize about my suggestions. Nevertheless, these data still warrant discussion since we are virtually ignorant of the anthropology or phenomenology of hunting, an absolutely vital part of Sambia male existence.

First, there are the techniques of hunting, what is handed down by a man's father, brothers, friends. We saw earlier how boys learn, step by step, the skill of preparing snares and traps. Add to this the countless memories of one's father entering the house of the lad's childhood (where he sits with his mother), bringing out a bag of game or a morsel of meat, getting his mother's praise, and surrendering part of that tasty treat for his meal. Or seeing his father traipse off into the high forest with his cronies, returning weeks later with a great prize of meat, like a hero. That man—if he is a good father—will carve his son's first bow, present him with arrows, teach him how to stalk game and knot snare traps. He entrusts him with his own hunting magic: spells and incantations that are heirlooms to be kept secret and eventually handed down to his own son. Here are the makings of a hunter in the child.

This seed gets special attention when the first initiations begin. Indeed, the first ceremony of the ritual cycle forces boys to reveal their potential hunting prowess by killing a possum. Men earlier trap the animals, break their legs, and then unleash them inside the frame of the ritual cult house under construction. Each boy must try to bludgeon a possum to death with a stick. Successful boys are verbally praised as *aamooluku,* "war leaders and good hunters"; weak and whimpering novices, however, are slurred as *wusaatu,* "soft men," rubbishy good-for-nothings. Boys get drummed into them the imagery of the hunt, too: its necessity and desirability if they are to be sharpshooting warriors. They are also enjoined to spit the blood of possum, in a later ceremony, and success or failure is again greeted by the same masculine stereotypy as before: adulation for the successful hunter, humiliation and shame for the incompetent. This pattern continues for years; so by the time of adolescence (third-stage initiation), youths are expected to be accomplished killers—hunters and warriors. Masculine pride and social esteem have their roots in this formula.

Third, there are spirit familiars (*numelyu;* or *numjentu,* also breath or steam), first acknowledged[11] at special initiation ceremonies and later through one's dreams. Here we face a particularly difficult concept with no ready equivalents in Western culture. Spirit familiars have a supranatural focus with an undercurrent of religious experience. In ritual, boys are made to undergo hunger, sleeplessness, prolonged excitement, and monotonous singing for hours and days. Several years later, at the shaman's initiation (*narangu,* the erection of a new men's clubhouse), another such experience is heightened by the ingestion of hallucinogens and the intoxicating, constant smoking of strong tobacco. Some youths fall into a trance, the telltale sign of a shaman's calling. Others (who do not become shamans) report the experience of sensing something alien enter them. The familiar's presence may be construed by shamans from a leaf, flower, feathers, or fur discovered adhering to one's skin. This is the familiar: an animal, plant, or spirit being believed to enter one's innards physically, and a piece of which dwells in one thereafter, animated and alive. It is said not only to heighten one's "strength"—i.e., prowess in war and the hunt —but to bestow good health and long life. The image of a familiar may be also revealed in dreams (*wunju*). Repeatedly recalling the dream image of a flower, tree, or person (interpreted always as a spirit or ghost), for example, is a symptom that one has been personally identified with a particular familiar. And new familiars may be thus acquired from dreams.

A whole range of familiars is advantageous for the cassowary hunter. But unlike all other familiars except those of the shaman—and most sha-

---

11. This choice of phraseology pertains to the complexities of how spirit familiars are experienced: some familiars are believed to be transmitted to the fetus from a father's sperm; others may be acquired as the boy develops (Herdt 1977:156). See Chapter 8.

mans are also cassowary hunters (although the reverse is not true)—the cassowary familiar par excellence is the female hamlet spirit. And according to belief, it cannot be acquired except by actual biological inheritance from one's father or male kinsman. So only certain individuals of selected families can become cassowary hunters.

Next I should mention the obvious: hunting is more than food-getting; it is also a sport. Obvious as this is, however, it is seldom paid serious attention in anthropological reports (see, for example, Wagner 1972: 155–156). Hunting is a rewarding challenge; it is a break in the routine of garden chores, as men note. It is exciting: one stalks a prey, overcoming and capturing it by means of bow and arrow, trap, or even one's hands. There is a standard of masculine prowess in this: it is judged more dangerous to stalk bigger game, such as wild pigs or cassowary, or to climb trees and hunt possum with one's bare hands.

For instance, fourth-stage initiation begins in a long ceremonial hunt in the forest, the yield of which goes to one's affines and betrothed in the final marriage ceremony (*nuposha*) prestations a few weeks later. Only possum are acceptable game; and those possum caught by hand, the hallmark of possum hunting, are especially honored meat gifts. Sambia thus know that each catch is a feat. So each catch—and there may be over a hundred animals collectively caught in the hunt—is lauded, and the story of who caught it, and where, is recalled again and again to peers, women, and children.

Fifth is the matter of who actually eats the game. Three taboos stand out. The meat must be given to others. A man may not usually eat his own catch, unless it has been trapped, and even this is permitted only for a small number of species (out of scores) not otherwise forbidden. Furthermore, many more meat taboos apply to boys and youths than all others. Only as a male matures and marries can he partake of a wider menu of game, such as rats, frogs, or lizards, until then considered polluted and dangerous to his health. Women of all ages have far fewer food restrictions than do men.

And next, a food taboo especially germane to this discussion: all women, young and old, are absolutely forbidden ever to eat (see also Barth 1975:165–166), or even touch, cassowary flesh. The taboo stands out boldly against the overall pattern of ingestion taboos, since women have much greater freedom in eating foods than do men.

Now we face a problem that particularly pertains to cassowary hunting and has a strong psychological component: individual predilection. Out of a pool of perhaps five or ten genealogically eligible candidates within a village, only a handful of men will ever attempt to stalk cassowaries; and among them, one or two or three, at most, will actually make some kills. This small number must be set against the general norm: all men hunt possums, birds, and other animals except the cassowary. And from a community's bank of cassowary hunters, only one will be fervent, acknowledged, and successful.

The cassowary hunter is a driven man. His special requirements must be accompanied by a special predilection: to dream frequently, report his dreams as omens, sustain sexual abstinence, and then, when he finally bags a bird, to surrender it to others since he cannot eat the meat himself. (He can, however, eat other meat and the cassowaries trapped by others.) The difficulties in this are great enough, and the event of snaring a cassowary uncommon[12] enough, for each killing to become a special triumph. To outwit a cassowary, he really has to desire to do it. That is how Sambia reckon.

Each killing becomes a special triumph: this leads to a final clue about the personality of a cassowary hunter. He must be willing to sustain (and perhaps even enjoy) the cumbersome taboos he assumes by pursuing cassowaries. While trapping he must halt all heterosexual activity because idioms allege that he becomes a danger to his wife. (Homosexual activity, however, remains appropriate, if otherwise acceptable, i.e., if he is not married and a father.) Once a cassowary snare is set and the magical spells uttered over it, the hunter becomes infused with the power of the spells. Unlike any other magical spells, even lethal sorcery, cassowary magic is also dangerous through contact with the magician; and it is dangerous *only* to females. Coitus with his wife (or other contacted women) could result in her falling sick, developing sores or incapacitating respiratory illness, or eventually dying. Likewise, if a woman accidentally trips a cassowary snare, she becomes endangered. Only a hunter's own healing spells are believed able to release her from this danger. So his wife, too, shares sexual abstinence with the hunter. No other hunting contains this inherent risk to women. (Men are advised not to copulate with women before possum hunting, but only because they can sully their own hunting prowess, i.e., animals are said to "smell" women's sexual fluids lingering on the hunter's bodies, thus eluding capture.) Once other males eat cassowary meat, moreover, they too are forbidden to touch (i.e., copulate with) women or to eat female foods like greens and pandanus fruit, for fear that such contact will hinder the cassowary hunter's future chances of bagging a bird. But these men are not dangerous to women: only the hunter endangers women, especially his wife. The cassowary hunter must sublimate his heterosexual activities, then, channeling those energies elsewhere. It is in the dream that he seeks proof of his predilection.

---

12. Clarke (1971:90) notes that four or five cassowaries were trapped in a year in a Maring hamlet (see also G. Lewis 1975:50). The figure was roughly double that in Nilangu hamlet for a year; many of the trappings were Nilutwo's.

This sketch has established some general points, but now we need to
see how these characteristic trends take form in the behavior of particular
individuals. What do they do, what do they say and think, what predilections lead to cassowary hunting, and how is it suffered and enjoyed? Of
the several cassowary hunters I know, two are shamans; three of them
spoke with me frequently; one of them I knew well.

Nilutwo, of Nilangu hamlet, I knew best. He was a constant informant
for eighteen months, and during that time I followed closely[13] his behavior and life history and dreams. A married man in his early thirties, an
accomplished cassowary hunter (but not a shaman), and a prolific dreamer
since his teens, Nilutwo was a gifted, difficult, and often troubled friend.
He had long suffered frequent nightmares. He had suffered mild bouts of
crazy behavior in his teens, what Sambia called *abrumbru* (madness), and
what may be akin to Langness's (1965) "hysterical psychosis."[14] An only
child whose father (toward the last, acting crazy and violent) had died
young, he was reared almost alone by his mother, a strong, thrice-married
widow, who saw to his premature initiation. Nilutwo's marital history was
a disaster; and his present marriage had been difficult from the start.
Women generally disparaged him as a "weak" man who was, nonetheless,
constantly in trouble over his ill-fated attempts at adultery. The woman
who was to become his wife often ignored him. He had brothers and
age-mates, however, who actually abducted the wife from another village,
locking the couple inside a house to ensure that the marriage was sexually
consummated. (As it was.)

This is Nilutwo, my sample. Drawing on interviews of a clinical type
augmented by social observations, I relied on him for investigating various
things, particularly his cassowary hunting. His experience and knowledge
answered a need for understanding; his personality complemented mine
enough to form a working alliance. In time we became friends. To learn
about his predilections, I was led into his dreams, although what follows
is still incomplete. But let us begin with his dreams.

There are many cassowary-related dreams but really only one Dream,
"the Dream": an image of "copulating with a woman I know, or have seen
before, sometimes my brother's wife, or a different woman," Nilutwo
said. "The Dream" often, though not always, ends abruptly with ejacula-

13. Closely means working at least three, sometimes six, sessions a week, an hour a day, when
possible.
14. It is my impression that this episode was similar to what Western psychiatrists label a
"psychotic break." In this and other respects, Nilutwo is unusual, but he is not unique. This
episodic acting out is common among cassowary hunters, and especially shamans. From such
a small "pool" of cassowary hunters, it is difficult to assess what is normative and what is
deviant except through case studies that note the unique and general aspects of each.

tion. Immediately after a "wet dream" (*wunjaalyu*), Nilutwo would awaken, sometimes shaken, sometimes elated, but usually experiencing some anxiety. (Should we call this a repetitive nightmare? Or simply a frightening wet dream, one he has often known, and experienced as spectacular, since puberty? I am uncertain.)

Now other men and youths have wet dreams too, although the topic is embarrassing (and exciting) enough to preclude easy access to knowing how frequently. When Nilutwo (and here, other men act the same way) awakens, he checks his genitals and grass sporran: he was at first careful to hide the evidence from others, including his peers (since wet dreams communicate pubescence and erotic desire, both fraught with conflict), and now his wife; and he is cautious in disposing of the seminal emission, since there is a danger of its being eaten by insects, a life threat. There is, too, a strong element of shame (*wungulu*) in this cover-up.[15]

Finally, there is the meaning of the dream: for Nilutwo, a haunting recollection of something past, like fleeting (and pleasurable) thoughts of erotic desire toward forbidden women, such as his sister-in-law. He dreams of her and several other women (some old) frequently. He has other sorts of dreams, too, some of which he treated as omens that a cassowary trap had been tripped and that a creature waited there in the forest ready for him to kill. But no other dreams have the stupendous implications of his "Dream."

Nilutwo perceives these wet dreams as a manifestation of his special relationship to female hamlet spirits. They are his spirit familiars. They may come to him disguised as his sister-in-law or other women, but they are still spirits.[16] Since nearing adolescence he has dreamt of them; since then he has been a renowned cassowary hunter. His dream women taunt him, reveal things to him, frustrate or seduce him, and he, them. He fears, resents, and enjoys them. Sometimes Nilutwo is chased by evil ghosts, pursued by giant snakes, or nearly overwhelmed by a great surge of water before he awakens, visibly frightened. Yet when he experiences a familiar woman in a dream, when they flirt and engage in coitus, and when all the elements of a "good dream" come together, producing a final ejaculation without frightening images, Nilutwo is ecstatic. He may lament the loss of semen, "water gone for nothing"; he may even deride the spirits for that; but he does so visibly composed, with a smile, soon ready near dawn

---

15. The reasons are complex: the wet dream is itself embarrassing because of the implication of sexual desire; as is the suggestion of having copulated with a spirit or ghost; ejaculation, alone, is shameful, i.e., men completely deny that there is masturbation, and nocturnal emissions are considered wasteful of one's sperm.

16. See Appendix B for a verbatim transcription of two of Nilutwo's dream reports, together with his associations to them.

to set off and examine his cassowary traps. "I saw a spirit, we played [had coitus] together; it was a wet dream. My *moyu* stick must be sprung. . . . I want to go examine it—have I caught one [cassowary] or not?"

On half a dozen occasions I have observed Nilutwo awaken from such a dream and then discover a cassowary in one of his traps. He journeys there alone, or sometimes with a companion. He seldom confides at first in other men and never in his wife.

Let us try to picture that forest scene. Soon after "the Dream," Nilutwo walks to a hidden spot, away from all human habitation. From a distance the tall spring-loaded stick is visible, but it is down, sprung. He comes across this dead carcass, the elusive cassowary stilled by his snare, literally strangled by its own attempt to free itself (see Wagner 1972:63). Or this female creature may be still alive, struggling, trapped. It is dangerous, it hisses, it stamps around; and it may even charge. Yet it is trapped, there is no escape. So he knows he must kill it. It is he who triumphs.

Nilutwo went into a dream; he saw his spirit; they had sex and he ejaculated; in waking life the cassowary was trapped; and so he had killed her.

This is a hypothesis about how Nilutwo may experience a stream of thoughts and feelings consciously[17] associated with a cassowary kill. All the necessary components convert the often frightening dream into a successful outcome: "This time, trauma is turned into pleasure, orgasm, victory" (Stoller 1977:6). We still know virtually nothing about the roots of Nilutwo's predilection. We do not even have enough data to confirm this suggestion nor to say how often it applies to Nilutwo's own behavior, not to mention its general applicability to the behavior of other Sambia cassowary hunters, or all men.

Nilutwo himself is successful on occasion, although his failures far outnumber his real triumphs. Never mind: that one moment of victory, once in a while, is enough to impel him to recreate it.

What Nilutwo experiences in his dreams are the productions of his own mind, psychodynamics, and past history. The inner experience is projected outside himself into the fantasy of a supernatural visitation, an omen, a female spirit that animates his dreams and waking life. His own "Dream" —shared by his peers—is projected into what he consciously experiences. It is supported, reinforced, and made useful by a culturally constituted pattern of Sambia masculine character, the role of the cassowary hunter. With this, let us now return to the hunted phantom and men's idioms that genderize the cassowary as a masculinized female.

---

17. Clearly, there is an interplay of personal daydream and fantasy (conscious and unconscious) with a culturally constituted interpretational fantasy system in how Nilutwo experiences and measures his dreams, though we cannot here take up that complex whole.

Masculinized Females

Sambia men refer to cassowaries as if they were only female. That remains true despite the ostensible awareness that the birds are of different sexes. And men's references involve more than metaphor. The trend of this one-sided genderizing—an assertion of primordial femaleness—parallels my earlier description of the pandanus, but surpasses it in the affect and detail of men's verbal behavior that equates women and cassowaries. In addition, there is a myth telling how cassowaries were once actually women (see Appendix C). Cassowaries are, after all, the largest animals Sambia know, a fact that understandably facilitates an anthropomorphization unparalleled for trees or smaller animals.

The key idiom is this: "Women are the age-mates of the cassowary." This identification, among men, goes beyond previous statements illustrating equivalence or similarities. The idiom's conviction is sustained by numerous beliefs, perceptions, and feelings (which are so firmly entrenched in masculine culture that it would be virtually impossible to find a man who disputed it and who could be used as a "control case" for investigating the null hypothesis that women are not like cassowaries).[18] Men's statements about the traits and behaviors of cassowaries are constantly lumped with observations about women. Likewise, this peculiar identification is focused back on women for whom eating cassowary flesh is taboo since "they are its age-mates."

To examine further this equation of women and cassowaries, let us now focus on the perceptual traits of correspondence between those two "species" that are desirable, and put to use, in ritual idiom and ceremony, considering point by point the focal projections underlying men's allusions to cassowaries.

Genitalia first. What matters principally is the lack of external genitals: without visible penis or vagina, men say, cassowaries are "unlike bird or possum or man." A trapped bird is at times assigned lexically to the male or female sex on the basis of length of legs and neck coloration. Nevertheless, the same carcass, its flesh, and other living cassowaries are called *kaiouwugu,* "the very same as a woman." This genderizing "attitude" has lexical, metaphoric, and perceptual components; and such statements are also arbitrary, for men profess relative (and convincing) ignorance of how cassowaries reproduce. The cassowary "has no penis of its own," men assert, and no "vagina" (*laaku*) from which to menstruate or give birth. So here is what I suggest occurs.

---

18. Among Sambia men one could, however, use cassowary hunters as a "control" for the maximum degree of involvement in the identification of women and cassowaries, or the espousal of associated idioms.

In the absence of observable genitals, men tend to *think* of the creatures *as if* they were female. Stress then gets placed on traits that correspond to women's secondary sex traits and behaviors. I noted a similar process at work earlier in pandanus idioms, but cassowary idioms are more lopsided in this respect. For instance, flowers and nuts distinguished "female" from "male" pandanus. The "male" secondary sex traits in cassowaries (short legs, red neck wattles) are seldom mentioned, have no secular or ritual significance, and are ignored alongside of the "female" aspects. In the matter of genitalia, then, all cassowaries are perceptually lumped together as "females," and two anatomical traits outweigh others in sustaining masculine viewpoints about the womenlike cassowaries. They come in the absence of genitalia.

There is, first, the cassowary's unusually large anus (*loopootu; loo,* anal; *pootu,* pathway; *loopootu* is generic for the mammalian [but not bird] anus). The anus appears to double as the cassowary's "vagina."[19] Men furthermore associate the lack of penis and vagina with its anus; for instance, Tali once casually remarked (when talking with me): "I think the cassowary anus is half vagina and half anus, like a chicken's." (A handful of men around him nodded agreement.) But then he denied that the cassowary has a vagina, noting that none can be observed. This is clearly problematic since Sambia unambiguously distinguish penis and vagina in all mammals (but not in birds). Tali's statement alludes to chickens as birds, and this underlies the anomaly that cassowaries are "not bird" and "not mammal." Comments about another, related anatomical trait—the cassowary's rump (*letn'omwalyu*)—complement these perceptions of its anus and give warning that the idiomatic boundary between women and cassowaries is fuzzy.

Second, therefore, men identify perceptually the cassowary's rump with the curved shapeliness of a woman's buttocks. Here is a cardinal attribute anatomically defining the relationship of age-mate, *ginyoko,* between these two types of females. (Recall the concept of *ginyoko,* which identifies men with trees. The term is used discreetly.) Several attributes are noted. The actual size (i.e., skin surface), weight, and curvature of the abdomen, and the girth of the hind end of cassowaries, are "identically the same as women's." (Male anatomy, men say, makes for a flat abdomen, bony hips, and less full and shapely buttocks.) The roundedness of the abdomen, to illustrate, is concretely associated with pregnancy and parturition, as we saw in pandanus idioms. The inverse holds true for men: males with distended abdomens are slurred as being "too womanlike"; if that condi-

---

19. There is no term for vagina or penis in the cassowary, and no metaphor known to me for either, except the anus, which is never called vagina (*laaku*).

tion persists, such men come to be labeled "soft and rubbishy." And idioms allege that these individuals have foolishly allowed themselves to become internally polluted by women's blood.

The cassowary rump is fundamentally associated with the egg-laying fecundity of its anus. The color of rump feathers plays a large role in this perception. The dark brown and black feathers of reproductively mature birds—the plumage covering their posteriors—are called "anal hair" (*kaiouwugu loopoo-aatu,* cassowary anal feathers, where *loopoo-aatu* is generic only for human anal hair and is never used elsewhere for feathers). Those feathers embrace the anus, and their significance is quite precise: men categorically refer to the rump plumage cluster as *kanyelaatu* (*kanyelu,* generic for woman's grass skirt; *laa-tu/ku,* vagina); in addition, the anatomy and color of the feathers are "identically the same as the color of our women's skirts." This correspondence leads directly into the relationship between reproduction and growth in cassowary development.

Idioms postulate a fixed cycle of changes in the coloration of cassowary "anal hair" that is thought to be correlated with their fast-growing reproductive competence. Three distinct stages are noted in the animal's life cycle and all pertain to reproductive maturity. First, there are the newborn chicks (for which there is no category name, though I have heard *tai* sometimes used). Chicks have soft, yellow-brown down, a color similar to the skin of newborn Sambia babies (though no one has pointed this out to me), and men emphasize how quickly cassowary young seem to grow. Second, the adolescent birds nearing procreative age are labeled *chenchi,* which term is a homonym for menstrual blood. Their hallmark is orange-colored rump feathers (*chenchi-aatu*). Those special feathers are ritually used only once, when they are mounted exclusively in the headdresses of prepubescent second-stage initiates (*imbutu:* compare *imbei,* young woman, also adolescent cassowary). (I noted earlier a form of this noun in the pandanus nomenclature, *aambei-walu,* denoting middle-aged "female" trees.) Last, there is the category of reproductively mature birds, *yowusiku* (after the name of the "cassowary mother"). These animals have black rump feathers, the earlier, brighter "anal hair" having disappeared (these birds are also the most frequently trapped). Idiomatically, the black feathers are associated with having procreated and passed into adulthood.[20]

---

20. I should note how anal hair is conceptualized. Private male conversations jokingly depict the occurrence of anal hair as a key secondary sex trait, but only of male puberty. Among youths this is characteristically embarrassing, and they take care in fastening their arse-covers so that "women cannot see our arses." Initiates are disparaged as "boys" (*kwulai'u*) if they do not wear arse-covers; and boys whose initiations have been too long postponed are disparaged as having anal hair, but still—shockingly—being with their mothers (an implication of incestuous intimacy). On one occasion I heard Weiyu wonder aloud to Tali and other men

Here I must note the semantically complex matter of these "colors of cassowary reproductive maturity" and their sympathetic analogues in ritual magic. Crudely, the colors fall into three categories: yellow (chicks), orange-red (adolescents), and black (adults). Yellow mud (*koonai-kwaku*) is identified with the soil in which pandanus grows and the cassowary roams. Recall that cassowary feces are mixed with this yellow mud and the solution is smeared on children and first-stage initiates (never on older males) to "help them grow quickly," i.e., like cassowary chicks. By contrast, the second-stage initiates wear the orange-red feathers and have red ocher, red pandanus fruit "grease"[21] (*moo-nugu*, the category term for semen and cassowary oil), or both, rubbed on them. That body coloration is forbidden to younger males; and it is forbidden for women to see boys painted red during the initiation. Against this focus on red, men compare the black feathers of mature birds with a dark blue-gray mud (*kai-kwaku*, in the high altitude forest). Here is Tali:

> The *yowusiku* paints herself with *kai-kwaku*, and she produces a child: she has black feathers. [A muddy-colored rumped bird] uses [its] leg to beat the earth, turning it muddy blue . . . this is its habit: when tearing up the earth it shakes its legs as it does when struggling in a trap.

The rump feathers naturally turn black in cassowaries. Sambia women, however, artificially color their grass skirts black, using *kai-kwaku* mud, to preserve the reeds against wear and rain. (In certain initiation rites, men, too, smear mud on their grass sporrans after they have attained marriageable age.) Finally, although mature cassowaries and women are "painted black," the *chenchi*, adolescent bird, "does not paint itself *kai-kwaku*" and, contrarily, it is absolutely forbidden ever to place *yowusiku* rump feathers on the head of initiates because "they are still growing [and] it will thwart them," men say. Among adult men, interestingly enough, only cassowary hunters or shamans wear headdresses of black *yowusiku* feathers (though forest spirits are also said to do so).[22]

---

whether women possessed anal hair, to which the audience gave conflicting opinions. See also footnote 29, this chapter.

21. This is followed by feasting on pandanus fruit, which ends the taboo imposed on eating that food at first-stage initiation.

22. Let me mention several other tangential points about this color symbolism. Yellow is the color of the yellow orchid-fibre bandoliers and waistbands placed on first-stage initiates, emblems of warrior status par excellence. Like the rainbow colors orange, red, and white, yellow is utilized in body painting and war-shield decoration, and Sambia exegesis concretely identifies those colors with the phenomena of sun and moon corona, and rainbow prisms. These skyward or heavenly colors contrast sharply with black, idiomatically pinpointed on the earth, mud, and the mature cassowary. Here again is a metaphoric differentiation associated analogically with short-legged male cassowaries who hide in the heavens and the

This material underlines the view that reproductive status is the key variable in accounting for men's perceptions of aging in animal species. Masculine idioms tend to embody their tacit knowledge about procreative changes in women to project culturally constituted gender traits back into a species. So cassowary sayings closely parallel those pertaining to pandanus trees. The pandanus life cycle was classified according to perceptions of "reproductive changes" (and color transformations) in grass fronds, aerial roots, and nut pods. Seasonal changes in "female pandanus trees" corresponded with procreation developments in women (skin coloration, pregnancy, etc.). Likewise with birds, whose transition from bright to dull plumage is believed to be a shift from maleness to femaleness. And so with cassowaries: from yellow-brown to orange to blue-black rump feathers—the final sign of having rapidly attained reproductive competence. (Recall that these types of feathers are ritually identified with the different categories of males.) The process of darkening and aging seems indicative of the consequences of giving birth as men see it. Black rump feathers link cassowaries with women having blue-gray grass skirts; neither type of "female" can climb trees, and they must forage the earth; both can, nonetheless, procreate: that is, I think, what the concept of *kanyelaatu,* "anal feathers," implies. This sets them apart from men, who do not undergo such parturition changes, ever. Like the pandanus, moreover, the dark-colored "female grass skirt" is singled out as a distinctive feature separating women, "female" pandanus trees, and all cassowaries, from "male" pandanus trees or men. There is more to be said about this process, but first we need to consider idioms of cassowary behavior, since these brutes are more humanly animated than pandanus trees.

To sketch what men say of cassowary behavior is to unfold still another dimension of precise focal projections directed toward the birds. Take its rootlessness and wanderlust: the cassowary has "no house of its own"; it does not permanently nest. Lacking a territory,[23] men assert, the animals roam and rest at will, never stopping to roost or construct a nest like the

---

long-legged earthbound females whose hiding place is the muddy interior of the forest earth. There are two other uses of black mud, too: one is the shaman's use of it in painting the bodies of people in a whole village to protect them against illness by "cooling them off." The other is cosmetic, since some women put mud on their graying hair to darken it and make themselves look younger. Finally, men occasionally refer to *yowusiku* cassowaries as *kwei-waku* (compare *kweiaalyu-waku,* cassowary grease); *kwei-waku* is also, generically, a "true" manly warrior; and *kwei-kwaku* (white earth) is loam-colored forest mud used as a war paint. Note how this configuration of associations concerns cassowaries, sky and earth, manliness and the powers that control thunder, lightning, sickness, death, and life. In that regard we must not forget that cassowaries are thought to be immortal, unless animals or men kill them.

23. Sambia do not recognize defined feeding territories among cassowaries (see Crome 1975), though its hunters know of certain forage routes.

bush hen. A similar idiom sometimes alludes to the sexual division of labor: only men build houses, only men own them. Women, "like cassowaries," move from their parents' locality to their husband's natal hamlet at marriage.

Like women, cassowaries are said to eat "rubbishy foods," hard seeds and soft "female" foods like greens and pitpit. Their huge piercing eyes enable them to scour the undergrowth, mucking about in the decaying, muddy vegetation for anything edible. They eat anything, that is, that they can swallow: large tree shoots, impossibly hard nuts, even old discarded bamboo torches and stones. "Like women," then, cassowaries "swallow whole anything they come across," and in great quantities. This insinuation is pointedly the subject of lewd joking among men about women (and sometimes boys) as fellators. Women are sexually slurred as wanton, indiscriminate penis suckers who hungrily crave semen selfishly to "strengthen themselves." Any man women come upon is viewed as a penis with "water to be drunk"; women seek the life-giving fluid from them, or so men assert. Then, too, the promiscuous cassowaries are as "mindless as women" (unintelligent, lacking prudence). Though swift and big, the bird can be snared once its feeding trail is discovered. There cornered, it is unruly, and even dangerous, like women. When touched the animal feels "cold-skinned," almost icy, as are women compared to their "hot-skinned men."[24]

Last, men focus on a somewhat more obscure and ominous behavior. The cassowary "mother" caretaker "abandons her young" as quickly as possible, men declare. The female lays her eggs but does not carefully tend them. She is believed to be the sole caretaker of the young. No Sambia in any way ever mentioned cassowary paternity, fathering, or paternal caretaking to me, a further indication of the absoluteness of the attribution of female sex to the bird.[25] Men assert that the mother raises her young and eventually "teaches them to recognize the traps of man," an insurance against capture. Yet nurturance one day turns into abandonment. Men say the "mother" eventually feigns entrapment, near the time its chicks become *chenchi* adolescents. After a while the young wander off or are chased off, deserted forever.

---

24. Since men rarely encounter cassowaries alive, or soon after death, I am uncertain about the significance of this idiom. But its thrust is clear enough: ghosts, hamlet spirits, and women are all said to be cold-skinned.

25. Sambia are ignorant of the cassowary male's role in courtship and breeding. "When ready to lay, the female disappeared with the male but she soon returned after laying. During incubation the males did not come to feed. . . . Each year the male brought chicks to the house for feeding. At about nine months of age, the chicks are abandoned and chased away by the male" (Crome 1975:9). Here is a clear case of empirical error: it is the male bird that tends and finally disperses the chicks.

The trend of these idioms raises the problem of culturally constituted fantasy. What part represents naturalistic observation, what part is erroneous interpretation of the apparent, or focal projection? The answer requires that we shift modes of description. Having illustrated the similarities and parallels men commonly amplify between women and cassowaries, let us now consider what is less obvious: the different qualities and traits that distinguish the "female" cassowary from women. It is the difference as much as the exaggerated identification, I believe, that makes the cassowary a perfect bisexual representation for men, one utilized in masculine idiom and ceremony.

Take anal birth, for example. This is the tacit implication of men's idioms and beliefs about that orifice they share with the cassowary. The cassowary is a female minus a vagina, the thing men most dread in women. The cassowary has a large anus, capable of emitting large, dark green eggs (weighing up to 1½ lbs.) and prolific fecal droppings. Women do not, of course, need to procreate through their anuses since they possess vaginas. Cassowaries, however, lack both penis and vagina, but they are empowered with a special anus, seemingly their only possible orifice having the capacity to yield life. That is the unspoken supposition of men's idioms that link men and cassowaries against women.

That men harbor this supposition is clear from their ceremonial use of cassowary feces to stimulate growth in children. It is obvious to Sambia that there is something special about these feces. Why else should whole tree seeds and nuts pass through the bird unscathed, and then, suspended in fecal matter, pop up new shoots? Hence cassowaries are equipped, willy-nilly, with the power to transfer plant life from place to place. So, from the haunts of cassowaries, soil is collected, pale yellow soil called *koonai-kwaku* (pandanus soil). Cassowary feces are mixed in it. The solution is smeared on young children, and occasionally on first-stage initiates too, to hasten their maturity. "It will help them grow," men assert,[26] like the cassowary chicks that grow so fast. The yellow soil itself is said to have an "infectious quality" enabling it to spread its color quickly when transplanted. And so shall children grow. The yellow mud, furthermore, is painted on men at several occasions:[27] the house-raising ceremonies of the ritual cult house at its construction; during the pandanus spitting ritual of third-stage initiation; and following a ceremonial feast upon a cassowary kill, privately, in men's company in the forest. Women, too, make special use of the mud, but only once: during their menarche ceremonies. All

---

26. If a boy seems too small for his age, the father may also place possum feces in the child's net bag to hasten his growth.
27. Recall that initiates have yellow mud painted on them at collective initiation, whereas men do not.

these events, including the cassowary feast itself, involve reproductive development and parturition.

Elsewhere I consider those other events, but here let me cite the unusual behavior concerning the cassowary feast. A glimpse at those data will illuminate the use of the yellow mud and how idioms reinforce the need to distance men from women and cassowaries. So let us return again to Nilutwo, one of his dreams having led him to discover a trapped cassowary—and the feasting that follows it.

Nilutwo makes his way to the hamlet quickly. He doesn't dawdle, he is excited. But he manages to contain his enthusiasm: he has trapped the bird; let others praise him for it. He quietly spreads word to his clansmen, who in turn tell a few more. The kill is, however, always referred to obliquely, e.g., "Let us go fetch some betel nut," men might say. So women, and other unwelcome strangers, are kept in the dark. Sambia men like it that way: this is men's business.

There, at the trap, the feathers are removed, the carcass is cut up, and its meat baked in an earth oven. Nilutwo gets adoring praise and he grins a lot (yet he remains mostly silent and stands aloof from the butchering). He gets to distribute much of the cooked meat. Most of it is eaten there, relished, gobbled down, in relative silence. The initiates get a share, but not of the posterior or anal part: otherwise they might "defecate too much" when next beaten at initiation rituals. Then the excess cassowary grease is rubbed on the initiates' faces and chests. No other animal products, and only one other human substance, semen, is ever used in that way (but boys do that to themselves, privately, after fellatio). Still, the reason is purportedly the same: boys' faces will be shiny-nosed, glistening, and handsome for youths and women alike. Each participant is then rubbed with stinging nettles. Nettles are intensely painful, so the boys grimace and yelp; but men bear it stoically as usual, a necessary curse to rid themselves of the smell and grease of cassowary flesh. The whole group is then painted with yellow mud. With the flesh in their stomachs, still feeling the sting of nettles, the private feast is concluded. They return to the village.

Once there, no mention is made of the feast, but women instantly know what has happened. Some men unveil tidbits of meat that they feed only to their tiny sons. They place the meat in the uninitiated lad's mouth, never allowing him, or females, to touch it. (If women touched the grease, they would ruin the hunter's magic.)

The men then raise a songfest in their clubhouse. This is their celebration: the triumph in the kill of a cassowary. Besides, prohibited by taboo from copulating with their wives for a night or two, there is little cause to return to their beds tonight. Let the women sleep alone: they are not going anywhere. (Elders again advise men that it is best to avoid too much contact with their wives anyway.) Soft "female" foods are taboo for a time, too, this prohibition one of many restricting the mingling of "male" and "female" foods in one's stomach. Till dawn the men go on singing apart from their women.

Back in the village the feasters were easily identified by their sallow skin color, the product of the yolky yellow mud. They are a visible reminder of what happened in the forest. Behind that, however, is a latent experience that most Sambia men have known: "the Dream." If they have not directly experienced it as a wet dream, they have heard mention of it, time and again, by Nilutwo and other hunters. A prophecy born of the Dream has again come true in the feasting. Like the Dream, eating cassowary can be exciting and disturbing, even dangerous. Cassowaries sympathetically resemble women, so it is dangerous to experience their flesh. Those are "female" influences: inside the dream, trapped in the forest; inside one's stomach, smeared outside on one's skin. The consequences of the Dream seem closer to men in their feast: the danger of eating the cassowary meat is exacerbated by the excitement of ceremonial secrecy, the pain of the nettles, and by being painted yellow—which is the color of female parturition.

Now we should recall how these images refer to hamlet spirits—otherworldly beings—and cassowaries, creatures of mystical origins and anal parturition. The external boundary between oneself, a product of women, and the cassowary, is temporarily suppressed and violated. Its unusual powers are incorporated into oneself. This is dangerous; and to insure that the risk is controlled and the cassowary caught again, there is a strict need to keep cassowary products and oneself physically separated from women until some hours later, when the excitement has been worn down by the singing into sleep.

Then "the Dream" comes again. Only in that world does one sensually experience "hamlet spirits," the go-betweens that dreamily link cassowary with real women. And while idioms fuse the identification of all three types of "females," Sambia dream interpretation culturally separates hamlet spirits from women or cassowaries in the secular world.[28] The behavior of taboo has the same effect for the cassowary eaters painted yellow and their women: the hunter's magic is, if only briefly, dangerous to all females. Women cannot participate in the feast; and men stay clear of them. And for once the tables are turned: it is women who must be careful lest they be endangered by male contact that could transmit cassowary magic. Dreams or no dreams.

---

28. This is affirmed in the subtle difference that cassowaries are sometimes said to be the "children" of hamlet spirits, the result of a union of male forest spirits and female hamlet spirits.

The psychological experience of the feast thus enables men to triumph over the aggressive female cassowaries, and their women, who are temporarily bypassed. There is a tension here. Yet the sense of distance separating men from women and cassowaries is kept intact and comfortably exciting.

Overview

Like other New Guinea peoples (see Barth 1975:54; Bulmer 1967; Gell 1975:224ff.; Mead 1968:84; Tuzin 1977:210–211; Williams 1936b:88n., 311–312, 390–391), Sambia are fascinated by the cassowary. Its nature enchants them; not just what the animal is or does, but what men wish it to be. We have already seen a similar process at work elsewhere: distinctively magical qualities are attributed to garden crops, animal categories, and the defenseless pandanus. Cassowary idioms are even more perplexing for an observer. Large and strong, with ambiguous genitals, odd habits and migration patterns, the cassowary combines several compelling mythological elements. This creature, which thus seems to me, a sympathetic observer, to be an asexual bird, is for Sambia a powerful mystical animal genderized as a "female." Men's viewpoints are accommodated by several naturally occurring aspects of perceptual correspondence that link cassowaries with humans. These correspondences are then channeled through focal projections: men attributing to cassowaries precise qualities of human maleness and femaleness as they know them. Behind this constellation of knowledge and experience, I think, lies a fantasy system.

It is not so remarkable that men have fixed on this phantom dame of the forest as a key representation of their culture. Temperamental, wild, masculinized females: what better bisexual image (see especially Tuzin 1977:210–211) for a group of men who so profess abhorrence of women? This side of masculine idiom is understandable; it is, furthermore, captured in the myth to which I previously alluded (see Appendix C). What is troublesome is the transempirical contents of cassowary-oriented behavior.

It is remarkable that naturalists so very astute as Sambia could actually believe in anal birth. How can they sustain such a stupendously erroneous thought in the face of their own clearly postulated link between coitus, sperm, and procreation?[29]

There is circumstantial evidence aplenty, like the subjective connection between dream experience and spirit beings and the allegedly immortal

---

29. I am speaking only of adults, and it is worth adding that anal birth (like oral birth) is one theory of procreation among Sambia children unacquainted with the biological facts of life, which are hidden from them.

cassowary; or like the conviction of mystical origins associated with anal birth. One problem is to understand at what level of experience the cassowary is "believed" to be a "female"[30] with an anus that procreates. This is a complex matter; and yet we know that fantasy is at play since individuals offer ready interpretations of experiences, like that of dreams, which come from within them, no matter how widely shared their interpretational elements. I still have little access to those fantasies, but do not wish to ignore them because Sambia do not. So like others I must speculate: how do such convictions—culturally constituted but personally motivating—come about?

Anthropologists have offered only three[31] answers to this old question: faulty technology, faulty politics, or faulty reasoning. Frazer (1911) and Malinowski (1954) after him saw in primitive magical belief the seeds of dormant technology, an attempt to explain the unknown on the basis of inadequate information or procedures. Faulty technology. Leach (1961, 1964b) and Douglas (1966) reckon somewhat differently. A flaw in the political order makes a magical belief or myth not only tenable, but necessary to maintain the status quo distribution of power. Faulty politics. And Tylor (1873), and those following him (see Horton 1967, 1968), see the conviction of faith in magical components as a product of cumulative understanding; individual percepts about the world become accepted, and distilled generation after generation, into revered custom. Errors in perception and explanation are thus recapitulated by the cultural system (see Lévi-Strauss 1966). Faulty reasoning. Each of these notions is sensible, yet each contains its own inadequacies (see De Vos 1975; A. Parsons 1969; Sperber 1975). The last possibility, faulty reasoning, is perhaps closest to a general explanation, but it is vague. Furthermore, it neglects an essential dimension about the maintenance of a magical conviction: the subliminal and institutionalized inhibition of contradictory information.

Insight is avoided to sustain individual and societal fantasy. A mystical conviction is entrenched by custom, is handed to us with our language, is plausible in the scheme of things, and it makes life easier for those who rule. It may even be verbally manipulated by the powerful who stage things in accordance with their own perceptions. Sambia men do this; women are allowed free reign in the gardens; since men warred, women

---

30. Inge Riebe (personal communication) tells me that the Western Highlands Karam recognize both male and female cassowaries, but they apparently mistake the caretaking male for the female, while still tending to think of cassowaries as "like women." This seems to be a situation similar to that of Sambia.

31. I am thinking of social anthropology. There is another, now defunct school in American cultural anthropology, the psychoanalytic culture and personality school (Kardiner 1939). Tuzin's (1976) recent work, "methodological individualism," is different, and it offers an alternative approach too (see Chapter 9).

provided needed food, and they were less meddlesome there, sullying themselves in the earth, which only added dirt to their pollution in the process. A belief also may be perceptually reinforced if no contrary information is offered or, if offered, is ignored. This is bad science; let us not forget how recently Western society clung to stupendously bad science, like spontaneous generation, or, even more apropos, the belief that witches gave birth to demons through their anuses. A fantasy system surely supported that magical thinking; but we still do not understand how custom eventually gave way to personal, or scientific, insight (LeVine 1973:254f.).

Here we must confront our own anthropological "bad faith" (Sartre 1956). We are vulnerable to charges of "bad faith" if we attribute the "causes" of tribal behavior (including myth and rite) to faulty technology, politics, or reasoning, and leave it at that. That stance ignores the wealth of information contained within a people's knowledge about the environment or their culturally constituted fantasy systems that incorporate it.[32] Nor can I agree with workers such as Barth (1975:225), who theoretically reject native insight on the grounds that it is, ipso facto, a contaminated communication. Methodologically, that remains an empirical issue in each case. But theoretically, it is in the details of such interpersonal communications that we may recover the tacit infrastructure of meanings.

The ethnographer should feel uncomfortable in this context only if he or she lacks a normative baseline with which to assess individual behavior. A behavioral (not just normative) description requires attention to individual behavior and subjectivity as well as to the norm. Our sociologically normative strategy has succeeded in constructing systems of kinship terminology and in counting garden plots or typologizing firewood. But symbolic behavior is different. Verbal behavior, and particularly the products of individual minds, like dreams or fantasies, requires that we persist in forming relationships with individuals that are *close enough* to ascertain what is ordinary or eccentric, recurrent thought and mood, duplicity or outright lie. Nothing is simple about this procedure, as the material of the last three chapters plainly illustrates. Nilutwo's experience

---

32. Perhaps because of their research emphasis on social structure, New Guineasts have tended to pay less attention to people's knowledge of natural species. For example, Lawrence and Meggitt (1965:12) stated simply that: "No Melanesian religion pays great attention to the total natural environment. Most treat it implicitly as something that can be taken for granted." Clearly, this does not hold for Sambia, as the last three chapters indicate—and those findings simply scratch the surface (see also Barth 1975:180–190; Gell 1975:128–133; Rappaport 1968:32–99). Of the more technical, ethnosemantic descriptions of indigenous classifications of animals or plants, Hays (1979:269 *n.* 2) writes: "With the exception of Bulmer's . . . publications on Kalam [sic] ethnozoology . . . New Guinea Highlands ethnobiology has been reported only in fragments or extremely restricted descriptions (cf. Bulmer 1974 for a survey discussion)."

of cassowaries and his meanings about cassowary idioms are undoubtedly distinct from those of other Sambia. Yet observations of his behavior are crucial for understanding the overall symbolic pattern. Unless we recognize this distinction, we are reduced to poetry. And the cassowary is not like a rose is a rose is a rose; it is both like and unlike what Sambia construe it to be. It is the ethnographer who must explain the measured difference.

The thrust of these chapters on the inward cosmos has concentrated on the manifest and tacit meaning of sex assignment and genderizing in natural species. Now let us turn to idioms of human femininity and masculinity, the greatest species of culture.

CHAPTER SIX *Femininity*

What do Sambia believe they know about the biological[1] development of the human animal? Why men should hold that the ontogeny of females is innately "natural" and easier than that of males, and how their viewpoint gets worked out in idioms and personal knowledge is at the heart of the final chapters of this study.

Femininity[2] should be our starting point. First, because of the biological

---

1. Throughout the remaining text, "biological" generally means ethnobiology, that is, the natives' own meanings about the growth, structure, and reproduction of humans.

2. I follow Stoller (1968) in arbitrarily distinguishing between sex factors, as biological elements (gonads, anatomy), and gender factors, as those psychological and cultural elements implied in identity constructs like boy, girl, masculinity, and femininity.

facts of parturition: females give birth. Second, because of masculine belief and secret ritual dogma: men hold that females naturally achieve reproductive competence through a means endogenous to female physiology. Femininity is thought to be an inherent development in a girl's continuous association with her mother. Masculinity, on the other hand, is not an intrinsic result of maleness; it is an achievement distinct from the mere endowment of male genitals. Masculine reproductive maturity must be artificially induced, by means of strict adherence to ritual techniques. These contrasts are basic in the givens of nature, and I shall try to show how.

This chapter, therefore, concerns idioms of femininity—men's views of women. Not all idioms are of interest here, only the fundamental ones impinging on ritualized masculinity. Those sayings tell what femininity is, how that is known, what it comes to, and how it affects a man's vitality. These verbal data only vicariously concern social behavior; they are also distinct from the thoughts and behavior of women themselves. E. Ardener (1975) has written that most ethnographic data pertaining to women actually derive from male subjects and represent a man's point of view. This is true of most New Guinea reports (see M. Strathern 1978), including the present one. Finally, like the following chapter, too, this material concerns idioms, and the natural design of feminine growth in men's eyes. It says nothing of the phenomenology of how individual women sense their femaleness, how they perceive men, behave, or what this means to them, matters to be taken up in subsequent writings. Masculine idioms are my focus: they depict women in remarkable and disparaging ways.

Prudish Chauvinism

A society of warriors tends to regard women unkindly, and Sambia attitudes have carried this emphasis to its furthest reaches in the relationships between men and women. Harsh even by the standards of New Guinea (see Langness 1967; Meggitt 1964; Read 1954), where sexual differences are sharply contrasted, the rhetoric and ritual of men represent women as polluting inferiors a man should distrust throughout his life. Men hold themselves to be the superiors of women in physique, personality, and social position. Indeed, survival for individual and community alike demands hard, disciplined men as unlike the softness of women as possible. This dogma of male supremacy permeates all social relationships and institutions. It forms the bedrock on which are based warfare, economic production, and religious life.

Men idiomatically refer to women as a distinctively inferior and "darker" species than themselves. The sense of this caste one hears constantly in the cliché, "Women are no good"; or, still worse, "Women have that vagina, something truly no good.''³ Men commonly relate female sex traits, as much as their disparaging conception of femininity, to this dogma, and its idioms find expression in the most negative language imaginable for Sambia.⁴ This point requires attention.

The harsh emotionality of masculine idiom raises a spectrum of ethnographic problems concerning men's attitudes toward women. These factors merit examination since they influence not just what men say but how they say it. Sambia men are excessively emotional about the subject of femininity (which they constantly link to eroticism). In previous chapters I mentioned a similar link between attitudes and idioms. For instance, cassowary idioms were charged with negative and positive undertones, as in men's sense of danger and triumph while participating in the cassowary feast. Yet the subject of femininity requires that I do more than simply allude to emotional attitudes. For women (unlike birds or trees) give birth to men, suckle them, and interact with them. Women are mothers, sisters, wives; women become lovers: sexual intimates, the source of erotic pleasure and of one's progeny. All these interpersonal relationships involve emotional experiences. They are capable of evoking thoughts and feelings conditioned by powerful, redundant masculine declarations. (As we shall see, the thrust of assertive masculinity stems partially from its tacit denials that men have feminine qualities, the antithesis of a phallic warriorhood.) Most Sambia men spout such clichés, but only some of them do so harshly, vindictively.

How, then, shall we distinguish the mere parroting of dogma from the harsher side of a psychosocial predilection toward destructive misogyny? This distinction is a central problem in New Guinea ethnographic reports and one that we dare not ignore.

Two of these postures represent extreme ends on the continuum of masculine behavior. They subsume somewhat different attitudes and separable psychological experiences. Nonetheless, it is not so easy to separate them in verbal behavior. That requires prolonged observation no less than elicitation. And somewhere, in the course of research and writing, it also means that we distinguish between "normal" and "abnormal" masculine

---

3. This latter saying, *aambelu-tuvo laaku maatnu-maatnu tokwuno,* one seldom hears, for men utterly detest saying the word *laaku* (vagina), preferring any number of metaphors such as "her bamboo" (vagina), or euphemisms, like "that thing below" (which initiates say). This avoidance is partly because men believe simply uttering the term vagina is contaminating: to speak the word, and then swallow one's saliva, directly invites pollution, sickness, and potential death.

4. I am speaking now of normal discourse and men's private talk, not the fever-pitched curses of marital squabbles that are disruptive and evoke even worse language. Interestingly enough, most men regard women as more foul-mouthed than men—and this goes especially for older women when angry at their husbands.

behaviors. For example: Sambia men tend to vilify women, it is true, but it is the deviant and, I believe, neurotic individual man who is so consumed with demonstrating ruthless masculinity that he constantly and destructively broadcasts misogyny. The consequences can be disastrous. Such behavior sometimes precipitates all the most terrible and spectacular human troubles: jealousy, revenge, wife beating, murder, and suicide. We dare not ignore this evidence for the meaning of femininity and masculinity among Sambia. Nor must we confuse idle clubhouse banter with pathological chauvinism. Few Sambia men are this openly violent (and yet in certain circumstances violence is still normatively permissible, by ritual edict, in a man's dealings with a woman). These differences represent statistical tendencies: most Sambia fall in between being petulant parrots and destructive misogynists.[5]

In conversation my adult male informants generally spoke of women as a category. They generally used demeaning, negative language—and not only in conversations on the general topic of reproduction or marriage or eroticism, where one would expect it. They also used it in speaking of individual instances of birth, nuptials, coitus, and even economic endeavors like clearing gardens. (This was, however, less common when they spoke with me than to a large peer group.) In male groups, men often become more chauvinistically arrogant and brazen, i.e., sexually slurring women more harshly than when they are with women or boys. When men refer to the contamination of women they implicitly exclude girls (if one asks them). Furthermore, mothers or sisters are rarely lumped with marriageable women in matters of pollution. To illustrate: not once have I ever heard a man specifically describe his mother as a "dirty polluter," a term men are prone to use about women more generally. Girls, like boys, are not considered polluting to others except through contact with women, e.g., their mothers. And girls or old women are rarely sexually slurred, unlike marriage-aged women.

In short, it is erotically and, especially, reproductively active, marriage-aged women who are the most dangerous polluters. Of them, one's own wife and one's brothers' wives are most carefully monitored as potential contaminators. Erotic access, then, or potential access (i.e., the levirate

---

5. A methodological note is in order here. I made assessments of the behaviors of men based on prolonged naturalistic observations and rather detailed studies of some ten different males of various ages. Field conditions did not permit me to choose a random sample of subjects, nor to elicit uniform responses from standardized questionnaires (although I did do this in focused studies of ritual experience). So I am limited in my ability to generalize and predict precisely the behaviors of all Sambia men. Even so, the case studies I did collect are perhaps more detailed and complete than a normative sketch—encompassing various independent variables a questionnaire might have ignored—and these data I mention below. But the material is thus far incomplete and therefore distorted.

permits marrying one's brother's widow), dangerously involves pollution. Even though men can easily enough make such discriminations, they ordinarily do not. Their chauvinist stereotypes take precedence over ignored or forgotten differences among "women."

It follows from this that *individual* men do not perceive all females identically, and they therefore act differently toward them. Little girls are usually treated with benevolence and care. Old women, one's mother or elder caretakers, can get respect if a man is alone, or older, or otherwise less constrained by the need to be seen as dominant. One's mother, sisters and daughters are usually treated with concern and consideration, for aside from genuine affection they are alternate suppliers of food. This is not universally true; and it changes when these women, too, become faces in a crowd of females who get lumped together by male groups and ritual rhetoric. As a rule, however, it holds as true as its converse: sexually active women are treated most badly. (It is difficult to generalize, even here, about men's behavior toward their wives, except to say that spouses are ambivalently treated, as sexual property and partners, provisioners of one's table, mothers of one's children, but still women with that "no-good something.") Clanswomen are better treated than female outsiders (i.e., inmarrying wives); and wives of one's natal hamlet find it easier than inmarrying, imported wives (mainly because their fathers and brothers nearby are potential supporters in marital squabbles; see Allen 1967:62–63). Older men usually, but not always, treat women better; and their older wives fare better than second or younger wives. Newlywed men are the most notoriously difficult, jealous, and quarrelsome, the most fearful of their (and others') wives' contamination.

In short, men differ in their interactions with and emotional responses to particular women.[6] Sambia men favor spouting chauvinist dogma over the messy particularities of their actual relationships with females. These differences between masculine idioms and interpersonal behavior need to be kept in mind when assessing the lexical and metaphoric significance of idioms depicting femininity. We must not forget that dogmas can hide such individual variations in attitudes or behavior (for whatever reasons). Women vary in age, in erotic, reproductive, and residential status, as much

---

6. This is my chief reason for arguing that we need to describe not only cultural stereotypes (Durkheim) but also individual action in regard to them. Clearly, Sambia men harbor pronounced stereotypical views and idioms about categories of women, and some understanding of them is necessary for later describing more difficult analytic problems concerning the meaning of individual masculine behavior and interaction with females. Despite the weaknesses in her data, and the lack of attention to social changes that have influenced the definition of gender roles among the Kafe, I still favor Faithorn's (1976:92–93) position in the recent literature.

as in personality. Men suppress these differences, in speech and interpersonal behavior, by reference to their sweeping idioms. (Such differences also tend to be forgotten when a male ethnographer is surrounded by all male informants who wish to reinforce the strength of one another's conviction that they "really understand" why women should be kept in their place.) With these cautions, let us now sketch men's attitudes toward eroticism before describing femininity.

Eroticism, especially heterosexual activity, is fraught with conflict in boys, youths, and men alike. Heterosexual conflict begins with the active attempt to keep children sexually naïve.

Prudishness is born in childhood, since men and women alike feel that children are best kept ignorant of all erotic matters. People are always careful to cover their genitals, and they avoid reference to them in heterosexual company. Coitus and fellatio (among spouses) belong only to the forest. Heterosexual activity should be hidden from children and should not (but occasionally does) occur at night within houses after they are asleep. Men say women are careful to conceal their menstruations from men and children.[7] Raucous humor or lewd stories are bluntly discouraged in the presence of children. People are self-conscious about any sort of risqué behavior. Both men and women, for example, use euphemisms for erotic matters in the presence of children (e.g., "water" for semen, "bamboo" for vagina, and "stick" for penis). Boys are allowed to go about uninhibitedly naked till they are three or four years of age. Girls, however, are from infancy completely covered from the waist down by grass skirts, whereas until initiation boys may have only a pubic cover (their buttocks can remain exposed until then). Boys are also teased and playfully taunted about their genitals in a way that is never done to girls. Clearly, girls are expected to hide their genitals, protect their femininity, and behave decorously, whereas boys act very differently.[8] Following infancy, boys and girls are encouraged to play apart, and all sex play is forbidden. All this is necessary, men say, because if boys and girls could "sexually play among themselves" they "would have no thought of being warriors or making gardens." (This ploy seems successful; most boys, at least, denied any knowledge of semen or erotic intercourse until they were initiated.) Men usually avoid even mentioning heterosexuality around initiates or women; and women do likewise toward adolescent girls. Yet

---

7. It is important that boys are first prevented (at around three years of age) from accompanying their mothers to the menstrual hut at the admonishment of other female caretakers, who warn that contact with the menses may block the boys' growth.
8. Here is one of the small details of socialization that lead, no doubt, to the origins of sexual excitement: hiding one's body purposely, to be feminine, and being allowed to exhibit, e.g., to be masculine, leading to sexual hiding and sexual looking in heterosexuality.

the degree of that avoidance of eroticism cannot compare with Sambia priggishness surrounding their children.

From these wellsprings boys are initiated into secret homosexual activities and come to the strictest avoidance of females. Even casual play between initiated boys and uninitiated boys or girls is forbidden. (Erotic heterosexual activities for initiates are unknown and virtually unthinkable.) Warrior games are taken up. To restate: boys must absolutely avoid all interaction with women, even their mothers, by ritual edict; and all heterosexual knowledge is formally denied to them. Boys joke among themselves (careful not to be overheard by their elders, who would punish them for such thoughts) about the tantalizing possibilities of married couples who journey alone into the forest. But in all respects their capacity to act on such fantasies is severely suppressed. For similar reasons, puberty is greeted with embarrassment, in boys and girls alike. Voice change and the appearance of facial hair are cause for both pride and dismay.[9] Boys and youths, like men, never expose themselves, even among their peers in the clubhouse or while bathing in streams. And boys are frantic about being thus observed by women. Boys ordinarily take pains to deny their erotic attraction to older youths, and yet that is nothing compared to the impossibility of even hinting at one's excitement regarding a girl. Among boys and youths, wet dreams are hidden and masturbation is denied.[10] Throughout all of this, peer group pressures support a boy's growing sense of becoming masculine during adolescence, meaning that they reinforce his homosexual activities and avoidance of females or heterosexual experiences.

Heterosexual interaction begins only after the marriage ceremony, if then, depending on the ages of the spouses (see below). Marriage has been arranged, and there is little personal choice in the arrangement. Hence the couple's interaction is understandably slow, awkward, embarrassing. Youths are cautioned from the start to be moderate in all heterosexual matters; so restraint is translated into wisdom. (The slant on homosexual experiences is unrestrainedly enthusiastic.) Girls, men allege, fear coitus because they fear the physical harm men may inflict on them. Once again, heterosexual activities are mentioned in idle gossip or risqué jokes—which men enjoy among their cronies, as do women in similar company; nevertheless, coitus is absolutely the most private act, one that occurs only in the forest, during the day, following sober precautions that ensure strict isolation and protection against female contamination.

9. Men say that Nilutwo once shaved off his pubic hair near puberty, peculiar behavior they joked about behind his back.

10. Wet dreams are common among males. Masturbation in fact rarely, if ever, occurs; I doubt if Sambia men ever consciously experience it.

Against this background of erotic ambivalence we come to the emotional attitudes embodied in the term "the shame of the vagina."

Coitus is capable of arousing shame, and masculine idioms remind men that this possibility must be kept constantly in mind. As a general rule, men rarely say the terms for "menstrual blood" and "vagina" because they provoke shame: "To call the name of the vagina is to become greatly shamed."[11] Here follow excerpts from a conversation in which Tali and Nilutwo themselves considered this subject.

> To call the name of the cunt[12] is to be greatly shamed. And all the women, if you see their cunts—if they remove it [grass skirt], to clean themselves of lice or remove feces, or something—the women can be ashamed. And we men: if we see the penis of another man, that's not the same, it's not shameful. It's [penis] the same kind as mine, a man's. Or if the women [among themselves] talk about the cunt, that's not difficult, they're not ashamed. But if we [men] call the name of the cunt, the women will be greatly shamed. Or for them all [women], if they say *laakelu* [penis], that's not shameful, it's acceptable. And if another man sees the cunt of your woman, she will be shamed. Or if another woman [i.e., not one's wife] sees your penis, you'll be ashamed. [Tali]

> We must not be *too* ashamed about this. This [vagina] is for making children. If I see the cunt of my woman, it is the pathway for my cock. Women, too, can think like that, "oh, that's the cock of my man, it is like my meat [food, semen]."

---

11. This fastidiousness suggests another point of method about the sensitive subjects that follow. Men usually regarded the discussion of female procreation as a difficult but fascinating task. Their feelings went beyond the common attitude that serving as my informant was respectable and interesting, but tiresome. This is because, to reiterate, it is actually polluting even to utter the words for "vagina," "menstrual blood," and "vaginal fluids." Men must unfailingly spit after saying each of these terms, else they risk swallowing their own saliva and, by implication, accumulating that "polluted" fluid in their stomachs, bringing on sickness and death. Once, in my house, Tali, Weiyu, and Nilutwo were discussing these topics, and they compulsively spat more than thirty times in less than three hours as a result of the conversation. This made such elicitation awkward and difficult, in a way such conversations were not when they normally used euphemisms. Their attitudes and dispositions were somewhat halting; yet their relationships to me, and their commitment to the research, facilitated by the action of spitting, overcame their reservations enough for them to reassert constantly their sense of not being contaminated by their own words. (I wonder to what extent their use of euphemisms is still conscious, or has now become subliminal, like other word taboos in Sambia life; and one wonders what this means for the fragmentation of their sense of themselves.) Did I come to influence what they said? Obviously I did; and therefore my data are distorted by my making it possible for them to discuss such troublesome matters more openly than usual. I have, however, tried to correct for this distortion by understanding that these informants are especially articulate and motivated, and more conditioned to such conversations than most men; and by comparing these data with observations of other men over a two-year period.

12. Sambia have quite recently imported this term from Neo-Melanesian slang, sometimes in preference to vernacular euphemisms, which women can understand.

We can't be too ashamed of it, otherwise we won't make a big family. [Nilutwo, quietly, straight-faced]

Stiff-necked prudery like this is therefore constrained, in part, by men's recognition that heterosexual compatibility is needed to create families, ensuring the full measure of adult personhood through one's progeny. But it is from innumerable comments of this sort, and the actions that follow from the values underlying them, that one comes to think of Sambia fundamentally as a "shame culture." This outlook, as we shall see, is woven into masculine development.

From prudery to masculine arrogance we are led to the sense in which men regard women as sexual property. To illustrate, I quote Tali on the subject of adultery and how men should treat it.

If a woman meets you on the path, flirts with you, you *must* copulate with her. If you don't, she can say that you have no water [semen], you're only a *kwulai'u* [i.e., a boy]. If you say no, she'll spit on you; then, or later, too, back in the village, she can hang herself [emphasis], for she thinks you don't want her.

This sparked Tali to recall a piece of ritual edict from fifth-stage initiation:

If someone sees you copulating with another man's wife, he may report back to the villagers. Back in the village, her husband may try to fight with you. But you must retort that it was the wish of the woman; her husband will beat her; and she may hang herself; yet the husband won't beat the adulterous man. For, if a woman wants to fornicate, you must do it; this is not open to question.

Here, then, women are viewed as sexual objects. If a woman initiates adultery, a man should accommodate her; it is unmanly for him to refuse. Moral responsibility, however, falls on the licentious woman. Her husband may beat her or she may hang[13] herself: these are ugly, touchy consequences of relationships between the sexes. Like shame felt in respect of the genitals, this area is troubling for Sambia.

Powerful experiences, then, emotionally envelop many of the following idioms of femininity and masculinity: this fact should not be forgotten when Sambia are presented through their words alone.

The Tingu

Men believe that a girl is born with all the vital organs and fluids necessary for her to attain adult reproductive competence naturally. This conviction

---

13. Sambia, both men and women, commit suicide by hanging; known suicides (and suicide attempts) by women are more than triple the number by men.

is embodied in perceptions of the girl's biological development from the moment following sex assignment at birth. What distinguishes a girl (*tai*) from a boy (*kwulai'u*) is obvious: "A boy has a penis and a girl does not." Yet the simplicity of that idea is belied by an ingenuous theory about female procreation and ontogeny to which men cling, and firm opinions about the natural divergence of male and female growth. Girls grow easily and quickly, outpacing boys. Women have it easy, men have it hard. These differences are thought to be innate, absolute, irreversible (see also Meigs 1976:398; Newman 1965:78–80; Poole 1980).

To comprehend what this theory of femininity entails, we must first note what the tiny infant's vulva communicates about her physiology: she has a menstrual-blood organ (*tingu*).

The *tingu* is the very essence of biological femaleness. This is true in two fundamental ways. The *tingu* is literally held to be the primordial structure of female physiology. The vulva can be externally viewed: behind it, linked by the birth canal (*kwulai'u-oolu,* male-child rope), is the womb (*kwulai'u-ketu*); behind that rests the fabled *tingu*. Each organ is biologically connected within a system. Furthermore, and what is essential, it is the *tingu* that is held to operate (make functional) this feminine complex, serving as *the* catalyst of its natural life-cycle changes. The *tingu,* men are convinced, is capable of manufacturing menstrual blood (*chenchi*), the key precipitant of adult femininity, in boundless quantity. In sum, the *tingu* is the endowment of femaleness and the capacity to function as a woman.[14]

Masculine doctrine holds that other mammals, like humans, regardless of sex, have a *tingu*. Precisely what it is that Sambia believe to be the *tingu* in the area of the lower human abdomen is unclear;[15] but men sometimes allude to it, for example, in possums. (And what people call a possum *tingu* women wear as an amulet of fertility.) What matters is the tremendous natural power of the *tingu* as a biological instigator of femaleness; its contrary functions in male and female ontogeny; and its invidious presence within males as a harbinger of sluggish masculine growth.

The *tingu* fuels women's bodies with a life-giving force. In girls, the organ is said to be "soft," like an "immature pandanus nut." It also

14. I need to reiterate the distinction between sex traits (genitals) and gender traits (e.g., feminine qualities and traits, like breast-feeding). Sambia do not make this distinction in this way; their view implies, again, that the biological component creates and is fused to the psychological and behavioral aspects of identity.

15. Since Sambia are not cannibals and they do not perform autopsies, it is doubtful that they could actually correlate one of many human organs with possum organs (e.g., uterus), on an equal basis for males *and* females, consistent with their conviction (and possums do not possess appendixes). Suffice it to say that they are convinced of the *tingu's* existence.

contains a small amount of menstrual blood transmitted intrautero from one's mother. Lodged within the *tingu,* this smear of blood is special. Boys do not possess it; their *tingu,* men believe, is like a small kernel, "hard and dry" (*yaalkoogu*).[16] Unlike boys, girls also have a womb, and the *tingu,* germinated by the blood smear, slowly alters its form.

> When a woman is born . . . she has a blood-filled round pool [*menjaak-boongu*].[17] . . . Tiny girls, they have got it. But the pool is small, theirs is not large. So when a woman is big, the round pool gets filled up and its blood is plentiful. [Tali]

Intuition suggests that Tali is referring to the womb. That is one possibility. Instead of the generic term for womb, *kwulai'u-ketu,* however, he used *menjaak-boongu,* which, in its literal sense, means "blood pool." Even so, for over a year I assumed that that idiom merely signified a metaphor for womb. That assumption was, after all, consistent with the Sambia theory of conception in which the father's semen and mother's blood coagulate in the womb, creating an embryo. This notion is, furthermore, common throughout New Guinea (see Mead 1968:48; A. Strathern 1972:13; Wagner 1967:64–65).

Native statements also lent some support to that intuition. For instance, there was Kanteilo, an aged sponsor, who told me about the dangers of menstrual blood.

> The woman's stomach is filled like a *menjaak-boongu,* from which menstrual blood flows and a child is formed. When a pig is butchered, women remark to us [men]: "Look: the pig's stomach is filled with blood; so is ours. It is for this reason that we [women] resist having sex with you so often!" And so it is taboo to have coitus with a woman when her menstrual blood flows.

Here again it seemed reasonable to infer that the ordinary speech reference to *menjaak-boongu* simply represented an especially apt metaphor for the womb. But on further search, that inference encountered problems: it could not account for all the other data.

---

16. *Yaalkoogu* is the same term and concept Sambia apply to mature pandanus nuts, trees that lack moisture inside their bark, and withering pandanus flowers (see above).

17. *Menjaak,* "blood"; *boongu,* "round pool or bog." Men sometimes refer to the womb metaphorically as *menjaak-boongu;* and instead of *kwulai'u-oolu,* or "umbilical cord," they can say *menja'-oolu,* "blood path." Occasionally, I have heard Weiyu abbreviate his references to womb to simply *"boongu."*

Three clues suggested a different line of thought and eventually a hypothesis.

The first clue is linguistic. Men usually distinguish womb from *menjaak-boongu,* or the *tingu,* in everyday speech. For example, Tali said monthly menstrual flows come at the "time of a new moon, [when] the *tingu* can become bloody [inside]." And when I asked him whether a barren woman (*kwoliku*) had regular menstrual flows, he gave the following response: "The *kwoliku,* too, she has them [flows]. The *kwulai'u-ketu* [womb], that's all [she lacks]; it is dry [*yaalkoogu*] and closed."

Contrarily, the term *menjaak-boongu* has another linguistic aspect nearly as common in its metaphoric significance as a cover term for womb. This is the *designata* of various dream images (*wunju-pookwugu,* literally, dream picture) to which men refer in dream reports. Bloody streams of water, huts that leak red fluids, and particularly, stagnant blood-filled bogs (*boongu*) that surge upwards, threatening to engulf the dreamer—these are nightmares from which a man starts up trembling (*kowuptu*). These images also are tagged *menjaak-boongu* in the dream interpretations of Sambia.

The second clue concerns the masculine theory of the differential growth rates in boys and girls. Girls almost always surpass boys in the development of speech and motor coordination, reaching physical maturity much faster. This universal human pattern has now been recorded in New Guinea (see Malcolm 1966, 1970), and it is apparently the subject of some consternation among other Highland peoples too (see Buchbinder 1973; Lindenbaum 1976).

Men say that it is the *tingu* that enables girls to grow quicker, achieving biological maturity earlier than boys. Here is a casual reference to this idea spontaneously expressed by (not elicited from) Tali.

> *Tingu:* It, only, can grow [*perulyapi*] women, it can make them grow quickly. . . . The skin of women is cold, it grows quickly. A man, he has hot skin, he grows easily [slowly], easy. If you put something—food—inside the house, it stays cool. It can grow quickly. A woman is the same as the earth; she is cold, she can grow quickly. The [menstrual] blood opens it, the skin swells up—on women, and the *tingu* . . . [is inside] so she grows quickly.

Contrast this with how the *tingu* functions in males as reported by Weiyu: "Of you and me, males, the *tingu* is *jerungdu* [hard]. And so it has no blood. But that [*tingu*] of women is soft. It hasn't much hardness." And further:

> . . . the *tingu* [is inside] . . . when she's young, she can expel blood [menstruate]. . . . This can open her skin so she grows quickly. When she's grown, is big enough, then, she can expel blood, she can *taiketnyi* [experience her menarche].

These remarks implicate the *tingu* as the source of women's rapid maturation. "Cold-blooded" as the earth is cool, women are innately fast-growing. The *tingu* produces blood, stimulating growth by actually expanding the body and skin surface. This culminates in the menarche, only a step away from feminine reproductive competence. As Tali hints, the prospects for male ontogeny are fundamentally different.

Third, there is the meaning of the psychological frame that embraces the terms *menjaak-boongu* and *tingu*. The two are affectively equated. Tali makes this clear: "The *round pool* of blood *is* [emphatic] the *tingu*. When a man is born the *tingu* is strong, and it contains no blood. The woman has blood inside the *tingu* at birth . . . the *menjaak-boongu* is *tingu*." This statement concretely identifies the *tingu* with the image of the blood-filled pool. What are the percepts of Tali's equation? Of the *tingu*, we can only be certain about the faith men place in an internal female organ believed to fabricate menstrual blood. Of the blood pool we can no longer comfortably hold that its designata is *only* the womb (although it includes that among its referents). *Menjaak-boongu* implies a generalized image tangibly referring to a round puddle, vessel, or accumulation of blood in one's innards, or in dreams. The multivalence of these designata suggests a subjective link between the inner experience of the image of a *tingu* or *menjaak-boongu*, and outer, corresponding perceptual forms.

These data are best organized by offering a hypothesis. I propose this: the subjective orientations (or "reference condition"; see Powers 1973: 45)[18] that govern individual perceptions regarding the *tingu* include the designata referred to in animals and dreams, as well as a man's sense of reproductive inferiority compared to women. The phenomenological manifestations of the *tingu*, in the Sambia world, are a "possum organ," menstrual blood, and verbal references to those things and feminine parturition. But the fusion of those cultural and tangible entities in the *subjective image* of the powerful *tingu* organ (in thought) operates as a symbolic filter that blurs the boundary between reality and fantasy. This idea suggests that other idioms bearing on the "essence" of femininity—namely, vagina, womb, and blood—are also best understood from this perspective. Masculine culture compartmentalizes (controls, filters) men's perceptions of female biological capacities by concretely delimiting and focusing idioms on the *tingu*. In other words, the *tingu* represents a focal projection: through it, men try to cope with human femininity. Menstrual blood anxieties, too, hinge on the imagery of *tingu*, womb, or *menjaak-boongu*, as I shall show. These idioms reveal *masculine reactionism:* individual and group behavior that reacts against women's much too tangible flows of

---

18. See also Gilberttson (1964), whose similar concept of "index values" takes the cybernetic perspective that subjective principles constrain behavior and perception.

menstrual blood, the "essence" of femininity and reproductive superiority. Now let us examine this idea in its details.

The Life Cycle of Femininity

Vulva, Womb, and Tingu. These organs are all that is needed to hasten a girl's advance into adolescence. Unseen changes are wrought by the *tingu* within those organs, overcoming their "dryness" (*yaalkoogu*) through the circulatory increase of that red fecund plasma that enlivens all humans and creates babies. Girls thus grows unfettered into maturity, whereas boys are blocked along the way. What needs telling is men's urgent concern that children are closely bonded to their mothers; that in girls this is unproblematic; but that in boys such an attachment stifles the unfolding of masculinity. Indeed, unless initiated and ritually treated, boys remain small and weak. In the next chapter I shall sketch the mother's part in the ontogeny of boys and girls; here let us examine the impact of *tingu* physiology on female adolescence.

Men notice that from the earliest years girls seem to mature faster than boys. Speech comes more quickly. Girls become taller, with bigger limbs, torso, and girth. Their buttocks start to shape and their eyes seem livelier. In all these things boys lag behind. Men privately attribute the difference to the girl's unseen but active *tingu.*

It bothers men that girls physically outgrow or "succeed"[19] over boys. This biological race does not refer to their occupations, although girls seem steadier and more dependable than their brothers, who dislike gardening and are prone to throw tantrums. In fact, by the time boys take to running about the hamlet throwing sticks or catching tadpoles, girls have already assumed garden chores and baby-sitting responsibilities. "The fashion of this region," Moondi[20] said, "is that women win men in growth size." Why this matters is a subject of endless preaching to boys. Here again Moondi comments:

> If a woman outgrows you, another [older] youth can steal her, your [betrothed] woman. Where can you get a woman then? Men can take two or three wives. Some steal women. Where can you obtain another woman from?

In short, it spells trouble if a girl outpaces the boy assigned to her in

---

19. As in the common idiom, *nuno-wuluwut'nji:* literally, she "can win over you," outgrow you.

20. Moondi was my best linguistic informant, and he served as a field assistant for a long time. A fifteen-year-old bachelor, eldest son of a happily married couple with many children, he was bright, articulate, and essential in the research.

marriage. Men fear the consequences: no wife, no offspring, no manhood.

Growth and Marriage. The protrusion of her breasts brings the first sign of adolescence in a girl.[21] The breasts swell and expand, and their coloration should match the skin tone broadly. The breasts are "upturned," an indication of nubile virginity (and evidence that the *tingu* is the agent of the girl's internal "swelling"). A girl's abdominal area and buttocks become enlarged. Although the vulva swells and grows, the hymen is said to remain unbroken.[22] (The clitoris, interestingly enough, is accorded no function, and is never mentioned by men.) These changes are based on long-range but avid male speculation: a firm lid is kept on heterosexual interactions for some time to come, by strict avoidance taboos that require maidens and all initiated males, until marriage, to hide (*ioolu*) their faces and bodies behind bark capes. Such avoidance so much characterizes normal heterosexual interaction that its behavioral concomitants are synonymous with the unfolding of femininity and masculinity. Men adamantly claim that they cannot relax these rules, else premarital promiscuity would become rampant, destructive. For boys:

> If women see their faces, they won't come up big. If boys removed their capes and walked around, they could look at women anywhere. They could see women, they could all fornicate around. So we [men] really hold onto the cape tightly, severely tabooing this for boys. And we think like this: when the father removes the cape [after marriage, at fourth-stage initiation], he [the youth] will act all right. If we didn't do this, boys would look at women's faces anywhere . . . and copulate with women anywhere.

And for girls:

> Our women are afraid. They're afraid that men will harm them. You white men give presents to women, they let you copulate with them. Our women are different: if you give gifts, they won't fornicate. . . . Women don't like to fornicate; we gripe [*chembootu cheruntu*, nose hot] at them! The old women tell the younger ones: "You must fence yourselves in well. You must cover up securely with your cape. . . . You can't play around with another man." [Tali]

---

21. It is significant that Sambia have no ready word for puberty, despite the tremendous significance they attach to pubescent changes. For a girl, puberty means the menarche; for a boy, it means especially the development of facial hair and enlargement of the glans penis.

22. Besides the vagina, the only term men associate with the hymen is *koondu-aiku,* "door," or "cover." Men metaphorically refer to the entire female genital area as *sambia,* or "shield." Vulva, *lundu-gwoapi,* is rarely used; and I have never heard men mention the clitoris (*lakandiku*) publicly. More generally, men simply speak of the vagina; see below. No manifest importance is attached to the clitoris, but the hymen is said to be specially mentioned in women's menarche ceremonies.

Being cloaked in a bark cape is, therefore, a positive means of keeping heterosexual virginity intact. This concealment illustrates men's prudish attitudes toward eroticism and underscores a general viewpoint: men consciously associate heterosexual body contact, even of a casual sort, with erotic interest.[23] Over the years, between first initiation and marriage (ten to fifteen years later), this attitude is constantly pounded into boys; and it is one that merits an aside.

Initiation means that boys and girls are not only separated but polarized, a distance that is vital. Undoubtedly it helps to keep girls (and, heterosexually, boys) virgins. Undoubtedly it enables boys to be disciplined into warriors whose lives are lived apart from women in the clubhouse. Undoubtedly it turns girls into the (allegedly chaste) gardeners and caretakers men need for the production of food and babies. And undoubtedly all these things are vital to Sambia society. Yet neither prudishness nor economics is sufficient to explain the severity with which boys are forbidden even to glance at women.

Women are pictured as relentlessly dangerous to masculine health. Their bodies (and no less so because of their puniness) are polluting; so all heterosexual contact, even touching, is deemed harmful. (The risk for men, at least, is not so much in the hand-holding that never occurs as in the many dangers of the coitus that might ensue.) For all males this danger is always present; but for youths, who lack defensive ritual knowledge of sexual purification procedures, succumbing to a woman's charms would be fatal, since unlike men they do not understand how to cleanse themselves afterward of a woman's contamination. It is remarkable how this fear regimentally takes over, psychologically and morally fragmenting a boy's eroticism. Premarital homosexual fellatio is constantly, secretly experienced by most boys; heterosexuality is pervasively condemned. (The consequences of this split we shall glimpse in Chapter 8.) It is thus with much trepidation that youth and maiden approach impending marriage. Only then is the initial step taken to bridge the distance created by those years of living apart.

Marriage is the first great ceremonial event in a girl's adult development. Unlike boys, she has not undergone initiations but has, instead, continued to live with her parents, her family. It is that institution (operating through her parents) that sets in motion the marriage as a formal contract with another, sometimes distant and hostile, family.

Many factors condition the marriage arrangements. All marriages are

---

23. There is evidence from individual case studies to suggest that, sometimes, *all* male/male body contact is eroticized; that is, different from obvious homosexual contacts leading to an ejaculation. This problem I shall consider elsewhere.

arranged,[24] and many couples (upwards of 50 percent in some hamlets) are betrothed at birth. Between these two points of birth and marriage, however, unforeseen events can delay or even cancel the prior contract: long wars and the social enmity they bred; political extortion by a stronger clan group over a weaker one in demanding a woman, even a *particular,* especially attractive woman (previously betrothed); unexpected deaths (either that of the betrothed boy or girl, or one of their fathers, whose absence may change the arrangements); not to mention personality clashes among the parents or clan-group leaders. Kinship links or political alliance may be enough to pull the marriage negotiations through these difficulties; but they may not be. And then, near the time of marriage, the groom, under certain circumstances, has a measure of choice in arranging a different marriage if he absolutely dislikes the assigned girl.[25] (This occasional happening is, I think, the only element of choice that exists in the matter of the nuptials.) Marriage, in short, is largely the grist of pragmatic circumstances, today as of yore.

The timing of a marriage ceremony depends on the advancing biological maturity of the betrothed, especially the groom. Following third-stage initiation and the visible attainment of manliness, a youth can be married. If a potential wife is agreed on, assigned, and if she is near puberty, the marriage formalities can be arranged. The girl is still classified as a *tai* who has not yet menstruated, and most brides are probably twelve to fifteen years of age. The groom should be older (by as much as five or ten years) than his bride; this relative age difference (and only at the first marriage) is considered appropriate and is even, in a subjective sense, enough of an edge that men describe the spouses as same-sized (*havalt-nunta*) persons.[26] There must also be at least one other couple, preferably three or four of them, for staging the protracted possum hunt and resulting marriage feasts. (The grooms are usually age-mates.) From such large-scale involvement, a marriage becomes a real happening in village life.

The betrothed approach marriage with ambivalence, and the reasons

---

24. Except, of course, in the case of wife stealing, which was quite rare.

25. The most common reason is the closeness of consanguineal relationship: some youths (not all) dislike the thought of marrying an actual FZD or MBD, i.e., cross-cousin, because it is "wrong" and "shameful"; this dislike goes even more for intraclan marriage. Morality is one reason, but another is erotic excitement (see below).

26. In other words, men feel that it is this difference that makes the spouses equivalent, as if to be closer in age would make the woman "too much of a person." In Bateson's (1958:175–178) terms, men think of this age difference as the necessary ingredient for creating a male-dominated complementary relationship (e.g., husband/wife) out of a potentially symmetrical relationship (i.e., male-female), by uniting spouses—a man and a woman—of disparate ages (asymmetry of age). Despite this common age difference, men and youths are extremely concerned that females not outdevelop males.

are easy to understand. The spouses are unfamiliar with one another. There is no courtship whatever. In the best circumstances, a youth and maiden will be only strangers—not total strangers—from hostile hamlets. (Some men, however, still prefer wives from outside their hamlets, professing that "local" women are not as exciting. For instance, Weiyu liked to say that "a man's penis won't get up for his [clan] sisters" or familiar females. This preference does not mean, however, that men like to marry from distant or hostile places, and, indeed, some men prefer local women, who are less dangerous. This liking for local women also raises problems about sexual excitement; see below, Chapters 7 and 8.) Nor can it be doubted that the strangeness between the spouses is uncomfortable. Youths tend to put off marriage as long as possible; near the ceremony they can get clammy hands and become panicky; and there are well-known instances of girls commiting suicide then, or within a few months after marriage.

Finally, the marriage is, at the moment when it occurs, mostly a ceremony, however excited are the participants. For it does not lead the spouses into immediate or comfortable interactions; nor to sexual intercourse (which may be delayed for months or a year or two); nor to cohabitation. Why get married, then?

Despite all its difficulties, marriage remains the measure of many social rewards. Perhaps the other possibility, not being married, is worst of all. Sambia boys and girls are reared in families, and they model themselves on their parents. To be a whole person, a human being, society demands that one marry. And to be fully masculine, a man must not only marry but father some children. A girl is prepared from infancy to be feminine in this way too. So there is really little choice: marriage is vital to one's identity and the "reproduction" of society.[27]

Feminine status and the nature of the marital contract between husband and wife are dramatized graphically in the *nuposha* ceremony. *Nuposha* is the name of the servile role a girl takes in the formalities and, characteristically, the act after which marriage is termed.

Nuposha: all the brides lie flat on their faces hugging the earth, obeisant in the dusty soil of the hamlet plaza, covered entirely by their new bark capes. There, in the groom's natal hamlet, the marriage bargain is formally sealed for life. The men have returned after weeks of possum hunting; a

---

27. What about men who never marry? There are a few; and there were some such "permanent bachelors" (see Bowers 1965) in the past too, the alleged victims of an alleged shortage of women. I think this claim needs close examination: most Sambia men really want marriage and a family, but there is that 10 percent who fear it. Similarly, large numbers of Kaulong men (Jane Goodale, personal communication) dread women and never marry because society does not force them to.

long rope, hung between tall poles staked across the plaza around the clubhouse, has suspended from it a string of packages of smoked possum, earmarked in payment of each bride. (Those meat gifts soon fall into the waiting hands of the bride's kinswomen.) The youths stand stiffly alert, in full warrior garb, overlooking their brides and the crowds, peering stone-faced into the sky (as they have been directed to do). This is, after all, their first public appearance before women; they must be careful not to contaminate themselves by looking directly into women's faces, or to betray their inner panic (*kowuptu*) and awkwardness at this drastic, long-anticipated moment. All the pomp and ceremony disguises this experience and is applauded by the onlookers, for Sambia dearly love such displays. There follows a great feast in celebration. (The newlyweds do not, however, join in; the meat is forbidden to them, and custom still requires them to remain apart.) In this setting custom also begins to alter the shackles that bind and divide the newlyweds.

For bride and groom alike the marital contract has this stony-hearted beginning. It begins in a mood of festive formality and rigid conformity to predetermined roles. Like clay figurines, carefully molded and colorfully glazed, the newlyweds have been pitched into a staged drama not of their own design. Afterwards, the groom continues to reside in the clubhouse. The bride goes to the hut of her parents or parents-in-law. And there they remain for the months or years until the girl's menarche. They may begin to interact, slowly, cautiously; and the effects of those social and erotic encounters are important for the next stage in the young woman's developing femininity.

It must be reemphasized that the bride is still classified as a girl, not a woman. She has not yet experienced her menarche (*taiketnyi: tai,* girl; *ketnyi,* completed). She is unalterably a virgin in two senses. First, her vagina is still considered covered (*koontu-aiku agikootnash,* door unopened), the hymen intact; second (and most important), her vagina is still said to be dry, since neither blood nor vaginal fluids flow from it. That virginity is positively valued. Her vagina has not been penetrated by a man, and it is unsoiled by her own contaminating fluids. Men perceive in this a biological implication for the tie between her and her husband: they are still immature and heterosexually inexperienced (another sense of being the "same size"). To wit, neither of their bodies (and especially the girl's) is ready for coitus (genital intercourse). Likewise, her mate (a youth also referred to as *nuposha*) should be *heterosexually* a virgin as regards coitus. Indeed, men say it is "bad" for a youth to marry any female but a *tai.* Married women should be avoided: their vaginas are "used, soiled, cold, not hot like a *chenchorai* [postmenses young women]." (Men assert that necessity might force a youth to marry a widow, but only a childless widow, one "less used and soiled.") Coitus can only occur, then, after the girl's menarche.

Early Heterosexual Fellatio. In the meantime, it is acceptable (but not widely practiced) for the girl and youth to engage in fellatio. According to male dogma, fellatio (*maambootu duvuno,* "bamboo-orifice penetrates," as distinct from coitus, *ilanyi* or *laakelu duvuno*) has nutritive and pseudoprocreative functions. (This value holds for both homosexual and heterosexual fellatio.) Fellatio serves as an erotic outlet for the youth, too, but that is not its primary aim, at least in masculine idiom. The girl acts as her bridegroom's fellator, supposedly at the behest of her mother. Here is Weiyu (who did not engage in heterosexual fellatio before his wife's menarche but enjoyed it afterwards):[28]

> The girl's mother tells her at the time of the *nuposha:* "Your marked man can shoot [copulate with] you, you can suck him. You can grow [*loropina*] quickly. . . . Your vagina will open quickly [precipitate the menarche]." We [young men] think this custom is outmoded, but some men still do it. Youths shoot girls any place, in the garden or bush.[29] A boy may want to coax his new bride, to shoot her . . . after the girl's mother talks to her, she'll be cooperative.

This practice, then, ostensibly precipitates the menarche in girls, but it has another significance.

Orally ingested semen has two other jobs to do in a girl's ontogeny as men see it. It first strengthens her body and later provides her with breast milk. We should be clear, however, about the native view of fellatio: it is not in itself responsible for conception or pregnancy or fetal growth. Men (and women) fully recognize that coitus sparks these developments, a point to which we must later return. And fellatio, either before or after the menarche, is universally practiced by Sambia couples and, likewise, it is felt to have the following effects.

Fellatio begins by helping to make a girl "strong" (*jerungdu*). Ingested semen is distributed to her body, "strengthening the skin, bones, and breasts," men say. This is accomplished by the esophagus (*koolei-pootu; koolei,* possum, meat, or food; *pootu,* a pathway connecting the mouth and

---

28. This topic was difficult to investigate. Men are ashamed to discuss it, in a way that is completely different from their openness about homosexuality. In part this shame is due to the intimacy of sex acts between spouses. Younger men also say that interest in this practice has declined with contact, whereas interest in homosexuality has not, an assertion that contains some truth. The major point here may be that initial heterosexual contacts are awkward and perhaps postponed.

29. Fellatio is permissible but coitus is strictly taboo within gardens, for fear that drops of sexual fluids will penetrate the garden soil and ruin its crops.

stomach).[30] The *koolei-pootu* takes semen and distributes it throughout the body, making the skin "taut and handsome," the feeble female bones "harder." This also aids the girl's frame in the task of childbearing (indirectly linking fellatio with childbirth), which labor Sambia universally describe as painful and difficult.

Semen allegedly does something else to the girl's body that is even more spectacular: it accumulates in the breasts, swells them, and there becomes milk. Ingested semen is carried by the *koolei-pootu* to the breasts. Tiny feeder organs (*aamoonaalyi-oolu*, breast-milk ropes) suspended in breast tissue are held to amass the semen and, somehow, to convert it into milk. Tali remarked: "A woman eats semen and it goes to her breasts where it is stored." Fellatio, furthermore, helps to change the breasts anatomically. "If a woman is vaginally copulated with first, her breasts do not properly fall down [*aamoondu meitnu-bolyokeno,* breasts droop enough], she does not get breast milk quickly." So it follows, according to Weiyu, that as the "woman sucks a youth, her breasts fall a bit; then, after a while, they can have coitus." Here is Weiyu again:

> In young women, the nipples stand up; they are brown-colored. In older women the nipples become black-colored [*aamdoot'nboolu,* generic term]. *Taiketnyi* and *chenchorai* [women] lack *aamdoot'nboolu*. After marriage, the husband gives semen to his wife and her breasts start to make black nipples [create a baby]. . . . Fellatio does not produce black nipples [create a baby] . . . only coitus does. [GH: Then why did their nipples turn black?] Because the woman already had breast milk.

These data illuminate the perceptual link between heterosexual fellatio and pivotal changes in a girl's femininity. But I need to sound a note of caution about them.

Premenarche heterosexual fellatio is not common. Despite the fact that youths enjoy homosexual fellatio, and postmenarche fellatio (with their wives), they generally disclaim erotic interest in the practice with their (premenarche) girl brides. Indeed, there is a definite trend of aversion to it. Whatever problems this posed before pacification, social change—especially coastal migration or contract labor—has exacerbated them. Since the 1960s, Sambia youths have left their hamlets for temporary work on coastal plantations as wage laborers. Perhaps 20 percent of unmarried males nowadays journey to the coast and remain for two to four years; then they return home with a little money in hand. This absence delays marital

---

30. All humans are held to possess an esophagus, but in females it has a special function: it can transport orally ingested semen to the breasts. (But what prevents boys from becoming pregnant is their lack of a womb.)

arrangements in an unprecedented way.[31] The marriage ceremony itself must be delayed until the youth's return (and such delays have, incidentally, been the source of much marital strife and litigation among clan groups). Consequently, marital erotic activities and cohabitation are delayed too; and this delay has had the effect of making it obvious that certain females are married long *after* their menarche—without having consumed any of their husband's semen, as girls—and yet they are still observed to "achieve" their first menses promptly, are still strong enough to bear children eventually, and they have no lack of milk for breast-feeding when the time comes. All of this occurs, of course, with only the benefit of postmenarche sexual intercourse. These observations puzzle men and contradict their belief that a woman's reproductive development (i.e., the onset of the menarche, successful birth, having milk) is a function of her inseminations. Nevertheless, in situations like this, men have their own explanations for what happened, and they do not worry much about the apparent inconsistencies.[32] The mythology of masculinity is more persuasive than anomalous perceptions.

One effect of these events, however, has been to make the youths' aversion to premenarche fellatio with their immature brides a more visible interpersonal concern. Among those youths who remain at home, the choice of their sexual relationship to the girl is no longer as silent as before. (Remember that Sambia are quite secretive about sexual intercourse though, nor do others—except, perhaps, one's father—ever ask about the young couple's sexual relationship.) So let us consider briefly why certain young men continue to avoid this earliest heterosexual fellatio, since the problem sheds light on several powerful points about the development of male gender identity. (I shall rule out the importation of a Western/Christian ethic, from the start, since men say this erotic aversion is a historic pattern, and because there is no discernible missionary impact on Sambia sexual morality as yet. Men do have their own moral

---

31. Disruptions in marital arrangements were not unknown in the past. Deaths and wars created problems. So did brother-sister exchange. An older sister given to a man was risky: if a boy did not mature fast enough to marry his assigned wife (his sister's husband's sister), then she could be used to obtain another wife for his brother-in-law (or the latter's clan), on the excuse that the assigned girl needed marrying quickly.

32. Tali and Weiyu, for instance, argued that a man who returned from the coast would want to copulate with his bride frequently, and these (too frequent, depleting, risky) inseminations would, in effect, "make up for lost time." In Western culture, we still have a few inconsistent values, and outcomes, of this sort. For example, a youth should not "spill his own seed," i.e., masturbate; should date and marry a girl of his own age and class before engaging in sexual intercourse: otherwise he invites any number of evils like insanity, blindness, stunted growth, not to mention the status of the outcast. Yet for centuries men have violated these beliefs and not suffered the threatened consequences, while only recently (and most thoroughly in urban areas) have such moral convictions been ignored or rejected.

standard, as I said, that condemns heterosexual activity outside of marriage while condoning homosexual contacts.)

Probably the strongest reason for the aversion to premenarche heterosexual fellatio concerns the loss of semen too early in a man's life. Fear of semen depletion is essential to the ,nale viewpoint, and it creates other consequences that will be examined in the next chapter. Here is the obvious principle: if a girl's body consumes semen for strength, the production of babies, and milk—her body a vessel of almost limitless need—it remains true that a man's semen substance is also acquired externally and is therefore limited. Although idioms stress that semen hastens the growth of femininity, then, laying unequivocal claim on jural status of the offspring, this very idea ironically harbors the seeds of men's great dread of semen depletion. This anxiety clearly enters into youths' resistance to early heterosexual fellatio. But there are other, "quieter" factors that contribute to it, and it is worth listing them in this context.

First, men perceive *premenarche females as children,* a category of asexual or not exciting erotic objects. (Could there, then, be a double standard applied to the even *smaller* boys who are enjoyed as fellators?) Second, *all initial heterosexual activity* may be anxiety-provoking to males, so they avoid it (and fellatio) as long as possible. Third, a premenarche girl may be *too much like a boy but with a female's body,* and is therefore unexciting. (We shall see below that the data demonstrate the opposite viewpoint.) Fourth, a youth may experience *his body as too small and weak* (i.e., not masculine enough) to engage in erotic intercourse yet, but only as regards *females:* he may fear their depletion of his semen and substance. Fifth, youths may resist early (not necessarily only premenarche) heterosexual fellatio for *fear of strengthening their wives too much:* the girls would become vigorous and aggressive women. Eventually we shall consider all these possibilities (except the first one[33]), but especially the last two in some detail. Now let us investigate how these marital events lead toward feminine maturity, the menarche.

From *tai* to *taiketnyi:* virtually overnight the girl becomes a young woman (*chenchorai*) by virtue of the menstrual blood (*chenchi*) discharging from her body. Her body literally "sings out for her man" (*kwei'n-diku*), i.e., is ready for coitus; yet it also screams of bloody pollution (*pulungatnyi,* generically), a poignant dilemma in which masculine culture is deeply rooted. Men assert that the woman's "vagina is now opened" (*laaku meitnu-koo'sokeno*), unleashing years of blocked-up fluids. Unlike the previous marital events, then, the *taiketnyi* ceremonies are triggered

---

33. This factor is involved in certain individual cases, but it is uncommon, so I shall postpone examining it until those studies can be detailed elsewhere.

only by the girl's natural chemistry. The turmoil and triumph belong specifically to her and her husband, two opposite-sexed individuals whose genitals will soon be united through coitus.

The solemnity of this impending change is stamped on each of them, separately, and in quite different places. The ritual doings of men are secrets that belong to the forest. They parallel, but are removed from, the secret covenant of women sealed in the menstrual hut. Only the vague outlines of the women's happening are known to Sambia men (and to me), and the reverse is apparently true. Nonetheless, men still believe they know the source of the women's secret: it is really the female *tingu* that yields the menarche. (Both men and women compare the menarche to the first-stage initiation of men, and later we shall see why.)

For the girl's part, she must be removed to the menstrual hut for two reasons: because of her dangerous pollution and because of her own "deep shame." Only that hut can physically contain the pollutants. Children are kept away. Dogs and pigs are chased off for fear that they may eat some of the fluids, poisoning their flesh and transmitting the contamination. There the girl is cared for, purified, lectured, and beseeched by her womanly elders. She is instructed in caring for her own menstruating body and in caring for her husband's needs. (Men believe this last is accomplished through the male elders' orders to the female elders—who must school the girl in the ways of sex and the steps taken to protect her spouse from her own contamination.)

The young woman also remains hidden in the hut for a few days to vanquish her "shame." Here is Kanteilo (a respected elder) telling why.[34]

We men say secretly that a woman's blood is really like a dog's [menstrual] blood—*chenchi* [female dog]. This name is greatly shameful for women and is never used in their presence. Women themselves use only the term *pulungatnyi-kantei* ["pollution walk," monthly period spent in menstrual hut]. . . . To say the name *chenchi* to a woman would deeply shame her. She could hang herself. . . . She is ashamed that she bleeds like a dog.

In masculine thought, the menarche is not only shame-provoking for women, it is also disgusting for men. Menstrual blood, in imagination or in reference, can evoke feelings of nausea and disgust. Indeed, I cannot overstress how very deeply ingrained is the revulsion with which most adult men react to things tinged with menstrual blood.[35] Perhaps the

---

34. Even an age-tempered, good-natured old man like Kanteilo (who was a war leader but remains an unreformed womanizer) felt compelled to spit and grimace as he said *chenchi* and uttered this remark.

35. See below, pp. 247–248, for an anecdotal illustration. Here is a long-standing and virtually unmentioned area of research. First, for women, what is privately experienced? Are women

strength of such emotions is matched only by the cool inevitability of the menarche that frets men into initiation.

It is given in the nature of female physiology that the *tingu* must eventually trigger that menstrual discharge. The process begins at birth.

> The mother gives her [girl] blood; it becomes a blood pool which fills up. Then the *taiketnyi* comes. Women are that group who make children, so they all bleed. The blood flows and her breasts are tight, her blood is filled up; so we say she has, herself, opened the door [her vagina is open] at her *taiketnyi*. [Weiyu][36]

Weiyu reiterates about the *tingu:* "At the time of a new moon, it can become bloody. Other times, you'll see it doesn't have that blood." Last, Tali sums up this theory in a single sentence: "The *tingu* is filled with blood—only it—it makes the menarche, and the blood flows." In short, men believe that the *tingu* naturally produces menstrual blood that gradually fills the girl's innards, including (but not limited to) her womb, eventually bursting forth from her vagina.

A man can do irreparable harm to his wife if he prematurely violates this natural cycle. Men note that the woman's body eliminates these fluids and thereby unblocks her vagina for coitus. Her own cycle "opens the door for his penis." What, then, if vaginal intercourse occurs before the menarche? The results would be harmful for the woman. (The immoral man would also be placing himself at risk.) The most frequently cited example of this, in Nilangu hamlet, is a middle-aged woman whose stomach is always distended. Men blame her husband.

> K copulated with her, in the vagina, before her menarche. He forced open her vagina. By doing that he didn't allow M's [his wife's] *chenchi* and *muguchelu* [vaginal fluids] to be properly eliminated. So the fluids remained stored up in her stomach even after she has given birth.[37]

Half a dozen times this story has been told me, and its lesson is clear: K was irresponsible and permanently disfigured his wife by preventing her

---

actually ashamed—as I think some of them are—and how, and in what degrees, is this sensed? For men, we must confront idiomatic attitudes no less than the psychophysiological emotions evoked by blood. What are the sources of such a disturbing experience in a life history and culture? In subsequent writings I hope to describe how such feelings arise, in masculine development, out of a childhood where they were mostly silent. See Chapter 8 for further discussion.

36. Compare this statement with Tali's view (below) that blood grows and swells inevitably in girls, leading to a bounty of blood.

37. M has had five children despite this condition, which may be related to maternal thyroid failure at the time of pregnancy.

body from expelling lethal fluids at the (natural) menarche.[38] It is important to emphasize, however, that K's premenses vaginal violation polluted his wife by damming up her own contaminating fluids. His penis and semen helped to do that, but they were not in themselves polluting: his action was stupid, but it was his wife's body that held the contamination. First menses fluids are contaminating to women. For healthy feminine development, these accumulated fluids must somehow come out of their own volition. Before describing these successive changes, though, a note concerning another concept, *muguchelu.*

Muguchelu (literally, *mugu,* mouth or lips; *chelu,* stone or seed) is vaginal fluid. It ranks second only to menstrual blood as an "essence" of femininity, and it is just as contaminating. Men spit compulsively after saying *muguchelu* just as they do after the word *chenchi,* and for the same reasons. (Although penile fluid is likewise termed *muguchelu,* men seldom mention it, and do not consider it polluting.[39]) Close to the menarche, men say, a girl's body also begins producing *muguchelu.* Tali has said: "A young girl is dry, she has no *muguchelu.* The *tai* makes her own *muguchelu;* none of it comes from her mother." Some men suspect that it is the *womb* that manufactures it, although *muguchelu* is said to be stored in a different place, the *kereku-kereku* (semen organ), which I describe below. What matters for the moment is the association between coitus and the fluid. *Muguchelu* (or *goolungat'aamoonaalyi,*[40] as Weiyu prefers) is "for helping open the vagina for the penis" during intercourse.

It follows that the menarche is "dangerous" for both the "afflicted" maiden and her husband. The young woman cannot feed herself; otherwise she risks contaminating food by her own touch. (Fingers easily transmit pollutants.) She is "sick," men assert; so she must be fed by her ritual sponsor[41] like an infant. This caretaking sets up a special, ceremonial avoidance relation between the older sponsor and the maiden. The elder woman not only feeds her (and in that context is forbidden to speak with her), but also helps the mother instruct her daughter in caring for the

---

38. This immoral and reprehensible act and one other (even worse) violation—breaking the postpartum taboos—are the only serious ways a man can jeopardize his wife's health. By contrast, there are many ways a woman can harm her husband's health.

39. The natural oils of certain leafy greens are likened to the *muguchelu* of women and sometimes called that. They are, incidentally, the key reason such greens are taboo for boys and men when they are especially cautious about what they eat, for example, at initiations or cassowary feasts.

40. The *goolungatnyi* is a species of small ground toad that abundantly exudes a white mucus from its skin. Women hunt and eat it, but its flesh is absolutely (and for life) taboo for men. It lives near pandanus groves and is associated with their harvest period.

41. This woman is often her brother's wife or father's sister and is called *nyetyangu,* as is the parallel guardian role for boys in initiation, occupied by an older man.

latter's maturing body, e.g., learning procedures for handling menstrual flows and coitus. Finally, it is the sponsor who collects stinging nettles and prepares a menstrual hut fire for the girl's ceremonial purification.

The husband too, who has been off in the forest trapping possum for the *taiketnyi* ceremonies, is endangered by his wife's menarche, and is likewise bound by rigorous taboos. Most liquids and foods (except taro) are forbidden. His age-mates, ceremonially bonded to him since first initiation, are also obliged to honor these taboos lest they also become polluted. After several weeks the husband and hunting party return to the hamlet bearing possum gifts. For the girl, her menstrual flow halted, the dangers are mostly past. Her husband, back again in the hamlet, renews the risk of contamination and must submit to purificatory rites that reduce his wife's body's threats to his health and life.

The most stupendous of these secret male rites is nose-bleeding, an event men furtively compare to the menarche, since it is believed capable of expelling the pollutants (see Chapter 7). Men think it necessary to nose-bleed themselves for three reasons. First, "The menarche is like our *moku* [first-stage] initiation," men announce: women's menstruations are linked with nose-bleedings. A youth is associated with his wife; they are said to be the "same kind" of person, reproductively; so, as the girl bleeds, her husband must do likewise, else he will become polluted, weak, unmanly. He is also instructed in the need for vigilance during coitus and his wife's menstrual periods. Second, a youth is compelled to "feel the pain" of nose-bleeding, a reminder that his wife is dangerous and needs to be kept "in her place." Third, youths are now said to "have a woman": they must be strong and aggressive warriors, fighters able fearlessly to attack, even kill their enemies. Those rites finally conclude his isolation and are followed by the public menarche ceremonies in the hamlet. (Again, the possum meat gifts are distributed to his wife for redistribution to her collateral kinsmen.) These events pave the way for eventual residence with his wife.

Cohabitation and Coitus. Cohabitation, the sexual bond, and a woman's monthly periods coincide as foci of masculine idioms in the next developments in a woman's femininity.

A couple are usually slow to take up residence together. All the same, in the weeks following the menarche they should begin steady[42] sexual activities to cement their marital contract. They usually have many problems. They are strangers to each other and new to heterosexual activities.

---

42. I cannot adequately generalize about the frequency of sexual intercourse in the population because my data are reliable for only a small sample of men, and among them the incidence and conditions of intercourse vary widely (but see Bulmer 1971:155*n*.).

Conflicts erupt. (To reemphasize: men feel women are scared of them, frightened of being physically harmed.) Marital squabbles, often over sex or sexual jealousies, occur, sometimes frequently, and are sometimes serious enough to embroil the entire community. So it is a sad joke (but still a joke) among older Sambia that the newlyweds will suffer much, as is their lot, before their cohabitation becomes quiet from a truce.

Elders caution youths to be prudent in heterosexual activities. Fellatio should again come first: only later, after several months, may coitus follow "safely."

There is not only an adolescent bashfulness in young women; they are also tightly prudish. This feeling is shared by men, and it frustrates the youth. On the one hand, girls are taught to hide themselves, as Weiyu notes: "Not good that men see the breasts of you women, or they'll want to hold them [breasts]. . . . It [breast] wants to come on top [grow, protrude]."[43] Understandably, there is a tension in erotic activities, then, more so at the start than later. When a bride resists too much, marital squabbles result. It is important to note how men interpret the bride's opposition. Here is Tali:

> If a woman is uncooperative, the elders talk to her mother and ask her: "Did you tell her the *taiketnyi* story [erotic teachings] or not?" The women [invariably] reply, "Yes, we told her, but she's strong-headed, she wants a different man."

A woman's unbending resistance to sex communicates dislike of her husband, then, and this attitude leads to many difficulties. The longer a bride resists, the more she compels her husband to use force. So men say that a bride may finally force her husband (if he persists) to thrust himself upon her, and in this act there is, as elsewhere too, a manifest connotation of rape.[44]

Fellatio again adds semen—which "strengthens" one's wife and adds

---

43. Until disruptive events following pacification ten years ago, it was taboo for Sambia girls and young married women to show their faces, and especially their breasts, to men (other than their husbands, and at marriage he had to break down this taboo *in her*). This taboo has, curiously, lost much of its force, but younger women are still modest about their bodies till after they have one or two children. Needless to say, men are attracted especially by women's breasts, which some admit are sexually exciting, a dynamic that forms a cornerstone of masculine heterosexual eroticism.

44. I cannot here enter into the murky subject of erotic fantasy or excitement, except to note that, in cultural idiom and men's private talk (which has a quality of the "locker room" banter among American males), there is a *tendency* to regard women as sex objects, fetishized bodies reduced to orifices for fornication; and men's individual behavior (in case studies) supports this viewpoint. But with only such fragments of data, and none on individual fantasy, I cannot describe the precise meanings of this cultural slant in a population of individual Sambia.

more breast milk (whether or not it occurred before her menarche). Vaginal intercourse is far more risky and exciting, as we shall see. Yet in any erotic exchange, the newlyweds face the difficulty of going it alone for the first time. Men claim that women are reluctant and that, for instance, they hide behind their gardening routines. Or they may stay sheltered in the shadow of other women (e.g., their mothers-in-law). Yet one sees, too, an awkwardness in the youth who hangs about the doorway of his bride's quarters, making idle conversation with everyone except the woman he needs to face. The young man's problem is how the devil to overcome the greater reluctance of his bride and coax her alone into the masculine forest.

Men ambivalently lament that now, as in girlhood, their women remain fickle and tiresomely shy. This behavior stems in part from women's timidity. Women are "weak and pliable"; their skins are "soft." They do not fight in war, cannot hunt, are too puny to scale trees. Women have cause to be timid, therefore, for they are inept at defending themselves or mastering the world. Another reason, too, is that men *expect* women to be shy and resist; otherwise they are branded as "easy marks"—potential adulteresses.

Why are men therefore persuaded that women become sexually aggressive as they mature? This appears paradoxical, but is not so experienced by Sambia. Men sense that women's behavior is basically deceptive. Behind a woman's mask of reticence, men are convinced, lies an imperious contradiction. Women are not really prudish, they are priggish and wanton. Women only seem to be shy; they are, at heart, not chaste but repressed. Sambia men presume that their *wives* are lascivious harlots who, when at last unleashed, develop insatiable erotic appetites. Weiyu scoffs:

> Woman . . . no, she's nothing! She won't think well of you [husband]. Truly not at all. . . . She's the same, exactly, as the cassowary! [Scoffs.] Whatever she smells she only swallows it! Whatever type of tree fruit, or small things, she can swallow the water [semen] of all men, wherever she sees them. If you send her [wife] elsewhere, she won't think about you. If she is with you [lowers voice], she acts good. But if you send her to another place, and she encounters *any* kind of man, at the toilet or anywhere, she will swallow [suck his penis]—that's all!

Here again cassowary and woman are equated in the same thought—to drive home the point that both are wretchedly promiscuous.

This leads to a dreadful and pervasive attitude that wants emphasis again: women as sexual property. Once you have copulated with a woman she is yours; and once she has had your child she is yours absolutely. This is transparent in the following comment by Tali.

> Of us [men] we've already smelled it [vagina] . . . So your penis, it won't rest

well. It can get up, easily. If you journey with a woman, you won't be so quiet [inside] or walk right. You can think of the cunt of your woman. You can be irritable. [But] if you walk about with a man, you will converse: you'll walk all right. It's only a walk, it's only a man. With women, no. Your sister—she's like a man, you won't think like that—she's a man. But your woman, she's your share. Whatever you want to do, that's all right. It is only *your* desire. And another woman, if she talks with you, tells stories, if she persists in talking, Weiyu and me know this: she is thinking about that thing [coitus] and she's talking with me.

This train of thought, at heart, portrays women as lecherous sex objects. Tali seems convinced, too, that sexual intercourse is entirely at the discretion of a man and for his pleasure alone.

Men admit of only one posture in coitus: the missionary position, the woman lying on her back. (Fellatio is different.) No other form of intercourse is acceptable, and men vehemently deny any other.[45] Foreplay is minimal; there is little touching. Pleasurable or not, coitus is essential. Tali states why: "It's for making a child. It's for making many children."

This view is, not surprisingly, complemented by frequent denials of orgasm (*imbimboogu*) in women.[46] (Or, more precisely, a lack of interest in it.) Men recognize that women have vaginal fluid related to their sex and erotic role. That fluid (*muguchelu*) has nebulous origins and functions. Some men say that it comes from the *tingu;* others argue that it is linked to the *kereku-kereku* organ, as is men's semen. But according to Weiyu, vaginal fluid is "not viscous like semen, it is more [watery] like mother's breast milk." Furthermore, Weiyu, for instance, was convinced that, somehow, "*muguchelu* is produced by semen, like mother's milk." The fluid is also "foul smelling," and that odor is referred to in idioms as the "vaginal smell" (*geruchentu*), "truly a bad smell," since women do not bathe.[47] Weiyu says, "A woman doesn't expel [ejaculate] this grease,

---

45. Sambia deride anal intercourse, which is said to be practiced by neighboring Fore peoples. Cunnilingus was unknown till (after a year) I asked about it and got bewildered stares and fervent spitting responses.

46. Here is a subject on which my inquiries are never matched by men's conversations among themselves. Orgasm in women is not a topic men discuss, and when I asked about it, the responses ranged from breathless, vehement denials (most common) to occasional claims of "Yes, it happens" or motions of lack of interest. By contrast, orgasm in males is a common, though lewd, topic (especially among fellators)—a measure of masculine virility, e.g., abundance of seminal emission—and it is never far from ritual rhetoric concerning heterosexual functioning and health, either.

47. Weiyu: "The vagina is filled with *muguchelu:* women don't wash. Women say they don't wash their vaginas because they would not heat up our cocks, we wouldn't really ejaculate. We don't mention the vaginal smell since women would hang themselves. For that [reason] we also don't spit [in front of them to eliminate the bad smell in our mouths] during intercourse." Men must always spit after intercourse out of sight of their wives, and they keep

it is only painted on the penis [inside the vagina]; we can feel it." Some men simply deny that women experience orgasms. Others disclaim knowledge, or hint of ambivalence about the subject. Tali's view on this point is unusually balanced:

> Women, too, can feel sweet [a metaphor for orgasm] sometimes, you can see that. But it's not a good thing. . . . [GH: What?] Their grease [*muguchelu*] is not a good substance so they [women] don't talk about it. Of us men, we just talk about that [sex], we do this, we do that; but of women, I don't know. . . . We don't know, does she feel the *imbimboogu?* Still, we don't know. That knowledge belongs only to women.[48]

Whether women do or do not experience orgasm takes us beyond mere idioms; what matters, at the moment, is the doubt thrown on this possibility. This doubt, I suggest, amounts to the denial of one function of femininity: to experience erotic pleasure in and of itself. That raises a different set of reactions: dread of pollution from vaginal fluid and fear of semen loss (see below).

For all its conflict, coitus forges a lifetime bond that Sambia silently measure as its own reward. Tali underlines how in simple and eloquent idioms. "When a couple walk together from the forest, and everyone sees you returning from the gardens, your family and friends are happy for you." Yes, the marriage has been consummated. That thought augurs good things to come: erecting a house together, jointly planting gardens, rearing a family. Such things can be appreciated and enjoyed in their own right; they are, furthermore, the foundations of respectable adulthood. Whatever motivates the attitude behind Tali's point—whether contentment, compensation, or rationalization—is ignored. But that joy is undeniably there for a moment. It suffices that when they see the couple return alone—husband leading, his wife dutifully behind him—men feel assured that things have been set in their right order.

Menstruation. From coitus to menstrual flows: here we reach the hub of budding femininity. The menarche ushers in regular menses. Menstrual

---

tree bark in their mouths during intercourse to absorb the smell and remind them not to spit. Spearmint leaves are also placed in the nasal septum to displace the smell of the vagina.

48. This last sentence is a standard way males disclaim knowledge *and interest.* It is inappropriate for Tali to say publicly much more than this, for how could he know what women experience unless he had discussed it with them? And to do so would admit of too much heterosexual closeness. But Tali *could* speculate: if I had urged him to speculate, had not been simply fobbed off by that answer, he might have offered opinion, experience, fantasy. Those would represent his thoughts, however, not someone else's.

discharges signify the core of feminine reproductive power, all that is uniquely strong and weak about women.

A wife's periods disrupt cohabitation. They also interrupt the family food supply. And although the woman goes abruptly to the menstrual hut, no verbal explanation is ever given and none is needed. She is bleeding and "ashamed," as she was at the menarche. Her husband may go to the clubhouse and forest. Her children she leaves behind. A woman's periods are so steady and visible that they serve constant notice of a powerful force alive and operating within her. Nothing else, except the waxing and waning of the moon, so dramatizes cyclical periodicity in the Sambia world. There is certainly nothing comparable in men; no endogenous indicator to show that a man's body is visibly empowered by a living energy that actively responds to inner periods.[49] Yet men compensate. They possess a secret: by thrusting sharp canes up their noses they painfully make their own bodies simulate what naturally occurs in women: monthly bloodlettings. Their conscious reasons are complicated; but the key is a desire to remain strong and masculine. An understanding of such rites, then, requires some knowledge about how men apprehend the menses.

A woman's periods are linked metaphorically to the moon's periodic "sickness" (*numbulyu,* sickness or disease). The "moon is the man [*kwolyangu*] of women," men like to say. "He goes from small to big and dies": the moon is "sick" as it wanes; then the "moon's sickness is finished." Men tend to associate feminine changes with this natural lunar cycle. Tali states: "Her skin is a little painful, it itches a bit. The moon does it. . . . They [women] all do that as they always have. And the moon, too, it rises, so the blood it falls out."[50] It is a common and public idiom, therefore, to allow that a woman "kills the moon," i.e., has a period, when she visits the menstrual hut.

Do these lunar idioms amount to a different theory of menstruation, or

---

49. This statement is not quite correct. Penile erection has a similar quality. It is relatively autonomous and uninhibited by conscious regulation. Sambia acknowledge this: "The penis has its own thought, it rises of its own accord." (See Freud 1963:155; Tuzin 1972:238f.) This is, certainly, all that is true of nocturnal emissions or erections. Here, too, there is a sense of periodicity for Sambia, who regularly recall night dreams. But there is an essential difference: menstrual *discharges* are lethal, discarded; semen (except from nocturnal emissions) must be ingested. (This is, incidentally, why masturbation goes so much against the grain of Sambia culture.) Expulsion versus ingestion: both processes are cyclical, but they are quite antithetical in what happens to the fluids and their intrinsic power for life.

50. Sambia, unlike us, do not fancy a man's face in the appearance of the moon; they nevertheless speak of it only as of the male gender. Myth tells that the moon's surface became discolored by a man's angry throwing of cooked greens, splatting and permanently disfiguring the moon's center. By contrast, the sun is, in idioms and ritual symbolism, constantly treated as if it were masculine and had no relationship to women at all.

are men simply voicing metaphor? Here again detailed verbal data are needed to make an interpretation. Throughout tribal New Guinea and elsewhere, it is common for humans consciously to link lunar cycles and the menses. The significance of this link among Sambia is clear: the moon is a convenient metaphor for casual references to a woman's periods. Sambia recognize perceptual correspondences between the two cyclical events. They also genderize the moon as a male. The lexical significance of idioms pertaining to menses, however, turns back on a woman's body: it is the interior workings of female biology that concern masculine theory.[51]

The imaginative association between menstrual flows and lunar sickness is not hard to understand. Blood and semen are the fundamental substances of health and life itself. Blood loss provokes anxiety. For instance, Weiyu casually remarked, "It's not good that lots of blood flows. . . . If I lose my blood, I die. When I cut a finger or something, I tie it quickly with a vine." And elsewhere he told me: "We think a sick man has dry blood; his skin is slack. A man with lots of blood is healthy, he won't die quickly" (cf. G. Lewis 1975:202). Here is a hint about the meaning of life-supporting, dangerous blood flows in women. Menstrual periods may be likened to a periodic female sickness. This idea disturbs men. But that blood loss is trivial compared to the overflowing pool that is its fundamentally female source.

Women's bodies have a great natural power to generate and regenerate blood in profuse quantity. Their bodily vitality is rich; their abundant blood repels disease. They are thus innately healthier and longer-lived than men. Women have "bountiful blood," men constantly avow, since they are "filled with a pool of blood."

> Blood keeps the body cool; sickness goes to a hot body. Women have cold skins *from so much blood* [emphasis]. Men are hot-skinned from too little blood. The *arukoogu* banana tree [very black-colored] is taboo for us men to plant since it's so cold. If women had bodies like us, they'd die quickly too. . . . But blood keeps women healthy. Women hold the source [*kablu;* tree base, source] of blood. They have a blood pool [*boongu*]. . . They have so much blood. Sickness avoids women, their coldness chases it away. Women don't die quickly, they are never ill. We men have small buttocks, we go up trees. Women have big buttocks, like tree trunks; they live a long time.

---

51. There may be some Sambia individuals who are actually convinced that the moon causes menstrual flows. Even so, I believe that if we took a wide sample, asking alternative questions and getting honest answers, few Sambia would be found to hold such a belief. Historically, some Westerners were no doubt convinced of the old wives' tale that a virgin must not sleep in the moonlight lest she become pregnant. Today, it might still be possible to locate Westerners who believed this, but they would be a decided minority.

Here Tali notes how blood is fuel for endurance. Even robust health is thus a by-product of one's fund of blood. Women are biologically gifted: they have it easier than men.

For moments like this men can forget that women lose some drops of blood, that they experience cramps and have to lie about uselessly in the menstrual hut for two or three days, weak and vulnerable. Yet they bounce back, seemingly unaffected by their blood loss. Females do not fall sick, not really, and they live longer than men to boot. (Semen ingestion contributes to this longevity, as we shall see.) This leads to the procreative functions of menstruation.

"Menstrual blood is for giving babies": this is an outstanding principle of masculine dogma and one that follows from all that we have hitherto examined. Tali is adamant (he was emotional, here, with tones of resentment in his voice):

> Menstrual blood is for giving babies, for making blood, like the gasoline you white men put in airplanes. . . .[52] Menstrual blood is for giving blood to women. The blood is the mother [i.e., provider] of women. That blood keeps women healthy; they hold the arse [base] of blood. Women can produce new blood for themselves. . . . Women give us [as a fetus] half their blood, while half stays inside them. Yet they always stay healthy.

Once more, this endless fountain of blood is linked to the notion of a blood pool. Weiyu says:

> The blood of women, it helps the child so she can create it [fetus]. Blood: it's the same as a round pool [menjaak-boongu]; for she [one's mother] has so much blood. The infant comes up inside [the fetus in a birth sac, moo-nupi, is contained inside blood-filled innards].

Such comments idiomatically attribute an intrinsic power for manufacturing blood mass to the adult female body. They support the interpretation that men perceive a naturally occurring, effusive blood pool as the source of womanly menarche and menstrual periods alike. This point needs emphasis.

The womb is vital in the functioning of the menses. Coitus is, first, said to "feed" semen into the womb via the birth canal. Vaginal intercourse deposits semen needed for actual fetal development within the womb. (Note the contrast with fellatio practices, which can only strengthen the mother's body and stimulate milk production.) There is so much blood

---

52. Sambia have seen barrels of gasoline unloaded for light aircraft at Mountain Patrol Station.

inside a woman, however, that these inseminations are thought to displace equivalent amounts of blood periodically; hence menstrual flows.

The infant [embryo] is exactly inside the blood. The womb opens a little, to make a place for the [developing] infant. . . . It [womb] shakes out a little blood, it [blood] flows out [i.e., as a discharge]. And later, with enough semen, the infant is formed then; and the birth sack blocks [the birth canal from which falls] the blood, so blood cannot fall out [i.e., monthly periods halt]. [Weiyu]

Here emerges an essential idea about femininity. The masculine viewpoint tends to *deride* femaleness while also *denying* its procreative functions. Semen is thought to dislodge some blood that becomes a menstrual flow; some femaleness (blood) must be removed to create a fetus. The fetus, in time, blocks the birth canal, whereupon menstruation ceases. The most female act—giving birth—arises from semen injections into the blood pool; giving birth halts the menses. This point, although powerful, is still only a piece of the broader system of focal projections centered on female parturition.

It is neither the womb nor the actual blood flow that concerns men most, but rather the overwhelming effusive mass of blood contained within a female body, a body capable of reproducing itself. For example, men recognize—reluctantly—that women do not need men to menstruate. Here is Tali again, responding to my question.

All women, alone [not cohabiting with a man], they too kill the moon. . . . They don't have men but they still *pulungatnyi kantu*. She [sic] is filled with blood and can release blood all the time. The elders say: "You men, if you don't lie with a woman and she kills the moon, you can't go harangue [your wife]: 'Who have you fornicated that you are killing the moon!' " No, all women can kill the moon. . . . The moon comes and she goes to the small hut.

In spite of their dogmas, men thus acknowledge that female bodies can, of their own volition, menstruate; coitus is not needed for that. (I should mention, though, that here [compare p. 207 *n*. 5] men suspect such women of promiscuous sex; even Tali has at other times said as much.) There is also the tacit acceptance of something else here: women can reproduce quite effectively so long as a man—any man—is available. All they need is a penis.

Take the opposite case, a barren woman (*kwoliku*). Since marriage and personhood and masculine identity are based on having children, what good could there be in a sterile human being? On this matter men are unalterably dogmatic: they absolutely deny that a man could be sterile (see

Read 1951:162). No category, cover term, or metaphor exists in reference to such a manly condition; sterility is exclusively a female failing.
Indeed, while men discuss barren women, they never, in my experience,
questioned their own fertility. Usually men say a *kwoliku* has been sorcer-
ized in vengeance by a jilted lover or ex-husband. Sometimes they mutter
that she is eating abrasive plants to prevent conception or induce miscar-
riage. (Older women with children are also believed to prevent conception after tiring of childbearing.) A barren woman is not a whole person;
she has no children. Yet it is equally certain that this inadequately feminine person still possesses enormous blood.

> A *kwoliku* [barren woman], too, she has it [blood]. The womb—that's all—it
> is dry and closed. We [men] question—that semen—where does it go in the
> *kwoliku?* [Great laughter.] Where does it go? They [lovers] fornicate for noth-
> ing. . . . A man who has no other *woman* [emphasis], he does it for nothing,
> to relax his penis, that's all. We wonder . . . does the semen go to the *tingu* of
> the *kwoliku?* She has no *kwulai'u-ketu* [emphasis]. . . . Does it go to the *tingu?*
> [Tali]

Without a womb, the barren woman still menstruates. Without a womb,
her husband's semen still disappears inside her. In such terms men question whether sperm goes to the *tingu,* providing a hoarded double vitality
of maleness and femaleness. This is what Tali hints. The implication is that
a *kwoliku* has all that feminizing blood and she gets masculinizing semen
too.

(In the next two chapters we must carefully examine how this overflowing abundance of femininity, pinpointed consciously on menstrual blood,
generally shifts the focus of a man's sense of incomplete maleness away
from his lack of internally produced semen onto fears about feminine
pollution.)

Each menses requires a man secretly to nose-bleed himself in the forest
alone. Of all manly rituals this is the most painful, traumatic, and intimately personal. Nose-bleeding is not, as is the menstrual period of one's wife,
shame-provoking. Yet it is secret. Tali says, "Not good that they [women]
become ashamed: women think this, so they hide. It's not the same for
men. . . . So he [husband] stays around the hamlet [until he must nose-
bleed]." Women are ashamed of their periods; men hide their nose-
bleedings. (See also J. Whiting [1941:64] on Kwoma "shame" about male
blood-letting practices.) A woman hangs special leaves around her neck
to signify she is in her period; a man paints red ocher on his stomach, face,
and limbs, following that secret ritual he has enacted in the forest. The
parallel of activities is striking. Sympathetic identification is at work; parturition is the focus.

Pregnancy. Pregnancy stimulates the next set of changes in a woman's femininity leading to adulthood. Coitus is instrumental in them.

Men vary, of course, in their estimations of the number of inseminations needed for forming a fetus. Fellatio may have occurred often over the intervening months, but only vaginal intercourse leads to pregnancy. (Men agree that precious little of the orally ingested semen finds its way into the womb, since the woman's body uses that semen in the other ways previously noted.) Vaginal penetration, however, brings the penis closer to the womb itself. Here may be a potential source of the greater danger and excitement most men associate with vaginal versus oral sex. The semen is said to be quickly absorbed into the womb, and after "forty or fifty ejaculations" the fetus is nearly formed.[53]

> A man and woman fornicate. The man has an ejaculation and his semen goes into the cunt. The semen is carried by the *kwulai'u-oolu* into the *kwulai'u-ketu*. The womb shakes; this causes some of the woman's *muguchelu* to fall out of her *kereku-kereku,* into the vagina. [Weiyu]

By this process, therefore, men do not recognize conception as such; instead, coitus simply builds up the fetus until birth occurs. There is no category for conception, and a single instance of coitus will not create a baby. In men's discourse, a woman's body is likened to a garden in which her husband implants a seed that germinates in the womb. Constant coitus, and the continuous relationship of the spouses, are thus the indicators of the newborn child's heritage.

Sambia see impregnation as a definitely dual sexual process in which both semen (maleness) and blood (femaleness) are vital. Coitus "plants the child" by slowly admitting an accumulation of semen[54] into the womb, displacing some blood. Yet blood must also combine with semen to create the embryo that "is exactly inside the blood." Hence men rather weakly imagine that semen "mixes" (or coagulates) with female blood inside the womb. They liken the process to the formation of a gummy mass such as when white milk sap of the *ngwuku* tree is collected in a vessel. Semen is the embryo's source of strength.

> He [embryo] doesn't eat sweet potato in the stomach. . . . The *kwulai'u-chemulku* [embryo], it hasn't opened its eyes yet, it doesn't eat. It has no food of its own. We say: semen goes to make its skin and bone.

---

53. Weiyu, speaking of his wife: "I wait two or three days . . . and then I copulate with her again." Other men assert that they wait five to seven days, and some wait as long as two weeks, between periods of coitus with their wives.

54. *Kwulai'u chemulka* (boy-child stomach) is pregnancy and is the nearest concept to cover the accumulated semen that I could find. The embryo or fetus is usually referred to as a "boy."

Still, the role of blood is no less vital. Tali continues: "Blood—your mother gives you. And bone, skin—your father gives it to you . . . just like that. For men and women it's the same. Blood comes only from mother." Father's semen creates skin and bone tissue; only one's blood comes from one's mother. (The growth of teeth is usually attributed to breast-milk.) The emerging infant is a composite of male and female fluids.

Pregnancy brings about visible changes in the young woman. The woman has been "fed" enough semen by her husband to alter her breasts. They become "tight" (full), with black nipples—a result of coitus. Weiyu says, "Fellatio doesn't make *aamdoot'nboolu* [black nipples], only genital intercourse does"; breasts now filled with milk. So the entire breasts begin to change to a darker skin tone. The limbs and face, on the other hand, turn dull "yellow," and the stomach develops a red hue. The overall effect, men assert, is a "nice" vibrant glow about the pregnant woman, at least at first.

The embryo inside the womb is described as blood red. At birth, the blood is expelled. (Until then, the full womb keeps the mother's milk from flowing.) It is this mass of blood, enveloping the fetus within the stomach, that gives the stomach its warm red hue. What do these physical changes mean?

> This is to produce a child [*kwulai'u imutnundikeinun-tokeno*]. The woman carries a belly, has a child [*kwulai'u imutnyi*]; she can develop loose skin [*cheruptu.*]. It's the same as pandanus [*kunaalu*]: we've told you many times [bored].[55]

Tali, responding to a question, said more than he would otherwise have needed to say: parturition changes in women perceptually correspond to the growth of a nut pod in "female" pandanus trees. In both, "pregnancy" is identified with a slackness of skin (*cheruptu*), a darkening of breasts or of the nut pod, and a yellowing of the overall body or foliage.

Coitus should continue until a woman can feel the child moving within her, near the sixth month of pregnancy (according to men's reckoning, though this is rough; Sambia do not keep count for pregnancy). The last few months of accumulating semen are still deemed critical for the child's health. Not only does that semen complete fetalization, it also lends more milk to the mother for the infant's postpartum sustenance. By seven months, however, all sexual intercourse must stop for a long time to come,

---

55. I asked a general question about why the pregnant woman's body changes and I got this specific, characteristic answer, which Tali incidentally felt was so obvious that he added pointedly, "We've told you many times." The concept of *kwulai'u-imutnyi* has much significance in male ritual, and this statement is theoretically salient because of how Tali has verbally linked pregnancy, pandanus, and coloration (see Chapter 7).

since blocking the birth canal with semen threatens the fetus and agitates labor.

Birth. Near birth the expectant mother is, ideally, removed to the menstrual hut. (In practice, labor sometimes begins in the forest or forest houses, where birth actually occurs.) Three reasons for this: birth is secret and, like the menarche, entails some element of shame; the birth-giving process is highly polluting; and consequently the infant's sex assignment is always the province of women. Myth has it (see Chapter 8) that "women originally hid their first birth, so now we men hide homosexuality." Then, too, a woman's body and innards are exposed, so only women should witness her labor. Children are also kept out. Elder women may ease the labor by serving as midwives. A difficult birth may require a woman shaman whose healing spells, as she massages the abdomen, address the fetus as a slippery eel so as to coax it from its cavernous hiding place (cf. Lévi-Strauss 1967: 186). When the newborn finally "breaks through" (*bungerapi*) and emerges, it is laid on freshly cut banana leaves. The infant looks "completely red and bloodied" from the birth sac (*ket-ivita,* net-string-bag bark cape). This mass of fluids now becomes the single greatest pool of pollution Sambia ever see amassed. And it is treated that way.

From this context arises the masculine viewpoint that birth is deeply contaminating. The menstrual hut is temporarily referred to as a "birth house" (*morum-angu*). Blood and the afterbirth are thus exposed to the open air in great quantity. Women are said to use their grass skirts to clean the infant, the mother, and themselves. The umbilical cord (severed with a bamboo knife) is even buried in the earth near the hut.[56] This house, these women, that infant: here lies the crux of men's genuine fears surrounding birth and the menstrual hut (which they passionately avoid). Nevertheless, out of this dark and tainted nest emerges a new human being.

And immediately upon birth, amid this untidy assemblage, women hastily clean the infant so as to determine its sex. The genitals are the only certain clue, and women, alone, examine them. There they pronounce the infant's sex, which is stamped forever; and instantly word of the birth— and the baby's sex—spreads like wildfire among the villagers. It is remarkable how, in a day or so, an entire region seems to learn about the birth of a boy or a girl. During the process, men stay away, completely removed from the scene of sex assignment; indeed, men (especially the new father) will probably not see the infant for weeks and sometimes months to come.

---

56. The huts are not raised on a platform like regular houses. They are built on the ground to prevent animals from foraging underneath and becoming contaminated.

198 Guardians of the Flutes

Men know that women arrange it that way. Nearly everything men voice at the time expresses the suspicion that women have ulterior motives in conspiring to keep men ignorant of the actual doings in the birth house. Birth is, after all, women's business: let the men have their wars and secret ceremonies; giving birth is the heart of female pride.

The birth of a girl can be a joy. The mother[57] appreciates that a girl will become a garden helper, that she will bring bride-wealth and food gifts, and that she will provide a girl in exchange for securing her son a wife of his own.

A baby with a penis is different. Men, they themselves say, always want a male child, a true heir, a warrior and protector of life and property. Indeed, "the firstborn ought to be a boy," and the young mother may adore and spoil him (knowing full well that he will be her means of support in old age). The next boy, however, may not be so welcomed. "Where will he obtain a wife without a sister to exchange? Won't too many boys fight over their father's land?" For such reasons, Sambia say, women used "secretly" to practice male infanticide (*mulu ruvraa-ketu;* death/hitting birth sack). Women allegedly took it upon themselves to suffocate the newborn. Men (and the father) were not only not told, they were told lies: "The infant was stillborn." Helplessly kept out, men say (without great conviction) that they have always harbored this uncertainty about the birth seclusion. There is another masculine anxiety about the birth, too: the possibility that the infant may be a hermaphrodite (*kwolu-aatmwol*). (We shall examine infanticide and hermaphroditism in the following chapters.) What matters, at the moment, is that birth and sex assignment are handled by women alone.

Giving birth and suckling the infant stimulate the final[58] biological changes in a woman's body, and their handling sets the infant on a certain developmental line. These parturition changes are important in idioms and simulated in ritual.

The exhausting birth leaves the mother's skin "loose and not healthy." Her breast nipples now turn "completely black . . . so the infant can see them better." The woman's stomach slackens, becomes "yellow," and is

---

57. Obviously personality, age, and other factors enter into any woman's response to pregnancy and birth, so I wish to reiterate that this material addresses masculine idioms much more than women's actual behavior.

58. I am obviously excluding menopause from this view, and for two reasons. First, Sambia men, at least, do not recognize menopause as a category in any simple sense (there is no term that means menopause, for instance); instead they prefer to think that a woman has, for different reasons, stopped bearing children. Second, not much importance is placed on menopause in male idioms, with this exception: old women are said to be "dry," like girls (*tai*), although this is also said of old men. Unlike girls, however, old women are "soiled" and "used up" from coitus and childbearing.

"very soft." Eventually, after a few days, the skin coloration will return to normal. With the birth sack expelled, a woman's milk is freed, so she can breast-feed. The infant itself is "very soft," with tannish-yellow (*kakaptu,* like immature pandanus nuts) skin. The initial milk (i.e., colostrum) is yellow, say men, and here is why:

> The umbilical cord contains blood . . . and semen. At birth, the birth sack breaks open and eliminates blood. The blood wants to dry up, so it turns into water. The water . . . has yellow fluid, and this is pushed [upwards] into the breasts at birth [after the umbilical cord is severed]. This water flows out of the breasts as new [yellow] milk [*chewvutnji-cherup'nha*], for three or four days. [Tali]

As Tali described this to me, another man, Kwol, cut in: "If you've seen the yoke of a bush hen egg, it's the same as the new milk of the mother. After that, the breast milk turns from yellow [*cherupnji-aamoonaalyi*] to regular white milk [*aamoonaalyi*]." As the child grows, in a month, it "is a little stronger" and still has "a yellow skin." The milk firms up the child. Men note that the child's nonsolid feces are also yellow while it stays on yellow breast milk.

The colors of this parturition process—in the bodies and emissions of mother and child alike—are, for men, a symptom of the biological closeness characterizing the maternal bond, inside and outside the mother's womb. The event of the birth leads to the final masculine initiation, too, performed for the father.

Parturition and Female Superiority

Now our attention must turn to the meaning of postpartum changes for men. Let us be more precise: Why do idioms especially focus on—like a symbolic filter—the birth metamorphosis of mother and infant and the colors of their fluids? There are two answers to this question, one simple, one complex. The perceptual phenomenology of birth comes first.

The female body actually undergoes visible changes near birth. The abdomen swells, the skin tones alter, the breasts bulge, the nipples darken. Sambia wonder about the internal causes of these events. Apparently, men reckon, it must be the process of giving birth itself. Skin coloration alters from its normal appearance to deep black, then reddish hues, followed by dull sallow. The female body is preparing for birth: femininity changes like this at birth. A female being must give birth to attain complete womanhood. This drive to birth is basic; it is innate; it produces life; and it is fundamentally female. Like the inner *tingu,* female maturation, the protrusion of breasts, and the menarche and menses, birth is immanent.

The only possible way to ignore these highly visible facts is to look the other way.[59]

Men perceive corresponding parturition changes occurring in the natural world. The signs are not so obvious in natural species. They require a special perceptual set. They require Sambia masculine focal projections. In fact, they are so obscure that only after many months did I sense their presence beneath idioms, despite repetitious allusions made by males in many settings. Once understood, the metaphoric and lexical significance of such perceptual correspondences became apparent.

Take the pandanus. The trees are dimorphically male and female, but only the female trees have feeder ropes, grass skirts, nut pods, and nuts, analogically just as women possess birth canals, grass skirts, wombs, and babies. The pandanus is driven to give birth; under the warm sun it changes from its normal coloration to darker shades, then yellow. Its nut pod matures and the nuts are harvested. Or the cassowary: it is lexically recognized as dimorphic, although men think of it as fundamentally female. Her tail feathers turn from tan-yellow to orange to black; then, at maturity, her anus emits eggs. We should not ignore the importance of these natural species as material resources. But they are also idiomatically significant "because" they visibly undergo perceptible cycles in their appearance, the outcome of which is biological reproduction. All female beings have this power; males do not. In short, the compelling, tacit qualities of these masculine idioms derive their force from perceptual correspondences linking women's parturition with these natural species.

The natural drives of parturition so evident in women are thus frustratingly dormant in men. Coitus, birth, and adulthood go hand in hand for Sambia. In myriad ways, Sambia society, the family, and ritual cult translate adult competence into reproductive competence. The birth of a child is the last step into adulthood and the achievement of adult status (*aatmwunu*) for man and woman alike. (This is, I think, why masculine idioms deny the possibility of male sterility.) Yet the place of the two sexes differs greatly in this development. Having a baby and suckling it are visible and what really count. Only females do this; and so every man must have a wife. Parturition is innate to femininity. Hence, body changes dependent on giving birth become tangible evidence of the irreversible push toward reproductive competence never so dramatically apparent in the bodies of men.

---

59. Here, too, is a phenomenological problem that needs research. Unlike men, Sambia women, nearly all of them, have distended stomachs, probably from thyroid failure. Pregnancy distends the abdomen further and creates the other symptoms too. So how do men confront women every day with their pseudopregnant stomachs, and how might this perceptual factor exaggerate the difference between manhood and womanhood?

Here, at last, we encounter the complex problem of what this form of female reproductive superiority means for individual men. And here one can draw from cultural idioms, but they do not in themselves provide enough data with which to comprehend an individual's sense of femininity and masculinity (i.e., gender identity). To say more we should need substantial evidence about how a Sambia man senses these changes in women's bodies: in his sense of himself and his maleness. Obviously this psychological issue takes me beyond my present objective and anticipates what will be said elsewhere; nonetheless, I wish to illustrate why those data cannot be ignored.

The birth of a child once again separates husband and wife and is finally celebrated by another possum hunt and feast in the hamlet. Childbirth inaugurates the postpartum taboos with their strict avoidence of sexual contact. The new father learns of these taboos and how to purify himself of birth contaminants in the men's secret ceremonies enacted in the forest on the day after the possum feast. Only one new ritual element, however, is taught the father-husband whose initiation, there, confers the stamp of full manhood. That technique is the use of a strikingly yellow tree sap (called *itmenjaaku,* tree blood). That tree sap, its use and meaning, is what concerns us.

The young man is taught to cut and tap a species of tree so as to smear the sap on his body. The bright yellow sap he puts on his navel, breast nipples, penis, and on the creases in his elbows and knees. Men say this: "The sap strengthens the skin, makes it strong, and prevents it from loosening." The sap is used, then, to coat the body and thereby defend it from the pollution of both mother and infant. This is immediately followed by another nose-bleeding, which expulsion removes his wife's contagious blood. Here is Weiyu, privately relating this experience not long after undergoing the rites.

The elders told us at our *moondangu* [birth rites]: "Before, at your *taiketnyi,* you had to walk a long way to find milk-sap trees to rub on your skins. Now you have a child and you can put *itmenjaaku* on yourselves, when your wife menstruates. This sap strengthens your skin. *Itmenjaaku* is [lowers voice, grimaces] the same as the infant's feces [*moondungaleku*]. We young men are afraid of putting *itmenjaaku* on our skins because we think it looks just like infant feces [expostulates]. [GH: Then why do it?] It's our custom, it makes us men [raises voice, emphasis]. . . . And after vaginal sex our skins are shaking [*guria*].[60] Rubbing yellow sap ends this feeling; we can feel good [*ilaiyu,* happy, pleasant] again.

---

60. This is a fairly common statement and an apparently common experience among men; Weiyu brought it to life and his intensity made it convincing.

This short communication unveils many of the truly great anxieties of Sambia manhood. Achieving final initiation and manly strength; menstrual pollution, contamination, envy and sympathetic identification with infant and mother; the disturbing anxieties of genital penetration and ejaculation —those concerns are all encapsulated in Weiyu's intimate remark. Why, out of all the possibilities, should men have ritually fixed on yellow tree sap? Why should Weiyu (and other men) consciously link this yellow sap to infant feces and the overwhelming excitement of heterosexual genital intercourse, which leaves him shaking? Such questions want answers that only Weiyu can provide, about himself, his subjective experience, and what it is like to be Weiyu and to be inside his skin, close to his wife's body. One thing is certain: those are the inner experiences that, for Weiyu, "make us men."

Since femininity is that overwhelming and innate, all that is left for men to do is separate and defend boys from women, while oddly simulating certain perceptually correspondent female changes by means of ritual. The *tingu*, menstrual blood, and birth are the keys for understanding masculine idioms about femininity. The thrust of these accumulated observations is that men implicitly recognize females as reproductively superior to themselves. Now we must examine the other side of the coin: how men perceive themselves in their own idioms, and how they reconcile their own theories with the virulent all-male mythology of the Sambia secret cult.

CHAPTER SEVEN

Masculinity

Men are manly and they must be that way. Warfare demands it, hunting requires it, women expect it. This is the Sambia view: it is the consuming impetus of masculine ritual.

A man is the sum of his forceful vitality or strength (*jerungdu*) and masculine behaviors. Strength is a product of heritage and semen and successive initiations, so it is synonymous with masculinity itself. And from strength comes manhood. Manhood can be observed: in one's proud bearing, fighting prowess, abilities to trap game and, from sheer muscle, to clear wild tracts of rain forest. A manly male knows how to perform painful rituals on himself and how to handle his wife and estate. There is much male arrogance in this outlook. (After all, male genitals set a man a cut above women.) Yet manhood is not a sham, and the fate of the weakling tells why.

For instance, a man, sitting in his forest house alone with his wife, is caught unawares by three enemies. They break in the door and jump on him, but not before he takes up a stone club, bludgeons one of them, and wounds another. He is then overpowered and at great cost killed; his wife is abducted forever as sexual spoil to a distant village.

Tales like this remind men and boys alike that the substance of true men is a force to be reckoned with and the only one that really counts. More than ourselves, Sambia must be vigilant enough to confront brutal destruction as a daily possibility. Without a sophisticated technology—guns or steel armaments or electronic barriers—Sambia cannot hide from their foes or life's constant dangers. A man's only certain protection against this world is his own unbending masculinity. For Sambia, far more than for ourselves, manliness is viewed as an individual achievement. Both nature and nurture are crucial for attaining manhood as Sambia see it. Nature provides male genitals and potentials, but by itself the male body cannot stimulate the vital spark necessary for masculine development or cold-blooded courage.

Masculine competence is the successful outcome of a lifetime of scrupulous ritual acts and teachings. Boys have penises, but they lack the secondary sex traits associated with puberty: a muscular body, pubescent glans penis, and behind that, semen. Semen, alone, is believed to cement these developments; but, paradoxically, male physiology is believed unable to manufacture it endogenously. Only strict adherence to ritual technique can generate that biological maleness; homosexual inseminations are a vital part of the process. This is men's perspective about their secret cult.

Sambia therefore stress initiations and homosexual experiences as ritualized supplements that increase a boy's maleness and build up his masculinity. This chapter is about the beliefs and idioms that tell of this process. Our concern is with how this Weltanschauung finds its way into the collective initiations that culminate in biological puberty (third-stage initiation). (I shall mention the last three initiations, too, in regard to their ideological consequences for adult masculinity.)

Ritual Masculinization

The ritualized simulation of manhood is the job of collective initiation, and that is precisely how men see it. Male initiation is a rigidly structured form of inculcating manliness step by step. It begins when boys are seven to ten years old and, in the ensuing ten to fifteen years, effects the transition from childhood to adulthood. This native perspective is sufficiently novel and arcane to justify using a special concept to aid description and analysis of the data: *masculinization*.

I shall refer to the initiation processes of separating a boy from his mother, ceremonially treating his body, administering homosexual inseminations, and the attainment of biological puberty (including eventual reproductive competence) as *masculinization*.[1] Sambia themselves speak of rituals that "grow a boy," "making him into a man." The process is believed essential to biological maleness, although biology, behavior, and personality are all equally involved. When Sambia men talk about masculine growth—and the context (ritual or nonritual) is an essential factor constraining what is said—they have in mind a person's physiological maturation, (mental) attitudes, personality traits, and conduct, elements that they may or may not disentangle. This is not because Sambia cannot separate these components, but because they form a constellation in (see Read 1952) one's developmental history and present behavior. It is important to reemphasize, then, that my analytic distinction between sex traits (maleness) and gender (masculinity) is not made by Sambia in any simple or unambiguous form.

It is apparent that Sambia hold a radical, ritually induced conception of the nature and ontogeny of maleness and masculinity. Neither adult reproductive competence[2] (i.e., biological behaviors) nor masculine gender (e.g., subjective contents) are natural products. Instead, these (postnatal) attributes must be behaviorally created anew in the individual boys of each Sambia generation. Oral ingestion of semen by boys is essential to the growth of their manhood. Adult ritual procedures, then, simply help sustain the masculinization brought on by constant semen ingestion and careful preadolescent and postadolescent initiation.

Nevertheless, men believe the maintenance of (biological) maleness is arduous, its resulting masculinity tenuous. Erotic activities threaten mascu-

---

1. Webster's *Third New International Dictionary* defines *masculinize* thus: "to cause (a female) to take on male characters (as by the administration of an androgen)." (By permission. From Webster's Third New International Dictionary © 1976 by G. & C. Merriam Co., Publishers of the Merriam-Webster Dictionaries.) This biochemical concept is directly analogous to Sambia men's stated aims in initiating a boy and modifying his body and behavior. Semen, I think, can be viewed as an androgen in Sambia thought. A little is "fed" to women to make them *strong enough* to give birth and suckle, but enough is held back so that women do not become *too strong* (i.e., pseudomasculine). More is fed to boys to develop male secondary sex traits (see below). Indeed, the notion of *jerungdu* has, among its various connotations, the overarching premise that masculine life force and behavior rest on a fund of semen (analogous to the androgens, which we know can induce male secondary sex traits in otherwise biologically normal females [see Stoller 1977:16]).

2. It is not male sex assignment based on possessing male genitals that is at stake; it is rather the internal capacity of male physiology to produce a biological and behavioral drive to acquire secondary sex traits, and hence reproductive (sexual) competence in adulthood.

line vitality, and loss of semen (especially in heterosexual activities) is a constant worry of manhood. Menstrual blood contamination through coitus is another great fear. Semen loss and blood absorption are thus the twin dangers against which a man must protect himself or face certain death. These fears are, indeed, the greatest culturally learned elements that condition a man's consciousness of secret ritual and misogyny. These entailments seem to follow easily, perhaps inevitably, from the ritualized model of maleness, for what is felt to be externally constructed can also be torn down. The other side of the coin of Sambia masculine ideology thus involves a rampant dread of male atrophy: the imminent loss of semen held to sustain maleness artificially; and hence the ebbing of masculinity and of life itself. We shall need to examine men's idioms regarding all these phases—the building up, maintenance, and ebbing of masculinity— starting with infant caretaking, where we stopped in the last chapter.

Monjapi'u: From Nourishment to Stranglehold

I have already noted how men see the natural growth of boys and girls in different terms: both are closely tied to their mothers, but they differ greatly in physiology. A variety of things trouble men about this situation, especially its impact on boys' masculine development. What initially concerns them—birth pollution, surviving birth, and the sex assignment—is out of their hands since they are kept away from the birth hut. Men are not so powerless during the prolonged years of female *monjapi'u,* or nurturance, following birth. (Though they sometimes like to think so.) It is the effect of this bountiful mothering on the physiological and social growth of boys that bothers men most. Let us recapitulate the early events of parturition and then explore *monjapi'u* idioms. This review will help frame men's perceptions about why the roots of masculinity are initially sparse and endangered.

We saw how the fetus develops "centered within the blood" of the womb according to masculine idiom. The intimate expulsion of the infant from the mother's body is the greatest fact of birth. From the fountainhead of a woman's womb, whose blood can create life or take it, the infant emerges red and wet. The pollution trails mother and infant alike. Some of it is externally removed, some of it remains. For a girl this poses little risk. After all, the mother's blood provides the infant's blood circulatory system, and a girl also needs that smear of blood in her *tingu.* Yet where boys cannot exist without the former, they are imperiled by the latter. Indeed, their mothers' excess blood (inside them) soon enough "blocks their growth."

Babies must also survive birth; and here, too, there is a greater risk that boys will succumb. Infant mortality from natural complications and illness is, in general, rather high. There is, however, the additional possibility that boys could be put to death. A curious myth also alludes to male infanticide (see Appendix D), and I stress men's conviction that it occurred and was, no doubt, always a concern at the time of each birth. (There was no female infanticide, and male infanticide was apparently infrequent.) Now a discarded custom, infanticide raises difficult (and perhaps unanswerable) questions about Sambia family life.[3]

The birth of twins led to a different kind of infanticide, since this event was greeted as an evil omen. Sambia (like tribal peoples elsewhere) regard twins with repugnance, as human anatomical oddities or disfigurations are likewise treated.[4] One of the twins (there seems to have been no sex preference) was put to death. It matters most that one of the twins was said to be fathered by the (male) forest spirits. "Visited" in their sleep, some women dream of copulating with men, which dream figures are usually interpreted as forest spirits.[5] So a mother of twins could claim such a dream to be the "cause" of twins: the forest spirit impregnated her (after her husband) a second time. Women "haven't enough breast milk" to feed both offspring; so one lives at the expense of the other.

On top of these concerns looms a more dreadful question concerning sex assignment: hermaphroditism. Was the infant really a male? was its penis visible? (The problem of wrongly assigning a male with a tiny penis to the female sex does not seem to worry men as much.) Into women's

---

3. This topic was hard for me to investigate among women, who often feign ignorance (see Bulmer 1971:153–154). Does so unusual a "custom" as male infanticide suggest that historically Sambia females were in short supply? The present birth-rate sex ratio of 120/100 (male/female) supports this idea. So infant betrothal and wife-stealing, too, might have been consequences of this imbalance. But how are the spouses, interpersonally, in conflict here? And is men's alleged ignorance really that, or is it duplicity or deception? Men's comments hint that sexual antagonism is at work, yet case studies are needed to say more; see also Chapter 8.

4. Sambia have an aversion to biological anomalies in general, especially human ones: blindness, albinism, cleft palates, etc., are treated as nature's jokes and are regarded unsympathetically. Yet individuals strong enough to survive are accepted in certain ways, even if they never succeed in obtaining a spouse or full personhood.

5. What is interesting for descent theory is that the idea of spiritual impregnation is loathsome, and the spirit's "child" is the one put to death. This is a far cry from virgin birth (see Leach 1969), among Trobrianders, for example.

   Behind the notion of supernatural conception lies a more frequent but disturbing thought: men are never quite certain of the true *genitor* of an infant. Here is Weiyu: "When a woman gives birth, you think it is your own child, but we're [men] never sure. It may be made from the semen of another man, too. Later, when the child is born, the mother will again go to copulate with that man who committed adultery with her. Some women . . . get pregnant after only two or three months, some do not. An older woman [can trick and] say to you: 'Yes, I'm old, but if you give me semen, I'll change my skin and be young again.' Women sometimes rub their hair with blue mud [like that] to darken it; they put on a [young woman's] noseplug, a necklace around their necks. You'll think she's young and you'll want to copulate with her. That's how older women seduce us."

hands pass the infant and its socially intractable sex assignment, but women are less trusted with this decision than entrusted with it by the default of their men.

I was surprised at how men actually express concern to one another that their infant sons may be hermaphrodites. When men discuss the problems of masculinizing their tiny sons, their wives' pollution, the boys' "weakness" (pseudofemininity), and hermaphroditism all emerge as factors. Sometimes in quiet moments (Tali, for instance, communicated this to me) men express trepidation that an uninitiated son might "change into a girl." (They assume that the child's "penis" may be very small or dysfunctional; there was never any suggestion that a female with an oversized clitoris could be wrongly assigned to the male sex.) Men say, at first, that an infant issues from within its mother and virtually remains an appendage of her body. Because of postpartum taboos and the interpersonal distance between spouses, men are removed from the infant much of the time. Some fathers may not even see their children for the first six months of life and only infrequently thereafter during the first year.[6] Second, men point to the existence of living hermaphrodites in the local population as proof of how "males can change into females," even though most of these persons today, as in the past, were classified as "males" and socialized as such.[7] Possessed of ambiguous genitalia, hermaphrodites are both pitied and ridiculed, and like anomalous persons everywhere their mystery makes them suspect. Hence these "male-females" come closest to occupying a true pariah category among Sambia; and understandably, in a society where sexual differentiation counts most, men fear that their sons may suffer the same fate.

What part fantasy plays in such expressions is uncertain. Its presence is

---

6. I should underline the obvious: that great individual variation exists in this matter—a result of the complexities of marriage harmony, residence, the mother's health, the father's social obligations, and the presence of other wives or children. Recent behavioral observations, conducted in 1979, also indicate that some mothers actually use their babies as a psychological buffer between themselves and their husbands.

7. Most of these persons are probably pseudohermaphrodites, biologically abnormal males with undersized penises. Of a dozen or so instances of persons classified as hermaphrodites (only four of whom are now living), most were assigned to the male sex and were reared and initiated as men. (Whether there is a genetically higher proportion of pseudohermaphroditism in the Sambia population is uncertain, but it is a possibility, and one that might also provide another means of understanding why hermaphroditism is a focus of masculine idioms.) The phrase "males change into females" has recently become a popular idiom among men because of a well-known, unusual case (I know of no other living instance) of a Sambia who was reared as a female, married (as a woman), and was allegedly discovered by her husband to have had a penis (see below). Government medical officers verified this case at the time (c. 1975). This case may have resulted from a possibility that men do not themselves consider: a pseudohermaphrodite with an undersized penis at birth could be assigned to the female sex.

clearly felt, however, as the confusion and worry about sex transformation in the myth of male parthenogenesis tell (see Chapter 8).

This leads to the central issue of postpartum mothering, *monjapi'u*. The attitudes and beliefs that address this concept are necessary for understanding the polarity of masculinity and femininity no less than what should happen through ritual initiation. Although I draw on behavioral observations in the following, my material is anecdotal and illustrative, not complete, since my aim is mostly to set a background for idioms.

Monjapi'u is a verb whose connotations embrace our terms "to nurture" and "to mother": both the provision of nourishment and overall caretaking are implied. Two principles stand out: early infant *monjapi'u* is women's work; only later in life does the father directly participate. "A woman *monjapi'u* her child till it has finished drinking milk and is breast-weaned," idioms acknowledge. A "man *monjapi'u* his dog," by feeding it table scraps or keeping it sheltered. People, in general, "*monjapi'u* pigs." Yet it is, unequivocally, a mother's milk sustenance that "makes a child grow big" (*angootu yungooglu monjapi'u*; big, gets up, *monjapi'u*).

It is the mother whose presence is vital for the early months of life. The father, who must be absent at first, provides his wife with meat and eventually helps out; but woe to the infant who loses its mother. She alone provides life's sustenance. Here are two elders:

When a child is tiny it sleeps with mother. It drinks mother's milk. She looks after it. When the mother bears another child, it [the firstborn] must stop drinking milk. The mother gives over the child who sleeps with its father, and eats [only] solid foods. Sometimes an older child tries to suckle milk, but after a bit the mother scolds him until he stops expecting milk.

And here is another senior man: "The woman *monjapi'u* her infant by feeding it breast milk and [masticated] greens. Only the man [father] cares for the child when it can walk. . . . He gives it solid food and meat." Why this becomes a vital factor is that, unlike ourselves, Sambia children are breast-fed beyond the second, and even third, year of life. Indeed, some informants cite the suckling of their mothers' breasts as their earliest memory.[8]

The father takes only a small role in early *monjapi'u,* as custom prescribes. Postpartum taboos are the chief bulwark here. Not only are they powerful, they are stringently enforced by the sanctions of male ritual edict. Coitus must halt near the seventh month, else the "infant will be

---

8. For some months I remained highly skeptical of such reports from adolescent boys. When I began to check with adult men, I found them independently reporting a similar memory. Whether fact or not, these males—not all males, I should add—reported being breast-fed as their first recalled experience.

born weak if its [internal] growth is interfered with." Later sexual activity thus rests on the infant's healthy development. Fellatio only is thereafter permissible so long as both spouses agree (there is a greater element of choice on the woman's part, here, so long as she is lactating). But vaginal penetration is strictly off limits, and I think this taboo is grudgingly observed by most men.[9]

The common rule for the resumption of coitus stresses that the baby must have grown big enough to enable him or her to "walk and carry out an instruction from his father, such as fetching a bamboo pipe" (see Bulmer 1971:146 *n.* 1). (Most men eagerly await this event, for unless they have a second wife they have had no erotic outlet, except wet dreams, for twenty months or more.) During this period, men universally affirm that their wives hide the newborn. There are two reasons. Women themselves say they must hide the infants (especially the face) following birth lest men, and especially the husband, see them prematurely and "think them ugly, become displeased." There is a wife's care in this expression that differs from later antipathy to postpartum sexual activity. If this rule is broken the infant's skin is said to "turn black" and unsightly. Besides that, the mother herself can be harmed: her skin, too, turns black, and her milk can dry up. Such possibilities not only endanger mother and infant, then, but they threaten to undo the cords of adult maturity—familyhood—to which the parents are now firmly committed.

Here is the key context of male beliefs about man-stimulated "pollution" that can injure women and children. Men can stunt the infant's growth and damage their wives simply by prolonged interaction with, or looking at, the child. Compare this belief with its inverse: that initiates' growth will be stunted unless they absolutely avoid women. The contagious imagery—black skins, weakness—is similar and is, I think, linked with the parturition changes described in the last chapter. Precisely why remains uncertain, but clearly what is important is that mother and infant flourish and the woman's lactation not be interrupted.

This postpartum avoidance has another side too: erotic interest. All sex is forbidden; violations harm baby and wife, potentially bringing humiliation and shame to all. So the husband must take steps to ensure that he avoids situations that erotically excite him and thereby jeopardize the postpartum taboo. Ritual edict does this job by prohibiting men from actually watching their wives breast-feed. Sixth-stage initiates are told they must not "watch the breast-feeding, become aroused, and wish to copulate with their wives": physical distance is not only desirable but essential.

---

9. Breach of this taboo is considered disgustingly reprehensible for men, and I have twice observed men being scathingly castigated by elders (unusual for adult rituals) in fifth- and sixth-stage secret initiations for violating it.

Here a remarkable focal projection needs stating. At final initiation (when a father is taught about postpartum taboos) men are warned to withdraw from the breast-feeding situation; otherwise, by remaining, they risk being excited and desiring fellatio with their mates. As men explain it, this means that they could "imagine" (*pookwugu:* picture, imagery) their wives (like the baby) sucking their male member (like the breast the baby suckles). This is not mere fantasy: individual men report such experiences.[10]

This talk does not seem much like the rumblings of misogynist men who dislike women's bodies. But we should recall that Sambia, too, are complex humans: that the husband is sex-starved; and that it is not yet clear what meaning men attribute to the breast-feeding act set in the context of their wives' sexual abstinence. Nevertheless, this taboo is a valuable clue about the subjectivity of being masculine and fitting into male gender roles. Fellatio carries a different load of experiences than does coitus, and male dogma speaks of the nutritive functions of fellatio; so its meaning no doubt links it to breast-feeding. After *one's wife* becomes *a mother,* this subjectivity (consciously, subliminally) probably shifts: there is something so intimate, arousing, and dangerous about the breast-feeding act that walls must be built around it. Yet it is this very distance—hostility—that helps maintain the family unit socially, interpersonally, and erotically; it further removes the father from his child; and, in various ways, it contributes to a prolonged, luxuriant mother/infant symbiosis. (Note how this perspective suggests psychodynamic motivations, such as the possibility that the postpartum taboos defend a man against his envy of the infant's situation.) In the next chapter we shall see how the myth of parthenogenesis seems to anticipate this situation, providing a secret script for triumphing over it.

The father still has only intermittent, cool contacts with the child during its second year too. Babies are women's work: at this point men seldom hold the child or feed it. The child may occasionally sleep with his or her father, otherwise remaining attached to the mother. A woman is constantly with her children and carries the infant in her arms or a net bag. Even when the mother is traveling or gardening throughout the day, the child stays warm against its mother's skin by being suspended in a net bag over her back, cloaked underneath her bark cape. Rarely is a baby left unattended, and even more rarely do men take it. Men's attitudes about this division of labor are important and merit comment.

A couple may walk from the garden, the woman carrying a big bundle of

---

10. Little fragments of references to erotic interest, like this one, can be checked with informants and pursued in case studies. Weiyu, for instance, has mentioned this kind of excitement to me at least three times, twice spontaneously. Such data provide rich opportunities for linking customs with the psychodynamics of character structure.

firewood, a pile of food, and the woman complains. [Her husband may be carrying nothing.] The man [still] mustn't carry the baby. The man will say: "I've given you [wife] that child—it's something belonging to you. I've given it over to you." If a man carries a child, his skin will slacken, he can become weak, age quickly. You [father] won't produce another child. . . . So you mustn't carry a child for her; if she gets angry, that's her fault. And when a couple go to the forest, that time, too, you shouldn't carry the baby. The woman can cry, let her: "I've come to hunt possum—why should I carry your baby?" [Tali]

We must not discount the glorification of manliness at play in this arrogant posture toward wife and infant; and this is also why the quality of early *monjapi'u* attachment stems partially from men's chosen aloofness in purposely avoiding the infant. Masculinity is always being tested, or so men think.

It is significant that the baby receives no childhood name until the end of the first year.[11] Until then, personal pronouns are used in speaking or referring to the infant. (Even after bestowing a name, Sambia still use personal pronouns more commonly, I believe, than do many American mothers.) Women say they are reluctant to name an infant earlier lest they grow so attached to it that its untimely death would make them "cry too much." (The high rate of infant mortality lends credence to this affective idiom.) The child, until then, is regarded as little more than an appendage of the mother's body. The bestowal of a childhood name thus recognizes the increasing mobility, or separateness, of the infant from skin contact with the body from which it emerged.

The infant's soul (*koogu*) is thought to be tangibly present in the infant's body at this time, as evidenced by its increasing capacity to verbalize and reason. Furthermore, the soul is believed to arise from within the womb while the infant is still an embryo. It thereafter follows the healthy baby into childhood and adulthood. This, a most remarkable acceptance of maternal-bonding effects on spiritual essence, is oddly at variance with the male-dominated patrilineal institutions and ties of descent that govern social behavior.[12]

---

11. Children have two names, an adult name conferred on them at the birth-house ceremony by the mother's sponsor, and this other (later-bequeathed) childhood name. Oddly enough, whereas boys lose their childhood name at first initiation, taking private age-mate names, some of them also get another, new adult name at the adult name-bestowing ceremony, toward the end of that initiation. Some boys do keep the "official" adult name conferred at birth, however; but the childhood name (and name song) is taboo for both girls and boys: that piece of early identity should be forgotten, and it is a violent insult to call a man by his childhood name. Women receive their adult names and lose their childhood names much later in life—at the menarche.

12. This belief implicitly recognizes how the soul is tied to the sentiments of social bonds: the

The infant continues to take all nourishment from its mother well into the second, and sometimes third, year of life. Breast milk remains the baby's key source of food and "strength." Daily gardening chores interfere with feeding, but this is made up for in the ready access the child has to the mother's breast at night. The child continues to sleep with her. Gradually she begins to feed the infant more solid foods. At first this type of feeding occurs mouth to mouth: the mother masticates food and feeds it directly into the infant's mouth from her own.[13] Whereas this masticated food is polluting to the child, milk is not at all (see Tuzin 1980: Chapter 1). Later, the child can feed itself. Yet it still gets the breast: women sometimes use it as a pacifier,[14] so men cannot help noticing how the child is too dependent on the mother and her breast.

Children remain strongly attached to their mothers after the postpartum taboos halt, and in most respects it is she who remains their primary caretaker. It is she from whom they still seek most food, solace, and companionship. Indeed, even with older toddlers, men feel it is unmanly for the father to show excessive interest in any children, including his own. The mother (and other women) handle toilet training. But there is little emphasis on bowel control, and infants are not discouraged until later from eliminating almost anywhere. (Here is another reason why men are reluctant to handle the child: they fear contamination from its urine or feces, in addition to the general stigma of birth pollution and feminine contact.) Most days, after children are older and walking, they follow their mother (who may or may not be joined by her husband) to the garden. Girls are given gardening responsibilities early. Boys may play alone or with other boys and girls; and they may as well do so since they are not of much help in doing chores until much later. So boys have an especially carefree and sheltered existence in those early years; that is, in fact, how their enviable state is viewed by men, who look back without any expectation of ever again being so much at ease.

This pattern persists till the third or (occasionally) fourth year. A child continues to have relatively free access to its mother and her breast until coitus resumes.[15]

---

child's "heart" (in our Western sense of emotional commitment) really belongs to its mother, whence came its "soul."

13. Rarely do men do this. Only once have I observed a man do it, and that was Nilutwo, whom I have already characterized (in Chapter 6) as unusual.

14. Marie Reay (personal communication) tells me that Kuma mothers (of the Western Highlands) enjoy breast-feeding and say they gain satisfaction from it. She has observed infants refuse and spit out the breast, only to have the mother force it back into the child's mouth.

15. Even afterwards, children cry for the breast when frightened. A few months after the rustic

Toilet training finally emerges through self-control and, if need be (as with weaning), shaming and slapped hands. Both boys and girls sleep with their fathers occasionally. But men—and here again it is careless to speak too broadly—tend to become reluctant about their growing sons sleeping close by them as they mature. For a year or two after weaning this is permitted; but the older a boy is, the more uncomfortable men become. The ostensible reason is linked to ritual belief: frequently sleeping next to men or boys, especially male children,[16] risks the loss of one's spirit familiars. A father is most vulnerable to his sons: they share in the same "substance" (semen), so the familiars may wish to "escape" into his sons' handsomer bodies. Most girls also sleep separate from but near their mothers after they are three or four years of age. By the age of five, then, girls seldom sleep with their fathers, and boys tend to sleep in the male space near their father but not in close contact with him.

Exceptionally close maternal attachment, prolonged orality, and physical and psychological distance from one's father are, therefore, key factors in early Sambia socialization.

In spite of this deliberately distanced beginning, most men are affectionate toward their older children, and they take a special pride in their sons. There is a peculiar *idealism* in this attitude toward boys: it is oddly one-sided (favoring sons, not daughters), oddly sentimentalized (compared to other masculine attitudes toward child-rearing), predictably defensive (for this and the reasons noted below), and also understandable.

This point informs many of the idioms concerning ritual initiation and therefore deserves to be explored in some detail. Here is Weiyu, somewhat emotional but to the point. His remarks were in answer to my question about the value of children but typify a common masculine attitude.

> We think that it's good to have children. Who can inherit my land? Who'll get my *belaaptu* [magic]? Who can manage your forest land . . . your pandanus? Women, no! She's [sic] nothing! . . . But your son! He's the same as the very cordylines [foundations] of the hamlet. He'll think well of you, he won't forget you. . . . If you die, too, he'll make good for you; he'll wrap carefully your bark cape, make a good bed [grave] for you.[17] We're pleased with boys like that.

---

medical-aid post was opened in the Sambia Valley (1976), I saw a boy, about five years of age, scream from fear of an injection. He instantly took to his mother's breast, sucking defensively, which she permitted.

16. Remember that men and women never sleep close together. Some initiates become reluctant as they get older to sleep near other initiates or men (the exception being their age-mates, but even this becomes inappropriate in adolescence). Here there is an unquestionable element of erotic tension.

17. Nowadays, government health officials require Sambia to bury their dead, whereas tradition-

But girls, they can go to another place. You won't be too pleased with her. When you die, your cousins, brothers, they'll put you on top [of funeral piles]. And your son, he won't work, he'll feel truly sorry for you, his papa. . . . Not so with women! Men say to their wives, when arguing: "You won't die first, I will! You'll pretend to wail for me and then get another man." But he [boy] will wail, wail . . . and on and on. He can cry at the burial ground; they'll bury you; and he'll cry into the night![18] He can come back to the house and cry more. He can spend a long time [wailing] . . . and at the funeral . . . all the same . . . he can hear the cry of the bull roarer, think of you, and cry more. But the women—no: they can fake it, pretend, only. . . . They can pretend to cry only.

In this long statement we see how children bear the fruits of manliness, even after death. Through his wife, his children, a man defies mortality. But whereas wife and daughters are devalued, a son epitomizes the best and most affectionate person who cares for one. A wife is a woman; a daughter is still only a woman. A boy is a son and comrade and ally. An essential sameness between them binds a son to a man: their masculinity.

Here is the crux of men's conscious, sentimental idealism in regard to their sons. Men let their wives and women rear their sons. But at three and four and five years of age there is a change: a father should begin to spend more time with his son. He should teach, direct, and push him, funneling his experiences in ways that separate mother and son and masculinize the boy. However weak this trend may be in certain families, its roots are still there. Some of it is compensation or reaction, I think: the father reacts to the luxuriant attachment between mother and child after the fact. Some mothers, too, no doubt foster this separation from the very start by rewarding masculinity in their boy's behavior. All of these responses make a difference in the boy; but all of them come about slowly, with perhaps a little too much difficulty, and a little too late. Men want ideal sons; that takes aggressive training and tough discipline, and something more: years of mastering experiences that can seductively create the idealized masculinity of a warrior. Ritual initiation provides all of these. A father cannot be close to his son in those early years, and after initiation their sense of filial closeness can never be the same as in childhood. Yet at least ritual initiation guarantees unspoken bonds between father and son through an ideally shared ritual experience.

---

ally the corpse was left atop funeral tiers until only a skeleton remained. Now the corpse is wrapped in a new bark cape for burial.

18. Sambia truly fear the burial ground, especially at night when the dreadful ghost can emerge. Weiyu suggests that the bereaved son is so overcome by grief that he is beside himself and transcends this fear because of authentic feelings of sorrow for his father.

The *kwulai'u,* then, is seen as a person with a penis who is polluted and stunted and not manly. He is still polluted from the womb. His mother has fed him (mouth to mouth), and he has ingested her food and saliva. He has been constantly in touch with the contaminated skin of her breast and whole body. He is entirely too dependent on her for protection and warmth; her body remains too much of a haven for him. There is more than a hint of femininity about him; he even wears the same type of grass apron as females. He is puny; undisciplined; openly bawls and throws tantrums when he does not get what he wants. At such times men are openly hostile to boys, taunting them till they cry, telling them to "go back to their mothers where they belong." A boy is flagrantly contemptuous of both parents and sasses them. He takes food without asking and provides nothing in the way of hunting or gardening. He is dreadfully useless in defense of the hamlet. Men cannot forget that their sons are carriers of feminine pollution; they must be carefully watched lest they accidentally pollute a man, his weapons, or food. They are too contaminated to have free access even to the public side of the clubhouse. And they are, of course, kept ignorant of cult secrets and chased away when ritual is performed. Such considerations come to mind when men discuss the need to initiate their sons. Another thought concerns them all and is the most salient, for masculinization is literally a matter of life and death.

A boy's body has female contaminants inside it that not only stymie his physical development but, if not removed, will weaken and eventually kill him. His body is definitely male: he has male genitals and his *tingu* contains no blood, nor will it activate. Yet for boys to reach puberty and manliness requires semen. Milk vitally "nurtures the boy"; sweet potatoes and other "female" foods provide his "stomach nourishment." They become only feces, however, not semen. Female development stems from possessing a menstrual blood organ and blood. Women's own bodies internally produce the menarche, the watershed of reproductive maturity. No comparable mechanism is active in boys to stimulate their biological secondary sex traits. Only semen can do that; only men have semen; boys have none.

What is left to do, then, but initiate boys and thereby masculinize them? Only through initiation can men collectively and immediately put a halt to the stultifying effects of *monjapi'u* mothering upon their sons. The mother's blood and womb and care, which gave life to and nourished the lad, finally thwart the growth of maleness. Her care turns into a stranglehold that threatens his very existence. To undo these feminizing effects, he must be drastically detached from women and ritually treated. He must thereafter avoid their engulfing contagion. The feminizing effects are turned back and are replaced by the idealized masculine behaviors of initiation that remold the maleness kindled in the mother's shadow.

Initiation and Male Ontogeny

A boy's body is perceived as an open vessel highly susceptible to environmental influence. Mother is the primary influence; father is a weak second. Nothing innate to male biology seems to resist or repel the feminizing effects of women. Girls are not at risk;[19] they simply succumb to their mothers' influence and the drives of their natural biology. They become feminine like their mothers. Boys must be separated from women. Still, separation, in itself, is not sufficient for attaining adult masculine competence. Boys must be wiped clean[20] of female contaminants—and by characteristically painful means. Pain and trauma thus become a sign of the hard-won path to manhood required by the ritual cult. Insemination can then follow but not come before; otherwise it goes for naught. Through successive initiations, steps must be taken that maintain the precious growing bud of manliness in the boy, since he (like men) forever remains vulnerable to feminine contamination and, hence, regression to a premasculinized state of being, and death. Against this danger a defense is needed; masculine rituals and taboos, forced on boys, provide just that.

It is, then, this cultural orchestration of male rituals, and the bodily changes they are thought to induce, that will serve as our focus. To comprehend the long-range "biological" effects, we must first examine how Sambia view male physiology.

The Kereku-Kereku. Three organs are primary: the semen organ, semen feeder ducts, and the penis. Together with semen, their governor, they form a physiological system. First to the nerve center—the semen organ.

All males possess a functional semen organ (*kereku-kereku*).[21] Lower mammals, too, such as dogs and pigs, have it (see also Newman 1962:134; Wagner 1972:40). Females are also said to contain the semen organ, but its form and function differ from that of males. (We saw how some men believe this organ in women can hold vaginal fluid.) It will be helpful to recall a final statement from Weiyu depicting an image of fetal development.

> Semen makes the infant, completely: bone, skin, brain [including the spinal column]. . . . One thing only—blood—your momma gives to you. Momma gives you blood; [but] everything else, only semen makes. The woman is filled up with blood—the *tingu* makes it and fills it up.

---

19. This is not quite an accurate rendition of the masculine view, for prolonged maternal *monjapi'u* also bestows the feminine personality traits of irrationality, suggestibility, and cowardice that men associate with women (see below).

20. This is an apt, literal translation of what purificatory rituals actually attempt.

21. A homonym for the immature pandanus nut: "It's just the same word, that's all," Tali said.

Blood and semen have complementary roles in intrauterine development. Semen is the more substantial component, although blood internally obscures it by "filling up" females' (and by implication, males') insides.

The male semen organ is initially "solid and dry" and only gradually alters after the ingestion of semen. Boys do not inherit semen from their fathers or mothers: their tissue is constructed from semen but otherwise contains none. (By contrast, recall how the *tingu,* initially holding only a smear of blood, gradually grows, engorged by its own blood, which also fills up the womb.) The immature semen organ is, ironically, called *kereku-kereku jerungdu,* "hard semen organ," meaning that its hardness comes from emptiness. The semen organ is only a container. It cannot, by itself, manufacture sperm, not in childhood, not in adulthood. A male semen organ only accumulates what semen is swallowed. Orally ingested semen does modify the organ's form. A pubescent semen organ is called *kereku-kereku imenyu* (where *imenyu* is a qualitative adjective denoting softness or pliability); and orally ingested sperm causes this condition by "opening" and swelling the organ from inside.

Women's semen organs are said to be filled by blood or vaginal fluid or both, not semen. The male *tingu,* by contrast, is simply inoperative: "Of you and me [men] too—we have a *tingu.* But it is *hard* [emphasis] . . . and women also have got a *kereku-kereku* . . . but theirs is filled with vaginal fluid." Tali sometimes says this and sometimes argues that the invisible female semen organ holds only blood; but in either case, it contains only female fluids.

Characteristically, as this viewpoint holds, even the male semen organ, depository of that vital fluid, becomes infected and taken over by feminine substances in women. The boy's semen organ, however, is hard and empty, as is his *tingu* organ. No semen or maleness there; so manhood is not possible. Only oral insemination can make these developments a reality.

How this development occurs is no mystery to Sambia. The semen organ is joined by "feeder tubes" to the mouth, navel, and penis. There are two such tubes. One, the esophagus, is shared by all humans.[22] Like food and water, semen can be swallowed; but unlike those substances, it

---

22. As I noted above, the esophagus transports semen in both women and boys, but to different places. Some (perhaps most) swallowed semen is siphoned off by the "breast ducts" (*aam-wilu* or *aamoonaalyi-oolu*) of women and converted into milk before it reaches the stomach or womb. Slight amounts of it may get into a woman's womb; none of it goes to her semen organ since she lacks the internal system of tubes associated with a penis. This is consistent with the view that orally ingested semen goes to "strengthen" a woman or provide milk, while semen "fed" into the vagina goes into the womb for fetal growth. Boys lack a vulva, birth canal, and womb; their ingested semen goes first to "strengthen" and then, as need be, into the liquid pool accumulating in the semen organ.

is thought to be funneled undiluted straight into the semen organ. The other feeder tube only males possess. This organ, the "semen tube" (*kweikoonbooku bwoot-oolu:* semen; *bwoot/bwutu,* navel; *oolu,* rope), "directly connects the navel with the penis and testes," and thus with the semen organ. The tubes therefore extend from that organ (in the upper abdominal region) upwards to the navel, and downwards to the stem of the penis. (Another, separate organ, the "urine tube" [*so-wilu*], connects the bladder [*soomdu*] with the urethra [*so-pootu*].[23]) Tali said this: "Both the semen tube and urine tube are joined at the base of the penis, so semen is ejaculated through the urine tube during intercourse."[24] In boys, all these semen-related tubes and organs are thought to be "closed, hard, and dry" at birth, and into childhood, until fellatio activities.

The prepubescent penis is sexually unimportant and reproductively immature, for the boy's body lacks semen. That penis is puny, like a "little leech"; it lacks the mature glans penis (*nungundeiyu*) and foreskin, masculine signs greatly stressed by Sambia. Men and initiates jokingly refer to the adult glans penis as that "ugly nose," and that "face within the penis [pubic] hair"; such idioms characteristically distinguish the (sexually) immature from the mature male. Semen has the biological power to change this immaturity. Here is Weiyu.

> Now when we [males] drink the milk of a man or that of a tree it goes down and *wolu-munjulupi* [paints] the *kereku-kereku*. It paints it and it [semen organ] comes up white. And so it makes *kweikoonbooku* [semen]. The penis [alone] contains nothing . . . it remains empty. But only the tube—it joins the *kweikoonbooku-oolu* and penis—it shakes it, and it expels semen [at ejaculation].

To reach this point of having a potent ejaculation requires years of semen ingestion and appropriate ritual treatment. What matters, to sum up, is that this result is not natural or inevitable, as is the push into female sexual maturity. Instead it derives from strict adherence to the male cult's formula. But I have gotten ahead of myself; more material is still needed to understand the careful steps that lead to this moment.

Pweiyu. Beginning with the native term *pweiyu*—ritual—and its connotations, we can decipher the idiomatic significance of initiation in the male life cycle. Sambia notions about ritual stress both the collectivity of large

---

23. Sambia recognize the bladder but do not distinguish the kidneys.
24. Sometimes men draw attention to the prominent blood vein (*moonerut-oolu*) on the underside of the penis. For instance, Weiyu said: "It fastens the speech pathway: when you laugh or talk or are scared, you can feel it near your testes." The testes have no reproductive function as Sambia see it; men feel they are vital, however, and if harmed, one "can die."

groups of men *doing it* and the initiates' pain or physical experience in *undergoing it.*

Pweiyu refers to "collective group initiation" or *mokeiyu.* These are grand events that assemble the biggest throngs of people in Sambia life. *Pweiyu* collective initiations are organized by and for men according to their calendar. *Pweiyu* means large groups of men, festive, dramatic excitement, and as much as that, reexperiencing the ostentatious mythology of stampeding manliness: that men are society's movers—warriors strong and proud—and that men can get grand things done.

The individual-centered *pweiyu,* however, have a different sense, less crowded and public. These initiations are inspired by the privileges they bestow. These rituals from the time of marriage, hinge on female life crises, as we saw. Their experience is restricted and out of the public eye; cult secrets are transmitted to initiates who suffer and enjoy their mysterious knowledge and ceremony.

The ideals of collective *pweiyu* experience stress the cleansing, radical resocialization, and psychological impact of its effects on boys. Here men's aim is for ritual to exercise "health-sustaining" constraints on the novices. One sense of the word, for instance (as Tali taught me), is drawn from the common verb *pweiyu,* meaning "to bind or wrap." When Tali first mentioned this, he said *pweiyu* was like "tying something up inside of something else." He illustrated as he spoke, which is his habit, pointing out how men "wrap game inside leaves and then *pweiyu* it with vines," securing parcels. As he spoke he made a wrapping motion with his hands as if to entwine invisible yarn around his fingers. Weeks later he demonstrated how the pandanus nut pod is also a type of *pweiyu* whose nuts are "bound" to a seed cluster not easily broken apart. Speaking of how ritual works, therefore, men distinguish two experiential modes: learning through verbal teaching (*imbwash*), and learning through looking (*woondoowalyu*). (This dichotomy seems to occur widely; see Spiro 1968b.)

Teaching is an important part of Sambia ritual, and it operates by means of conventionalized ritual "stories" (*pweiyu koongundu,* where *koongundu* means talk, teaching, and moral lesson) whose norms bind thought (*koontu pweiyu,* thought restricted).[25] Through these teachings boys are verbally taught (*imbwash*) masculine values, taboos, and meanings (e.g., attributed to ritual and dream images) cloaked with a fabric of conventionalized rights and duties. Each grade of initiation subsumes particular instructions of both a public and a secret kind. Seniors who teach at initiations invariably raise their voices. They physically poke, push, or slap

---

25. Inge Riebe (personal communication) has also noted that the Karam have a similar idea: they contrast ordinary "unrestricted thought" with the "restricted" thought of ritual contexts.

boys, to frighten and excite them, rhetorically demanding: "Listen! Mind our words! Is your ear path blocked by stones that you act the way you do!" Thus boys are deliberately frightened and made distraught, setting the right mood for ritual instruction.[26]

It is the other form of ritual experience, learning (emulating) by observation, that will mostly concern us here. Elders stress that initiates are like "babies"; they cannot think or recollect clearly, follow orders, or observe rules. They are not masculine in that way. The initiate must learn this manner by observing the customary ways of initiation.[27] Specifically, we shall focus on the cultural manifestations of rituals designed to coordinate with changes in masculine ontogeny. Ritual makes use of physical, instrumental routines in restricting, cleansing, and ingesting things; and the ritual behaviors funnel subjective attachments to conventions, persons, and natural species.

These ritual routines must be broadly classified—a simple enough task, it would seem, that in fact is far from straightforward. Indeed, to establish such a classification is tantamount to a functional description of ritual beliefs and actions. This outline will thus serve as our necessary road map for the following sketch of ritualized masculinization. Please note, however, that this will be merely a convenient *modus operandi,* an imaginary paramorph (Harré and Secord 1972) for model-building, not a point-by-point correspondence with the actual ritual behavior or its psychological experience.

Modes of Ritual Experience

Five types of ritual can be delineated in Sambia initiation. They occur at different stages of male development, with distinct experiential goals and behavioral effects. We can label them as follows: (1) stretching rites; (2) egestive rites; (3) ingestive rites or taboos; (4) insertive rites or avoidance taboos; and (5) confirmatory rites. These ritualized behaviors also undergo transformations as males mature. The simplest rites (type 1) are dropped; the ideological aspects conveyed in the teachings (types 2, 3, and 4) become more sophisticated and secret; more emphasis is placed on one's private experience; and, by adulthood, ritual procedures are no

---

26. Elsewhere I describe the interaction of ritual belief, radical cognitive resocialization, and initiation behavior. Sambia believe that consciousness is directly linked to hearing and speech; their theory of awareness is strongly sociocentric. For instance, madness (unlike self-induced shamanistic trance; see Herdt 1977) is viewed as a stoppage in the ears that distorts effective hearing and thinking.

27. Custom (*pasindu*) is the expected routines of tradition known to stem from the thoughts and dreams of ancestors. For example, men say how Numboolyu, their ancestor, originated dreams and passed them on to his children, men's "fathers" (see Chapter 8).

longer forcibly induced by others, but rather are voluntarily (as a means of conscious self-regulation) performed on oneself.

It is fundamental to the male ethos that men invariably attend to the concrete transactions between the body and ritual techniques or paraphernalia. The body is treated as a vessel: the impact of ritual on body functioning and development is men's overwhelming concern. Like a microcosmic stage, Sambia ritual scoops up and encloses past experience, sheds past influences, and sets a course of future actions. Instead of stressing this body function, Sambia might have stressed ritual symbols, like an art form, detached from the superseding body experience. Or they might have placed stress on the intellectual experience of ritual; but they do not.[28] Like most Highlanders (see Newman 1964, for example), Sambia attend to the practicalities of life, and this has its "positive" and "negative" poles. The body, and housed within it one's thought and soul, is defended by ritual techniques against alien contaminants and the death they bring. Yet these measures also represent an affirmation: the body is stimulated, built up, and freed of its shackles. In simplest terms, then, masculine ritual is not only a culturally constituted defense mechanism (Spiro 1965), it also has a life-enhancing quality. That is how men see initiation ritual, and much conceptual mileage can be gained from this viewpoint; so I shall outline it, hazarding a partial interpretation later.

Stretching Rites. This simple ritual mode, a thrashing technique, occurs early, in first- and second-stage initiations. Sticks, switches, or bristly objects (according to the particular ritual, of which there are four) are thrashed or rubbed against the group of boys' bodies. The aim is to "open up" or "stretch" (*perulyapi*) the initiate's skin surface. The uninitiated boy's skin is thus perforated and may even bleed; skin flakes are also rubbed away. Sweat and the fine down of the boy's cheeks, arms, and legs are said to be removed. With these substances goes the external contamination of women. The boy must literally "change skins"; this change is essential for the biological acquisition of a manly facial and bodily appearance. These things become key signs demarcating handsome initiates from the "ugly, puny, black-faced" *kwulai'u* who continue to live in their mothers' shadow.

---

28. Precisely why there is this experiential stress on the body and its boundaries is unclear, but the answer to this question deserves attention. Here is where I think we should question the neo-Durkheimian (see Douglas 1966, 1975) poetry about "the body being a symbol of society." From men's concerns and expectations is constituted a collage of body rituals *cum* "symbolic" behaviors that, if one wished to do so, could be elaborated and frozen as but one moment in the grand sweep of a society's symbolic code. But that analysis would much distort the data (especially the Sambia perspective) and, through its grandness, trivialize the actual experience and behavior of individuals.

Stretching rites are an initial stimulus to spur masculinization. Both external purification and physical growth are their explicit goals. They are crude and a bit dangerous, however; the lads must be carried on the backs of their ritual sponsors, and the boy can be injured or his soul so "frightened" from the beating that it might attempt to escape from him. Surviving these challenges is an accomplishment. As boys get bigger, it also becomes difficult to hoist them on the sponsors' backs. They are somewhat more unmanageable. So stretching rites are abandoned after second-stage initiation, and at any rate their job has been accomplished: to remove external pollutants and thereby pave the way for inside changes.

Egestive Rites. It is internal maleness that is most affected by the ontogenetically early egestive rites. The focus is on expurgating the body innards to remove internal, essentially "foreign" material believed acquired through intimate, prolonged contact with one's mother (and other females). Two techniques are used: cane-swallowing, to induce vomiting and defecation, and nose-bleeding, to remove contaminated blood. Both rites are introduced in first-stage initiation; they are secret, and are performed collectively in the forest before teaching about the sacred flutes and homosexual activities. Cane-swallowing has been abandoned (c. 1964), and I have never seen it performed.[29] Nose-bleeding, however, along with homosexual fellatio, still remains the bedrock of first-stage initiation.

Cane-swallowing differed from nose-bleeding in several respects. Cane-swallowing was performed only at first-stage initiation: men considered it excessively dangerous, and one experience was "enough" to do its job.[30] Nose-bleeding is performed subsequently, in third-, fifth-, and sixth-stage initiations. Its ostensible purificatory aspect—to eliminate menstrual blood pollution—remains important throughout all those ritual performances. Its secret teachings change, becoming more convoluted, and eventually entail the pollution of vaginal intercourse with one's wife. (First-stage novices know nothing of that later meaning or its experience.) Nose-bleeding becomes one of a handful of techniques that must be included in an individual man's repertoire of purificatory rituals. Once married and engaging in coitus, men assume personal responsibility for voluntarily

29. Cane-swallowing was last performed on Weiyu's age set (c. 1963–1964). It was abandoned without external coercion. Men say they took it upon themselves to give it up because it was "bad" and "too painful." But why they abandoned this rite and no others remains uncertain.

30. This may be a clue to why nose-bleeding was not also abandoned. The canes had to penetrate a foot and more inside, whereas the nose-bleeding grasses penetrate only a few inches, and one can clearly follow them and manage them since they are shorter. Eliminating blood and stressing its relationship to interaction with polluting females seem more vital than food pollution and eliminating feces, which are still eliminated whether or not one swallows canes.

nose-bleeding themselves, in secret, following each of their wives' monthly periods. Masculine health depends on this individual ritualized self-regulation.[31] What is of most interest, for the moment, is the purely egestive function of these two rites in the collective initiation ceremonies.

Cane-swallowing (*wusaam-menyereiku:* sweet potato/food; elimination) was a necessary prerequisite for masculinization. Two things needed doing. Tali said: "This is for removing the food belonging to the mother; you must expel the feces produced by that food quickly." The canes are said to have "pushed the food" into the "bottom stomach near the anus." From there it is ejected through the large intestine (*letn'dei-oolu*). Likewise, the "bad talk," actually "ingested" from contact with one's mother, is also "pushed out with the food." Through elimination, a boy egests "female food" and his mother's nagging reprimands and insults that stultify and "block his growth." This is a concrete thought. It is also worth noting that idioms of defecating and defecation control vividly impinge on masculine autonomy and a man's sense of being an effective person. For instance, when a man is angry and expostulating, his fellows may joke: "Don't talk so strong or your feces tube may pop outside!" This is said to humor him, to calm him and restore his *normal* demeanor.

Cane-swallowing had as its aim, then, physical elimination, and (less commonly) vomiting. But this emphasis on physiological egestion clearly has a subjective component too. Out with the feces pass the depreciating "words" of the mother to whom the boy was subordinated.[32]

Nose-bleeding (*chemboo-loruptu:* nose; *loropina,* a verb for physical cleansing and expulsion) is nowadays the single most painful ritual act. It is secret; so when first performed on boys by surprise, it turns into a forcible, violent assault that is probably close to authentic physical and psychological trauma (see Read 1965:128–133). The technique is simple: stiff, sharp grasses are thrust up the nose until blood flows. Men always perceptually focus on the actual blood flow, which they prefer in abundance. In first- and third-stage initiations, each novice is nose-bled in turn; and as blood flows from each boy in sequence, men greet the expurgation

---

31. By contrast, cane-swallowing elsewhere in the Eastern Highlands (see Berndt 1965:84; Salisbury 1965:62) apparently takes the place of continuous, life-preserving, nose-bleeding purification rites among Sambia. Furthermore, Sambia do not practice any other form of ritualized bloodletting, as from the penis (J. Whiting 1941; Tuzin 1980), the arms (Meigs 1976), or the back (Bateson 1958).

32. It is also worth underlining the explicit association, here, between defecation and masculine behavior. I think these idioms express the concern that a man subjectively sense himself as a separate, effective person distinct from his mother or father, or the active memories and fantasies of them that live on inside him. What we should then want to know, from individuals, is the meaning attached to these eliminative functions in a man's perceptions of himself, his fellows, parents, and wife.

with a collective war cry[33] (unlike what is done in any other collective ritual focused on body treatment). In *moku* initiation nose-bleeding symbolism is complex and esoteric. (For instance, hidden, but in close proximity to the group, some men also blow flutes, which have not yet been shown to boys when this event is held midway during the initiation. Hearing the flutes certainly changes the meaning of the ritual experience.) For the present let us survey the idioms concerning nose-bleeding as they are conveyed to boys during its teaching.

Three elements are emphasized, in this order: being punished for insubordination; removing the "bad talk" and "bad blood" of one's mother; and learning not to fear the spilling of blood during warfare. At the 1975 *moku* initiations I observed, elders first demanded that boys obey orders and thereby "act like men." Initiates were instructed always to be hospitable and offer water to men visiting their hamlets (or offer to fetch it). Then an elder reprimanded the novices, saying that when they were children they made "bad talk," mocking old initiates. He further asserted that if the boys remained defiant and disregarded their elders' instructions to fetch water or betel nut, they would be nose-bled again. For those acts, he continued, "We now pay you back."

Here we see clearly the use of nose-bleeding as a powerful means of coercing the unruly and selfish boys into a subordinate position.

Next comes the purificatory element of nose-bleeding. Like cane-swallowing, bloodletting is a necessarily painful way of getting rid of inner maternal influences. Here we can again draw on ritual rhetoric.

You novices have been with your mothers. They have said "bad words" to you. Their talk has entered your noses and prevented you from growing big. Your skins are no good. Now you can grow and look nice; we have helped you to do this.

Ritual teachings, besides terrorizing boys, thus turn the significance of painful nose-bleeding back on the boys' own bodies in the next instant. Of both cane-swallowing and nose-bleeding Tali said this: "Bad talk [of women] enters the nose; it goes inside our noses. Our blood belongs to *that* [bad talk]. Your mother curses you; you swallow the two of them [saliva and words]; so it [contaminated saliva] then stays in your stomach and nose."[34] Men are doing boys a favor: that is the drift of masculine

---

33. This collective sound is called *aambi'u-pweiyu* or "song ritual," as distinct from *aambi'u-mulu,* "song fight," for war, but the sounds are quite similar. In both cases, the cry is an expression of triumph at some conquest; here, over women's control of boys, and at men's control of the novices themselves.

34. Men say they do not punish children. They say that women punish them and particularly scold and curse boys more. This scolding is believed to retard physical development in

idiom. The surprise and trauma of the act are directed at the boys' contaminated innards, which, alas, must be violently penetrated to cleanse
them.

Proof of this need is what happens to women, who do not (as far as men
know) nose-bleed themselves. Boys and girls alike are affected by maternal *monjapi'u*. This lack of nose-bleeding is the chief reason why women,
unlike men, are so thickheaded. Tali notes: "It [bad talk] goes inside the
noses of women. [So] women don't have good thinking. They don't
remove blood, and their thought is blocked up." This comment alleges
that although the mother's blood does not retard girls' *physical* growth,
it does thwart their powers of reasoning.

It is, however, a matter of urgent concern that the mother's contaminated blood be removed from boys; otherwise male biological development
is impeded. Boys are screamed at for being "weak and sickly." Without
nose-bleeding, "their faces will remain like ashes," dull, unmanly. The
experiential effects of nose-bleeding, moreover, assume greater psychological force when we understand that, for Sambia, the nose is constantly
stressed in relation to the genitals in the things that count: personal appearance, sexual attractiveness, and ritual adornments (a subject to which I
return below). Inside, there are said to be active, negative female materials at work: mother's blood, "dirty food," and "bad talk," which keep
one's face "black like ashes."

The sense of these negative female agents in male ontogeny should be
clear enough now. They have stymied the blood and the internal and
external growth dependent on blood. Males, unlike females (who possess
the active *tingu* organ), have no abundance of blood; nor do they possess
a physiological mechanism, such as the *tingu,* to stimulate the blood circulation needed for pushing maturation. (This stimulation, as described
above, is what men believe the *tingu* does in precipitating female maturity
and the menarche.) So male ritual simulates these changes, through nose-
bleeding, substituting other substances, as we shall see, for the lost contaminated materials.

Finally, nose-bleeding provides the first direct example of how boys
must strengthen their resolve in the field of warrior life. One component
of ritual rhetoric stands out: "You [initiates] must not be afraid of seeing
your age-mates' blood [spilled]. If he [enemy] kills your mate, you must
be *strong* and *kill him* [emphasis] as revenge." This idea is spouted in
first-stage initiation; it comes more as a warning about the future than
anything else. But by third-stage warriorhood, this nose-bleeding idiom

children; so this idea becomes a piece of masculine idioms used in ritual and in men's rantings
against women too.

epitomizes budding manhood. By then, youths ought to endure nose-bleeding or battle with dignity and self-control, without flinching. That message, I think, helps the youth transform his early, personal nose-bleeding trauma into an expression of masculine triumph. "In battle you needn't dread the sight of blood since you have expelled blood yourself. You know how that is controlled, and you have survived it." Violent nose-bleedings are thus a form of warriorhood training vital for masculine character.

Ingestive Rites. Once a boy's body has been "stretched" and physiologically purged, he must then swallow and absorb substances believed vital to spark masculine growth. Ingestive rites follow these earlier procedures for plausible reasons. First-initiation ingestion taboos prepare the boy for appropriate treatment, through restricted intake of all liquids (water is prohibited till the last day of the rituals) and foods, since only taro and yam ("male foods") are allowed in small quantity. Then, his stomach empty, feces eliminated, and blood expelled, and only then, is the boy ready to consume what can help make him a man. Of all such substances, semen is the most valuable.

Ingestive rites have an antecedent long before this—at the time a woman is pregnant. Her husband can feed her (illicitly, through foods given her) special secret leaves or flowers in the hope of fathering handsomer (usually red-toned skinned), healthier children. Such plants contagiously affect the growing fetus.

Ingestion rites and taboos act in the same way to change the novice's appearance and physical size. From first initiation on, boys are told what to eat and what to fear eating. Initiation teaches boys the names (some of them secret) of myriad leaves, grasses, and cordylines, which materials help "strengthen" their skin and overall body functioning. Some of these special leaves contain an invigorating fluid (*i-aalyu,* tree water) absent from other plants. Some of the plants are also rubbed on the skin; of these, a few are eaten but most are not. In general, trees that are referred to as the "same" as boys—their "age-mates"—are specially set aside by ritual identification[35] and are not eaten.

The opposite is also true: a range of foods, like some plants, is taboo (*kumaaku*). Many of these foods have negative "feminine" connotations

35. We could label these trees "totems," since they have this ritual focus, are not eaten normally, and, in exceptional cases, do play a part in the social attributes assigned to kinship statuses. Indeed, great clans are credited with the corporeal rights of use and ownership of particular rituals, and such rights are fiercely protected. Nonetheless, as Lévi-Strauss (1963) has shown, the notion of totemism is so loaded with ambiguity that it serves as much to confuse as to enlighten, so I usually avoid the term. Elsewhere, I shall return to this problem in regard to how totemiclike items are related to local politics and ethnic identity.

either by virtue of their coloration (particularly red, yellow, and black tubers and leaves) or their soft, pliable character. Contagious and sympathetic thought processes are again at work. The boy *is* what he eats: he will be "black and mushy" if he eats the soft black forest mushrooms, for instance.[36]

A broad trend in masculinization is the initial imposition of hundreds of negative and positive ritual taboos that are gradually removed as a male grows, attains manhood, and passes into senescence. In each subsequent initiation he is taught about new "strength"-bolstering plants to be eaten secretly. There is a parallel shift away from flora bordering the hamlet, toward stress on ingesting high forest leaves, tree bark, and the like. (This shift mirrors a maturing preoccupation with the deep forest as a setting for ritual as one nears adulthood.) The high forest is, after all, less frequented by women, so its flora is "cleaner" and more vitalizing than that of hamlet surroundings. Likewise, subsequent initiations derestrict many foods as a male proves himself by attaining manliness. By the time of sixth-stage initiation, then, a man intimately knows hundreds of plant substances that may be consumed; and far fewer domesticated foods are prohibited.

Among the forest substances vital to adult masculinity, the class of white milk saps exuded by forest trees is absolutely essential to the maintenance of one's semen organ and biological maleness, and I shall return to them.

Another kind of ingestive procedure stems from painting (*wolu-mun-julupi*) the body with ocher, mud, or grease. "Ingestion," in this sense, is not confined simply to swallowing materials, as we should expect of a culture so reliant on sympathetic and contagious ritual procedures. A pervasive trend in Sambia thought is that any substance that brushes and, especially, is directly rubbed against one's body becomes quickly absorbed through the skin into the innards. For example, the earth surrounding the menstrual hut is polluted from women's periods, so it is avoided like the plague.

In addition to the initiation enforcement of ingestion taboos and requirements that certain foods be eaten, initiation custom requires pigments to be smeared on novices for body decoration and "strength." Each of these pigments has a job to do. We have already seen how yellow pigment is mixed with cassowary feces to stimulate physical growth in children; first-stage initiates, too, are smeared with this mixture. Red ocher

---

36. Barth (1975:162–171) has questioned the "logic of meaning" in the food taboos of Baktaman, essentially arguing that there is no rational (as distinct from logical) calculus of their complex of food taboos. This is a large topic: one could, indeed, take food taboos as a vantage point for describing the whole of Sambia *ritual* (not individual experience or behavior), for instance. But with few exceptions, food taboos, better than other sociocultural patterns, follow rather closely sympathetic and contagious associations with gender qualities (see M. Strathern 1978).

is placed on third-stage initiates and men; it makes them "strong" and "fierce-looking," brilliant like "fire light." There is a great difference between yellow and red pigments: red ocher does not physically stimulate growth (*perulyapi*) as does yellow pigment.[37] Second-stage initiates, however, have red pandanus fruit grease smeared on them (rather than yellow or red pigment), and of this men say, "That is enough . . . they [initiates] don't need nose-bleeding" because of that. (Recall the earlier noted equivalence between blood and pandanus juice.)

In short, each of these behaviors is an efficacious (i.e., "symbolic"), instrumental act as Sambia see it: strategic materials of the natural world are acquired and added to one's budding male body. This requires an aside about male fertility and the supernatural.

Simulating Potency. The same form of "contagious ingestion" technique is also extended to encompass even more esoteric, ceremonial body treatments. Two special kinds of ritual activity occur in first-stage initiation (and then only). Both are fundamental to masculinization. Although they take different "supernatural"[38] forms, their underlying processes are much alike. The first event focuses on a brilliant red ritual object called *kwolyi-mutnyi*. The object is about 1½ feet long by 3 inches wide; it is completely wrapped in red-dyed bark cloth of the kind used by shamans in healing ceremonies and is wrapped around the initiate's head as a headband in collective initiations. The second activity concerns a unique, edge-land forest hut (called the *mor-angu;* compare *morum-angu,* birth house) built expressly for attracting spirit familiars. Let me briefly introduce both of these.

Sambia are not a people who put much store on religious or ceremonial objects inherited and faithfully treasured from one generation to the next. Their life is harsh and their material culture, even by the spartan standards of the Highlands, seems unimpressive and even dull. Perhaps this dearth of material culture is because they were always at war and needed to be able to abandon their homes quickly. Perhaps they were, historically, more hunters than farmers, and so they still have little interest in such things. Whatever the reason, men's few shell decorations are valued, and they do get passed down from father to son; but otherwise, there is little

---

37. It is, understandably, "absolutely taboo" ever to place red ocher on first-stage initiates, who "still need to grow," who are not yet men.

38. It has now become nearly a truism of anthropology to assert with Tylor (1873) that the "supernatural" means the other world of ghosts and spiritual beings. Spirit familiars are of this form in Sambia eyes. But neither familiars nor ghosts are supernatural in the sense that they are not always present; unseen, yes, but real, and hence as much a part of nature as are the trees (see Schieffelin 1977).

material wealth except the land itself, and there is virtually no cult paraphernalia of enduring, sacred value: no great spirit houses, totemic poles,
or masks such as one finds scattered up and down the Sepik River (see
Forge 1973). Even the sacred flutes are made to be used only for collective
initiation rites, and are then discarded in the brush.[39]

For this reason, as much as for its magical powers, the sacred *kwolyi-
mutnyi* stands out as a curious hand-me-down of the Sambia male cult. This
small red bundle is thought to reek of great and overflowing potency.
Myth tells how long ago the object was created spontaneously from the
pool of blood of a Sambia warrior; a war party of neighboring tribal
enemies killed that ancestor from whose blood emerged the *kwolyi-mutnyi.* Sambia tell how they acquired their first *kwolyi-mutnyi* as recently as
forty years ago from a different tribal group, by trading shell valuables for
it to a neutral hamlet that acted as their agent. In the entire Sambia Valley
only two such objects now exist. Today, elders and ritual experts, like Tali,
know that its powerful ingredients, as much as its mythological origins, are
why the object is ceremonially struck against boys' chests in first-stage
initiation. Among its contents,[40] a female possum-bone awl is extraspecial.
Elders believe that this awl replaced a human-bone awl, as used among the
originally owning enemy tribe—who were said to have been cannibals—
in piercing the nasal septums of its initiates. What matters (for those
privileged to know) is that the object contains a *female* bone awl, as if to
underline that there is something intrinsically powerful in that femaleness
itself, and as if to encapsulate how femaleness lies hidden in the core of
men's most powerful ritual item.

The *kwolyi-mutnyi* is so potent that that one ingestive brush with it, at
first initiation, helps inculcate prodigious masculinity. Tali noted how the
mutnyi is for "making you come up with lots of children." This power is
precisely why the object is so treasured by its owners: it has become a
secret weapon in the drive to outpopulate and overcome opposing groups.
So powerful an object is naturally dangerous, and recent legend tells how
its misuse resulted in terrible death. The men of Nilangu hamlet say that
a deceased senior man traded for a *kwolyi-mutnyi* but "did not know how
to use the power correctly." He kept it hidden in his house and therefore
bade men to be careful in sitting, spitting out betel juice, etc. He grew
careless, gradually took sick, and out of desperation threw the object into

---

39. A pattern like what Tuzin (1980) reports of the Ilahita Arapesh and quite different from the
corporeal, smoke-blackened, stuffed-with-pig-fat fetishes of the Gahuku-Gama (see Read
1952:10f.; Salisbury 1965:67).

40. These include a red seed, stalks of wild ginger, an eagle feather, and red ocher, besides the
bone awl. The object is used by someone (e.g., Tali) who knows a special spell, too, that
enhances its efficacy.

the river. But to no avail: his stomach bloated and he died shortly thereafter, proof to Tali and others of the power of the object and why it must be carefully handled.

In describing its effects, Weiyu likened the *mutnyi* to the womb of a woman: "It is the same as a net-string bag or womb. Do we [men] ejaculate our water [semen] just anywhere? No: it is poured inside the wombs of women." (This statement links pregnancy idioms and procreation to the *kwolyi-mutnyi;* see above.) At which Tali, almost beside himself (uncharacteristically so), excitedly cut in:

> *Mutnyi* means [is at "base," *kablu*], like this: to come up with a child in the stomach. Like *nyu-mutnyi sumai;* like *kwulai'u sumutnyi-mai;* or *kwol-imutnyi.* A man is the same as *kwolu;* and woman is the same as *imutnyi; kwolu-imutnyi* is man-woman, and *kwei-mutnyi* is semen-woman:[41] to make many children.

All these semantic constructs correspond to the linkage between maleness and femaleness, and their imagery (like that of pregnancy constructs) draws on a red mass (*boongu,* red pool) that stimulates fertility; only here, that fertility results in the manly sexual capacities of puberty.

We need not engage in clever symbology to understand that for these two men, at least, the red object is consciously bound up with semen, blood, and the womb, and a ritualized drive to create in boys the stuff of many progeny.

At first initiation there is also another ceremonial event whose "supernatural" effects have a more personalized dimension and are, in a different sense, more vital and no less masculine. It is the "birth-house" (*mor-angu*) ceremony, an experience that occurs but once in a life and whose cultural goal is to attract spirit familiars into the boys' innards. "Birth house" is a doubly apt metaphor for this rustic shelter: a baby cries there, and spirit familiars are "born there."

Toward the end of first initiation, after days of ritual and fasting, the novices are nearly worn out. They are led from the cult house into the edge-land forest. They are lined up before the *mor-angu,* which is contextually likened to a "birth house" (taking a similar name and the metaphoric significance of a menstrual hut at birth). Boys hear high-pitched cries from within that are said to be a squawking newborn infant (but are actually produced from the bamboo flutes). Once inside, novices are made to lie on myriad ritual leaves, placed on new bark capes, which overlie various ritual decorations and paraphernalia. Inside and outside, the house

---

41. The *kwolyi-mutnyi* is less frequently referred to as *kwei-mutnyi* and *kwulai'u-mutnyi. Mokei-mutnyi* is the generic term for "he who sings out for the *mokeiyu* initiations," i.e., a ritual expert, like Tali.

is bedecked with ritual leaves to attract "new" familiars from the forest environs into the boys' bodies. After a night of lying perfectly still (but kept awake) they are removed to the cult house. There, they ingest hallucinogens amid a songfest, and shamans divine which boys have seduced familiars inside them, beings who will enable them to become renowned warriors, shamans, or hunters (see Herdt 1977:157–158).[42]

Here is a beautiful example of how Sambia culture has provided for the psychological needs of these displaced little boys. Out of their parents' homes these children are thrown into a fierce and sometimes cruel ordeal of manliness. That security is forever lost; they must now be as warriors. But it is one thing to dress up an eight-year-old in ritual garb, and quite another to get him to forget what he has lost, not to mention to get him to sense himself as a man and really believe in that. Sambia communities require this belief because pseudowarriors do not make good fighters.

Spirit familiars help to build this subjective sense of maleness. Familiars are personalized; they belong to *individual* boys. They are esteemed; shamans and elders praise the boy for his good fortune at having acquired them. They are invincible; they make a boy "stronger" and smarter, contributing to his masculine longevity. They can even be envisaged; during the ceremony, and in a semihypnotic state, the boy may visualize them; or, later, he may recollect them from his dreams, as the shaman predicts. Visible or invisible, the familiars live inside oneself, in that space left empty by the loss of one's mother and her expurgated blood.

It is not surprising, then, that most women (except female shamans) lack spirit familiars. They are not early separated from their parents; they are not initiated; and they do not engage in the spirit-familiar ceremonies, at least not directly (see Herdt 1977:159). Women's bodies are not open vessels: they are filled with the blood of their mothers. They do not need familiars because their own "natural" biology is maturing them. From inside that cavity, where dwell familiars in men, will one day spring infants.

Homosexual Activities and Semen Ingestion. Now we come to the most important early ingestive rite of all: fellatio. Oral insemination ought to be viewed as an ingestive rite, within initiation, and there is substantial evidence to suggest that Sambia believe the novice must be ritually prepared before consuming semen for it to have its desired effect. My aim is to survey the key idioms describing such effects.

Homosexual practices are introduced through the most secret of all

---

42. A few years later, toward the end of third-stage initiation, a more complex spirit ceremony (*narangu*) is held for its initiates, and older men, at the construction of a new men's clubhouse, which also attracts new familiars and is the basis for initiating new male shamans.

rites, the "penis and flute" ceremony. In the initiations I observed this rite followed nose-bleeding by several hours. For the first time novices are shown the flutes. Indeed, it is the bamboo flute that is used to illustrate the mechanics of fellatio: its tip is inserted into boys' mouths. Along with the secrets of the flutes, they are told of the urgent requirement to consume semen. Their bodies are decorated and painted, a highlight of initiation. The novice receives a new *choowinuku* grass sporran, a thin bark cape buttockcover (*bichoowi'u*), and other warrior garb. During the subsequent teachings about erotic life, the boys' old childhood pubic apron is dramatically cut with a knife. By this act, boys are absolutely enjoined to keep homosexual practices secret and to adhere later to heterosexual fidelity. Boys are lectured about the dangers of semen depletion. Men threaten castration and murder if they break these taboos. Afterwards, all the novices, amidst the troop of men, parade down from the forest onto the dance ground where their mothers watch them dancing for the last time. Thereafter, they are enclosed in the cult house; afterwards, for some weeks, they remain secluded in a special ceremonial forest lodge; and finally, they later return to the clubhouse of their own hamlet where they live and must avoid all women.

Like the *kwolyi-mutnyi*, the flutes are first bumped against the novices' chests, here, to harden them. Elders then scold the boys for their childish insubordination in allegedly "imitating" the sounds of the flutes as a game. Boys are commanded to "suck the penis" if they wish to grow big and live a long life. To illustrate, I cite fragments of observations of this rite made in 1975. Here is how I recorded the first reference to it:

> All of you boys look at this elder [referring to an old man standing nearby]. What do you think he has done? Heard this teaching this moment and grown *big* [emphasis]! All of them [men] ate the penis . . . and grew big! All of them can copulate with you; all of you can eat penises. If you eat them, you will grow bigger rapidly.[43]

It is in such dramatic circumstances that homosexual activity is begun. And this initial emphasis on biological male growth always remains central to fellatio practices.

But actual fellatio never occurs in that ritual. Sambia are far too prudish for that. Fellatio, like all sexual intercourse, occurs in private, between individuals, and usually under cover of darkness. (There is, however, a bacchanalian air about the nighttime activities that fall between the rituals. Some flirtation, erotic antics, and foreplay occur among males in the cult

---

43. This elder's rhetoric was too sweeping: bachelors are the main fellated partners; a few married men may join in, but older men—especially elders—never do so.

house, and also less openly in the men's clubhouse.) A boy's first fellatio experience (specified and assigned by elders) should occur during the initiation period, however, and it is reckoned critical for a successful transition into his ritual role. Furthermore, it ought to occur (and usually does take place) many times with bachelor youths during the following weeks of seclusion in the isolated forest lodge. It should, over the coming years, occur often—as regularly as "eating sweet potatoes," men say—day in and day out. In short, while fellatio begins with ceremony, it is scarcely a formal interlude: it becomes a whole way of life.

It is urgent for boys to ingest semen to "grow big." Unless they do so, their bodies will stay "small" and ugly. "A boy who doesn't drink semen still has a *kwulai'u* skin," Tali said. And here is Juvu, talking about the functions of fellatio as he was taught them, and as he teaches them, now that he is an elder.

> If you boys don't drink semen, you'll stay in the fire [metaphor for vagina]. You won't grow big. Your nose will be completely black; you'll die quickly. Black ashes on your nose will completely cover your face. If you don't drink semen, your penis will stand up and bump your own chest. When I first heard this talk [at *moku* initiation], I was very scared. . . . That very night I went and did it [fellatio].

Initiation, alone, is not enough. As Tali remarked: "You boys can't just fasten *moogu* [waistbands] and *mooniglu* [warrior bandoliers; decorations worn after initiation]. You must also drink the semen of all men."

The proof of this need for semen is evidenced by their past retarded development. Their mothers' food was inadequate. Men constantly tell boys that tubers and greens are only "stomach food," not material for building "strength." Such idioms would soon become dull cliché if it were not for the mark of urgency that constantly animates men's rhetoric.

> A boy *must* [emphasis] consume semen to come up quickly! You won't come up quickly if you eat sweet potatoes or sugarcane, *your mother's food* [emphasis]. A man who doesn't think of this thing [swallowing semen], he won't come up quickly! [Weiyu]

Invidious comparisons of crop foods and semen are common enough. Women's food is paltry against the needs of boys. This raises a fundamental point about men's psychological frame surrounding homosexual behavior.

Fellatio insemination is likened to maternal breast-feeding. Semen is for growth: *yungoolu-monjapi'u* (men "must grow boys"). In other words, fellatio is a latter-day male *monjapi'u*. This fact is less startling than it might be since we have already examined men's preoccupation with prolonged mothering, and the nutritive ideas concerning heterosexual fellatio. What matters is not so much the choice of idiom—dressing up fellatio as a form of breast-feeding—but rather the psychological involvement in homosexual contacts that goes beyond spouting metaphors or acting out social roles.

Semen is the substance closest to breast milk, and it provides the next sort of ("biological") push that boys require. Elders reiterate that boys should ingest semen every night, as if it were breast milk or food. In the midst of the penis teaching, for instance, elders exclaimed:

> When you do "sleep" with men, you should not be afraid of "eating" their penises. You will soon enjoy eating them. . . . If you try it [semen] it is just like the milk of your mother's breast. You can ingest it all of the time and grow quickly.

Initiates, among themselves, refer to semen as *neimi aamoonaalyi,* "our breast milk." And the boy's actual consumption of semen is likened to *monjapi'u* feeding by a mother of her infant. As a mother's early breast-feeding (and overall care) hastens a boy's development, later ritualized fellatio (and ritual procedure) is also extended to masculine figures whose semen helps him "grow big and strong."

In the fellatio context the *monjapi'u* process is thus redirected to embrace a kindred idea, *moo-nungendei* (literally, milk food, glans penis). As a man's semen is introduced into a woman's womb, creating milk and the fetus, the boy differentially makes use of semen for manliness. For instance, Tali said to me: "We men *moo-nungendei* women and their children. We copulate with a woman and she produces breast milk; then she feeds the infant." And again:

> We men complain: we give semen to a boy, we *moo-nungendei* him. And he turns around and copulates with a younger boy. We big men copulated with him and we said: "We completed his *moo-nungendei,* but he has gone and given his share to other boys."

Here we see a conscious continuity in men's views about copulating with women and with boys. Semen produces pregnancies and milk in a woman. To participate in the boy's *moo-nungendei* is tantamount to masculinizing him: it precipitates his puberty and makes him manly enough to inseminate boys and women.

Ingested semen passes down into the semen organ where it is absorbed. As noted above, men believe that semen is actually "painted" on the organ. Like pigment smeared on the outer skin, the semen seeps through the walls of the organ and accumulates inside.[44] Each act of fellatio deposits a few more drops. And although men recognize that the accumulation is bewilderingly slow, they counter by asserting that a boy has years to acquire semen, every night. They also add, with contemptuous smiles, that a boy who fails to acquire it must suffer his dark fate alone.

Men never tire of saying why insemination is essential. One example: when a few men were discussing the subject, one of them mentioned the initiate of a neighboring hamlet who had recently fallen from a tree. "He didn't drink semen, we know, he didn't drink semen: that's why he fell," Tali cut in. To which Juvu, a middle-aged man with two wives and ten children, spontaneously responded: "I still never stop thinking about semen or eating it," turning away, his voice falling off. Tali retorted with a smile: "A married man who didn't play around [swallow semen] enough will die quickly, like an airplane without gasoline!"

Repeated inseminations create a pool of maleness: the boy, it is believed, gradually acquires a reservoir of sperm inside his semen organ. Men say that initiates should take their semen from many bachelors (as if to emphasize that "strength" is based on multiple donors to this pool). The semen organ changes from being dry and hard to fleshy, moist, and then firm. Tali compared this change to the perceptible modifications in pandanus nuts, which change from being immature and fleshy to solid kernels. (The same analogy chosen for the *tingu;* here is a clue to their tacit linkage in idioms and thought.) Semen gradually transforms the initiate's body too. It internally strengthens his bones and builds muscles. Externally, it cleanses the face, making the skin taut and tough. Aside from sheer body size, one other visible trait—facial hair (*mugaatu,* mouth hair)—is judged the best sign of manliness (pubescence). Voice change and youthful musculature are noted, but the growth of a beard tells that an adolescent is ready for bachelorhood (third-stage) initiation. This emphasis on facial hair deserves a side note.

One striking theme, a combination of fantasy and belief, seems to be woven throughout the latent and manifest ritual symbolism of Sambia. This is the notion that the mature glans penis does not "naturally" develop but must be ritually simulated. Facial hair is a sign of biological maleness in a redirected sense: it suggests the hidden presence of a mature penis and glans penis, that "ugly nose" men say is "there down below." (Else-

---

44. Semen is also rubbed on the fellator's face, privately, by himself, and from personal choice, after fellatio. This makes the nose "nice"; so it shines (*doowungulu*) as if it were oiled. The only other substance smeared on the *initiate's* face is cassowary grease, as we saw above. (Unlike Gahuku-Gama or Fore, Sambia never rub pig's grease on themselves.) These substances "cleanse" and "brighten" the skin; they are also believed to be absorbed into the skin. Elsewhere I try to show that this treatment of nose and face is felt to have a latent, sympathetic effect on the development of male genitals.

where we shall see how men attempt to foster the emergence of these sex traits through the ritual rebirth of initiates; and we shall also see the converse: how body treatment and ritual paraphernalia are believed to inhibit the development of female secondary sex traits in boys.) The constant allusions to nose and penis, one suspects, impinge on an underlying preoccupation with creating and maintaining masculine potency (recall the idiomatic allusions to the nose and pandanus nuts described in Chapter 4). The sources of this ritual behavior and symbolism remain to be seen.

Yet we cannot avoid their psychological consequences in the minds and behavior of Sambia. Consider an obvious possibility: it would be surprising if initiates were to ingest semen and experience no concern about becoming pregnant, considering the idiomatic link between parturition and fellatio. Of course children are alleged to be sexually naïve; but once they learn of semen and experience fellatio, that begins to change. In fact, during first initiation some boys, in private, *are told* not to worry about becoming pregnant. Here is Weiyu.

> He [the fellator] has a penis; the semen he eats goes for that. A woman fills her womb; this fills with semen and makes a child. [GH: But what about (the myth of) parthenogenesis?] I think about that too; what is it about?[45]

Most initiates "know" (in some sense) from the very start that they cannot become pregnant, since they are told that they "lack a womb." Yet fellatio is secret and hidden (therefore dangerous); it focuses on the erect, excited penis and mouth, (just as giving birth and menstruation focus on the vagina and babies), and not just that, but a man's erect (implying psychologically excited) penis. (Not to mention the fact that the elders' emphasis on the impossibility of male pregnancy positively plants the opposite suggestion in the boys' consciousness.) These points are obvious; are they authentic concerns in boys' experiences?

There is but one way to investigate: I must form close enough relationships with boys to allow them to tell and retell what they feel they have actually experienced.

Individual case studies have thus shown (see Chapter 8) that despite the assurances of father and elders, boys still express early fears about becoming pregnant from fellatio (and related hesitations about reaching puberty and being inducted into masculine erotic practices). In short, the experience of being on the receiving end of semen entails some rather traumatic and endless adjustments for boys.

---

45. See Chapter 8, where myth describes how a pseudohermaphroditic male, following fellatio, gave birth.

Fellatio is governed by sex taboos similar to those surrounding heterosexuality. The idea of fellatio with one's father or biological brothers is
completely abhorrent and not discussed. Ideally, all male kin, including
cross-cousins, are taboo. In practice, however, this taboo applies to bilater-
al kinsmen with whom one frequently interacts. (Distant kinsmen can
sometimes engage in homosexual practices.) One's ritual sponsor and
age-mates are severely prohibited as sex partners. As a rule, then, fellatio
is permissible only with males from outside one's "security circle" (Lawrence 1965), i.e., with unrelated, potentially hostile males. (With true
intertribal enemies all social interaction, including sex, was traditionally
quite restricted.) Appropriate affines in other hamlets are acceptable
homosexual partners. Indeed, it is judged "good" that a boy serve as a
sister's husband's (older brother-in-law's) fellator (see also Layard 1959),
before the birth of the man's first child, since spouses are drawn from
hamlets of potential enemies. Nevertheless, there are occasional violations
of these restrictions (as there are of rules governing heterosexual intercourse) that should not occur but do. Aside from the shallower incest of
homosexual contacts among cross-cousins, for instance, these violations[46]
are bad signs because they suggest a lack of erotic restraint on the part of
a youth.

> If you promiscuously "play around" [with prohibited categories of boys], when
> you become a *nupos* [married man] then you'll want to adulterously copulate
> with all of the women. With some enemy boys, only with them you can forni-
> cate. [Tali]

So we see how, for Tali, homosexual restraint augurs appropriate heterosexual fidelity. This link between hostility and homosexual fellatio is important and pervasive. Fellatio is expected of males who are potential
enemies, not friends. This expectation leads to the next point, the "meaning" of insemination for the fellated.

So far I have concentrated on the constructive functions of fellatio and
its capacity to build up a boy's masculine "strength." The fact that fellatio
is prohibited among friends and permissible among potential enemies is
a sign of the rather visible conflict within homosexual relationships and
activities. (The same is implied, in varying degrees, for Sambia heterosexual relationships.) If semen is the essence and function of maleness, if the
body doesn't naturally produce it, if it must be swallowed and stored for

---

46. There are physical sanctions and, for want of a better word, "magical" ill effects, like
sanctions, resulting from having fellatio with a kinsman or tabooed male; e.g., the nose will
turn black. Homosexual promiscuity is not as immoral as heterosexual promiscuity; and some
kinds of homosexual incest (among cousins) are not terribly reprehensible.

later use, and if masculine potency rests on that reservoir of semen, then it is easy to see how ejaculation (loss of semen) is not only worrisome, but dangerous. (This applies to all ejaculations and perhaps, at a different level, to the experience of erections, too.) Semen depletion is, consequently, always a concomitant of every instance of sexual intercourse. Someone gains semen when someone loses it.

Boys know this, as is shown in their uneasy idiom that fellatio is like "drinking your bone" (*goomeru yungdu-tuv kwiandokeno*). Elders chide boys that they must literally "capture semen" (poignantly referred to as "stealing a man's strength"). There is little altruism here: no more talk of *monjapi'u* or infants suckling and the like. The stress is on a struggle: competing with one's age-mates to "outgrow" (*nunu-woluwutnji*) them, acquiring more semen than they do (like the implicit test of a boy to outgrow his assigned wife), and ingesting a youth's semen at his own expense, depleting some of his vital "strength." The implication is that there is only so much masculine "strength" in the population pool to go around: someone's loss is someone's gain. Isn't this Sambia viewpoint an understandable result of an erotic tradition deeply ingrained in a warrior's way of life?

This is a facile question. I have been describing ritualized fellatio in the setting of initiation. Homosexual practices are, for many reasons, a stupendous, touchy subject among Sambia. Fellatio is not only a ritual, since its meaning embraces the politics of life and death. Let us summarize the main reasons why: homosexual practices are vital to the processes of maternal detachment and masculinization; they are forced on boys whether they like it or not; they are hidden absolutely from all women; they begin as arranged, alienating encounters of a one-sided erotic nature[47] with a strange, older man, alone, and usually in the dark; manliness and existence hinge on them; and death awaits boys who reveal their secret, or women who stumble on them. It is also certain that this tragic sanction has been used against transgressors in the past. All these things impinge on the secret, shared tradition of homosexuality, and they are powerful reasons why boys act as fellators and consume semen.

But what about the fellated, their "donor"? If ejaculation is that threatening, then why and how should youths engage in homosexual fellatio? Here we face a key problem of male gender identity and masculine culture. Here we shall need to investigate a man's sense of himself, and the part that erotic attraction to boys and women, and the secrecy of homosexual behavior, play in that sense. First, though, we need to complete the outline of male initiation rites.

---

47. As boys mature, other factors also motivate them to engage in fellatio, but the original experiences always underlie that later behavior.

Insertive Rites. Now we can quickly glance at the next category of rituals that are said to build up maleness. Since they are so heavily used throughout initiations, our only concern here will be with how they operate as transitional techniques in achieving manhood.

Insertive rites are the çonverse of the elaborate ingestive rites described above: body substances are literally inserted into or attached to trees and plants. The body and ritual interactions focus on spittle, skin flakes, body hair, sweat, snot, and urine. In short, all the body's products, except semen, are deposited in their right order as ritual dictates.[48] Such techniques have a dual function: stimulating masculine development and purifying the body, thereby preserving it against contamination.

Two forms of insertive rituals predominate in the cycle of male initiation. *Akovanyu,* the simplest type, is the earliest technique introduced by initiation (associated with the first stretching rite). Once "stretched," the body is rubbed with the shaman's headband;[49] so the body and face are rubbed against the leaves of many trees that are also identified as the novices' age-mates on the basis of perceptual attributes like size, coloration, and rate of growth. Once again, idioms hold that these plants have the "same kind" of tree skin or anatomy as the boy, not a "different kind" (*jentu-kelatnuku*). These rites begin in first-stage initiation and continue throughout all the other initiations; only different plants are substituted as one matures. *Akovanyu* rites (in first-stage initiation) begin with a slow-growing, immature black palm, then proceed to a quick-growing, rugged, flexible, wild sugarcane. (Note the mixture of desirable "male" qualities: longevity, strength, speedy growth.) Typically, these actions occur early in the morning, just after dawn; initiates thus get dew rubbed on their faces and torsos, which makes their skins shine clear and "bright, like the white light of sunrise reflected in the dew." At the same time, bits of skin flakes and sweat adhere to the plants. This rubbing also cleanses boys. It is "like your soap," men told me. (They were thinking of how Europeans use bar soap in washing themselves.) The leaves, still attached to the trees, are rubbed against the boys' faces and bodies; again, as the trees grow, enduring into ripe old age, so will the novices.[50]

The other insertive type, the "spitting rites," exclusively employs forest trees and only begins with puberty (third-stage initiation). Usually, wild pandanus or black palm are selected as "age-mates" (although the redwood is also used once, in fourth-stage initiation, when its bark is chewed

---

48. I should also mention what is less obvious: that one's eyes and speech focus on trees; so the words and glances also penetrate (are deposited in) them, and not elsewhere, i.e., women.

49. Used in many *akovanyu* rites as a material means of connecting trees to the body.

50. Some of the initial *akovanyu* rites occur in the gardens, but in subsequent initiations forest trees are used exclusively, a pattern noted before.

and spit against its own trunk). We have seen (in Chapter 4) how novices stand atop specially constructed platforms adjoining these trees so as to spit into them masticated materials. Their instruction on sexual matters and purification involves the use of sugarcane and special leaves; and this spitting procedure serves as a conscious reminder that they must never "swallow their saliva" during heterosexual intercourse, especially coitus. This practice in adult life prevents them from unwittingly contaminating themselves, since the polluting "smell of women" is said to enter their noses and mouths during sexual intimacy. Their body substance, attached to the sturdy tree, also ensures them of longevity. And then (as later they may do on their own) they insert pubic and head hairs into the tree trunk, further fortifying themselves.

In both these ritual techniques we again see focal projection at work in modes of sympathetic and contagious identification with forest trees. Trees are genderized: certain traits are selected as masculine. These qualities stimulate and also cleanse. The underlying notion is simple: as a tree grows, fares, and wanes, so does a man. These techniques are used by individual men and can therefore be subsumed into their personal designs for purification following coitus or their wives' menses. In these many ways ritual makes use of "male" trees to stimulate and nurture masculinity.

Avoidance taboos concerning females also belong to this ritual genre. Aside from the various rites that result in boys' shedding, eating, or eliminating body substances, there are also rigid injunctions prohibiting direct interaction between themselves and women. The taboos are enforced by men collectively in first-stage initiation; thereafter, initiates are monitored carefully for a few months till men trust that the lads have internalized these taboos and that they voluntarily avoid women. This avoidance means never talking or looking at women and never eating or drinking in their presence. It is inconceivable for boys to sit with women or enter their houses. These are not merely traffic rules: they are sternly enforced threats against one's person and life. After all, they protect masculinity. (We can guess an ulterior motive, as men themselves express it: if boys were to spend time with women, how could ritual secrecy be ensured?)

Avoidance amounts to the opposite of ingestion. One "hides from women"; so boys should physically insert themselves into the clubhouse, its groups of men and strictly male associations. Boys can be impaired by women. They can be polluted, grow weak, lazy, ugly, or *wogaanyu*. As Moondi remarked: "Suppose you eat in the women's house, you eat part of a tuber and some [of it] falls down; all the women step over that, then you won't grow big quickly." Even distant interaction can stultify. As Moondi continues, "If all the women look at you, [then] you won't come up quickly. . . . Initiates must hide their faces or become *wogaanyu*." There must not only be a willful association with males, there must also be a constant aversion to interaction with women. Hence, boys characteristically grasp at the bark cape around their heads; run at the sight of women; avoid women's trails and haunts; and hide their voices and faces when women call into the clubhouse. Not to mention how boys and youths examine the women's food given them (through men or children) for the slightest evidence of foreign material (which is reason enough to throw it away lest there be the slightest chance of contamination).

All this prolonged avoidance behavior, too, belongs to masculine ontogeny.

Adult Confirmatory Rites. With each successive initiation maleness is thought to surge and become more firmly rooted in initiates. What a boy does and does not do are behavioral signs of how internal maleness is taking hold of him. And the conscientious youth will have ingested semen enough for him to demonstrate, in innumerable ways, his personal "strength" and its manly by-products.

The puberty rites of third-stage initiation recognize this achievement and transform the pubescent initiates into bachelor youths. To restate this: the male cult then requires the new bachelors to assist in rituals as fledgling initiators. They should serve as younger boys' dominant fellateds. Bachelors are allowed to don more warrior garb, twirl bull roarers, and play flutes for the first time. The youths' participation is then sought in a war-raiding party—cardinal confirmation of aggressive, masculine prowess. By the time of fourth-stage initiation and marriage, it seems, the youth is visibly masculine in the things that most count, except for heterosexuality.

So the final three (ego-centered) initiations carry the youth into full-blown manhood based on marriage, cohabitation with his wife, and fatherhood. There are still many things for him to learn. Kept largely ignorant of women and heterosexual intercourse, for example, the youth must be openly instructed (at fifth-stage ritual) in coitus and how to guard himself against feminine dangers. So as he approaches coitus and fatherhood—the peak of maleness and manliness—ritual techniques are shifted to defend and maintain the maleness built up inside him. Unless the newlywed adheres to certain rules and procedures, men believe, what maleness he has acquired will become infected and snatched away from him.

What matters most in ensuring strength is the individual's use of ritual techniques as a defense against masculine debilitation. Leaves are eaten still; foods are carefully inspected and ingestion taboos, though fewer, must still be observed; youths still avoid women in certain respects; and indeed, the last three initiations could be viewed as a means of deritualizing relationships with women. This does not mean that male and female relationships become casual and unconstrained by taboo; but more interactional possibilities with women are opened up, including erotic activities, flirtation, and mundane encounters. The ebbing of maleness has two foci. Manifestly, it stems from the fact that women are so dangerous that sex (for fathering children) and other intimate contact with them contaminates and depletes. Tacitly, however, there is recognition that warring and other masculine activities simply sap one's vitality. Nonetheless, men's rhetoric is preoccupied with women, and it is fair to say that men end up discounting the wear and tear of life itself as dull happenstance compared to one's draining encounters with ogress females.

There are a variety of these "defensive" procedures, but three types stand out. Nose-bleeding is regularly repeated because it egests internal pollution. Other activities, like rubbing stinging nettles on the hands after sex, aim to remove external contaminants. Last, the milk-sap ingestions are thought to restore "lost" semen after ejaculation. These individual-centered ritual techniques invariably take concrete body contact with women as their ostensible focus.

Yet, if we investigated individual behavior and discovered what men actually do, say, and think about these rites (for themselves) I suspect that we should uncover a normal statistical distribution concerning the psychological motives and effects (catharsis) they experience.[51] Toward one extremity of the distribution we might encounter individuals for whom such techniques are little more than social routines: they do them because they were taught to do so. At the other end we might locate a few individuals who scrupulously observe every tiny rule and so deeply experience a sense of relief that they feel subjectively calmed and restored by the action. (For example, several case studies revealed that individual men

---

51. The use of this statistical analogy, i.e., a bell-curve distribution of behavioral attributes and corresponding psychological experiences, in reference to the male population, is meant only to convey the possibilities of individual variations within the Sambia cultural pattern. Derek Freeman (personal communication) has correctly pointed out that this speculative model implies a steady-state perspective on Sambia culture and individual consciousness, generally ignoring the *descriptive* problem of innovation and individual choice in such matters. This point is more than pedantic: for example, a radical or revolutionary Sambia—a true prophet —may someday, at the right time and place, stir people to make choices that radically diverge from the ritual "baseline" of custom sketched above. Or, as is beginning to occur now, the changing circumstances of socioeconomic necessity may lead men to make quite different choices leading to behavioral divergence in ritual. With this *theoretical* view I concur: to argue, as do some workers, for a completely "fixed code" of rules and meanings pertaining to sociocultural patterns (i.e., ritual behaviors) implies that personal goals, choices, and consciousness are external variables lying beyond our purview of the human systems under investigation, a model that has led to an impasse in explaining transformations in culture and behavior (see Bateson 1972:415–422; Freeman 1970; Piaget 1971:117). My aim here is simply to argue that the institutionalized pattern of male ritual probably shields both qualitative and quantitative differences in its prevailing manifestations within individual behavior that Sambia are either unaware of or ignore.

found themselves trembling and anxious immediately after coitus; these men feel that the action of privately plunging both legs in cold mud, as required by ritual, helped them stop shaking and restored an outwardly controlled demeanor.) Between these extremes lies the majority of men, who hold complementary motives, who are generally convinced of the plausibility of their beliefs, and who are compulsively satisfied by performing the rites. These psychological aspects are as important as the social functions, in short, since outward ritual behavior entails an expectable inner psychological experience.

All these rites are thus self-contained and rewarding for masculine character structure and behavior. Whether we choose to emphasize the cultural or psychological aspects, these individual-oriented ritual techniques can certainly be viewed as an end in themselves (in contradistinction to the collective initiatory activities). For the individual is, at one and the same time, not just protecting maleness and health but confirming (to significant others, to himself) his manhood (personhood) by the very doing of them. In contrast, earlier initiation rites are but a means to an end: creating maleness and manliness.[52] Let me survey the techniques that follow marriage and associated rites to conclude my description of confirmatory ritual and male ontogeny as a whole.

At their secret nose-bleedings in fifth-stage initiation men compare the woman's menarche to their own *moku* initiation. The woman's periods have come; her vagina is "opened up" and she can engage in intercourse. This fact is of great significance for understanding the many meanings of nose-bleeding in male thought. Menstrual blood is contaminating in itself; but when, in vaginal penetration, the penis comes in contact with female genitalia, internal pollution is possible. Blood and vaginal fluids can enter the urethra and then lodge in a man's stomach.

We aren't afraid of anything else: we [men] are afraid of the blood of women which can enter the stomach; the stomach will swell up; and we fear [the resulting] short-windedness. Another [fear] is this: we are afraid of the earth close to the menstrual hut: it would not be good for that "germ"[53] to enter inside our skin. [Tali]

Weiyu carries this thought a bit further.

---

52. The hermeneutical view of culture as the embodiment of what humans do, and therefore of how they define themselves, is best known from the writings of Geertz (1968, 1973). This perspective has now been vividly depicted in Schieffelin's (1976) study of Kaluli and in Tuzin's (1980) incisive study of the Sepik Tambaran cult among Ilahita Arapesh of New Guinea.

53. Tali, who speaks only Sambia, has acquired this Neo-Melanesian term from men who have labored on the coast and returned to the village. There is no simple Sambia gloss for it, and it is predictable that "germ" should be used as a cover term for female pollutants.

The woman [at her periods] expels her blood, so you, her man, must also expel it. Your stomach is not well; it will swell up: you'll get a bad skin and short-windedness. Not good that a man swallows his spit when he copulates with his wife: he must expel his blood. . . . It's not male blood, but the bad talk and menstrual blood of a man's unclean wife. It [blood] doesn't belong to us; it belongs to women.

Coitus is contaminating: it can cause the stomach to distend and a man's skin to blacken and lose its taut, masculine quality. Unless, that is, one takes these precautions, including periodic nose-bleedings and spitting one's saliva after sexual intercourse.

Recall again men's psychological frame regarding nose-bleeding. Women "naturally" menstruate. Since husband and wife engage in coitus, and a woman's body "naturally" eliminates blood—apparently enlivening her —men must artificially do the same. When I asked Weiyu to tell why women do not nose-bleed, he remarked:

It's not right for women to nose-bleed. We have penises, they don't. Women have their cunt . . . the cunt, it [by itself] expels blood. We men have no pathway for eliminating blood. We work hard to expel blood from the nose. Women have the menstrual hut, we don't; we, by ourselves, remove blood from the nose. Suppose you and I had no penis, we wouldn't spear our noses; we'd perhaps take women's way; kill the moon [menstruate]. . . .[54] We think about the bad talk of women—it goes inside our noses. We bleed ourselves because of that.

At the fifth stage (menarche-related) rites of men there are allusions to women's menstruation—sympathetic remarks—oddly at variance with men's normal chauvinism. I have heard men say, then, that the married initiate's (fellatio) intercourse with his wife has helped precipitate her "pain of the menarche." In this sense, men feel driven by the need not only to purify themselves but also to simulate what women are doing; in part, from some sense of responsibility[55] for menstruation in the lives of their women. In other words, ritual nose-bleeding does painfully to the nose what (men and) women's physiology does to her vulva: expel blood.

On the other hand, ritual idioms simultaneously make use of menstrual

---

54. Weiyu seems to say that men must forcibly bleed themselves, whereas women do what naturally comes to them, passively menstruate. This stress conforms to the masculine view that male ritual is hard, that masculinity is hard to achieve; whereas femininity comes easily to women. Furthermore, since men associate their ejaculation sensations with what women experience in menstruation, we could hypothesize that men feel women have it easier in erotic activity, too.

55. Does this entail: empathy; identification; sympathy; reaction; care; projection; social maturi-

246 Guardians of the Flutes

pollution dangers in compelling men to be tough with their women and fierce in their war-making. Elders angrily exhort youths to recall the "pain" of nose-bleedings in their dealings with the "dirty, foul-mouthed women."

> You initiates, you cry [from nose-bleedings]: do you feel the pain? Later, when your wife talks bad to you, hit her. It was because of her that you were nose-bled [by senior men]. *She* [emphasis] doesn't nose-bleed *herself.* Your wife's menstrual blood can enter your nose. A man who doesn't nose-bleed is *wogaanyu.* If your wife's menstrual blood goes inside your nose, you'll be sick, age quickly. [Tali]

Furthermore, youths are urged to be courageous in battle now that they can nose-bleed themselves.

> You mustn't be afraid of seeing your age-mates' blood. You have expelled blood: we now mount your armbands [signs of warriorhood]. If you see your age-mates' blood you mustn't run away, you must fight. . . . [You] must be strong toward enemy men: you now have a woman. You must fight enemies. [Weiyu]

These references, in sum, show vividly how elders suggest that youths cope with their menstrual-blood anxieties and nose-bleeding trauma in two ways. They are urged to transform their fears and anger through self-control: by managing their wives and by adopting a fierce warrior's posture toward enemies. (Here we see a continuity of ritual idiom from first-stage nose-bleeding rites through this event, years later, at the fifth stage.)

Does this formula work? Do men's behaviors actually conform to these edicts? Elsewhere I shall have much more to say about this question, but it is necessary here to give an inkling of how subjectivity accords with outward behavior in the developmental lines of masculine life.

Take menstrual-blood anxieties in secular life, for example. Similar beliefs have long been reported from the New Guinea Highlands. Yet little has been described about the actual behavior correlated with such attitudes and beliefs. How do individuals internalize this information and how does it "constrain" or "motivate" action? Sometimes? Always? In what circumstances? For all men, in similar, or complementary, ways?

---

ty; guilt; enactment of the masculine gender role; and how many other traits or qualities of the marital tie too easily subsumed under a word like "responsibility"?

Among Sambia, menstrual-blood anxieties can find expression in everyday behavior as befits particular persons and circumstances. Here is a mundane anecdote.

One day (in August 1975) I was walking with my friend Weiyu and his older classificatory brother down the mountainside from Nilangu hamlet to the river. Weiyu was then about twenty years old, married but still childless. The steep trail was muddy from heavy rains on the previous night. A conversation about local politics had absorbed us until we reached a moss-covered pig fence near the water. Two of us climbed over the fence as we continued talking. Yet when Weiyu reached the top of the pickets he shrieked and jumped to our side, visibly shaking. He hopped beside the trail and began shaking his limbs and entire body, as if to free himself of a dog that had sunk its teeth into a limb. We were both taken aback; I could only imagine that a snake had bitten him.[56]

Pointing to the mossy, damp fence top, Weiyu cried, "Look!" We approached the pickets and found soggy red blotches in the moss. (They could have been either betel-nut juice or some sort of blood, since the two look alike.) I said nothing. Meanwhile, Weiyu assiduously inspected every inch of his midsection (where he had slid over the fence rail) for red stains. He said, "Ooh . . ." repeatedly, grimacing and shaking himself; then he began spitting, squinting his eyes and mouth. He pleaded with us: "What do you think? Is it . . . ?" (his voice rising and trailing off). His brother immediately sensed Weiyu's suspicion that it was menstrual blood and that he had, therefore, inadvertently polluted himself. Realizing Weiyu's alarm, he tried to calm him, saying, "No, it's not *that,* Weiyu . . . it's not what you think." But Weiyu had been visibly shaken; he could not be dissuaded. His brother told him several times not to worry; and I joined him in trying to play down Weiyu's alarm.

Weiyu then began to curse women, denouncing them as a "bloody crazy lot." In the next three hours he harked back to the incident, sometimes examining himself, sometimes gesticulating about women, sometimes wondering aloud to us if he would become ill.[57]

It is remarkable that none of us—Weiyu, his brother, or I—ever mentioned menstrual blood by name during the incident. Only hours later, in the evening, did Weiyu come around to mentioning his fear that those red

---

56. Sambia, men more than women (by their own reports), are prone to panicky, phobic reactions to snakes, even small garden snakes and lizards. In other contexts, I have observed similar although usually more humorous reactions.

57. In ritual belief, Weiyu's only means of eliminating such external contamination would be to bleed his nose, eat certain leaves and milk sap, and coat some of the exposed skin with milk sap. As far as I am aware, Weiyu did not immediately do that; but he regularly bleeds his nose.

blotches were really a female discharge of blood. In the following months I never again heard him allude to his experience.[58]

Yet it was really unnecessary for any of us to mention menstrual blood. The two Sambia shared a lifetime of experiences, and I knew enough to sense what Weiyu feared. Weiyu was distraught; his friend wanted to dissuade him, not to externalize Weiyu's fears by naming the thing that so worried him. Such observations were uncommon; in two years I observed men visibly anxious about menstrual blood on only half a dozen occasions. Maybe a score of times other incidents were reported. But the number of times menstrual blood got mentioned in conversation was legion.

Men have available to them a rather extensive set of guidelines and techniques for sustaining their health against heterosexual coitus. Nosebleeding, after each of their wives' monthly periods, is a dramatic procedure. And there are other things men can do. Restricting the frequency of sex itself comes first to mind; a few days up to a week or two should elapse between one occasion and the next. Before the act, men can also ingest special leaves to strengthen the stomach and skin. They can masticate special substances, like redwood bark, to cleanse the mouth. They can (illicitly) place spearmint leaves in the nose to prevent inhalation of women's "vaginal smell." And during actual intercourse they can keep bark or a red seed in their mouths (again, illicitly, as a reminder to themselves not to swallow their saliva).

Coitus itself, men say, can be arranged to give men greater control over sexual intercourse, thereby reducing its dangers. This notion comes down essentially to a man's maintaining authority over the frequency and timing of coitus when his wife has not recently menstruated. In addition, men are ever mindful of their physical ascendance over women, and this awareness has a concrete focus too: men's dogmatic assertions that they can accept only the missionary position when engaging in genital-to-genital intercourse with women.[59] The man must always be on top. This position allows him the greatest physical leeway in initiating and terminating sexual intercourse. When he has ejaculated he may arise at once, since there is no need to maintain skin contact. (I remind the reader of men's unequivocal lack of interest in orgasm in women.) Though a woman may try to

58. If Weiyu had fallen sick, however, I am certain that he would have brought up the incident again, especially if a shaman had intervened with healing ceremonies, as is expected.

59. Of course, this position is the only kind of genital intercourse Sambia know; men, furthermore, always physically prevail over fellators, be they boys or women, since boys are usually smaller, and since heterosexual fellatio is normally practiced as a man stands up (whereas homosexual fellatio is sometimes practiced while youths and boys are lying down at night, side by side, in the clubhouse).

"coax the man on longer," men say they usually resist and arise quickly, and that intercourse is brief. Some men say they are concerned about remaining inside their wives too long. (Nonetheless, this did not prevent Weiyu and Tali from saying that they either think about or would like to engage in sustained coitus more often.)

After coitus the number one concern is to "replace" (*mugerutmonji*) the ejaculated semen. Men can do other things too, like rubbing their hands and skin with stinging nettles (where they have touched the woman), or eating and smelling leaves, and cleaning their fingernails with cassowary quills till they draw blood (so that female "materials" accidentally picked up under the fingernails will not later fall into their mouths or food). But drinking white milk sap outstrips everything else in the maintenance of health and longevity.

Maleness arises from creating, inside a boy, a "limited fund" of semen. Semen is the substance of life, like blood, and the spark of masculinity. But it is artificially acquired and accumulated, is a runny liquid, and is, therefore, exhaustible. Men thus harbor terrible anxieties about the depletion of their semen. "Semen is hot; it makes the male body hot," men say; whereas women, without their "own" semen, are filled with blood, cold blood, and so they are "cold-skinned." A woman is thought to "consume" a man's semen: first to "strengthen" herself and then to produce children.

> What does an infant come from? No, he comes from the water [semen] of we men, that's all. We give all of our water to the women. And it goes and goes . . . till the water of our bone and semen it is gone. [A moment later, he blurts out:] We give our water to women, only! We strengthen only their skins. . . . Women have no water of their own, only we do. [Tali]

From semen, then, boys and women acquire strength. This saps a man's maleness, debilitating him. So men see all sexual intercourse, homosexual and heterosexual, as an inherently unequal exchange: a man's semen leaves his body to enter the body of another.

It is also true, however, that heterosexual intercourse is, as men see it, more draining than homosexual fellatio. Tali said, "A man loses *all* his semen in vaginal intercourse, just like [plain] water. In fellatio with boys he loses only *half* his water." (It happens that some married men find coitus more exciting than fellatio, and heterosexual fellatio more exciting than its homosexual form.) There are various expressions about this difference, yet one stands out and seems fundamental. For example, when I responded to Tali's preceding statement by asking why, he quickly retorted: "But, the milk [semen], it goes inside the woman's womb, and that isn't a place you can see." And when I asked a group of men where semen went in coitus, they responded by roaring with laughter; then Weiyu said:

The semen goes inside the woman. Women consume semen, it passes into their womb. . . . She's like the earth. She doesn't shake [*kowuptu*]. Only men shake [after coitus]. Then, a man goes to the forest; he puts his legs in the mud; rubs mud on his stomach to stop the shaking.

The drift of these idioms thus suggests that a prime source of men's fears is the belief that semen disappears into the womb, becomes hidden and locked inside women's bodies. Never mind that semen is also consumed by boys. It seems to be feminine bodies that cause worry.

The situation is more complicated than this since, in the course of a marriage, the same man and woman have innumerable erotic encounters from which come children. My old informant, Kanteilo, said something close to this notion many times.

Semen isn't strong [*jerungdu*]. You give your semen to the woman by copulating with her. By that you die quickly, age quickly. If semen were strong, like a stone, and you gave *that* to your wife, you'd live a long time, not age fast. You'd still be strong at death, too. Semen is like water. Man is made from it, made only from semen. As a man gives up semen, he grows weak, ages, deteriorates, and dies.

This viewpoint is complemented by a saying that in a woman's body, only the "vagina is hot." It "heats the man's penis," so his semen is ejaculated. Men say that the vagina is so hot, in fact, that they must watch that their penises do not become "overheated and cooked by the bamboo [vagina]," so that their entire pool of semen (from inside the semen organ) does not "boil out" into the vagina. In some men this idea becomes a preoccupation, bordering on morbid obsession, that their wives are in effect "eating" their biological strength and thus gradually killing them. As farfetched as this idea sounds, it is not uncommon.

Men fear masculine atrophy. The gist of the Sambia ethos is that first boys, and then women, drink from a man's vessel, reducing and diminishing that precious fund. These concerns about depletion have given rise to a culturally standardized means of artificially replacing one's semen believed to have been ritually acquired from fellatio. This is effected by ingesting the white milk saps mentioned earlier. This milk sap is, in various respects, compared and equated to semen, mother's milk, and pandanus nuts. Kanteilo speaks of the mythic origins of this practice:

A man's children come from his semen only. The first man who came, Numboolyu, thought to himself: "If I fornicate with my wife, and give her semen, where can I get more? He found *aamoonaalyi* [mother's milk; K means tree sap] to replace his semen.

Even bachelors must replace the semen initiates take.

> Bachelors drink the milk of trees sometimes. They "catch their breath" from copulating with initiates. Some fathers still tell their bachelor sons: "You can't 'play with' initiates too often; it could finish your 'water.'" [Tali]

This act is performed, therefore, after each occasion of heterosexual intercourse. (Youths are not as scrupulous about homosexual fellatio, nor does ritual edict require it.) The ingested white sap has three jobs to do. It is used to coat the penis after vaginal penetration to purify it. It is swallowed and is said to coat the inner lining of the stomach, protecting against menstrual blood ("ingested" by the urethra). And it is thought to "replace" ejaculated semen, substituting for what was lost from the semen organ. As long as men adhere to this practice, they say they can stave off morbid depletion. Otherwise, atrophy is certain: all their masculine characteristics will imminently recede in the face of impending death.

There is no doubt that most men actually "believe" in this dogma about the substitution of tree sap for semen. Yet this statement still begs a number of questions like: What is a belief? a conviction? are there "false" beliefs and "true" beliefs? in what ways are men conscious of the differences in these substances and their origins and functions? and are they able or willing to describe them? They are, in fact; and Sambia men are prone to need the comforting *experience* of swallowing tree sap after coitus. This is true despite men's sense of "incomparability" between body products, like milk or semen, and tree sap, which men themselves sometimes note, and despite some doubts that semen has any true substitute. Nothing is as "powerful" as semen. Nevertheless, what else is available to restore it? Ritual provides that measure of reassurance.

The Erotic Transition

It is ironic that Sambia men, who doubt the innateness of their maleness and are so much at home in their forests, should have hit upon tree sap for the replenishment of their semen pools. This kind of "symbolic" process is intriguing. But we should not lose sight of the overall Sambia perspective: one kind of external substance is being replaced by another kind of external substance in the functioning of biological maleness and its ritualized product, masculinity. Mother's milk and food nurture; semen extends maleness and manliness; and white tree sap helps maintain the results. This developmental cycle has three interlocking dimensions: sexual customs, erotic experience, and the origins and changes in a man's sense of himself and his maleness (gender identity) that give rise to all behavior, including his desire and capacity to perform as a "normal" man in the ways other Sambia expect and demand.

Sambia boys are initiated into a secret cult that severely constrains sexual experience along definite lines. Boys first become fellators. Initiation counteracts maternal influences and requires fellatio ingestion of semen for many years. At puberty boys' roles are reversed; youths become fellateds. They are prodded into it. They are heterosexually suppressed and have no alternative sexual outlet. Yet they still have some choice: they are not compelled to copulate with boys, and each time they do so they know that they are "depleting" their semen. For some years, youths continue living in the clubhouse, engaging exclusively in homosexual fellatio. After marriage they have a woman available as a fellator too. For a brief period of a year or two, youths can be truly bisexual. But once the wife's menarche occurs and they begin coitus, homosexual activities should halt. To introduce the penis (contagiously infected by the wife's vagina) into a boy's mouth would be a dangerous, polluting act. Most men do in fact become exclusively heterosexual after marriage. But a few do not. They continue to desire homosexual fellatio more than heterosexual fellatio or coitus.[60] This is, in sum, the transitional pattern of Sambia sex customs.

Much in this cycle is awkward and dangerous, pleasurable and necessary, and matters of life and death for Sambia boys as they mature. Much is cause for consternation, turmoil, and even desperation, as the threats of secret ritual testify. The secret cult demands allegiance; it creates warriors and is the basis of men's domination over women and children. So boys and youths alike must conform; either that, which rewards manhood, or else oblivion by weakness, female contamination, or death. Put in these terms, the male developmental cycle seems more understandable.

Nevertheless, there remain dazzling questions about the erotic reversals

---

60. Let me underscore this point. Transitional homosexual fellatio contacts are a regular part of male development, but there is some individual variation in their performance and subjectivity. A small number of "deviants" (in Sambia terms) diverge from the normative transitional pattern at either extreme of the erotic continuum: thus, there are a few extremely heterosexually inclined males—individuals who experienced early, intense heterosexual interest, and associated lack of interest in homosexual activities, with low participation in homosexual fellatio; and there are a few extremely homosexually inclined males—individuals with an early, intense interest in homosexual practices that continues into adulthood, so that, as men, they enjoy, or even prefer, homosexual relationships with boys regardless of the availability of women as sex partners. The total number of these "deviants" probably constitutes no more than 5 percent of the entire male population. Some of these homosexually oriented men, after marriage and fatherhood, still continue to engage in homosexual activities even though they are disparaged for doing so. Please note, however, that they act only as inserters, not as fellators to younger boys—which is strictly forbidden, is immoral, and would be regarded as unspeakably unmanly. (I know of only two reported instances of older males acting as fellators for younger males, out of scores of cases investigated.)

—behavioral and subjective "flip-flops"—among Sambia males that are, for most Westerners, simply mind-boggling. What do these changes in erotic behavior imply about gender identity?

If, through my choice of research focus, I can reduce this problem to its usual anthropological interest, there is little cause for wonder. When anthropologists turn to such developmental experiences, our writings turn not to eroticism but to social customs (but see Levy 1973, who is exceptional). Now the problem of sexual transitions becomes so easy that it nearly vanishes. Our vantage point becomes *institutionalized* social relationships and sexual practices. "Society" takes precedence. Society requires sexual intercourse for its "reproduction." Sambia society's organ is a male cult. The cult has a socially regular cycle of expected, necessary rituals. So Sambia men hold that the male body lacks a mechanism for overcoming maternal effects and manufacturing semen, a belief that men cling to as the *raison d'être* of masculinity. So be it: that is simply one New Guinea society's ingenious means for creating social relationships and perpetuating the family and cultural order. That human solution may be repugnant to some. But homosexual fellatio is what boys and youths do, "normal," average males. So when ritual demands that men turn to women, they conform. Even if they still copulate with boys; even if they happen to prefer or enjoy it; even if they savor women or detest the vagina; even if coitus occurs but once in a blue moon—as infrequently as every five years (see Heider 1976)! This is ritual custom: it is what men must do to be men, even if they must be dragged into manhood screaming all the way.

Readers may sense that something is amiss in this structural-functional perspective, since it ignores the humanness of Sambia eroticism: love, anger, or warmth, sexual excitement and behavior. What if instead of examining only a great tradition of social customs, we also focus on the experiences of its individual purveyors? Now we must again question those erotic reversals in behavior and their meaning for a man's sense of himself. Sambia are then not so different from us; let us completely erase the boundary for a moment.

Why do I feel that my mother's blood has thwarted my growth? How can I remain convinced that my own body cannot make me a man: produce semen? If ejaculation is so terribly threatening, then why am I urged to engage in intercourse? If it is so dangerous, then how can I get erotically excited? If it were not that dangerous, could I get excited at appropriate times? How do I have the psychological capacity to be aroused by the thought of copulating with an eight-year-old boy, with his mouth or with a woman's mouth? And how can I manage to become excited by a woman after so many years?

Here we face problems of the origins of sexual excitement, masculinity, and femininity, and of the part secret initiation and ritualized homosexuality play in these origins. The resolution of these problems requires more than knowledge of idioms and cultural ideology. In the next chapter, then, I anticipate that broader study of individual development by describing the central myth of male parthenogenesis and its complex meaning.

CHAPTER EIGHT *Male*
Parthenogenesis:
A Myth and Its Meaning

Men begot humanity through homosexual fellatio: this is what men's myth of parthenogenesis communicates in secret. Our investigation began with Tali's assertion to that effect; in a single communication, he drew on myth, belief, and idiom in explaining the present order of things—the natural reproductive competence of femaleness and the urgent need that boys be homosexually inseminated. This chapter examines the *meaning* of that myth: its role as a collective system of fantasy, perceptions, and value orientations, and as a personal script ordering the experience of Tali and other Sambia individuals.

It is essential to stress the relationship between meaning and personal experience in crowning this study of Sambia idioms, for this spectacular fantasy pinpoints all the great contradictory currents of masculine culture.

The myth heralds the attainment of full manhood in two distinctive ways: first, it is told only to men who have climbed the ladder of initiations and finally fathered a child; and second, it is communicated in absolute secrecy as sacred knowledge. Viewing the myth as a communication medium makes it apparent that the psychological frame of the myth-telling context is as significant as its textual contents. The meaning that the creation myth holds for individuals derives semantically from both these aspects. In terms of the previous classification of ritual, then, the transmission of this myth to adult men is but the final confirmatory rite (after sixth-stage initiation) in their transitional achievement of masculine reproductive competence.

All these facts about an unusually secret fantasy suggest that it has powerful functions in adult male identity and behavior, particularly erotic life. Hence we shall consider the myth not only as a cultural institution but as a source of psychological functioning and character development. But first the story of the myth and what it tells—how mankind came about.

THE MYTH (Part 1)

Numboolyu and Chenchi[1] emerged from the trunk of the *dowutu* [softwood] tree. Numboolyu came outside first, and he was followed by that other "man," Chenchi, a Nokwai [tribesman], his age-mate. This occurred at Kokona.[2]

Numboolyu was the first man. He had a very small penis.[3] He did not know what his penis was. It was so small. He kept it hidden with rubbishlike things. One day Numboolyu pulled his penis out from his pubic area. It became a bit longer. He continued to hide his penis several days more. But he did not sleep well at night for his penis was intensely erect.

Then Numboolyu had his first ejaculation by masturbating himself. When he ejaculated, his semen fell on the ground. Later he urinated nearby. He compared the two substances. The urine, he noticed, was only water. But the semen looked just like snot [*chenamnu*]. He thought it looked just like the juice of pandanus nuts. So he knew it was something good. Then he decided to copulate with his partner.

Numboolyu showed his age-mate "woman" [who is verbally transformed at this point from male to female gender] his penis, asking, "What is this? I don't know

1. The secret name married men also use in referring to menstrual blood and the vagina of the dog. Numboolyu is the putative ancestor of many of the great clans of the Sambia River Valley phratries. He is also a culture hero.

2. Nokwai is the Sambia name of a Menya-speaking tribe of Menyamya. Kokona is the legendary Sambia homeland.

3. One informant, Nilutwo, illustrated the penis size by pushing the knuckle of his index finger about an inch between and above the fingers of his other hand.

why it [penis] won't rest." Then Numboolyu began copulating with the [age-mate] woman in her mouth. But soon she complained to him, objecting that the intercourse was not enjoyable. She said this was because Numboolyu's penis was too short. Whereupon she fetched a bamboo knife and slit open his foreskin, exposing the glans penis. The penis grew bigger and nicer. The "woman" declared: "Now it is good; I will eat it [suck the penis, ingest the semen]."

At this time both Numboolyu and his partner had enlarged breasts [like a normal woman's]. As Numboolyu began copulating with the woman in her mouth, however, his own breasts fell "flat" [like a normal male]. Yet the "woman's" breasts grew larger and swollen. She had no genitals at all; she possessed only a mouth and an anus.[4]

The woman's stomach then began to swell. The couple wondered what could be the cause: "What has produced this great belly? Has she eaten too many sweet potatoes, or what?" The woman started having abdominal pains, and from the pain she began screaming. She screamed and screamed. She retired to a small, shabby house—the *pulungatnyi-angu* [menstrual hut]—that the couple had built away from their house. The woman continued to scream from her stomach pains; then Numboolyu thought to himself: "What can I do to relieve her pain?" So Numboolyu entered the menstrual hut. With his bamboo knife he made a vertical slit in the woman's pubic area. When he made the cut a child fell outside. Some of the birth blood splashed onto Numboolyu's face. A female child was born, and when he saw it, Numboolyu proclaimed: "Another kind [a female person] has come out!" Then he covered the child with banana leaves.[5] He then used his hand to remove the birth fluids from his brow.

The birth blood flowed into the river Tekutaalyu ["taro place"] at far away Menyamya. Now the Green people [a Sambia hamlet in the Lower Green River Valley] are forbidden to drink this river water when their wives have menstrual periods.

Our women, at their menarche, go to the menstrual hut. Their menstrual blood flows and they have the fashion of sleeping in that house. When women kill the moon [menstruate], they go to the menstrual house. This means they are ready for marriage since their menstrual blood is flowing.

When women give birth, they do not let us [males] see the birth. This is because

---

4. In another telling of the myth, I heard Tali and Weiyu say something quite different about the genitalia of the fellator age-mate. They remarked that "she" had a microscopic penis that was like a hermaphrodite's until the fellatio began. "His" [sic: fellator's] penis was all right till fellatio, but when his breasts and stomach grew tight [like a pregnant girl's], this pulled that [penis] back inside the skin. Later, when Numboolyu cut open the skin, creating the vagina, he slit the remainder of the penis apart, so that "its nose [glans penis] went on top, becoming the clitoris [*lakandiku*], and the foreskin was split apart to become the vaginal lips [*mugu*], the testes being absorbed into the [vaginal] tissue."

5. Midwives use banana leaves for retaining the child during the delivery, as we saw above. In another version of this myth, a male child was the firstborn. This contradiction may be related to the fact that Sambia women practiced male infanticide when there were no female children. But that is my view: no Sambia suggested it to me.

at the first birth [of Numboolyu's wife], when the "man" had a child, Numboolyu didn't reveal the child, he hid it. Likewise, women today do the same: they hide during childbirth.

Since a girl child was the firstborn, girls always grow faster than boys now. The firstborn girl child "grew" first; now girls grow faster than boys. Boys would grow faster than girls, but the firstborn child of Numboolyu was a girl.

The woman [the new mother] continued to live in the menstrual hut. Numboolyu went to the forest. He felt it was wrong to have cut open the woman and he wanted to be in the forest. There, Numboolyu trapped possum and birds.[6] He brought his catch back to his mate. The fur of the *wakoogu* possum Numboolyu and his "wife" used to cleanse their hands [of the birth-blood pollution]. Now our wives use this possum fur to cleanse themselves following birth.[7]

Numboolyu speared birds for his wife and child to eat. Because of this, now we men have the bow and arrows [for hunting]. Numboolyu also cut a digging stick for his wife. Now our women use them for planting sweet potatoes.

After the birth, Numboolyu's wife had a vagina [where he had made a vertical slit at the pubic area] so he could copulate with her down below.[8] He proceeded to copulate with her—sometimes in fellatio intercourse and sometimes in vaginal intercourse.[9] In time his wife became pregnant again. This time she produced a male child.[10]

After he had created the vulva, Numboolyu said he then had two pathways [orifices] for sexual intercourse: the mouth and the vagina. First he had copulated with his wife's mouth[11] for two years. Then he made her vulva. But now we know that a woman must be copulated with in her vagina to produce a child; fellatio

---

6. At birth, masticated meat of the morning lark is fed to the infant to induce in him a clear and melodious speech like the bird's song.

7. During the public birth ceremonies, in the mother's house following her emergence from the menstrual hut a few days later, the smell of the burning possum fur cleanses the new mother and child of the birth pollution, enabling her husband to sleep in the house without fear of pollution.

8. During the telling of this sequence of the myth, my informant, Weiyu, spontaneously likened the transformation of the male age-mate, through homosexual fellatio, into a biological female as the "same thing" that had occurred to a Sambia "transsexual" now living at Mountain Station. That person was reared as a biological female; but following marriage, her husband discovered that his wife had a penis. I should note that Weiyu had referred to a case that is the precise inverse of what the myth states: the Mountain Station "transsexual" man was reared as a woman and had "changed" his identity to the male gender; see below.

9. In the first version I collected, Numboolyu is portrayed as caring for a girl child until she was grown and had experienced her first menses. Then he proceeded to copulate with her, producing many children. In the other version, a male child was born, and Numboolyu continued to copulate with his original wife.

10. When telling this myth a second time, Tali suggested another facet. He said: "Because of this [a male child being second-born], a man initially has fellatio intercourse with his wife and this produces a female child." This is of course a logical inversion of his original version, in which fellatio actually produced a female child. Nonetheless, I have heard both versions told, and men seem to have no difficulty in entertaining them.

11. This odd semantic construction aptly characterizes the thought of men, who are prone to make a fetish of the fellator's mouth as distinct from the whole person.

alone will not produce a child. Before there was no vulva; now women have the vagina. The semen of Numboolyu alone created the pathway into the vagina.

THE MYTH (Part 2)

One day Numboolyu's eldest son came to him. He said, "Father, my penis is erect. What can I do about it?" Numboolyu thought to himself: "My wife is here, but she is my scale [sexual partner]. I can't send my boy to my wife."[12] The son reiterated to his father: "Father, I have no woman, but my penis is erect; what can I do?"

Numboolyu instructed his eldest son to go and copulate with his younger brother [in homosexual fellatio].[13] [In telling the myth, Tali interrupted at this point and said: "If Numboolyu had sent his oldest son to copulate with the boy's mother we (men) would also give over our wives to our sons when the boys reach puberty! But he didn't, so we don't share our wives! Had Numboolyu sent his son to his wife, she wouldn't have refused him; she wouldn't have said no. She would have copulated with the boy."[14]] Later, Numboolyu thought to himself: "It would be bad if the boy became pregnant from sucking his older brother's penis." But their father decided to wait and see what would happen. He thought that if the younger boy did become pregnant, he could then tell the older son to cut open the boy's stomach to make birth possible [as Numboolyu had previously done]. But Numboolyu did not tell his wife about this. He thought that if the younger boy became pregnant then he would tell her.

So Numboolyu waited, but the younger boy did not become pregnant. ["Now we can copulate with boys without worrying that they will become pregnant," Tali said. "We do not tell women that we do this. For Numboolyu first hid it (his sons' homosexual fellatio) from his wife."] If the younger boy had become pregnant then Numboolyu would have told his wife: "Oh, wife, before we had intercourse [fellatio]: this boy, he did the same to his younger brother, who has become pregnant." But the younger boy did not become pregnant and Numboolyu hid the boys' homosexual practices from his wife.[15]

The elder son did not go to his mother and ask her what he could do about his erect penis. He went to his father instead. And his father sent him to his younger brother. Numboolyu thought: "Why should I send my boy to my wife? She is my scale. I have two roads for my penis [vagina and mouth]!" Numboolyu

---

12. Here is another convoluted construction: "My wife is my sexual scale. I can't send my boy to her." See below.

13. Later I asked the men this question: "Did Numboolyu's son copulate with the younger boy to 'strengthen' the latter or because the other boy's penis was erect?" They quickly chuckled and replied: "The elder son had a 'tight' penis; he wanted an *imbimboogu* [orgasm]."

14. This statement provoked intense and sustained laughter among the men for the first time, breaking the serious mood in which they had begun.

15. Of this, Tali said the following: "Originally boys did not grow quickly; the boy was the second-born. Only fellatio can make boys grow quickly following initiation. So boys must have semen to ingest and help them grow."

thought: "It wouldn't be good if the boy copulated with my wife and then the two of us [father and son] fought." [Tali: "If he (Numboolyu) had not done this, now we would copulate with our mothers and sisters." [16]]

Parthenogenesis and Masculine Idioms:
A Hypothesis

The purpose of this pat story is single-minded and bluntly insistent. It leaves no room for fallible doubts about the "true" origins of mankind, maleness, or femaleness: men created all.

This myth is rendered as a powerful exemplar of the social scheme of things. Numboolyu, putative patrilineal ancestor, is its hero. Like all heroes, he confronts momentous "problems" in life and discovers "solutions." Numboolyu was the first "man"; it was he who created masculinity and femininity in their present form, and who fathered us all. Hence this ancestor—"our father," as Sambia fondly refer to him—patterned the male cult, ritualized homosexuality, and the right order of relationships between the sexes.

Malinowski (1954) would have seen in this tale a timeless "charter" for the present-day institutions of Sambia society. Such a sociological viewpoint is undeniably important. It helps account for the cosmology surrounding men's rituals no less than the political functions of male initiation or the perpetuation of the economic division of labor among the sexes. The myth sanctifies and normalizes ritual custom for the privileged few by appealing to ancestral authority. And surely there is no greater claim to obedience than that of social authority petrified in dogmatic myth.

If all this is correct, and I think it is, then why is this revelation such a closely guarded secret?

There are many kinds of secrets in Sambia life, some of them so transparent that their discovery could easily set off an explosion between men and women. This myth is not that kind of screaming secret, although some aspects of homosexual activities may be of this sort. But if women know *some things* about male ritual, if they know enough to suspect the existence of homosexual activities, I believe they are completely ignorant of this myth. The myth is an unqualified secret; it behooves us to explore the significance of that fact.

The myth comes at a critical moment in a young man's life. He is married. He may still engage in homosexual fellatio, too, if he can get a

---

16. My informant Nilutwo repeated this idea several times while laughing hysterically. (The other men were laughing too.) Nilutwo remarked that copulating with one's mother is no better than the habits of a dog, but he continued to laugh.

boy to go along with it. (At least until the time of his wife's menarche.) But when he finally fathers an infant, his homosexual activities should forever halt. Otherwise he gets branded as "odd."[17] It is at this point, full manhood won, that the myth is revealed to him.[18] The young father becomes a new recruit into the deepest "mystery" of the male cult; the context and "story line" of the myth ask a man to capitulate to that secret.

Putting the problem of individual meaning this way requires us to investigate an enigmatic contradiction between this simple story—which holds that maleness is at the root of all things human—and the constant trend of masculine idioms, which convey an opposite view.

The manifest attributes of natural species like cassowary and pandanus, for example, are genderized, but their reproductive competence is tacitly associated with female traits. In humans, too, men see females as naturally able to achieve maturity on their own. In boys, however, the fragility of maleness is underlined by the requirement of ritual treatment, i.e., masculinization. Male rhetoric reflects male worry about the overwhelming female influences of the boys' mothers, which must be counteracted for boys to reach manhood. This "tension" between the predominance of femaleness or maleness in males, lies, I think, at the heart of this myth. Consider a cultural interpretation of this puzzle.

The story of male parthenogenesis appears to suspend this ideological tension. It asserts that maleness—penises and semen—came first in the mythic past. The myth is therefore reactionary: it turns back the pervasive pressure of femaleness by reinforcing the innateness of maleness and the primordial solidarity of men. Hence the enigma appears to fade: while masculine theory recognizes the dimorphism of species, and the dual sexual nature of fetal development, male rhetoric protests against the femaleness of things, and this myth secretly resolves any doubts about the origins of human reproductive superiority in favor of men.

At first glance this cultural interpretation looks convincing. The myth reiterates masculine parturition idioms that men impregnate women, help create the fetus, and provide for the infant's milk. Men not only feminize females; they also father heirs and perpetuate patrilineal kin groups. Furthermore, it attests to the need for men to engage in coitus and steer their sons into transitional homosexuality. Indeed, we sense that to have knowledge of this myth means that one has carnal knowledge of both boys and

17. There is individual variation, as noted above: some men continue to engage in homosexual activities after fifth-stage initiation, when ideally they should stop; a few men continue after fatherhood, too, but Sambia consider them deviants, a subject of later writings.

18. Nowadays men are told this myth when they are engaging in regular coitus, or when their wives are pregnant but have not yet given birth. Weiyu was told this myth a few months before the birth of his wife's first child.

women. Manhood means that one has successfully held that inseminating power over both. Men are in charge, then, and masculinity is the well-spring of the family and society. Such virulent dogmas of male solidarity are commonplace throughout New Guinea (Allen 1967; Langness 1974; Read 1954; see also Chapter 9).

On closer inspection, however, this view is incomplete: it cannot account for all the data. It conveys, like many ethnographies, a truncated description of the outward ideology and stereotyped action of male solidarity, not an accounting of the meaning of men's actual behavior. For we are still left with the nagging problem of the myth's secrecy. This is, I think, our most important clue about the overall meaning of the story and its behavioral context.

It might be objected that the myth's secrecy simply protects the secrecy of homosexuality itself. This is partially true, yet it is also incomplete. Why is the myth also hidden from younger initiated males? Why not lay to rest their doubts, too, about their lot in life before the final stage of fatherhood?

Barth (1975:219) has suggested the following solution to a similar problem: collective secrets of this sort are mysteries necessarily inscrutable, and hidden, until one has achieved admission into the inner sanctum of a ritual cult.[19] Without mystification, Barth reasons, there is no inexplicable, seductive force to sanctify the secret power of male rites or the need to distance males and females (see also Langness 1974:209).

This view makes the assumption that all men, including New Guinea men, have a compelling need—be it ideational, political, or psychological —to harbor secrets and exploit mysteries. What are men secreting— property or self—or taking pleasure in through such mystification and ritual domination? For example, why do men need distancing mechanisms in their institutional and interpersonal relationships with women? *And* with youths and boys?[20] Nor does this intellectualistic view enable us to understand why, for Sambia, homosexual practices are also secret. It is not only that men hide this myth through ritual secrecy, but also that the affective behaviors—excitement, frantic exclusion of women, shame—

---

19. Barth's (1975:219–221) work provides some insights into the uses of secrecy among Baktaman that parallel the characteristics of Sambia ritual secrecy. But Sambia mystify their ritual symbols more in relation to women than to initiates, compared to what Baktaman apparently do; nor is suspiciousness among males as rampant among Sambia, who nonetheless engage in deception (see below).

20. Langness (1967) suggests that, traditionally, warfare required several clamps to be placed on male and female relationships in New Guinea societies, a point with which I agree. His 1974 paper, however, stresses that men are naturally attracted to women and that secrecy and mystery keep men powerful over women. He does not explain the uses of secrecy in regard to younger males; see below.

through which they do so require an explanation. In short, to suggest that male secrecy (or ritualized homosexuality) is what men do to be solidary or control women only avoids these other problems, which go unanswered for want of more descriptive observations.

I wish to take a different approach in tackling these psychosocial questions, one in which we include qualitative data about individual experience. Contrary to the conventional anthropological view that New Guinea male myths and idioms only represent the collective assertion of male superiority and solidarity over women, I suggest that this story, and its particular form of secrecy, actually disguise men's deep doubts about their maleness. Not until males are older can this fantasy be passed on without overwhelming them.

It is my hypothesis, therefore, that this myth helps convert a man's nagging fears that he has feminine attributes into a positive conviction that he is masculine.

This dread I shall refer to as the transsexual fantasy (see Stoller 1977: 138–145) in masculine thought and behavior. It arises from the inability to be convinced that one is really a male and not a female. (Indeed, few adults ever consciously question the possibility, or existential results of, belonging to the opposite sex.) This possibility is disguised in the myth, momentarily entertained and then vanquished, as I shall argue. The myth has the characteristics of a daydream, a shared fantasy. To an outsider it seems fantastic, overstated, and even comic. The tale is highly condensed; indeed, like a daydream, its compactness is its chief strength. It is more than an ideological signpost: it is also a personal reality, one that is prescribed religiously, and may be reexperienced again and again.

Thus we shall need to unravel the myth's capacity as a culturally transmitted *structure of thought* (Lévi-Strauss 1967) as well as a *personal script* in the lives of men.

The myth embraces three semantic components in its naturalistic context: namely, the context of the myth-telling itself, its narrative style, and its textual (especially ideational) contents. Meaning can be attached to all three aspects, and they no doubt semantically overlap in individual experience. Of the three elements, ethnographers normally ignore the behavioral context, only mention the style, and usually concentrate on the logical structure or "story" of a myth. Initially, I shall speak schematically for the most part; then I shall illuminate the style and contents with observations of individual behavior.

The Narrative Context

The context of the myth-telling is a time near sixth-stage initiation and the birth of a man's first child. The myth can be told in the men's house or in forest houses out of hearing distance of women, children, and younger initiates. Several elders, other interested men, and the new *aatmwunu* (fathers) recruits assemble. But what matters most is absolute secrecy.

So guards are posted. The handful of times I heard this myth told in its entirety, men were stationed around the hut (where sat the elders) to guarantee that intruders were kept away. Younger initiates were chased off. Women, who on one occasion happened on the scene, were angrily reprimanded and cursed. The sentries simultaneously chased them off with the warning that we were discussing *pweiyu-yungalu*, "men's ritual talk." Such defenses also surround secret initiation rituals. (There is seldom a need for guards, however, since the noise of so many men and the knowledge that ritual is being staged in the area are reason enough to keep intruders distant if they know what is good for them. What does occur is a guarding against the opposite possibility: boys running away.) These safety measures do not embrace myth or storytelling in general, though, and as far as I know, this is the only Sambia myth that is absolutely secret.[21] This fact merits an aside.

For Sambia, posting guards to guarantee secrecy is hardly extraordinary. Ritual secrecy is a recognized dimension of men's collective ritual action. Indeed, it is simply impossible to comprehend Sambia life without an appreciation of masculine secrecy and its hidden eroticism. Aside from rituals, the clubhouse and most of its doings are shrouded in mystery too. Secret matters are not, of course, discussed in the presence of women and children. Furthermore, a whole corpus of ritual things have secret names,[22] so even the native language is entangled in secrecy. This secrecy means that an entire world of men's experiences is forever walled off and hidden from their wives, mothers, sisters, and daughters (but not their male children).

Methodologically, the design and meaning of male secrecy is, by its very nature, difficult to describe, since its threads lead everywhere and nowhere. This is (unfortunately for the ethnographer) an understandable paradox. For the "reality basis" of secrecy is its status as a silent subjective convention. Only when men collectively gather for initiations are secret communications objectified in ritual teachings or actions. (That is why ritual and the myth context are dangerous to outsiders.) Otherwise, secre-

---

21. Most origin myths, like those telling of how tuber crops or animals came to be, are public knowledge, and women also know of them. There are also anecdotal stories, mere fragments of myth, telling how women first invented the bamboo flutes; and while they have a secret quality, less so than the flutes themselves, such tales are not absolute secrets. Even mention of parthenogenesis sets men to taking serious precautions.

22. As distinct from mere word taboos that prevent people from saying the names of things, i.e., the vagina, or of categories of persons, i.e., the names for one's ritual sponsor or age-mates.

cy depends on the conscious self-regulation of every initiated male and his commitment to an unspoken conspiracy. Men must be constantly watchful of their own behavior (verbal and nonverbal) lest they unwittingly disclose secrets in the presence of women or children and thus disclose a piece of "themselves" that is secret: here is the rub of masculine secrecy as a context of communication.

Only among men, and then only in secret, can men let down their guard. This fact is, for men, exciting, necessary, and burdensome. "Women don't know about our rituals," men advise. "Women, they don't know that we play around," initiates say, grinning, impetuous, spontaneous, as if they were putting one over on the women. Consciously, ostensibly, verbally, then, secrecy is, at heart, the exciting labyrinth of homosexual fellatio and its trappings.

Ritual stands like an edifice that harbors its own mysteries. One mystery surrounds the flutes, which we shall examine shortly. Another mystery is how men manage to take the puny boys and transform them into handsome, vigorous warriors. But the myth of parthenogenesis is a very different sort of mystery; for unlike pieces of ritual, or perhaps homosexual relationships (which men feel that women suspect), this story remains a complete secret, with not even a hint of it outside the actual myth-telling, as men unequivocally attest. Now let us return to that setting.

With guards posted, it is safe for men to retell the myth. The narrators and the male audience need hide nothing. They are free, that is, to be "themselves," meaning that they can emotionally respond to the "story line" in ways otherwise forbidden. And the myth is psychologically compelling in this way.

So let us examine the emotional characteristics of the participants, and their behavior in the myth-telling situation. This will help establish a context for analyzing the myth's thematic contents. "Shame" (*wungulu*) and its tense silence first come to mind. The story opened with Numboolyu, who was said to have "had a very small penis," which he hid among "rubbishlike things." When I observed the men, they fell silent during this segment, except for the narrator. (When Sambia hide things from others, it is usually because they are embarrassed.) Our hero masturbates himself, a perfectly shameful act (which males universally deny doing). He copulates with his age-mate, another shameful, taboo act. The ancestor then tolerates his "wife's" operation on his precious penis; he enters the forbidden menstrual hut; there he delivers the baby and is polluted—all unthinkably humiliating, shame-inflicting acts. Finally, Numboolyu chooses to hide the baby; his heterosexual coitus from his sons; and eventually his sons' homosexual relationship from his wife. These hiding behaviors, we shall see, entail only one *hostile* posture toward the polar forms of secret eroticism: the "shame of homosexual fellatio" and the "shame of heterosexual coitus."

Next there is what I shall call phallic potency and its pride. Numboolyu can copulate with his partner's mouth, but not vice versa. His dominant erotic role (as inserter) increases the size of his penis. On the other hand, his inseminations *feminize* [23] his age-mate, increasing her breasts and impregnating her. He "creates" her vulva so that she can give birth. During the myth-telling, the young recruits sat wide-eyed and stone-faced; but some of the older men began to snicker at this point, as occurs during lewd jokes. Then, as I noted above, Weiyu cut in, remarking how much this was like the hermaphrodites' "changing their sex." The men discussed this thought; their talk grew more animated. As if to assent that his wife is sexual chattel, then, Numboolyu remarks that he has "two orifices with which to copulate," a common idiom applied to women as wives (and also a metaphor for heterosexual cohabitation). Men definitely became more restless and excited at the next point, when the myth tells how the ancestor had "created the vagina." One other major mood overtook the men after this point.

Amusement, then laughter, emerged when the storytellers declared that, for want of a homosexual outlet, the son would have copulated with his mother. The elder son first presented his pubescent erotic needs to his father. Numboolyu was perplexed but stern: he couldn't lend his sex partner to his sons, not even if they were in need. Men were momentarily severe; the ancestor didn't want to share his wife. The hero thus shrewdly taught homosexual practices and hid what his sons were doing from his wife, men smugly communicated. Because the younger boy was not impregnated, the "trick" (hiding fellatio) worked: that is the emotional sense of that mythic element. Tali said, "If he had not done this [instituted homosexual activities for bachelors], now we would copulate with our mothers and sisters," which might lead to patricide, an outrageous thought that provoked a storm of laughter within our group. In Nilutwo, especially, this laughter became hysterical: he was beside himself, laughing so hard for several minutes that tears streamed down his face, and he halfway fell off his chair.

We need to account for these emotional elements. The three mood signs (let us label them thus), namely, shame, mastery or pride, and deceptive humor, were behaviorally attached to the myth-telling experience. Here I wish to establish a simple but crucial dimension of these data. These affective behaviors are communicative signs that reveal different

---

23. I am thinking of the converse process of masculinization: here, fellatio (and then coitus) enhances the femaleness and femininity of the ancestress. The myth states the premise of male idiom: semen strengthens female bodies for childbearing and provides milk. Semen consumed by male bodies becomes strength and semen that masculinizes; and vice versa.

senses of men's responsiveness to the story. We should remember that men have stationed guards to ensure secrecy. Then it becomes clear that by so doing they have been made *comfortable enough* to vent feelings communicated by tense silence, snickering, and piercing laughter. At the very least this situation plainly illustrates how the myth opens up a part of a man's experience that he wishes to keep hidden from women and youngsters. Another way of saying this is that a man feels compelled to hide pieces of himself, and his maleness (his gender identity), from others who differ greatly from himself. This sense of identity can be comfortably experienced in the narrative context only so long as a definite distance is kept from women. A distinct boundary must be maintained between the part of himself that can roar with laughter and the usual, reserved comportment of manliness in public.[24] There is individual variation in such experiences, of course, and to state that the group of participants achieves an emotional "identification" with the ancestral hero should not obscure the differences in ideas or feelings individual persons attach to the experience. Conversely, this is a shared myth, not only a private daydream,[25] a distinction that helps explain how the myth, as a culturally constituted fantasy, engenders feelings and thoughts that are so personally real and frightening that they require a group context and sentries to make possible this level of individual emotional involvement.

The capacity for spontaneous identification with the story raises the next aspect of mythological meaning, the narrative style. As an oral tradition, the narrative mode of this secret story differs from other forms of Sambia tales. One way of clarifying the differences is to examine how the mythic narrative is experienced (intended, felt to be) as a metaphor versus concrete reality. What part of the story goes beyond the "just so" and comes to life within one's self as an uncanny resonance of one's own past? Three examples follow.

First, in war tales, a narrative form quite unlike our myth, men recount events in which they are alleged to have taken part. There is a sense of cool immersion in war tales at the start. Soon enough, however, the narrators' voices speed up, becoming more emotional and frantic. (We know that experience when we think of our own brushes with death,

---

24. For example, men characteristically feel it is unmanly to laugh or joke in public since only boys, not warriors, do that. Although this cultural value is changing today, there are still certain forms of masculine laughter that are strictly forbidden or humiliating, e.g., laughing at one's elders.

25. A point that the Freud of *Totem and Taboo* (1955a: see especially pp. 195–196, 201, 203–204) never fully appreciated. On the concept of identification, I think of Leites's (1970:54, 55, 58, 65, 86) distinctions concerning "achieving a realistic likeness" with another person, i.e., "imitation that is faithful in its favorable strivings"; or in the "adoption of someone else's properties," including the internalization of "true" and "false" beliefs.

especially when death is the object of a deadly "game" like war.) Such tales differ from the myth in their embellishments—the adding of details and little side stories—which tend to humanize the warrior characters (at least those who were on one's side!). Here is a striking stylistic element missing from the myth. For unlike the epic Greek myths or Scandinavian sagas, our secret story virtually ignores character development or poetic imagery for its own sake. Nor does it take much interest in human ambivalence. This style is characteristic of Sambia myth in general, which is shallow and poorly developed compared to that of other New Guinea peoples (see Burridge 1969; Mead 1940) or even Highland peoples (Lawrence and Meggitt 1965:12–23). Parthenogenesis, then, seems like a contemptuously simplistic model of reality; the ancestor emerges, he fornicates, children are born, and he invents the "ways of men." The myth has little time for the ins and outs of Numboolyu's personality or reflection on his lot in life. The story pours out all there is to know about that.

Second, the narrative style of ritual teachings more nearly results in the sense of emotional involvement displayed in the myth of parthenogenesis. Ritual, in fact, is really a communicative frame in which crucial information about reality and survival is thought to be imparted. Like initiation rites, the hearing of the myth is prescribed. Ritual experts do what is esteemed and expected: they impart collective secret wisdom to boys. When, in the nose-bleeding rite, men say they are expelling mothers' blood, the statement is not taken as metaphoric: the blood is concretely said to be her blood. (The question of the degree to which the *individual* feels this to be true is another matter, requiring case studies.) In the penis teaching, however, the bamboo flutes are clearly represented as a phallus; not the penis itself, but a metaphor of and sign for it. So reality and metaphor can meet in ritual.

Third, in the dream report, a common enough event in Sambia life, we are perhaps closest to the narrative style of the myth. In the dream, of course, we hear of an experience that was "actually lived." By this I mean that the dreamer experienced the image and sensations of the dream as another kind of reality (see Appendix B). Sambia dream theory, unlike ours, holds that the soul, moving apart from the person's sleeping body, actually experiences the recalled events of the dream. The dream narrative puts the memory into verbal form: the account becomes a consciously designed "reenactment" of what can be recalled.[26] The shaman's recounting of ghostly encounters in trance states is similar (see Herdt 1977:163). Sambia listeners may sit up and take notice of such reports around their

---

26. Here is one of the numerous questions of informant selection in ethnographic reports. Why

breakfast meal, since dreams hold clues about what has occurred or soon might. The dreamer's submersion in the narrative is dramatic but not complete (since he is awake). Nor does he need to embellish its characters: listeners know the dream's maker. The listeners' responses can vary according to their interest, from fascination to indifference. The key to their identification, I think, is their personal knowledge of having uncannily experienced the dream themselves (or finding it in something that presses on life at the moment).

In other words, Sambia experience a "shifting" sense of consciousness and mythological identification, one contextualized and less scientifically oriented, or stabilized, than ours; and these experiences are reinforced by a perceptual system that easily applies the stamp of factuality to statements that an outsider might construe as mere metaphor (see Price-Williams 1975:91). War tales, ritual teachings, or dream reports all convey elements of truth about reality: our reality, my reality.

An individual can attribute to these narratives varying degrees of what he perceives as a metaphor for actual events. The narrative reinforces this feeling by its contextual claim on truth and in just how vividly its narrator brings the experience to life. Such narratives probably span a gradation of possibilities, for individuals, between the poles of artful metaphor and concrete history.

There is, however, no mistaking the cultural intent of our myth: it is a communication of factual truth that is sacred, awe-inspired, and precious enough to be kept secret at great cost; truth that releases a sigh of "aha" in the listeners; a privileged truth. A culture hero, Numboolyu, is credited with the marvelous invention or discovery of many things in Sambia life. What draws men together is the uncanniness with which this factual truth touches on not only another's life, but mine. In a tribal world spanning but a few miles of forest, an island where every individual is known, named, and understood, human narratives are experienced directly, not vicariously; so parthenogenesis—specially communicated at a special time —makes a great claim on the young men's history and present realities.

Mythological Recapitulation

In such a world, male parthenogenesis is more than a simple fable, and it is greater than an allegory. It is a literal mode of necessity and mode

---

does someone like Nilutwo recall dreams and communicate them (with that implied emotional catharsis) to others far more frequently than is the norm? The most disturbing dreams Nilutwo had were usually disguised or kept secret; therefore, their meaning never becomes public knowledge.

of reality (Cassirer 1970) approximating the world and one's development within it. Yes, the story is fiction, a contortion of imagination and thought; but it is more than a myth—if by that term we mean only a veiled symbol or explanation for truth instead of the resonances of experiences also living inside oneself.

The disguised secret of male parthenogenesis is that it mirrors the developmental history of most Sambia men. It recapitulates what they have experienced and may have felt as children, initiates, youths, and now as men. Indeed, it strikes men as so uncanny in its meaning for their sense of maleness that it provokes equivalent emotional responses in most. The story helps a man to surrender his reluctance at becoming a fully masculine Sambia man and all that entails: the capacity to bear shame, pride, and constant deception alike. Moreover, through his participation in the fiction of male parthenogenesis, a man risks humiliation at the hands of women if these secrets were to get out. Men are rewarded by a deep sense of pleasure in reliving the story's collective delusion: the fantasy that men, alone, created all that is human.

Now let us examine the ideational contents of the narrative with this thought in mind.[27] For want of space I can attend only to the principal elements, particularly those that concern the idioms of masculinity and femininity that we have already noted.

1. The story opens with two males, age-mates, emerging from a garden tree. Numboolyu was first. Age-mates are social equals, as stipulated by initiation. That softwood tree is the first tree used in initiation for the *akovanyu* insertive ritual. So this seems to be the image of the primordial "family": that tree and those two males.

2. Even though Numboolyu is a "man," unlike an adult he has a "very small penis," a child's penis. This thought is reinforced by the next sentence, that "he did not know what his penis was." Besides that ignorance of his own maleness, his penis was prepubescent, a reproductively incompetent penis. So he kept it hidden. He was "ashamed of it," Tali commented (more like how women are alleged to feel ashamed of their genitals). His penis was so embarrassing, in fact, that he hid it amidst rubbish (sweet potato peels), a childish thought.

It was so small that by himself he had to "pull out" the penis from his "pubic area." (Here, "pulling out" was linguistically represented by the metaphor for masturbation; for instance, boys can "pull on the penis" of a fellated to stimulate him manually if he does not have an erection before

27. My perspective in the following section has been much influenced by Stoller's (1977:63–91; 1979:68–86, 205–218) work on erotic daydreams, which I appreciatively acknowledge.

fellatio.) In other words, the penis was "microscopic," and the hero had to manipulate it to enlarge it. But he continued to hide it. Once he gained knowledge of his penis, however, he began to get erections, and his erotic impulses kept him awake at night.

The "discovery" of his own eroticism led him to masturbate. This act, like others in the myth, contravenes standard morals (see Turner 1968b:577), since men and boys alike not only deny masturbation but usually respond to the idea with consternation or disbelieving laughter. Masturbation led to the discovery of semen, too (a substance that boys continually deny knowledge of before their initiations). Noting the perceptual correspondence of semen, snot, and pandanus nuts (unlike urine), Numboolyu acclaimed semen to be "good," i.e., "valuable." Hence, Numboolyu attained puberty, and he decided, matter-of-factly, to copulate with his age-mate.

3. Now we arrive at what I regard as the most compelling secret content of the myth, its transsexual theme. These elements impinge on the developmental scenario of early gender identity formation and eroticism in boys. The myth communicates in plain terms a male's gender confusion: namely, his incapacity to sense unambiguously his maleness, the erotic function of his genitals, or the difference between himself and females.

The hero exhibits his erect penis to his age-mate, who is transformed into a female at that moment in the narrative. Numboolyu implores his partner to "explain" for him the function of his own penis, and pointedly, the meaning of his erection. This interaction results in their first fellatio intercourse. The initial experience of penile erection, masturbation, is thus followed by his first interpersonal erotic activity, fellatio.

As a side note, it should be stressed that the myth does to the transsexual age-mate what initiation does to the boy novice during the penis and flute ritual: it converts him into a "wife" of the flute and an erotic partner for bachelors, fetishizing his mouth as an orifice for sex. Both Numboolyu and the real-life bachelor initially have but one erotic outlet, the age-mate's mouth. And like the ancestor, Sambia bachelors customarily turn to prepubescent boys in trying out—and thereafter anchoring—their pubescent male sexuality and manly gender role in homosexual intercourse.

But the mythical age-mate "complains" that Numboolyu's penis is "too short." "She" does the "unthinkable": slits open the foreskin encircling the glans penis, making it more prominent, like an adult man's. (Using a bamboo knife, she releases the glans from the foreskin in the way women sever the umbilical cord of a newborn infant from its mother's body.) The penis "grows" more. She praises it, that greater protrusion of maleness, declaring that it is then "good" for "eating."

Fellatio, then, produces a larger, maturer penis (and glans penis), and a heightened sense of a male's capacity to perform as a potent male.

This thought leads to a revelation: both Numboolyu and his age-mate had female breasts. Here is another symptom of transsexualism in the scenario: both males originally had female breasts.

Fellatio also changes this. Numboolyu, who now possesses a mature penis, gradually loses his female breasts as a function of copulating with his partner. The last vestige of the hero's femaleness fades away as his penis grows. Conversely, as he copulates with her, his age-mate's breasts expand. So fellatio insemination further clarifies anatomic maleness and femaleness in the couple. The ancestor's inseminations *feminize* his partner as a result of her acquisition of his semen (which becomes a store of milk, expanding her breasts). This completes the transformation of Numboolyu from an unfinished pseudohermaphrodite with a small penis and female breasts into a reproductively competent, masculine male.

It also stimulates his partner's femaleness but still leaves her incomplete. "She had no genitals at all; she only possessed a mouth and an anus." This picture is, in an oblique sense, an image of the ungenitalized body of a Sambia fellator (male or female): he or she possesses a mouth and anus, but the genitals are avoided (note the one-sidedness of the erotic relationship). (Is that also a primordial fantasy about one's mother and women in general? We can only speculate for the present.)

4. The next element, the woman's pregnancy, shifts the couple into the scenario of adult marriage. She develops a swollen stomach, a pregnancy. She goes into painful labor but is without a vulva or birth canal with which to relieve herself and give birth.

Numboolyu himself creates her female genitals. He now uses a bamboo knife (as was used on his genitals) to deliver the infant. Some men particularly stress the hostile element here, that the ancestor physically cut open his wife.[28] So it was his actions that pushed his mate into an adult female state: a "metaphor" for the procreative, marital functions of sexual intercourse between spouses.

His actions, however, pollute him: the birth fluids "splashed onto his face." This "charters" the initiation beliefs about the avoidance and purification rites vis-à-vis menstrual blood and birth, as the reference to prohibitions on drinking water (which men must now observe) clearly shows. Menstrual flows, or the menarche, are thus linked to coitus and marriage

---

28. After completing this manuscript, I conducted further research in 1979. One day, when talking about the myth, Weiyu told me that he spontaneously thought of Numboolyu's actions when he had coitus with his wife: "[When] I walk around . . . Yea! Now, I walk around and copulate with my woman; I think the same thing; oh, this thing [vagina], Numboolyu cut it in her, like this [the way I penetrate the vagina] . . . and I walk around, I copulate with her, too, huh? It was our Numboolyu, it was so very good that he showed us how to do that. . . . [That is how I think about] that something [vagina] belonging to my woman."

in the present scheme of things. It is worth adding, too, that by connecting the ancestor's presence at birth with his pollution, the fear of such pollution is contemporaneously reinforced, as much as by his "unthinkable" entrance into the menstrual hut to deliver the infant.

5. Now we must consider the first of several curious cultural inversions that occur within the myth. Because Numboolyu hid the first birth, women now hide childbirth. The myth is used as a mechanism for inverting responsibility for the present order of male and female relationships. Men first hid birth, so women do so now. (It is as if men were abrogating responsibility for birth itself: here is a parallel with rhetorical idioms that undermine the role of female parturition.) Yet this thought harbors open hostility toward women.

For example, men consciously and vociferously utilize the secrecy of birth as a mundane rationalization for keeping homosexual practices secret. "Women hide childbirth, we hide homosexuality," I have heard men say privately. Contrary to what the myth tells, women are made responsible for hiding childbirth, and then this reversal of the story becomes a rationale for the secrecy of homoerotics.[29]

In a different way, men blame women for the mythical loss of immortality. This event also refers to our myth but is not mentioned in the context of the parthenogenesis narratives described here. Men say that originally, after the first birth, a pool of blood remained on the floor of the menstrual hut. Neither Numboolyu nor his "wife" cleaned it up. A rat entered the hut and ate some of the blood; then the creature disappeared into a hole. Because of this, "we men now die," whereas before, men did not. So it was from the life-giving birth fluids of the ancestress that humanity lost its immortality.

6. Another manifestation of this psychological process occurs in the myth segment surrounding the first infant's birth. An alternate segment holds that the first born was a male. The ancestress, Chenchi, grew "angry" about her labor pains, so she killed the child, an act that then chartered male infanticide. Her anger, men say, also led to what men do today (see Appendix D): they must beat boys in male initiation ceremonies to toughen them for the constant war that becomes an additional hand-me-down of the ancestress's action. Once again, men displace responsibility for initiation and war—fundamentally masculine activities—onto women. (Masculine mythology thus denies men's own part in those warrior institutions, simultaneously distorting the passive nurturance associated with the female gender role.)

---

29. See Schieffelin (1976:224) and Van Baal (1966:493) for strikingly similar idioms among other New Guinea groups who utilize ritualized homosexual activities.

In a similar vein, the fact that the myth makes the firstborn a female provides a handy "explanation" for why girls develop physically at a faster rate than do boys. The myth thus enables men to deflect liability for virtually all of masculine existence onto women's shoulders: male infanticide, initiation, warfare, and the slowness of boys' growth befell men because of that primordial scene.

7. After the birth, Numboolyu goes to the forest for solace. "He felt it was wrong to have cut open the woman." This is a culturally appropriate expression of shame for what he had done—his erotic actions, his wife's impregnation, and his genital surgery on her—that led to the birth. He rewarded his mate (relieves his guilt?) with meat gifts and ceremonial purifications. These events thereby chartered their contemporary counterparts. Consequently, the ancestor's actions led to the present division of labor: men hunt and women garden.

8. Finally, to consummate their marital contract, the myth recognizes how Numboolyu's creation of the vulva made possible genital-to-genital intercourse as occurs only in heterosexual relationships. He no longer had to rely solely on fellatio; he also had a vagina to penetrate. This mythic choice of erotic outlet has tacit significance, for it contains an invidious message also present in the idioms that married men sometimes comfort themselves with: "I now have two orifices [i.e., wife's vagina and mouth], and no longer need to depend on the capricious initiates [fellators] for relaxing my penis." In time the ancestress became pregnant, and again she gave birth to a male infant. Men recognize, as they state, that coitus is necessary for conception; fellatio alone will not impregnate. (This association also links fellatio with the birth of male infants, and coitus with the birth of female infants.) The summing up of the first part of the myth is a masculine assertion: that the ancestor's penis and semen alone completed the female breasts, vulva, and vagina, a married man's erotic object.

9. The last segment of the story recreates how homosexual practices came to be secretly institutionalized. The setting is Numboolyu's family some fifteen years later.

First, his eldest son approaches Numboolyu with his budding manly erections. The youth asks his father's advice about how he can relieve himself. The ancestor is made to confront an image of himself in those years before marriage, and this leads him to ponder his son's growing maleness in a remarkable but obvious way. He thinks to himself that his wife is his only erotic outlet, whom he selfishly prefers not to lend—even to his own son. The youth reiterates his lack of a female mate, demanding that his father advise him.

The ancestor thus sends the youth to copulate homosexually with his younger brother (an incestuous relationship that is another "unthinkable" thought). The hero hid the sons' erotic relationship from their mother, his wife. He worried only that the younger boy might become pregnant, which would force him to cut open the boy's pubic area. This did not occur, however; and since boys do not now become pregnant, it is easy to hide homosexual activities from women. The myth thus charters the secrecy of ritualized fellatio among unmarried males.

We can hardly ignore the Oedipal content of this last part of the narrative. Incest is constantly hinted at. The myth states this concern in a peculiar idiomatic construction: "My wife is my property, I can't let my son copulate with my own sexual partner." Underlying this thought is the psychological frame of kinship and marriage. A boy and his father belong to one clan (local descent group), his mother belongs to another. Sex among clansmen is incestuous and prohibited: a boy can copulate with people of his mother's group, not of his father's group. (Particularly if his mother's kinsmen reside in another hamlet, although matrilateral kin are still not preferred for sex or marriage.) This possibility still does not mean, of course, that his mother is an appropriate erotic partner. Incest taboos and social norms (e.g., spouses should be of similar age) make such an idea preposterous and unheard of, but apparently not unthinkable: that is the latent implication of Numboolyu's thought.

On reflection, the stranger part of men's reactions to this use of incestuous homosexuality as a way of thwarting mother/son incest is men's insistence that the youth's mother would not have denied him sexual access. (The myth implies that women are such lascivious creatures that even maternal care would succumb to wanton eroticism.)

The myth-tellers make it clear, therefore, that homosexual activities came about for only one reason: the need for a transitional erotic outlet. To avoid incest, fighting, and patricide, Numboolyu gave his sons secret fellatio. (The myth still does not explain why it had to be secret.) Only as an afterthought did the narrators think to add that because boys grow slowly, semen ingestion is needed to help them along.[30]

Male Identity and Eroticism

Since men need this myth as a guiding fiction, we should wonder why they hide and postpone its revelation until after fatherhood. Most of the an-

---

30. Recall the secret context of our myth: the initiates are excluded and men are free to "be themselves." Does this point—that only the erotic outlet got mentioned—indicate that eroticism is, after all, a more powerful motive for ritualizing fellatio than men normally say? Here is a fragment of evidence to support the purely erotic function of homosexual fellatio for the bachelors, whose part in it also confirms their manhood, initially in a ritual context.

swers, I think, are buried in the story itself and what its script reveals about the development of a man's sense of his maleness and erotic excitement.

This approach throws weight on the psychodynamic functions of the myth, a viewpoint nowadays regarded as passé in anthropology. Despite its inherent risks,[31] there are three reasons why I believe that these data require that treatment. First, I have already described the sociocultural background of the myth as it concerns prevailing customs and institutions. Second, the story is a shared masculine secret: its behavioral context draws on male developmental experience and fantasy. Third, the ramifications of secretly sharing in this myth are manifest through men's characterological conduct in the wider society; although ignorant of the myth, women and children are still dominated by men and the mythic fantasy that motivates them. The most important observations now requiring attention, then, should focus on these last two psychosocial perspectives: namely, male developmental processes and masculine personality structure.

I therefore want to consider the myth in its capacity as a personal script for individuals.[32] A script, like our myth, has clearly identifiable actors, even if they are faceless. It has a story line: a sequence of precisely defined thoughts, predicaments, and resolutions. It is dramatic and risky, else it fails to excite us. It is timeless. For as long as Sambia society breeds men and women who must suffer and enjoy its warrior roles, our myth provides a formula for triumph, even if the cost is a masculine identity which bars personal fullness.

Viewed in developmental perspective, the myth, like a personal script, is an ingenious blending of the reality and fantasy of male ontogeny. It evinces the truth about the great moments of trauma and mastery in a man's life. The fiction is also personalized by the greatest culture hero, whose presence enhances imagination. Narrating the story are old men to whom one has always looked for knowledge and wisdom. Hence the story has three seductive stamps: official history, paternal affection, and the

31. In a review of Roheim's (1974) work, Kracke (1979:228) warns of the risks of psychologizing myths: "It is a risky business, similarly, to interpret myths as if they were the fantasies of an individual. Myths, certainly, embody fantasies; they are, after all, created and transmitted by individuals. But Roheim analyzes them as if they were fantasies, produced not by individuals but by some communal psyche. This they are not. Some fantasies may, to be sure, predominate in a society's mythology; fantasies that are in tune with the beliefs and values of a culture, perhaps, or that can be most easily given a form in harmony with those values and infuse them with emotional significance. But myths are created by numerous individuals, and embody the varied fantasies that may occur in a variety of different people." Likewise, in relation to individual behavior, myths and fantasies are no doubt experienced differently, according to particular cultural contexts and the changes that follow from one's movement through the life cycle.

32. We cannot investigate all the meanings of the myth as a script, for that would require individual case studies and more data; I take up this point in Chapter 9.

privileged feeling of being admitted into the chosen circle. Even so, the myth has a banal, unfinished character, as I noted. It is almost as if it were a "just so" story: too pat and too transparent. The effect is portentous.

The script enables men to identify with its figures but simultaneously to keep a distance if they so wish. Indeed, both these capacities—to identify and disidentify with the mythic experience—are necessary. Individuals respond emotionally as if to suggest that they can imagine themselves inside Numboolyu's skin. Their shame released that identification too much, while their laughter counteracted that release by helping maintain a tenuous separateness representing men's personal histories. If the myth is to capture and excite men enough to become internalized as a secret script—resonating in thought and character functioning—it must uncannily cradle their sense of themselves without undermining the need to fear and obey its autonomous voice.

This is a delicate balance. And parthenogenesis is a powerful myth, for it unveils the greatest of all mysteries: the origins and divergence of the sexes, and how their genitals came to be. A frightening revelation is made: the ancestor's body—my body—began as a composite of maleness and femaleness. No certain difference existed back then. A lingering fear is crystallized: the first men had female traits. The myth tells what should have remained hidden; and for a single instant men stand silent and helpless before the unfolding mythic scenario.

Those guards posted nearby: Are they there to keep women away or to prevent the youths from fleeing in panic? A function of sponsors and guards in first-stage initiation *is* to prevent initiates from escaping to their mothers bearing ritual secrets. Initiation introduced the homosexual practice that the myth here describes as a man's first and foremost erotically pleasurable sex. It is between two males of complementary age. Men attest that the sentries are to keep women away and protect those secrets. The myth surrenders this understanding only to adults, and it requires them to capitulate. They, too, must keep women at a distance.

The mythic script exposes that old separation and union with women. It amplifies men's preoccupation with the difference between maleness and femaleness: a conviction that femaleness is a self-propelling, competent principle in natural species and humans; a feeling that maleness is not naturally competent nor an internal stimulator of masculinity in men. Ritualized homosexuality is the corrective measure needed to instill maleness and masculinity.

The script directs us back to the "problem" of ritual secrecy. Secrecy prevents women from "knowing" that men innately lack semen, the essence of masculine potency. There are two ways of understanding that statement. One is to recognize the Sambia theory as their explanation of their reality: the male body is biologically inadequate. The other general viewpoint would subsume the first one and argue that, along with the rituals, semen, homosexual interpersonal experience and relationships, a boy also acquires the psychological sense of being a Sambia warrior. He is kept physically distant from women long enough to develop an adult masculine identity that is maintained thereafter through psychological distance. Internalizing the myth sanctifies[33] this process—a process in which one finally masters the nagging fear that one is less than masculine, that one could change into a female. This anxiety I have labeled the transsexual fantasy in masculine behavior.

Now I wish to hypothesize that this transsexual fear is a primary element of scripting that lies behind men's compulsive ritual secrecy. Men have a need to keep a distance between themselves and women. The political power lying behind this secrecy is, of course, the traditions of the male cult. The cult is a conventional compact, an interpersonal code among men. It is the threat of men acting in concert, men armed and capable of violence, which is the never-ending threat that defends ritual secrecy. That menace, or hostility, toward women is the means whereby men can barter and marry women, forcibly separate mothers and sons, and conscript boys into secret homosexual activities. It is this open power that constantly defends an individual man's right to a secret identity in his relationships with women and children. Developmentally, then, the ritualized (interpersonal) use of secrecy and its erotic trappings is a continuity in a male's ritual transition from boyhood to manhood, and the distance of secrecy facilitates adjustment into the ideal masculine role.

This ontogeny of meaning is implicit in masculine idioms and explicit within the mythic script. This leads to the next point: the hostility (see Stoller 1979:31) of secrecy is also a psychodynamic underpinning of eroticism, both homosexual and heterosexual. Secrecy is a key factor in a male's personal script stimulating erotic excitement.

The collective secrecy of male ritual stands between women and the mysteries of masculinity. It protects and nourishes two of the precious mysteries mentioned earlier. One concerns the flutes; the other is how initiation turns the scrawny boys into virile youths. The two mysteries really disguise only one experiential secret, however: manhood, and its supporting sense of maleness, comes *not from within,* but from the external, humiliating process of having been another man's sexual insertee, thus enabling one eventually to become a woman's insertor.

Let us now glance at some behavioral observations that illuminate this

---

33. See Freud (1961:41) and Rappaport (1971:69). While imprecise, "sanctifies" is preferable to other notions, like "symbolizes," "objectifies," "ritualizes," since it implies elements of religious faith, group expectations, projective identification, and the externalization of ego functions within a collective fantasy.

secret and its erotic dimension in the myth. These data involve the male cult's two mysteries of ritualized growth and of the flutes, but they will also help round out my interpretation of the mythological script in male psychodynamics and character structure. Ritual experience comes first, since its outlines will clarify the more exotic meaning of the flutes.

Male initiation attempts to offset the effects of prolonged maternal *monjapi'u*, which, according to men, threatens the growth of maleness. The mother's influence is too protracted and overwhelming. Her milk becomes more than a metaphor for femaleness. Milk takes on a meaning, for boys, as an affective representation of mother, her loving nurturance and exasperating superiority, subjectively living within the child as the earliest presence. Men must compensate for that presence through ritual separation and treatment. To undermine her influence, semen and the bachelor's penis are forcibly substituted. If a boy can be coerced and caringly seduced into male associations and homosexual experience, it may be possible to implant those masculine entities (semen) as affective symbols, too, inside and outside a lad's felt existence. Prolonged years of female avoidance and secret activities provide the time and space for this ritualized "design" of masculine individuation to take hold.

First-stage initiation begins in maternal separation, and boys characteristically express a feeling of loss at this split. Novices often hark back to this traumatic break, and a feeling of helpless loss seems to surround their perceptions of events following the *moku*. Even old men, like Kanteilo, have spontaneously said to me: "I felt sorry to lose my mother." A fourteen-year-old novice, Gaimbako, related his mother's parting words to him: "You won't see my face now." Then he added: "She cried for me, my momma. Later in the cult house I felt, why have I lost my momma?" And Moondi, talking about his feelings of separation, said this:

I felt sorry. I thought, "Why should I lose my mother! [Intense.] Why must I leave them [parents]? Why do I have to be initiated? I wanted to remain a *kwulai'u* with her. I thought of sleeping with them in their house. . . . They didn't beat me the way the men do.

What Gaimbako and Moondi communicated provides an insight into the situation of novices: that they are separated from and thereafter forbidden to be with their mothers; and how they must now be only with their fathers and other males.

Between this separation and their exposure to the bamboo flutes, boys experience many ritual ordeals: purification rites, long hours of dancing, fasting, and sleeplessness, beating rites, nose-bleeding, and a formidable list of little ceremonies, feastings, and dramatic teachings. We would be foolish to play down the complexity of these events: they are experienced, by boys, as frightening, wondrous, shameful, even though it is trauma and resentment they feel toward their fathers (and elders) well ahead of the love and respect that later combine with those early emotions. To recount the ritual secrecy and eroticism of first-stage initiation we must unfortunately do violence to this complexity. (Subsequent writings should help extend this material and correct that distortion.) Here is only a snapshot of that experience.

Nearly all boys perform their first act of fellatio during the initiation, and their subjective constructs of the experience are tremendously important for understanding how the myth relates to their own personal scripts as males. Let me cite from the case study of Kambo[34] to illustrate this powerful developmental experience.

Kambo remembered that his first fellatio experience occurred on the night after the ceremony that reveals the flutes and homosexuality. The elders had assigned an older bachelor from another hamlet to be his fellated partner, pointing him out to Kambo. They were total strangers.

> The big men marked him for me. . . . When I was a *kwulai'u* [however], I didn't know anything about fellatio. One boy held his own penis once [in childhood]. That was W [playmate in his hamlet]. . . . I told him: "That's not good for you to hold it." I didn't know about semen. I thought, oh, children come up from nowhere.

The older initiates, too, pressured Kambo into fellatio, as he and other initiates attested. They said to him, as he recalls:

> "You mustn't spit it [semen] out. It's the same as the milk of pandanus." And at the cult house, M [older initiate], he showed me what to do. I felt, what if they [men] are lying to us about this . . . I don't want to vomit from it [fellatio], I don't want to die! [Grimaces.] Not good that I get sick, or I throw up. That's [penis] not for sucking that they are discussing it so much. . . . But the young initiates said to us: "You must hold onto the bachelor's penis. You mustn't let go." . . . But I didn't want to become sick. And the initiates still urged: "When you sleep with them, they can poke their finger inside your mouth. [A sign, if accepted, that a boy will act as fellator.] So later he [fellated] poked his finger in my mouth, I thought, but it was really his penis. He *held* onto my head

---

34. I should add that I formed a close understanding of Kambo's experiences because he was an articulate, trusting, and unusually well-adjusted initiate. His limited exposure to Western experience (he had never been out of the area), his age (about twelve years old in 1976), and the recentness of his initiation (1973) made him an invaluable informant whom I depended on in my focused research on initiation. Nonetheless, despite our rapport, it was months before Kambo trusted me enough to relate the following experiences.

[emphasis] and pushed in and out. When he is close to ejaculating, you must open your mouth to drink. You can drink it, it's like water, like mother's milk. The younger initiates told the bachelors not to "shoot" us too hard. That was our first time. They had to be gentle. . . . But he wasn't very gentle with me! I worried when he ejaculated. I didn't want him to give me urine. But he didn't. The first time it [semen] tasted bitter. Later you can feel that it tastes sweet. . . . Yes, that's true: I felt it was bitter at first but now . . . it is sweet to me. When I first ingested it, I was afraid. Not good that his semen makes a *kwulai'u-oolu* [birth canal], and I have your child. Not good that he [sic][35] becomes pregnant. . . . I looked carefully at my stomach for a while. But later I heard some men say that [pregnancy] wouldn't happen.

From Kambo's remarks we begin to glimpse the extraordinary world of anxieties, emotions, and fantasy aroused by that first fellatio act. Kambo tells us how he first felt morbidly anxious. He feared pollution (urine), sickness, and vomiting, even death. But he eventually countered his own concerns with the construct that semen is "nothing more" than mother's milk. And in time, he asserted, its bitter taste turned sweet for him. Last, Kambo unveiled a fear that he might have a birth canal created within him, that he might become pregnant or give birth. That fantasy, a free-floating anxiety that semen ingestion might effect female traits in a boy, is a prevalent response in young novices. Indeed, Kambo's report, although its details differ slightly, is rather typical of what most boys report.

And here, in the independent report of this twelve-year-old boy, we find an uncanny correspondence with two elements in the myth of parthenogenesis years before Kambo will learn of its existence: first, the fear that he could have acquired female traits; and second, his own fantasy that he might have become pregnant.

In most initiates, the sense of involvement in the fellator role also changes as they approach puberty and bachelorhood (following second-stage initiation). Now they are placed in the role of helping motivate younger boys to serve as fellators alongside themselves. These older initiates long for increasing autonomy and "strength" as a means of transcending their subservient position under the thumb of bachelors. So they gradually become more aggressive fellators. We have already seen that there are multiple reasons for boys becoming fellators. Even so, near puberty some initiates are reluctant to abandon the safety of that status.

Moondi was like this at the start. In 1975, near his third-stage initiation, he resisted for weeks all the efforts of his father and others who urged him to be voluntarily initiated. On the night before the ceremonies began, his

---

35. Kambo sometimes makes unwitting slips of the tongue like this.

lineal grandfather implored him to "use his head," strengthen his resolve, and be initiated into the bachelorhood. I heard him reply: "I can't be initiated yet, I haven't grown yet. I'm still small. It will thwart my thinking." (Even though he was already mature and had reached puberty.) He eventually submitted, was initiated, and, in the ensuing weeks, began to engage enthusiastically in fellatio as the dominant fellated. In addition, through observations and conversations, he communicated that he enjoyed the erotic activities. In short, both a push and a pull were needed to stimulate Moondi's acceptance of the erotic side of masculine relationships. The formula worked.

A final descriptive note about the context of Sambia homosexual activities is warranted. I wish to stress again the coercive background of these early fellatio practices. Ritual taboos severely restrict interaction with women, and all heterosexual relationships are suppressed. There is, furthermore, a large element of power and dominance behavior influencing homosexual activities. Indeed, this element lends an appearance of similarity to the phenomenon of "prison homosexuality" known in Western societies,[36] although Sambia boys are never physically coerced into sex during initiation, and in most instances they retain some choice in homosexual activities. We must therefore be cautious in designating conscious (or subliminal) motives for males' interest in homosexual fellatio. And yet it is a truism that the vast majority of Sambia men developmentally experience both modes—fellator and fellated—of homosexual activities. Although initiates vary in their interest, most engage in fellatio on a regular basis. Furthermore, and although initiates, like youths, are initially impelled into this act, their later participation (e.g., choice of partners, frequency, interpersonal tone) is mostly a matter of personal interest. Bachelors tend to engage regularly in homosexual fellatio. They seem (impressionistically) excited by it, joking among themselves about especially attractive boys whom they prefer as fellators, but are often willing or wanting to have sex with any appropriate initiate. Last, most youths continue homosexual practices for as long as they can do so (until their wives' menarche or first birth), having bisexual relationships for a time; whereupon those same men prefer coitus once they have made the transition to heterosexuality.

To summarize, the erotic secret of male development is this: masculini-

---

36. But we should not push this comparison very far: observations show that some 50 percent of initiates, in a 1975 first-stage initiation, took eagerly to fellatio without much extra (in addition to ritual rhetoric) pressure, and they appeared to enjoy it without much conflict. (This, in eight-year-old boys.) Further, the strong social acceptance of secret homosexual activities at such an early age has far-reaching effects on Sambia gender development that differ fundamentally from the effects of prison life in late adolescence or adulthood, with its bitter, deadly stakes (see Davis 1969).

zation occurs under the hegemony of asymmetrical homosexual relationships. Ritual secrecy prevents women from knowing that fellatio is what transforms their fledgling sons and husbands into handsome youths. It is the bamboo flutes that become their *other*"mother" and "wife." And now to that second mystery.

The flutes also stand for men's secret rites of masculinization, but they harbor their own mystery. The flutes are used to frighten women and children, so they are also political weapons. Of greater importance, here, are their fetishistic qualities, which make the flutes diffusely erotic for men.[37] Male cult paraphernalia, the flutes and their tunes, are owned (as property) by different phratries. They are associated with political and kinship affiliations and identities. Women and children are supposed to fear them and hide from their haunting cries. This is not only because men would harm them if they uncovered the flutes' secret (see Berndt 1962: 51; Newman 1965:67; Read 1952:5). It is also because the hollow bamboo tubes, when blown by men, are thought to be vitalized by a mystical being, the female hamlet spirit, who is hostile to women.[38] It is she who animates the flutes with her cries. Men are her intimates.

The flutes have a fetishistic quality because their uses and meanings polarize the erotic traits of maleness and femaleness. The flutes are always played in pairs. Men say they are like "penises": the longer flute is referred to as "male" and as a "penis"; the shorter flute is called a "female." (The latter is also compared to the "glans penis.") The flutes are blown in pairs of rhythmic chords of two notes, rising and falling. The flute is used for teaching about fellatio in the penis and flute ceremony, and in that context the bamboo flute becomes a sign for the penis and an icon of the cult. What boys suck, in first-stage initiation, is the tip of the "female" flute (which is sometimes referred to as a "female breast nipple") protruding from the containing "male" flute. Fellators (initiates) are forbidden to play the flutes (or to twirl bull roarers), since these acts are proud masculine assertions that one has achieved sexual potency and warriorhood. (They can also dissipate a boy's semen if he is immature.) So not until puberty are these ceremonial acts permitted.

Flute-sucking and flute-playing graphically represent the dyadic homoerotic relationships between boys and youths. The flutes themselves are said to be "married." Since they are played in pairs and placed one inside

---

37. I mean that the flutes have an erotic fetishistic quality (Stoller 1979:8–9) distinct from their supernatural and kinship aspects; the flutes are not, however, a genuine erotic fetish, at least so far as my data reveal (but see Read 1965:115–117).

38. Similar ideas are reported from elsewhere in Highlands New Guinea by Berndt (1962:55–56), Lindenbaum (1976:56), Read (personal communication), and Salisbury (1965:60). I consider this material elsewhere.

the other, men refer to them as "spouses." Boys are said to be the flutes' spouses, meaning that flute players perform as fellateds for the younger flute-sucking initiates. The boy, then, becomes a receptacle for ingesting the bachelor's semen and a subordinate in all interpersonal encounters. Ingesting semen masculinizes; playing flutes is manly behavior.

The flutes thus represent a threat to women, secret erotic relationships among males, and a fantasy system entailing spirits and heterosexual and homosexual components. The fantasy system is objectified in male initiation.[39] Ritualized fellatio erotically fetishizes parts of the bodies of persons. Initiates come to fetishize the bachelors' penises (the source of semen); and bachelors fetishize boys' (and later women's) mouths as erotic orifices. For example, initiates secretly (and coquettishly) refer to a favored fellated as *mi dakolu* (*dakolu* is the hammerhead arrow); and bachelors respond to their favored fellator as *mi nungenyu* (my bamboo orifice).[40] Men actively perpetuate these—the behaviors that make the flutes erotic—in ritual and idiom.

The mythic script of male parthenogenesis involves these erotic secrets. Men spontaneously appeal to the myth as validation of their customs, sexual practices, and the secrecy of those things. Tali did this in the statement I quoted at the beginning of the Introduction. Here is another illustration of the same personal script at work. This time, Tali was responding to a question of mine: "They [elders] place the arse cover on boys and tell them not to reveal the secrets.[41] How does the arse cover 'mark' that [secrecy]?"

> The arse cover, *bechoowi'u,* makes the boy a *choowinuku* [arse cover completed]. Its pull string marks the place on his neck where the fellator's penis can descend. He cannot reveal the secrets, especially fellatio, to women and children. Without this [pull string] he might forget. [GH: How so?] The boy must hide his face well *because* [raises voice] he has the arse cover. We don't want to reveal fellatio to women. . . . They'd rubbish it, they wouldn't marry us. They'd say: "You all copulate with each other. Why do you hide? Have fellatio among yourselves?" But the practice [homosexual fellatio] is hidden by the banana leaf.[42] Before, Numboolyu had fellatio with the man-woman; she got

---

39. This system is symbolically complex; elsewhere, I also describe the impersonating behavior of bachelors who, during initiation, ceremonially identify themselves with the female spirits; and how boys come to attribute both masculine and feminine traits to those bachelors, as they do elsewhere, in homosexual relationships.

40. Men also refer to their wives' vaginas as "my bamboo orifice," only they use a type of bamboo (*nilyu*) as a euphemism for the vagina.

41. During the flute ceremony of first-stage initiation.

42. An implicit reference to the mythic delivery of the infant.

pregnant, gave birth, had the child. Because she[43] hid the infant in banana leaves, we now hide homosexuality.

The myth is used as an authority, a reference to the fabled past, in accounting for ritual custom and secret homosexuality. Secret fellatio is associated with the women's cloistered birth process, as if the mystery of birth "explained" the secrecy of homosexual practices. There is another element, too: that women would "rubbish" men, "wouldn't marry" them, if their homosexual practices were known.

Now we are back to the heart of the mythic script, its secret homosexual fellatio. What of the shame and silence I mentioned about the myth-telling context? Elsewhere, Weiyu said to me, quietly:

> It would be bad for them [women] to know. The women would say to us: "You men have no semen of your own . . . you copulate with us 'dry' [don't ejaculate], without semen . . . you're all spineless." And if they all said that, we'd be shamed.

There is no doubt that this fantasied insult expresses deep fears and ample reason for a Sambia man to be shamed. No semen, no manhood.

But in spite of this reference and all the stupendous, nagging concern about keeping homosexuality secret, it is also true that many men feel certain that women really know of it.

Men have recounted stories telling how women in times past accidentally stumbled upon men in compromising situations.[44] For instance, a boy and youth were once discovered engaging in fellatio near the pathway of Nilangu hamlet by an old woman who told them to "go away." So men mutter things like this:

> We think that the old women tell girls not to talk out [publicly broadcast what they know of homosexuality] at their menarche ceremonies. Old women say [speculating]: "Fellatio is a part of men's rituals. They hide it well. They hold the axe too. You girls can't talk out: not good that they kill you and throw your bodies into the river." We're ashamed that women know we "play" around. But they'll never speak out: they know we'd *kill* them [raises voice] and make it look like an accident [drowning, a falling tree]. We can't *really* kill women [quietly] now, now that the white man has come. So we just put up with it. . . . If women spoke out now—"Those men turn around [*mugerutmonji,* to give

---

43. An inversion of the myth: Numboolyu really hid the infant.
44. In several cases the men are still living, and I have verified the stories.

it back] and play amongst themselves"—we'd be deeply shamed. [Tali]

Not until a year after I learned of secret homosexual activities did Tali surprise me with this statement. Until then, men had fervently argued that women were completely ignorant; my own observations left me genuinely baffled about whether women knew or not. Even after his admission, Tali's words left me wondering about the plausibility of men's views. (And some men completely deny that women know; it is unclear whether they are aware of women's possible knowledge and are denying it, or whether they believe that women are unaware.) The ambiguity is rampant.

How can this be so? The answer lies in a phenomenon virtually ignored by New Guinea ethnographers: duplicity.

Even though men can recount such stories, and some of them will affirm, with Tali, that women probably "know," most Sambia still privately insist that women are ignorant of ritualized fellatio. (This insistence underlies all ritual rhetoric.) The conscious actions of men aim at keeping the situation this way, hiding homosexual behavior. Men are, therefore, certainly the perpetrators of a double deception: of women and of themselves. I must nevertheless insist that most men also sense that homosexual fellatio is a screaming secret: women keep silent out of fear, sustaining the duplicity.

Several reasons impel male duplicity, and, when men grudgingly allude to them, they come as threatening facts, shameful possibilities. The first one Weiyu hinted at in his remark above—that women would slander men as semenless. That would be shameful, for it would imply that manliness is a sham. No semen of your own: not just the semen but the bluster of manhood itself is contrived and not what men's unbending pride makes it out to be. Maleness, unlike femaleness, would then be perceived for what it "is," not a natural product of one's own body, but rather the artificial process of puny boys being turned into nubile youths by serving as fellators. If that manliness was acquired from outside oneself, then why can't it "dry up"? That is the awful implication of Weiyu's statement, and we have examined that notion before. Masculine atrophy: the widely shared fear—piece of personal scripting—that one day, somehow, one's semen might evaporate altogether and hence, no ejaculation. No semen, no inseminating, no manhood.

As if this were not already a dreadful enough burden of shame-provoking fears, Weiyu adds another. Women must not be given all a man's semen, or else they will become too strong. This possibility is so embarrassingly obvious that it took much of Weiyu's trust to say this:

It's not good that semen goes only to women and they look smart. For they would grow *too big* [emphatic]. . . . They would say bad things to us, "You're all *wogaanyu*" [soft, weak]. They could *push us around.*[45]

What a possibility!

It is not enough that homosexual practices must be hidden because women would slander men. Semen must also be diverted lest women be given too much male substance and become too strong, i.e., masculinized. (Here is a fragment of data that also concerns the earlier discussion [Chapter 6] about bachelors' distaste for premenarche heterosexual fellatio. Weiyu, at least, avoided that early erotic activity because he feared that he would deplete his semen pool too quickly and that he would masculinize his wife. Another factor also enters—youths prefer boys as fellators.) This idea is consistent with the theory of semen ingestion. Then there is the next allusion, that women would start pushing men around. That fantasy seems preposterous. Are men really afraid that women could overpower them?

Elsewhere, Weiyu ironically hints at this possibility. I heard him half-heartedly bemoan to a group of men:

> Younger boys drink the semen of older boys. They can spend years like that. . . . but then, a man goes, is married, copulates with his wife, but only *part* of his semen is left [grins]. We'd send boys to women sooner, so they'd [women] get lots of semen, only we think about the scarcity of women. Some boys have no wives, or they have to wait . . . such a long time for the *taiketnyi* [wife's availability after her menarche].

Here again is the sense that men are putting one over on women. Boys need semen for masculinization. And bachelors, because of the "scarcity" of women and Sambia prudishness about vaginal virginity, need an erotic substitute for women in the meantime. All three points are valid, namely, boys' homosexual inseminations, the fear that women may become too strong, and the bachelors' homosexual pleasures long before coitus. All three are shameful possibilities, all are implied by the myth.

The last point needs critical examination, however, since it is only a partial truth. Bachelors "need" a sex outlet (can they accept needing women's bodies?), Weiyu says. Until the menarche, they are given boys. Note, however, that there is choice involved: and yet most youths still

---

45. Compare this to a remarkably similar comment by Barth's (1975:48) informants. Barth nonetheless argues that the Baktaman practice "not a male cult but a communal cult performed by men" (1975:47–48).

"desire"[46] sex with boys. Not just any sex; for what comes to excite the bachelor is a certain mode of structured (governed by rules and taboos) erotic encounter between *unequals;* first with boys, then with women. Secrecy and duplicity maintain this situation. Men hold erotic privileges in both worlds, but only so long as they can keep women and boys under their authority.

> You and I, *nuposha,* are in-between men [bisexuals] exactly. We know how to fasten the door on the two groups [women and boys]. Not good that women come inside, not good that boys go outside. . . . When the boy gets a woman and they decorate the newlyweds at *nuposha,* then we older men speak out to the youth. . . . This time we tell the *nuposha* initiates, thus: "Now, you are married to a woman. You can't play around . . . you have your own share [sexual chattel, wife], and you can't go rob the initiates [fellators] of bachelors."

This statement (and the ritual teaching it mentions) recognizes that men are not simply biding time by fooling around with initiates. Boys were their first erotic partners. For this reason, and other personality factors, bachelors are sometimes passionately fond of particular boys. It is with preadolescent underlings that men first experience sexual excitement leading to a conscious ejaculation. (We still do not know what creates that excitement, but one factor may be a "romantic attachment" that transcends the use of another as a mere erotic outlet.) Homoeroticism is exciting; satisfying enough, apparently, that several notorious men cannot turn their backs on it. A few cannot, but most do.

This capacity for behavioral transitions, erotic reversals that leave behind homoerotic practices and relationships, is the crux of the adult man's dilemma hidden in the script of parthenogenesis.

That simple myth is about the continuities and discontinuities in a male's sense of masculinity, its developmental relationship to homoeroticism, and the resulting bisexual capacities of Sambia men. The myth's solution to the societal and personal problem of giving up homosexual fellatio is communicated at immense risk, for men may reach a frightening insight into the origins of their own maleness, while women could humiliate them if that secret were discovered. These precious data are implied by this brilliant mythic creation: an anthropology that ignores interpersonal communications or psychodynamics would have, I believe, passed over their powerful significance in favor of mere surface appearances.

This myth is about deep and prolonged personal repression. Men, if

---

46. The quotation marks are meant to underscore the many complexities covered by the term "desire," and how it comes about—a thick intersection of identity and behavior still not understood, but too easily dismissed by the word's apparent simplicity.

asked, would generally agree that women and boys are sexually repressed. I also think, however, that a good number of men, if they trusted us enough, would also add what some have shared with me: that they, too, feel repressed, erotically. (Do they feel repressed in other aspects of their lives too?)

The myth-telling context itself reveals that, obviously: men who have all known homosexual and heterosexual excitement band together momentarily to communicate a grave story that requires boys and women to be kept distant. As in everyday life, boys and women must be kept separate (and ignorant) so they cannot freely communicate about their sexual activities with one another.

Sambia masculine eroticism is geared to that secrecy and distance. Men have the upper hand. They must keep women and initiates powerless to get done what needs doing: separating mothers and sons, building a warriorhood, keeping boys heterosexually repressed, providing a homosexual outlet for bachelors, trading women like pawns, and using them to sire children. Those are difficult problems and perhaps cruel solutions. Let us not forget that the warring life of Sambia was ruthless and hard (though this fact does not, of course, explain those solutions). Men demand a one-sided erotic encounter: essentially asymmetrical sex concerned mostly with their own pleasure. Homosexual acts are never erotically mutualistic; and my impression is that many women seldom (if ever) experience an orgasm. Some boys and women may want more: more semen, more pleasure, more interpersonal involvement. (There are exceptional men who do give more.) But most men deny them. Neither women nor boys as erotic partners can be too strong, too masculine, for that is threatening. Male erotic excitement, I suggest, is tenuous, and it is based on limited closeness and empathic involvement.

The enforced duplicity of both women and boys is tacit acceptance of men's erotic domination. This viewpoint makes it apparent that repressive secrecy and duplicity are necessary *both* for the maintenance of the male cult and for individual male identity and the eroticism based on it.

Sambia society constrains masculine growth along a particular developmental line (A. Freud 1963). The maternal bond is the most salient and sensual relationship Sambia know. Men believe they are doing boys a favor in forcibly separating them from their mothers and in homosexually masculinizing them. This, they think, is all part of a necessary countermeasure to thwart the mother's negative impact and positively remake the helpless, clinging, dependent boy into an aggressive, manly warrior. Women must be suppressed and avoided. Boys must have their imitative and responsive behavior redirected onto older males. Not mother but father must be the cherished ideal human being. There are no exceptions since Sambia admit of no alternative routes to manhood.[47]

Contained within the urgent need for this ritualized repression may be another powerful fact—that the nature of the child's tie to his mother is so powerful and seductive that it has lifelong effects on a man's capacity to sense himself unequivocally as the kind of person Sambia warfare, ritual, and women demand.

Parthenogenesis says this plainly. Men must themselves "create" the differences between maleness and femaleness, men and women. Manliness is created first through a pleasurable homosexual fellatio. In that mythic time, the anatomical and genital differences between man and his mate were minimal. Numboolyu's penis is what counted, and it set the first couple apart (as did "her" ambiguous genitals). His age-mate's act of fellatio performed on him is what stimulated his maleness, the growth of his penis. The ancestral hero became more competent, manly.

The myth transparently disguises a man's personal script. The myth's evoked responses—shame and silence, pride and laughter—are symptoms of the uncanny identification with experiences long forgotten. The mythic content, with its emphasis on shame, pain, fears, cutting the genitals, pollution, and deception, seems to indicate so much trauma in the origins of men's eroticism. How is this linked to early infantile development? The differences between "me" and "mother" were ambiguous; the differences between males and females were blurred in the child's mind.

Uncanniness strikes that chord: it simulates how a child "had not yet marked himself off from the world" (Freud 1955b:236). An infant boy does not fully sense himself to be a male and not just masculine. The risky message of the myth is that within the symbiotic relationship with one's mother a boy may have felt a deep wish not to separate from or lose her body but, indeed, to merge with her. Parthenogenesis tells how manliness was created out of a pseudohermaphroditic body, and how the first female came from the body of a male transsexual. So that frightening wish comes again; only this time, it is disguised enough to satisfy a deep need whose meaning, in the myth context, is transformed from danger to uncanny triumph.

Does the transsexual theme in this myth mirror the constant preoccupation with sexual differentiation in male ritual, beliefs, and idioms at large? We cannot yet know. Nevertheless, men's immediate associations to the male-turned-female in the myth context are an important clue. Weiyu did not mention only hermaphrodites. He cited a well-known instance of a rare happening in Sambia life: a person who, though reared as a female,

---

47. Except, perhaps in limited ways, for the shaman, a matter discussed elsewhere.

was discovered after marriage to be an anatomically normal male. Transsexualism: that person (whose assigned husband then fled to the coast out of "shame") now dresses and attempts to pass as a male on the Mountain Patrol Station where he[48] now resides away from the village. This is an unusual case. What about men's general perceptions of the hermaphrodite?

Here we find further evidence in support of the transsexual element in the mythic script. A year after first hearing the myth I was talking with Tali about hermaphrodites. Some other men joined in. Tali said that a hermaphrodite, at first, "looks just like a girl. Their scrotum lacks testes, it's the same as a vagina. . . . Their penises are hidden inside the stomach." At that moment, spontaneously, the men nearby referred to the myth; Tali joined in.

Numboolyu he cut open the stomach of the other. This eliminated the infant. It left only testes, no penis [in the "woman"]. Numboolyu cut open her stomach, that prevented the penis from growing. Like hermaphrodites . . . [they] have testes, but no penis.

Then Nilutwo interrupted, adding that D, a known hermaphrodite, was said to have recently "developed" a penis.[49] It was microscopic, though, like an "immature banana." (This he knew from local gossip.) "How is this possible?" I asked. Tali immediately replied: "The *tingu*, it swells up and comes outside, and becomes a cock." He added his belief that hermaphrodites also "have wombs," since they "don't lose them," and that their femalelike breasts slacken, the milk being absorbed into the skin. The penis is still "too small" to insert, however; besides, since hermaphrodites "didn't drink semen as boys," they "have none" and "cannot ejaculate." (This does not logically follow, of course; as an initiate, a person like D probably served as a fellator.) When one of the men joked about copulating with a hermaphrodite, the men laughed. Tali and Nilutwo quietly talked together, after which Nilutwo joked: "We wouldn't fornicate him [hermaphrodite] anally either; we're afraid he'd turn around and try to penetrate us!"

We cannot be certain about the meaning of all these comments, but

---

48. We have to assume that this remarkable change of identity and behavior arose from the deep conviction of being male, not female. Medical examiners at the Station identified the person as an anatomical male. I have seen him once and, like a hermaphrodite with whom I work in the Nilangu area, his facial features and body build have an androgynous quality.

49. D was officially married (very late, long after his age-mates had been given wives) in 1976, after he announced that he was "ready" for it; men said privately that his penis had finally "come outside."

what matters is that hermaphroditism is not so distant from the myth of parthenogenesis or men's ordinary consciousness. Tali cited the myth, adding a detail, that Numboolyu's age-mate, the ancestress (Chenchi), really was a male too. The cutting of her vulva for birth halted the "woman's" masculinization. Then, to explain how hermaphrodites can develop penises late in development, he drew on beliefs about the *tingu.* The source of menstrual blood itself can be, somehow, projected out; and its protuberance becomes the hermaphroditic male's penis. There could be no more fantastic bisexual image than of that *tingu*-penis.[50]

That these men could casually spin off such a fantasy, humorously entertain it, and then set it aside, becomes a sign of the psychodynamic difference between themselves and younger initiates. That the myth can be reexperienced and rescripted like this provides confirmation of the certainty with which adult men sense themselves as separate, masculine persons.

The most remarkable thing about this myth, for me, is the willingness of Sambia to accept hermaphroditism in the ancestor and how primordial fellatio transformed him. Being a homosexual fellated masculinized the hero; being a fellator feminized his mate. Fellatio can create both maleness and femaleness. The initiate is not yet there; but men have triumphed over that danger. As adults, then, these men have become so entrenched in their ritually sustained sense of masculinity that this revelation evokes uncanny, sober interest, but not panic. It is my hypothesis that the myth would simply overwhelm those younger males, turning them frantically away from females as erotic objects. The mysterious revelation must be denied them till later.

The myth seems to establish that the difference between maleness and femaleness must be constantly exaggerated to reinforce masculine individuation after marriage and to create the heterosexual excitement that must eventuate in coitus. At fatherhood young men thus confront new challenges to their sense of themselves that the experience of this myth helps them bridge subjectively.

The focus of those changes following the birth of his child is the myth's injunction that a man keep distant from the mother and infant. He must not allow himself to slip into the same mode of luxurious dependence as his infant enjoys. He must deny himself the sensory gratification and sensual involvement (Lichtenstein 1961:206) with his wife that the baby receives. Numboolyu is a "double"; like him, a man should avoid the

---

50. This thought raises many possibilities unconsidered before. For example, is there, somewhere in a man's awareness (in daydreams, or in subliminal or unconscious thoughts, i.e., in dreams), a sense of the *tingu's* actively being a feminine organ within him, or a phallus in women? Individual case studies, as always, may eventually provide some answers.

tainted birth context and remember that whatever gratification he has lost, or however blissfully the infant now lives, the boy must eventually travel the same hard but worthy route of masculinization that he himself did.[51] Against his wife's visible parturition, a man is comforted by the secret thought that it was really males who originated everything. Women are not reproductively superior, the myth confides. It is imperative that the myth take hold of the dangers of seeing mother and infant together: the young father must resist any thought of wishing or needing to be blissfully attached again.[52] The myth makers take a gamble in revealing how pain and transsexualism and incest were all present, back then. But that risk is necessary. If the myth experience is to succeed, a young man must identify with the triumph of his double in overcoming those risks and thereby free himself of the transsexual fear once more. (See Chapter 9 for a theoretical discussion.)

The story can do this job, to repeat, because it is both a "myth" and a "reality." It is not I that is experiencing those things: it is Numboolyu. The myth is uncanny, frightening, and shameful; it speaks of unspeakable things, like incest; and it pronounces all the manly dangers and offers the new father solace in his child, wife, and marriage. It appeases his envy with the knowledge that his son will soon enough be removed to the safety of homosexual relationships, and secretly (by the male cult, coercively) at that. Yet the myth is still a story. That difference of denial—"I am not I"—is the measure of projection into another man and another time that guarantees the script's success. This projection frees a man to reexperience the story, or pieces of it, over and over, splitting and cementing acceptable meanings and responses in himself as husband or father, as a sharer in the secret cult.

The myth's frantic secrecy adds one last measure of safety and danger needed to shepherd the man's necessary distance from wife and children. The myth-telling context is a pseudo risk. That is why guards are stationed.

---

51. See Rank (1952): To resemble one's same-sexed parent is the most "intense and portentous wish of the child's early years" (p. 64), a wish that leads to the substitution of the myth for one's father: "the over-valuation of the father of infancy" (p. 67). My argument, here, concerns the birth of a male infant, as the firstborn, which is a Sambia ideal. A female infant changes the situation, I think, since the nature of the family dynamics of identification (child to parents, father to the girl, father to the mother/infant pair) differs from that of a male.

52. I am thinking of those corresponding ritual practices that come into play at the sixth-stage initiation rites, following the birth, and that are mentioned in the myth or hinted at by it: the ceremonial decoration of the young fathers (see Weiyu's comments, pp. 125–126); learning about the use of the yellow tree sap (see Weiyu's remarks, p. 201); and the postpartum taboos forbidding men to watch the breast feeding act lest it arouse them (see Chapter 7). Each of these ritual contexts concerns the separateness of the father and the mother/infant pair, as well as the man's changing sense of his masculinity and identification with (including envy of) his wife's and child's situation.

There is a danger, obviously, that women may penetrate their secrecy and discover the "truth" of masculinity: that maleness is not a natural state; that homosexuality is erotically exciting for men; and that men give up homoeroticism to attain marriage, fatherhood, and this myth. The guards are there to foster that risk: they reassure one that men really are dangerous, and that the cult's existence will always prevent women from learning the secrets that would humiliate the proud men. As long as females and boys are removed, men can sustain the splitting of subjective consciousness that denies: "I am not I." If women were to stomp over the guards it would shatter the cosmos (and provoke violence) because men would then be forced to breathe life into their secret illusion.

The distance created by ritual secrecy is exciting, necessary, and burdensome for men. The myth is a defensive script: it displaces responsibility for many of the great products of the male cult onto women. Is adult masculine character, then, as much an exciting reaction to this need for distance between the sexes?

The myth goads men to cease clinging to the last vestiges of childhood; never to stop contending with the women out there; and to surrender themselves to their fathers' myth of Sambia manhood. That psychological capitulation is the key to a man's continuing capacity to remain distant and thereby function as a warrior, a husband, and a father who can be erotically excited by women without wishing to merge with them. What ritual has painstakingly built up must not be undone at the coronation of autonomous manhood.

In an Amazon myth (see Appendix E), men tell of naked women who are alone and unguarded except by a great old tree and the sticks with which they are armed. These women kill their male infants. The tree magically impregnates them. So women have no need of men or semen, and male intruders are chased away. Even though they hold only switches, the Amazons have always succeeded in keeping men away, and overpowered, like little boys.

This myth is, for Sambia men, erotically exciting. The reason, they say, is obvious: the women are "naked" and "unguarded," men told me. And they stand alone armed only with switches. That thought, I think, is what makes the fantasy tantalizing. All one need do is overpower the women and take them. The myth, like an erotic daydream, confronts men with a pseudo danger—of being whipped and overpowered by the women. As a mythic script, it is not so hard to see how men could relive that humiliating trauma, converting the risk into the arousal of eventual triumph. That excitement is also uniquely Sambian and masculine, for men know that the tale is only a story, and it will never happen. Even in this script men are excited—at a distance—by their women.

CHAPTER NINE *Conclusion*

In a study prefaced by one person's remark, a communication that blended myth, idiom, and personal experience in reasoning out the elements of male growth, it is fitting that we now summarize the general implications of Tali's meaning for the origins of masculinity and femininity among a people so absorbed with the polarity of maleness and femaleness in themselves and nature. How has a behavioral approach—which focuses on actual behavior, not just norms—enabled us to appreciate better the Sambia fabric of reality and fantasy in these matters, and how are the findings relevant to reports from other New Guinea societies?

Studies of initiation ceremonies hold a special place in the history of anthropology. For those customs are common throughout the tribal world; their psychosocial processes provide a means for assigning statuses and roles to individuals, and anthropology's chief task has always been the creation of a theory of society, culture, and the individual among non-Western peoples. Durkheim and Van Gennep got us started; Freud was also there; Radcliffe-Brown, Malinowski, and their many students carried us further; and recent workers, like Victor Turner, have not only continued their efforts but explored new ground. These studies form a paradigm of research that communicates—to other disciplines and the general public—the viewpoint that human institutions, behavior, and existence are embedded in a sociocultural matrix: the behavior of individual tribesmen cannot be considered apart from the ritual traditions of their society. Such studies also carved out an intellectual discipline whose subject matter restored some of the humanness of tribesmen to Western thought. These great contributions, however, stopped short at one point: firsthand reports about the subjective experience of ritual initiation. This book has addressed that additional dimension of meaning.

Neglect of the actual behavior and subjectivity of initiation rites has had a special effect on New Guinea studies. Our best-known reporters, Bateson (1958), Mead (1968), Read (1965), and J. Whiting (1941), all mentioned pieces of individual behavior in its ritual context, but none *systematically* described that behavior. We still lack a treatment of ritual behavior as a system having sociocultural, psychological, and economic components. This matters because of the pervasive link between male initiation and gender role behavior that has been reported throughout Melanesia. The earlier studies, and later ones, too, have invariably referred to the relationship between initiation rites and gender polarity ("sexual antagonism") in myth, secret activities, and interaction between the sexes. Whiting and his colleagues (Burton and Whiting 1961; Stephens 1962; Whiting, Kluckhohn, and Anthony 1958) discussed this relationship in their seminal cross-cultural studies. But their ideas were not pursued in ethnographic research on particular New Guinea societies. The reasons are obvious: correct inferences about gender subjectivity also require focused observations of individual behavior, and these are precisely the data ethnographers in Melanesia have not collected.[1]

---

1. Although this study concentrates on ritual initiation and gender identity, specialist readers, especially sympathetic Melanesianists, will recognize that the above point (the omission of data on individual behavior) may apply with equal force to other themes of research in the region. Two come to mind: sociopolitical control and the stereotyped "big man" figure that still pervades the literature following Sahlins (1963); and the characterization of New Guinea social organization as being "loosely structured" (see Watson 1970). Whether these problems reflect empirical factors or are simply artifacts of our present paradigm will not be clear until we have better systematic studies of individual experience, cultural ideology, and institutionalized relationships in particular Melanesian groups. For this suggestion, and helpful comments on the following survey, I am grateful to my colleague Fitz J. P. Poole.

Sambia provide a unique "natural experiment" for examining the link between ritual and gender behavior in a New Guinea society, since sexual polarity has been pushed to its furthest extremes. I have tried to describe some of the details of the personal and cultural background of masculinity and femininity—gender identity—in male behavior. My primary interest has been in verbal behavior, what men say about the natural and human worlds. I have observed individual behavior more closely than anthropologists usually do. That is because my ultimate interest lies in subjectivity (meaning) and the origins of individual gender identity and eroticism. Analytically and methodologically, however, it is also because many of my data stem from working with individuals or groups of them (see also Tuzin 1976:xxv–xxx); the research pertains to those intersubjective conditions. That also means describing my own presence more fully than is usual, since the data were collected that way, and I believe that data presentation should reflect the form of data collection. At times this has been tedious and difficult; at times it has required inserting technical points which debate the merit of the approach within the book's contents; and at all times I have still had to edit and contextualize the material, trying to do so in ways that least distorted observations. I did not fully succeed; and too much is left unconsidered; but later work, I hope, will help rectify those inadequacies.

Before summarizing the substantive material on Sambia masculinity and the meaning of its developmental pattern, I wish first to adduce several general points about the medium of their expression—verbal idioms—since my own work has been exploratory, and others may envision finer ethnographic techniques and concepts with which to study that cultural mode and the symbolic dimension of related behavior.

Idioms—informal constructs of speech—constitute a naturalistic, intersubjective system of cultural knowledge and personal, pragmatic experience. Idioms are probably a universal of human language, but their meanings are bound to particular persons and their culture. The verbal form thus incorporates "semantico-referential meaning, pragmatic rules, and hierarchically ordered cultural premises" (Keesing 1979:30), all distinctive to a people who characteristically communicate with idioms. Idioms thus set up shared frames for perception, culturally transmitted boundaries with which individuals tacitly recognize or ignore patterns of phenomena. Their semantic bases derive from a lifetime of personal experience (and the resulting subjectivity) of an environment, customs, persons. They are communicated too easily, understood too effortlessly, with only slight shifts of meaning in referring to other persons known from birth in rich biographic detail. Tribesmen know more than they need tell; so they can tacitly hold, rearrange, or subscribe to new elements of idioms as the actors and situations change.

With Lévi-Strauss (1966:161), I believe there exists a "local logic" within a people's naturalistic system of communication; but it has a creative aspect, and its idiomatic parameters do not merely express a hard and fast set of "closed" rules for conveying meanings (Wagner 1975). Unlike Lévi-Strauss's (1966:17–21) *bricoleur,* moreover, Sambia do more than simply putter around with signs and symbols, shifting the signified into the signifying, as I hope I have demonstrated. Others have made similar points about the negotiation of meaning.[2] And on the New Guinea scene, the process of intersubjective communication can be "closed" only if one disregards historical diffusion resulting from trade, conquest, and cultural borrowing, not to mention personal innovations, all of which events change the means and ends utilized in the transmission of meaning. To study these processes of meaning requires detailed observations of the actual communications, not just inferences from the crystallized "structure" of customs and myth. Piaget has cogently summed up this point:

> If the concept of self-regulation or equilibrium has any sense at all, the logic or pre-logic of the members of a society cannot be adequately gauged from already crystallized cultural products; the real problem is to make out how the ensemble of these collective instruments is utilized in the everyday reasoning of each individual. . . . What we want to know is about individual inventions. [1971: 117]

This psychosocial perspective raises an equally important facet of idioms, their affective dimension, which I believe links them to the underlying fantasy systems of individuals. As we saw time and again among Sambia, idiomatic communications are not affectively neutral. Men's remarks are often subjectively endowed with connotations and feelings that draw on past experience, color intonation and syntax, influence the choice of metaphor and lexical terms, and simultaneously result in body gestures and actions that signify tacitly shared understandings. For instance, in the dramatic idiom, "Women have that vagina, something truly no good," men refer to ideas and values concerning women, femininity, and coitus, and they compulsively spit following the utterance so as to "cleanse their mouths." Here, meaning is attached to the idiom, its ideation and affect,

---

2. "By explicitly articulating semantic analysis to ethnography, and hence to pervasive cultural assumptions about the cosmos, causality, time, and being, we begin to capture not only the subtleties of meaning accessible to native speakers but the creative powers of language in metaphor and symbolism as well (Basso 1976). And in doing so, we begin to explore inter-connections between cognitive realms that too easily remain hidden if we map a single domain at a time" (Keesing 1979:27). The analytic problem, here, is one of "interlinkages" (Frake 1969:125), and in relating concepts like "idioverse" (Schwartz 1978)—or "individual culture"—and meaning viewed as completely shared "equivalence structures" (Wallace 1969:27–36; see also Tyler 1978:462ff.).

all of which are subsumed within the behavior of the intersubjective context. There is undoubtedly a "logic," or rather "analogic," of affects underlying such behavior (compare Barth 1975:224–225); it may be universal, as Freud (1953) believed; and it certainly has both manifest and latent meaning. Cultural training, childhood socialization, and a lifetime of experiences combine, developmentally, to forge the sense of such communications for individuals. Fantasy—personal and culturally constituted—persists throughout; so individuals can easily enough utilize affects and gestures (e.g., frowns, silence, spitting) to fill the gap between an idiom's use and the speakers' or listeners' meanings. When we ignore those data we misread even manifest behavior. Their inclusion will help build a theory of context (see Keesing 1972, 1979).

The ethnographic value of this approach lies in its closer presentation of how individuals draw boundaries around their perceptions of phenomena (e.g., persons and entities), better revealing the mix of fantasy and reality. No one has more thoughtfully confronted similar problems than LeVine (1973:223, 237ff.), who has systematically explored this area of research in his call for "grammars of interpersonal communication" and in his thoughts about the representation of ideas in communicative acts. Behavioral studies of these acts rest on normative descriptions, but they can go further by more clearly separating the natives' from the observers' views. Such accounts also equip the researcher for better handling of an absolutely essential psychodynamic principle of most human behavior— gender identity. The subjectivity of one's sense of maleness or femaleness, and the mixture of femininity and masculinity in one's behavior, influence most interpersonal communications at some level, whether they refer to other persons, events, or oneself, and regardless of whether they utilize pragmatic ideas, ritual or secular idioms, or myth. And in this way, intersubjective communications put into action shifting modes of identification and metaphoric imagination.[3]

With this in mind, let me summarize the main attributes of idioms as I have inferred them from Sambia behavior. Four trends stand out: (1) perceptual correspondence: the tacit and manifest responses to patterns of family resemblance (e.g., sympathetic or contagious "magical identification") connecting different classes of phenomena (e.g., women and casso-

---

3. "What is being inculcated [in tribesmen] is a mode of awareness continuously creative, indicating a fluid activity that avoids the tendency to select any one thing from a constant generation of images. We note again the tendency to regard consciousness not as an entity but more as a process. Our term 'set' might apply if we could look upon this process as multivalued. At any rate, the notion of looking at the contents of mind as some kind of mental furniture to be inventoried is as inappropriate in these cultural psychologies as it was for post-introspection psychology" (Price-Williams 1975:90).

waries), either in global or particular terms; (2) genderizing: a form of anthropomorphization in which men are prone, lexically, metaphorically, and subjectively, to polarize many natural phenomena and predicate their behavior on the basis of human male or female gender traits, which are read back into cultural constructs (M. Strathern 1978); (3) focal projection: precise isomorphisms pinpointing subjective links between human organs (or traits) and other phenomena (e.g., the pandanus flower is equated with the human penis); and (4) perceptual splitting: the categorization of phenomena into manifest or tacit subtypes based on subjective premises or images (the perceptual filter) that affectively polarizes (splits apart) the meanings attributed to members of the resulting gender classes (e.g., "girl" versus "boy," pandanus "flower" versus "nut pod). Various factors, contextual, interpersonal, and biographic, influence the significance of these idiomatic principles for verbal behavior. So does the observer's presence. In each instance the ethnographer must evaluate differing possibilities for the individuals involved, whose use of the precepts and concepts patterned in idioms provides evidence for various modes of identification, or disidentification, with the related designata of the idioms.

With perceptual splitting, for instance, we face a range of challenging psychosocial issues in symbolic analysis. Why are Sambia men prone to phobia-like responses to red fluids, as if such fluids were blood or menstrual discharges (see Weiyu's reactions, Chapter 7)? We might hypothesize that somewhere, in the course of male development, certain experiences (and their subjectivity) have affects habitually attached to them; some are acceptable, some are not; so conflictual forms of subjectivity (e.g., pieces of identity, mood signs, etc.) become detached from acceptable masculine behavior. Unacceptable affective responses about blood and danger, one's mother, her (or one's own sense of) femininity or reproductive competence, come to be associated with, and projected into, red fluids, which are thereby kept distinct from other "things," including images of one's own body. Certain affects (at manifold levels of subjectivity) are thus split off from one's sense of self and become feared, denied, or adored as "things" holding a dangerous power beyond oneself. Perceptual splitting is thus a symbolic mechanism having feedback effects in individual experience, cultural ideology, and social relationships.

It is with hoary problems like this that our conventional social anthropological approach proves to be inadequate (Spiro 1979). Earlier I noted three general viewpoints in regard to their "solution": faulty technology, faulty politics, and faulty reasoning. Each position has some merit, but none has succeeded in establishing a reliable methodology for demonstrating what part of individual "symbolic behavior" is "symbolic" versus instrumental or institutional routine. More attention should be paid to the subjectivity of identification.

Perhaps instead of faulty reasoning, for example, we ought to consider the "faulty optics" conditioning Sambia idioms. A defective lens produces a distorted or secondary image: the culturally transmitted idiom subsumes a set of subjective resonances. Idioms are socially contingent on equivalent expectations. The phenomenological parameters of an idiom are mentally constrained by residues of developmental experiences built up in one's perceptual and fantasy systems. Like a primitive "choice machine" (Hoyle 1966:42),[4] an idiom subliminally creates artificial boundaries between inner awareness and external reality. So by choosing an idiom, men tacitly assert certain possibilities, thereby inhibiting recognition of other choices. Cultural idioms are seldom perceptually neutral, either in metaphoric or lexical significance, since they affectively funnel memory traces resulting from past experiences that were suffered and enjoyed. The intersubjective context of idioms may thus trigger a proneness to sense again past wishes, others' expectations, and the outlines of one's own personal scripts. These resonances may produce a distortion in perception if related past experiences involve conflict, interpersonal or intrapsychic. Does all irrational[5] perception stem from conflict? Clearly it does not, but our progress in understanding this problem depends on the development of a more sophisticated treatment of culture and consciousness.

These analytic principles lead to the more important psychosocial focus of the contents of masculine idioms, the meaning embedded in the "false optics" of Sambia gender polarity. Let me summarize their broad and pervasive symbolic trends. (1) Gender distinctions concerning natural species transcend simple dimorphism, attributing to female beings a natural reproductive competence greater than that of male beings. (2) Women, like garden crops, "female" pandanus, and cassowaries, undergo rapid and visible parturition changes "naturally" (i.e., not ritually induced); men do not. (3) Sambia clearly postulate a dual sexual role for men and women in procreation. (4) And while two hypothetical organs—*tingu* (menstrual-blood focused) and *kereku-kereku* (semen focused)—are polarized as opposite-sex biological mechanisms that motivate sexual maturity and gender role competence, the *tingu* is self-activating and internally self-sustaining, whereas the male *kereku-kereku* organ is not. (5) The innate difference between these organs is accepted as a fact of nature in explaining why girls physically mature faster than boys. (6) Women are

---

4. For this and related references, see Freeman (1977).
5. See also Sperber (1975:3–4). I am not referring to convictions that are the result of temporary situational or personal factors (e.g., tiredness, anger) or the product of a lack of scientific knowledge (e.g., male cassowaries, not females, care for the young); rather, I am referring to those that clearly transcend a people's own trend of understandings and are of the order of dogma (e.g., cassowaries give birth from their anuses).

thus reproductively superior to men since femaleness (e.g., the menarche) results in feminine reproductive competence (i.e., childbirth). (7) Masculinization is, however, a product of ritual activities: separation from females, and constant homosexual inseminations that are consciously compared to a form of "male breast-feeding" (i.e., semen-feeding). (8) Ritual secrecy and female avoidance taboos indicate that a behavioral and psychological distance from women, along with homosexual experiences, is necessary for the creation of a warrior's sense of masculine gender identity and manly comportment. (9) After initiation, men must still continue to defend themselves against the overwhelming contagion and depletion of women's bodies through constant adult rituals of nose-bleeding and milky tree-sap ingestion. (10) In blatant contradiction to men's own heterosexual theory of procreation and the trend of male idioms, the secret myth of parthenogenesis nonetheless denies the primordial existence of women, affirming that males, alone, created humanity.

In analyzing the myth I pointed to the disguised transsexual theme within it. Males were the original creators, but they were pseudohermaphrodites whose female secondary sex traits did not alter until the invention of homosexual fellatio. That act had a dual function: it masculinized the ancestor and feminized his mate. I hypothesized that it is the essential inability of males to sense themselves as fully masculine, sufficiently phallic, in the ways required by their community, that provides the subjective impetus for this myth and its secrecy. Reexperiencing the mythic script, entertaining the risk of having been hermaphroditic, reliving the ancestor's traumas, and then overcoming them through the secrecy and danger of the myth-telling context, with its triumphant outcome, provide a personal script for assuring the necessary formula of successful heterosexual excitement and distance in adulthood. (This is only a general sketch; we still do not understand the precise elements which constitute that formula.) The myth stands for a developmental dilemma; sharing in and subjectively experiencing the fantasy is an attempt to channel certain conflicts, old and new, into precise masculine outcomes.

A primary one is erotic. To be effective, male initiation must convert small, puny boys, attached to their mothers, into virile, aggressive warriors who are first erotically excited by boys and then by women. Through its institutionalized and subjective dynamics, the myth is linked to that behavioral pattern. It can evoke powerful memories and fantasies, and thereby reconstitute that subjectivity, making it available to the demands of masculine secrecy and everyday behavior. The mythic script disguises its correspondence to one's personal history by means of faceless fictive characters, a stamp of authoritative factuality, sharing in the tale with others, and its secrecy.

It is that subjective tension—between the adult imperative of always acting like a fully masculine warrior, competent in fighting, hunting, and erotic activities, and the core childhood sense of having been a helpless small person, male but not manly, who was once intimately a part of one's mother and her femaleness—which I believe informs the predicament of Sambia masculine identity and culture. That tension comes through in idioms. Yet I think that its most striking manifestations are concealed in the secret experiences of myth and ritual, where men are removed from women. If this is so, then we should expect that those structured, transitional experiences gradually split apart (ritualize) a man's adult behavior from what he felt back then as a child.

How shall we then explain the roots of this stupendous dilemma in male idioms: that femaleness is natural and more basic than maleness, and that boys must be homosexually inseminated for years to attain even a tenuous biological and social manhood? To interpret below, I serve notice that I must sometimes speculate, and that I am offering hypotheses, not facts. The reality and fantasy of men's idioms make this an intellectual necessity from the start. Here, in addition, I shall contrast the Sambia with other New Guinea cultures so as to generalize about their male developmental cycles.

We shall go wrong from the start unless we again underline how deeply rooted is Sambia culture in a history of constant war. Warfare, to repeat, colored virtually all facets of social life and dictated the need for certain kinds of men and women. This point I cannot emphasize too strongly, since I fear that recent workers have neglected it—not its sociology or politics so much as its powerful psychological effects (but see F. Young 1965, for a comparative study). Twentieth-century intellectualized researchers have not emphasized how catastrophic war can be, socially, economically, and psychologically, especially that primitive form of warfare that depends on stone-age weaponry—through man-to-man combat— which we have never known (Schwartz 1973). Such facts relentlessly condition the very meaning of male existence. Such a warring society needs omnipotent, dependably fiery soldiers; yet these soldiers were once, as children, long suckled by women. The effects of this behavioral fault line on male gender identity we have only begun to uncover, but they are without doubt deep, long-lasting, and profound.

In her study of *Sex and Temperament in Three Primitive Societies* Margaret Mead concluded:

If a society insists that warfare is the major occupation for the male sex, it is therefore insisting that all male children display bravery and pugnacity. Even if the insistence upon the differential bravery of men and women is not made articulate, the difference in occupation makes this point implicitly. When, however, a society goes further and defines men as brave and women as timorous, when men are forbidden to show fear and women are indulged in the most flagrant display of fear, a more explicit element enters in. Bravery, hatred of any weakness, of flinching before pain or danger—this attitude which is so strong a component of *some human* temperaments has been selected as the key to masculine behavior. [1968:265]

Here, in Mead's insightful remarks, we see the predicament of little boys who must become reluctant warriors (see also Mead 1949:95ff.).

Perhaps Sambia male babies are cared for and expected to become rugged warriors from their first days of life. Perhaps they are cradled, adored, and frustrated in ways that ensure aggressiveness. But perhaps, too, those individuating experiences are delayed, made secondary to the mother's fear for the child's health; nurturance and gratification come first. For months the baby owns the breast, has no rivals for its milk, is constantly, blissfully cuddled, remains enveloped and nameless, a piece of his mother's body and existence. And younger mothers, at least, respond to the baby's demands far more from love than from duty: this cherished infant is her greatest achievement; he rewards her femininity with the great moments of motherhood she has been made for throughout her whole life; and he provides her with little joys and sensual contacts often missing from her sometimes thankless, dutiful marriage. Moreover, the infant does not possess his father, who is not so much physically as psychologically absent. So the first part of life is spent away from one's father and other men; at a sufficient remove for the irreversible message, "You are a male," to be mixed with other messages; and the effect is to soften, not harden, the infant's own constructs of maleness.

Now suppose that, along the way, an infant's awakening senses and motor coordination are still rapidly stimulated—all except his sense of separateness, which constant maternal care dulls. Mother and infant are close, too close, for the even-paced divergence of maleness that is necessary for a male infant's individuation. So something stays blurred, as one notices in the hidden breast-feedings. (Although still unmeasurable, there is little doubt that countless maternal responses "fix" [see Stoller 1979: 235–239] powerful bonds, within the baby, that are so visible in the later, glowing, eye-to-eye contact that psychologically merges mother and infant.) Father's presence grows, through the stages of crawling, toddling, and walking. Nevertheless, trailing along after the child is his mother, her fragrances, her body and its pollution—all of which classes him, for the time being, with his mother, not his father. The father watches, then occasionally holds the baby. Then, as even later, a man takes the child—but only briefly—and then sometimes he communicates a humiliating message, which may never be forgotten: "I am a man, you are something different"—a message that maintains the father's necessary distance, but guarantees trauma for the child. Then, too, these experiences may be set in the midst of family conflict: the hostility of silence, bickering, or open fighting between the parents, conflict in which the father always wins, and no one wins; or the mother's responses to aggressiveness in a growing boy whom she ambivalently identifies too much with his father; and the boy's treatment as too much his mother's baby by his father. But despite the enormous subjective and behavioral significance of these facts, neither father nor mother need worry much about the fate of the boy's masculinity.

For in a couple of years, as both parents know, radical resocialization is inevitable: what mother and father would not or could not do gets irreversibly done through ritual initiation: abrupt maternal detachment, separation-individuation, and routinized masculinization. That trauma helps instill manly pride, but it leaves scars. And like a primitive form of behavioral surgery, it remakes the most available, the most visible parts of the boy's gender identity: feminine behaviors are ruled out so that only masculine ones may rule; other needs go underground; and ritual fills in the gap of unfinished maleness.

All of these factors pertain to the normal pattern of Sambia male socialization. They suggest the general viewpoint that society's "insistence" (to use Mead's term) on turning maternally attached infant *males* into the psychological beings identified as *men* creates an insufferable dilemma. What is insisted on repudiates what is inside. By the age of seven to ten years (first-stage initiation), the early months of the "critical learning" period are long since past; the formative years of childhood development are virtually complete; the core sense of identity is set; and so the late procedures of ritualized gender surgery must rattle the very gates of life and death to effect the desired modifications in even visible masculine gender behavior. Although ritual dogma ignores this problem and ritual behavior disguises it, we can see its outlines in mundane idioms and the myth: the quiet mixture of femaleness and maleness projected into the world is different from the stampeding public rituals of men. Contrary to other workers, then, I hold that boys are reluctant men; and even Sambia men take pleasure in the stereotypical fantasy, far more than the hard-won reality, of an aggressive warrior's life.

The symbolic behaviors of ritualized masculine development can be seen in this way. Men are genuinely convinced that biological maleness and manly reproductive competence are not inherent; that mother's continued care and women's pollution threaten masculine life; and that homosexual insemination and ritual procedures are the only salvation of maleness. My view is that this symbolic complex is a culturally constituted response to the situation of most Sambia men's need to sense themselves as unambiguously masculine in the ways demanded of them by their warring communities. Where personal history stops short, the male cult takes over.

Whiting et al. (1958) and Burton and Whiting (1961) tried to confront similar issues in a cross-cultural survey of gender identity and male initiation rites, and their work will serve as a theoretical springboard for contrasting Sambia with other New Guinea societies.[6]

Whiting and his colleagues were concerned with the relative incidence and "sociopsychological" functions of puberty rites in tribal societies. Arguing from certain prevailing assumptions of psychoanalytic and learning theory (Whiting et al. 1958:361–363), they wanted to correlate the relationship between child-rearing practices and initiation customs in widely dispersed societies. They began with the idea

> . . . that a long and exclusive relationship between mother and son provides the conditions which should lead to an exceptionally strong dependence upon the mother. Also, we assume that if father terminates this relationship and replaces his son, there should be a strong envy and hostility engendered in the boy which, although held in check during childhood, may dangerously manifest itself with the onset of puberty, unless measures are taken to prevent it.

Their literature survey seemed to confirm this suggestion (but see Norbeck et al. 1962).

They then described several broad implications of their findings: the more exclusive, or intense, the mother-infant relationship, the greater the child's "emotional dependence"; the stronger the dependence, the greater the resulting hostility and envy (social and sexual) toward the father or his substitutes; at puberty this leads to (Oedipal) "rivalry" with the father, and "incestuous" approaches to the mother; initiation forestalls these developments; and, regardless of the relative strength of infantile dependence, there will remain a need for initiation to exercise authority over boys, thereby assuring identification with adult masculine figures.

---

6. This is fitting, since Whiting et al. (1958) cited various New Guinea reports and amplified their points with an ethnographic sketch of the Kwoma, a Sepik River people of New Guinea with whom J. W. M. Whiting (1941) lived. What follows is not, however, intended as a critique of all of the related work of the Whitings and their students; this is not the place for that, nor does space permit adequate treatment of their ideas (see Barry, Bacon, and Child 1957; Harrington 1968; Lambert, Triandis, and Wolf 1959; Longabaugh 1973; Munroe and Munroe 1971, 1973; Munroe, Munroe, and Whiting 1973; J. W. M. Whiting 1961; B. Whiting 1965; and see also J. Brown 1963; Cohen 1964b; Stephens 1962:152–159; and F. Young 1965). In their most recent work, the Whitings have shifted their viewpoint compared to the earlier papers, and their conclusions support my own work among Sambia, especially in regard to the effects of "aloofness" on male gender-identity development (see Whiting and Whiting 1975:190–199). Because of its historical and theoretical place in the literature, however, I treat only the Whiting et al. (1958) and Burton and Whiting (1961) papers directly in the following review.

Burton and Whiting (1961) further refined this argument with their "status envy hypothesis." First, they defined identification by its *consequences* (not its motivations) as a process consisting "of the covert practice of the role of an envied status." Second, their *sociological* definition of identity ("a person's position or positions in the status system of . . . [a] society" [Burton and Whiting 1961:87]) was based on a counterintuitive psychological proposition—that a "completely satisfying complementary relationship between two people will not lead to identification." (We shall see in a moment that present research in gender identity does not support this position.) Third, the authors distinguished between "three kinds of identity":[7] attributed identity, those statuses that society assigns to a person; subjective identity, those statuses a person "sees himself as occupying"; and optative identity, statuses a person wishes to occupy but from which he or she is blocked. Concentrating on the last "type," Burton and Whiting (1961:87) add:

> Obviously, one's optative identity derives from status envy, and nothing much would be added to our theory by introducing the concept if one's optative identity were always objective and realistic. . . . however, this is frequently not the case, and people often feel "I am what I would like to be." In such a case, the subjective and optative identities merge and become discrepant with the attributed identities. *It is our thesis that the aim of socialization is to produce an adult whose attributed, subjective, and optative identities are isomorphic:* "I see myself as others see me, and I am what I want to be." [My emphasis]

This rightly led Burton and Whiting (1961:88ff.) and later workers (see Allen 1967:14–27; Harrington and Whiting 1972:487–491; B. Whiting 1979:321–323) to draw attention to the effects of prolonged mother-infant relationships on male identification. They argued that intense "dependence" leads to "primary identification" in infancy, whereas later childhood and initiation experience creates a different, "secondary identification." Care of the infant exclusively by the mother thus brings about a "primary cross-sex optative identity," the result being problematic intrapsychic conflict between the two layers—primary and secondary male gender identity. That would potentially create grave problems in the segmentary, patrilocally-based societies of New Guinea, with their male-

---

7. This typological conceptualization differs from the view of gender identity used in my own analysis above. Splitting up aspects of identity into different types of this sort is a convenient heuristic device, but it often tends, in theory formation and writing, to reify those identity categories as "things" existing outside in the world instead of placing them in the totality of a person's subjectivity and behavior. Except in the simple sense of "social identity" (which is a special case), it is more parsimonious to think of various levels or attributes of identity, or similar concepts that recognize a constellation of identity parts that make up a system (see also Erikson 1968:15–43; Katchadourian 1979:13–34).

centered institutions and need for men unambiguously to serve a community's political and military needs (Allen 1967; Shapiro 1979:293–295). Burton and Whiting (1961:90–91) therefore advanced a hypothesis still very much with us: puberty rites resolve "cross-sex identity conflict" by psychologically "brainwashing" a youth's "primary feminine identity," replacing it with a "secondary male identity."

To sum up, this work was important, and it set us on the right track. It explicitly linked initiation customs with their cultural background in early socialization, indicating some of the psychosocial factors that influence gender-identity formation. It drew attention to the critical nature of the child's tie to his mother, also stimulating needed research on the problem of the absent father and male identity (Biller 1970; D'Andrade 1973; Lamb 1976). It must be made clear these twenty years later, however, that we still lack sufficient or adequate material with which to test their ideas: Whiting and his colleagues were theorizing about complex psychosocial issues based on variable, rough, and disparate normative accounts of initiation customs. To do justice to their suggestions would require extensive behavioral observations of mother-infant interactions and the family unit, and of ritual behavior, as well as focused studies of individual gender identity (topics I take up elsewhere). Nonetheless, recent advances in research on sex and gender, and on ritual behavior in New Guinea, point up several shortcomings in the thesis of Whiting and his collaborators and allow us to ask new questions about those old problems.

Let us consider in turn five different factors that pertain to the Whiting work, illustrating new perspectives on the role of ritualized gender identity in masculine development. According to their ontological and ontogenetic status, they are: (1) the biopsychic status of "emotional dependence" and identification in childhood; (2) Burton and Whiting's assumption of "isomorphism" in the developmental stages of gender-identity formation; (3) the dynamics of ritual secrecy and the meaning of different levels of subjective identity; (4) the incidence of institutionalized homosexual behavior in New Guinea; and (5) the relationship between childhood, ritual experience, and subsequent adult behavior, especially erotic activities. (I hope it will become apparent that most of this reformulation complements the earlier Whiting work, expanding on what was previously assumed or unknown.)

Mother-Infant Bonding

In the same year as the initial Whiting study, Bowlby (1958) published a seminal paper on "The Nature of the Child's Tie to His Mother." In it, and in later work (1969, 1973), he drew on psychoanalytic, learning, and ethological theories to study attachment behavior: the child's tie "is a product of a number of behavioral systems that have proximity to mother as a predictable outcome" (Bowlby 1969:179). As an outcome of behaviors such as crying, smiling, and sucking, the infant effects physical proximity to his mother. Observations show that the presence or absence of the mother is the most critical variable in accounting for the activation of attachment behaviors (e.g., clinging) or separation anxiety (e.g., protests, despair) (see Bowlby 1973:46). Among subhuman primates, attachment behavior is readily visible soon after birth (see Bowlby 1969:227, 230–245, 259–264); and rhesus monkeys, for instance, usually prefer female to male caretakers (Sackett 1972). Observable attachment behavior in humans emerges later (Bowlby 1969:228), in part a function of neotony. Both children and nonparental figures can become the focus of attachment, and without the use of rewards like food (Bowlby 1973:265). Various conditions can later reactivate attachment behavior, and in all normal children stressful situations tend to provoke clinging, sobbing, unspecified demands, and searching behavior (Bowlby 1973:22–27).

This research has definitely shifted the theory and methods used in understanding maternal bonding and its effects on identification. It calls for more emphasis on direct observation of children and their culture, less reliance on inferences from adult behaviors or symptoms. (Children are not simply impoverished renditions of the adults that anthropologists mostly focus on.) On the one hand, Bowlby's behavioral approach encourages interdisciplinary perspectives on development in lower mammals and humans.[8] On the other hand, it allows a critical look at the value of Burton and Whiting's concept of "emotional dependence." Indeed, Bowlby himself (1969:228–229) debated the merits of that term, rejecting it and kindred terms (e.g., affiliation) because they were not measurable or parsimonious enough to be used as descriptive units. His reasons are worth citing:

. . . in this account the terms "dependence" and "dependency" are avoided, although they have long been in common use by psychoanalysts and also by psychologists who favor a theory of secondary drive. The terms derive from the idea that a child becomes linked to his mother because he is dependent on her as the source of physiological gratification. Apart, however, from their deriving from a theory that is almost certainly false, there are other strong reasons for

---

8. The literature on this subject is burgeoning and exciting; for studies that relate to sex and gender, see Ainsworth (1972), Green (1978), Johnson, Gilbert, and Herdt (1979), Jolly (1972:214–246), Klaus and Kennell (1976), Money and Ehrhardt (1972:65–94), Reynolds (1976:119–125, 151–166), and Stoller (1968:3–16ff.).

not using them. The fact is that to be dependent on a mother-figure and to be attached to her are very different things. Thus, in the early weeks of life an infant is undoubtedly dependent on his mother's ministrations, but he is not yet attached to her. Conversely, a child of two or three years who is being looked after by strangers may show the clearest evidence that he continues to be strongly attached to her though he is not at that time dependent on her.

This is more than mere semantics. At issue is our research paradigm—theories, concepts, data—with which we think about the effects of prolonged, exclusive maternal bonding on gender identity in groups like Sambia. Understanding the child's tie to his or her mother as one of "emotional dependence" obscures the need for observations concerning the effects of that bond which live on in a person's behavior and subjectivity. "Emotional dependence" is temporary and inconsequential.[9] It implies that such a state of being, no matter how exclusive or prolonged, blissful or traumatic, remains tractable, easily modifiable, as but one stage through which one passes into another. A significant stage, to be sure; one resulting in a primary identification with mother, and hostility or envy toward father—disastrous inclinations if unchecked. But that dependency—those inclinations in subjectivity and behavior—is like an old crutch of support to be put on the shelf as one is initiated and "outgrows" (forgets? represses?) those "childish needs."

If the psychosocial consequence of initiation rites is the masculine dismissal of dependency, then we have a number of unexplained problems on our hands. Like: the early age and severity of Sambia initiation, years before puberty; attachment behavior redirected toward masculine figures during initiation; prolonged ritualized homosexual behaviors; secret identities; and the adult tendency to stamp gender into everything. These factors indicate that the "dependency" model of gender-identity formation is too simple. Can initiation simply relieve the "pressures" of "cross-sex identity conflict" by brainwashing away (eradicating? disguising? converting something into something else?) those early maternal bonding effects? On the contrary, Bowlby's work should lead us to respect the profound neuropsychological and behavioral-structure effects of that willingness to maintain proximity with the mother; for, long after dependency vanishes, the effects of attachment remain in force.

If maternal bonding can be so powerful, precipitating lifelong behavior patterns, then we should wonder whether any techniques—even the dayslong primitive forms of initiation treatment, such as beatings and threats—

---

9. ". . . whereas dependence is maximum at birth and diminishes more or less steadily until maturity is reached, attachment is altogether absent at birth and is not strongly in evidence until an infant is past six months" (Bowlby 1969:228).

can effectively transmute the underlying structure of subjectivity. Here we need precise observations of ritual behavior, and postritual developmental experiences, to measure the immediate and long-term shifts in individual responses or inclinations toward masculine gender behaviors.

This is where the concept of a "critical period" in human infancy must come into play (see Luria 1979; Maccoby 1979:195–197; Money and Ehrhardt 1972:176–194). What occurs in those first six months of life is unknown: we still have no way to probe what the infant feels, thinks, or represents. Even the following two years of life are not well understood. So we must rely on inferences from other sorts of observations. (Bowlby, who generally ignores identity, identification, and fantasy, is least helpful here.) The research of psychiatry and psychoanalysis provides our most powerful tools here, since theirs are the only means of acquiring accurate data on that early subjectivity.

Gender-Identity Formation

Stoller (1968, 1973, 1975) has repeatedly addressed the difficult issues surrounding the earliest sources of gender-identity formation. His thinking represents a long synthesis of clinical work on sex and gender, allowing for an interactionalist model of psychodynamic, cultural, and behavioral factors. (The complexity of these matters requires a certain sensitivity to interdisciplinary research; Stoller respects that, while admitting of only tentative formulations—something essential at this stage of such research.) In a recent work, he begins by rejecting the idea that infants inherit intrapsychic conflict or fantasy, arguing for a "conflict-free phase of development." He continues:

> . . . in humans, as in all other species of animal life, there is nonmental learning, such as conditioning and possibly—as in birds—imprinting . . . The capacity of cells, organs, and organisms to modify behavior in the absence of mental involvement, even in the absence of a central nervous system, is unquestioned. The human infant's tissues, like those of humans of all ages and those of any other species, are prone to such influences. Permanent behavioral styles, automatisms, call them what you will, are inserted by mothers from birth on into this congenital matrix, to form a foundation for behavior. These biologic ("instinctual") and biopsychic ("conditioned," "imprinted," what else?) anlagen will serve as vehicles for playing out the intrapsychic conflicts that in time arise. The point here is not that a behaviorist or ethologic model must be an alternative to a conflict model, but that both are at work.
> . . . these biopsychic phenomena are present, shaping the infant's responses within its mother's embrace, becoming habitual, automized fundamentals of later character structure. Not only are they not the product of intra-psychic

conflict, but many of them are the result of *gratifying* experiences that the infant "learns" to repeat (the quotation marks are to indicate that we do not yet really know what the word "learn" means). [1979:236]

This view has important implications for Sambia and similar peoples. What if in addition to an early and prolonged period of these naturally gratifying experiences—which impart "critical learning" and shape character structure—the father remains removed from the infant in the early months of life? The consequences for the processes of identification are large.

This perspective contravenes the Burton-Whiting position on identification. If nonconflictual, gratifying experiences are *also* present in earliest childhood, then there are no theoretical grounds for continuing to hold a theory of identification which argues that a satisfying, complementary relationship between two people cannot lead to identification. (Or envy: see Bettelheim 1955:17ff.) Before later experiences, verbal-cognitive learning or speech, and before pre-Oedipal and Oedipal conflict, there may be that other special era which is "biopsychic" and free of conflict. Once more Stoller is helpful:

> The term "conflict" needs to be clarified, for it refers to two different processes. The one that especially concerns analysts is intrapsychic conflict, wherein one part of oneself is fighting against another part of oneself, intersystemic or intrapsychic (antithetical scripts). There is another kind of conflict—more interesting to nonanalytic theorists—in which the conflict is between one person and another (as with a child fighting against its mother). After a few months, probably all conflict with the external world has its intrapsychic-conflict ramifications, but at the beginning of life, I do not think that is the case. At first there is just the mindless brain, vulnerable to external stimuli that permanently emplace—fix—some aspects of psychic life. After some of this earliest biopsychic experience is embedded in brain and psyche, fantasy begins, its task to modulate the impact of the outer world and inner stimuli, protecting us from—*giving us explanations for*—otherwise unmanageable forces that impinge from outside and from within. [1979:236–237]

If one's core gender identity is rooted in this soil of strong mother and tantalizingly distant father, the question is not simply one of a "primary feminine identification" but rather one of a primary sense of existence whose feminine qualities are deeply part of the earliest subjectivity that impels character structure and adult behavior.

The anthropological significance of this viewpoint lies in its implications for the meaning of continuities and discontinuities of male gender-identity formation in New Guinea societies. Stoller (1973:314; see also Money and Ehrhardt 1972:176–178) has noted that core gender identity is well formed by a year and a half or two years, and "almost irreversible by around age five or six." In the Highlands, as elsewhere, this is more problematic and risky for boys than for girls. In an insightful review, Lidz and Lidz make this point, stressing the differential gender formation of males and females in Melanesia. They also observe that:

> The fundamental task that must be carried out in all societies is the differentiation of the child from the initial symbiosis with the mother . . . and then in guiding the boy to rescind his initial identification with his mother and gain a firm identity as a male. Whereas the girl must establish boundaries, she does not rescind the initial identification with her mother as a female. Herein lies one of the reasons why Freud's early efforts to describe the girl's oedipal transition as a mirror image of the boy's failed. It also seems to be one reason why in New Guinea it is believed that the girl matures naturally and female puberty ceremonies celebrate the girl's maturation whereas the boy's initiation is required to induce maturation. [1977:28]

Other psychiatric researchers have concentrated their efforts on understanding these processes. What Mahler (1968) calls separation-individuation is a characteristic developmental phase in which the infant establishes a sense of him- or herself and body boundaries as distinct from the mother. The mother can either help or hinder these processes, whose outcome is psychosocial individuation for the child. Conflict arises from a reluctance on the part of either mother or infant to do this. In males, unlike females, there is an added difficulty. Boys must not only separate from their mothers but must also disidentify (Greenson 1968) from them and early symbiotic union. And this process implies their capacity to wish to identify with available masculine figures. Girls, on the other hand, must separate-individuate, but their core gender identity is feminine, like their mothers' (see also Chodorow 1974). If this critical psychological development is blocked, any of a number of basic gender disorders can result. (Primary male transsexualism [see Stoller 1968, 1975] is perhaps the most spectacular form, as noted above: a biologically normal male can be absolutely convinced—i.e., without intrapsychic conflict—that he belongs *in* the opposite sex.) Consequently, only if a boy can "grow beyond the feminine identifications that resulted from his first encounters with his mother's female body and feminine qualities" (Stoller 1968:98) can he become a "separate masculine individual."

This process can be hindered in two obvious ways. A woman may persist in blurring the boundaries between herself and the child; or she can use him as a means of filling a void in her relationship to others (especially her husband; see Stoller 1975:57–68). The child, too, can resist relinquishing the protecting, warm sensuality of his mother and his sense of wishing to be like her (see Green 1974). In either case, a child faces marked difficulties in establishing his individual sense of maleness and transition into the masculine gender role.

The Whiting-Burton focus has also deflected attention away from another important and puzzling ethnographic fact: some New Guinea tribes stage initiation rites for males well *before* puberty. Some, like Sambia, begin in late childhood and continue in stages of progressive status advancement for years, into adulthood. A partial listing of similar groups would include societies as widespread as the Baktaman (Barth 1975), Baruya (Godelier 1976), Wogeo (Hogbin 1970), Bimin-Kuskusmin (Poole 1980), Gahuku-Gama (Read 1952), Marind-Anim (Van Baal 1966), Trans-Fly (Williams 1936b), and the Ilahita Arapesh (Tuzin 1980). In short, whatever else the rites may effect in the sociocultural functioning of these groups, early initiation has psychosocial effects that take firm hold during childhood.

Here again we must speculate. Are the early age, severity, and exclusiveness of maternal detachment within these initiation systems sociocultural indicators of the underlying core anlagen of male gender-identity formation in these groups? I believe they are; for reasons still unclear, a greater tension works within the gender subjectivity of males of such groups, with intense maternal attachment effects pulling one way, and a converse psychosocial need for perhaps even fiercer masculinity (than in other groups, possibly because of local warfare and other social conditions) pulling in the opposite direction (Langness 1967).

Our anthropological approach on this account needs to be reconsidered. We would, out of hand, reject the biological determinist argument that anatomy is destiny. And yet we have, since before Mead (1928, 1968), seemed to accept an implicit cultural determinism in regard to gender identity and erotic behavior.[10] There is no question that cultural factors influence the development and maintenance of masculinity and femininity (see Rosaldo and Lamphere 1974). The cultural constraints (e.g., attitudes, gender role norms) are there in the adjustment of individuals to cultural institutions or roles. But so are psychological and behavioral factors that the New Guinea materials underscore (see LeVine 1979).

It should be clear that the Sambia pattern of sex and gender development differs radically from our own. Men are adamant: the sexes have quite different "problems" in attaining adult reproductive competence. For women, biology and behavioral development are fused; feminine

---

10. Mead sometimes shifted her views on this problem; see *Male and Female* (1949).

behavior and female reproductive capacity are natural outcomes of a female's anatomy and cultural training. Men are different: anatomy and behavior are split up; neither biology nor early learning experiences ensure the development of masculinity or the capacity to act as a reproductively competent man. Instead, men perceive masculinity to be the product of *female-influenced conditions* (biological, psychological, and sociocultural). This constellation of developmental patterns leaves boys too susceptible to femaleness and femininity. And these conditions not only thwart biological ("male") growth and the capacity to act in a masculine way; they are also lethal if left unchecked.

These are, according to ritual ideology, the conditions that force men to intervene with initiations. Boys must be detached from their mothers and thereafter strictly separated from all females. Ritual taboos and secrecy help maintain the physical, social, and psychological distance between males and females. Boys must be radically resocialized and traumatized. What is done and said to them—and what they are released into feeling— constitutes the ritualized socialization of emerging adulthood. Ritual-based knowledge and action, idioms and emotions, all come after the age of seven to ten years, following first-stage initiation; as does ritualized homosexual fellatio.

Masculinization: that is the concept I applied to that second experiential "layer" of socialization implemented through ritual life. Its experiences differ fundamentally from those of infantile and childhood socialization. Ritualized masculinization makes use of active teaching, rhetoric, and rapid behavioral conditioning, more persistently cognitive elements than those of the preverbal affective anlagen of infancy. Initiations provide the years-long extra push needed by boys in making the transition from maternal attachment to rugged adult warriorhood.

Sambia is a society that is culturally disjunctive to an extreme in the developmental cycle of its males. Early infantile experiences inaugurate the closest interpersonal relationship known to males and females. Ritual does its utmost not to build on this experiential core in a man's sense of himself but to redirect and repress it as far as possible. So we face the difficult task of describing how a male's sense of himself, as a child, is synchronized with his social behavior and sense of adult masculinity. The two experiential "layers" are not necessarily in harmony; and whatever personal dilemmas, conflicts, or contradictions are embedded in this highly fragmented developmental pattern are difficult to observe on the surface. This is, I submit, the prime reason some reports of New Guinea initiation rites are misleading: the observer took secular dogma or ritual behavior as the most visible, the most important, phenomena informing masculine identity, behavior, and ideology. In other words, a theory of culture must attend to the differences between, and integration of, these conceptual levels; symbolic meaning cannot simply be inferred from one level.

Ritual Secrecy

It is not surprising, then, how many workers have followed Whiting and his colleagues in taking ritual secrecy for granted. Not only the dynamics but the behavior of masculine secrecy has been neglected. Indeed, I suspect that if the cross-cultural materials had been rich enough, the Whiting et al. (1958) study would have clarified further discrete patterns of male initiation by distinguishing those tribes in which ritual secrecy is intense from those in which it is weak or absent. The forms, contents, and meaning of ritual secrecy, I believe, hold significant clues for the relationship between male identity and initiation.

A major point about Sambia initiation, in this regard, is its creation of a secret dimension of masculine identity. That subjectivity seems to be an intended outcome of male initiation experience, as I argued above. Precisely how that secret sense of oneself fits into gender formation and adult behavior remains uncertain, but its force is tremendous, and the implications of that are pervasive.

For theory the implications are also profound. On this count, there is no reason to concur with Burton and Whiting's assumption that all societies aim to make the various parts of identity "isomorphic." From either a psychological or a sociological viewpoint, Sambia socialization not only does not aim to effect this "isomorphism," it positively resists it. The reasons are clear: such a continuity would probably not deliver the kind of warriors the ritual cult demands. Boys, at birth, are assigned to the male sex, but they are male, not manly; attributes of both the male and female sexes are ascribed to them. How should we characterize that subjective sense of core identity in a boy? (Never mind that for theory formation no such data exist in the New Guinea literature.) Does the child choose to be masculine? At what point, how unambiguously, and what does "masculine" mean—either more or less of some qualities or behaviors? In other words, there are different levels of identity, multivalent subjectivities belonging to public and private behaviors, and there is no necessary fit between those facets of an existence that should be described as "isomorphic."

It may be, as Read (1952) originally noticed in his study of Eastern Highlands cults, that ritual secrecy is itself a primary datum that must be explained in its particulars. By means of "deceit" and "conscious falsification," Read believed, the Gahuku-Gama male cult shielded essential, glaring contradictions between masculine ideology and ritual behavior. Here we are on less convincing ground in arguing that ritual secrecy *only* maintains male solidarity (Read 1952), sanctifies ritual knowledge (Barth 1975), reflects the need for power or control over women (Langness 1974; Lindenbaum 1976), supports the economic division of labor (Godelier 1976), or disguises male envy (Bettelheim 1955; Hiatt 1971). These points are all relevant; we can omit none of them. But taken alone, rather than as parts of a psychosocial system, they have not been shown to account for the early age of initiation and the secrecy it brings; the intense or weak elaboration of secrecy, or its pervasiveness within various segments of a society; or the hostility and distance that are its consequences in relationships between men and initiates (Langness 1974:206–210; compare Tiger 1970) and between men and women. We need an approach that better accounts for the cultural and psychological factors that make excitement out of secrecy.

The Sambia data recommend that we rethink the meaning, forms, and functions of ritual secrecy in Melanesian groups. If my thesis is correct— that initiation effects radical maternal detachment plus discontinuities in male development—then we should look to those secret aspects of identity for clues about the contents of subjective excitement that psychologically power ritual symbols and activities. Secrets thus become a hidden, disguised compound of self, which developmentally bridges the discontinuities between core gender identity and manly behavior. As Simmel (1950:307–308) argued, secrecy consolidates a "personality unity" of knowledge; here we could add that it also utilizes fantasy systems and ritual behavior. In a face-to-face society like Sambia, this is effective in many ways. Not only does secrecy, like discretion (Simmel 1950:321), compel one to stay away from the knowledge that others conceal, but, in such close quarters, it is also "hard to confront liars" (Simmel 1950:313). For masculine secrecy, then, there is bound to be feminine duplicity, and ritual guards against the upsetting of the political status quo in Melanesian societies (see Allen 1967:6–7; Gourlay 1975:103–120).

In short, many different kinds of secrecy permeate Sambia male and female identity and behavior, and we are far from understanding the intricacies of these phenomena in Melanesian groups as a whole. At the very least, we must clearly distinguish between screaming secrets and whispering secrets in relationships between the sexes (see also Langness 1976:98–99). And that vast difference is negotiated in various ways— conscious, subliminal, situational, and, yes, unconscious—through fine nuances of communication that inform what part is *meant to be,* public or private, screaming or whispering, true or false. We are fairly ignorant, for instance, of the problems of duplicity in connection with what women and men do or do not know about one another's activities. Our research thus requires a model of human action and consciousness that can incorporate the varieties of subjectivity in such intimate quarters. The distinctions between these different experiences, e.g., screams and whispers, add up to the methodological point that we may no longer justifiably use the simple contrast between public and secret. And for theory, both personal and shared significance (in Durkheim's sense) endow myths and rites with their power to direct behavior.

Ritualized Homosexuality

Various factors have led to the neglect of ritualized homosexual practices in anthropological studies of Melanesian initiation. Our research paradigm, the skimpy and anecdotal reports, not to mention personality factors —all have contributed to our ignoring such behavior. Then, too, research over the past fifteen years has made known the presence of transitional homoeroticism in more areas than were available in Whiting's day. Today, in addition to the older contributions of Deacon (1934:171ff.) on the New Hebrides, Landtman (1927:237) on Kiwai Papuans, and Williams (1936b) on the Keraki Papuans, there are reports from Godelier (1976:276ff.) on the Baruya, Kelly (1976:45ff.) on Etero, Schieffelin (1976:124–126) on Kaluli, and Van Baal (1966:834ff. and *passim*) on the Marind-Anim tribes of Southern Irian Jaya.[11] Not all of these societies performed initiation ceremonies in the same way. And it must be made clear that this sample is small in view of the hundreds of different tribes known from Melanesia. Nonetheless, it cannot be doubted that these societies reveal, at one end of the spectrum of sexual polarity, the edges of a powerful, neglected, developmental pattern, now reported from scattered parts throughout the region.

While ritualized homosexual behavior links Sambia to the above groups, it also divides them from most other Highland societies, from which it is apparently absent. Hence, although their ritual cult strongly resembles what Read (1952, 1954) and others have reported from the Eastern Highlands, Sambia differ in their prolonged institutionalized fellatio practices. Not just in form but in content, then, Sambia ritual development belongs to its own place and time.

I wish to underline these differences as much as the similarities, for my intention is not to suggest that ritual initiation always embraces homosexual activities or relationships—it does not—but rather to suggest that this special psychosocial pattern is more common than once thought and that we must not ignore it in explaining the meaning of male initiation and relations between the sexes in Melanesia. In most of these groups there is an expectation, a push, a political conscription of boys into male initia-

---

11. This is only a partial listing; see also Dundes's (1976) review.

tion; there is little or no choice. Homosexual practices, too, in varying degrees, are coerced. And that enforced role component, in addition to boys' great need or desire to "become men," is enough to determine that Sambia (and the others) are not homosexuals, not in our Western sense. (To reiterate: homosexual behaviors do not equal a homosexual identity.) They themselves would not accept that label, for their experiences lead mostly to exclusive heterosexuality and fatherhood.

Viewed this way, there is no reason to ignore the fact that ritualized homosexuality is also a personal, eventually erotic experience. However much it is a ritual, a cultural form, an institutionalized social relationship, fellatio is also an erotic act. Who would dare deny that fact? For example: those who would argue that prepubescent boys are simply complying with their role obligations would be only half right, for we should still need to explain the individual differences among boys regarding their interest in and excitement about fellatio, not to mention their personal choice of certain bachelors over others. In the older youths, these personality differences are even more important. In them, fellatio is much more than a matter of erotic duty (as in boys), since whatever else occurs, their necessary erection is, and it represents, subjective sexual excitement. I don't mean an erection resulting from genital masturbation of the bachelor (that's too easy); nor do I mean using boys as the only available sex outlet, which becomes a kind of de facto masturbation (that's too obvious); I mean particularly the youth's fantasy, his erotic desires that create an erection before the pleasurable sex whose fetishized focus is fellatio with a boy (and then, years later, with a woman). It is that erotic component in male gender identity and sexual behavior that I regard as fundamentally bonded to Sambia ritualized homosexual relationships.

That ritual bond is highlighted in some other Melanesian societies too. Two illustrations should suffice, one older, one recent. First, F. E. Williams on the Keraki Papuans:

> The bachelors had recourse to sodomy, a practice which was not reprobated, but was actually a custom of the country—and a custom in the true sense, i.e. fully sanctioned by the male society and universally practiced. . . . It is actually regarded as essential to the growing boy to be sodomized. More than one informant being asked if he had ever been subjected to unnatural[12] practice, answered, "Why, yes! Otherwise, how should I have grown?" . . . It is commonly asserted that the early practice of sodomy does nothing to inhibit a man's natural desires when later on he marries. [1936b:158]

---

12. This kind of old-fashioned prudishness has no doubt inhibited some field-workers from investigating sexuality.

And here is Schieffelin on the Kaluli of the Great Papuan Plateau:

> The male influence is concentrated in semen. . . . Semen is also necessary for young boys to attain full growth to manhood. Kaluli men maintain that women attain maturity by themselves (first menses?) but that boys do not. They need a boost, as it were. When a boy is eleven or twelve years old, he is engaged for several months in homosexual intercourse with a healthy older man chosen by his father. . . . Men point to rapid growth of adolescent youths, the appearance of peach fuzz beards, and so on, as the favorable results of this child-rearing practice. [1976:124]

In both these reports we see striking similarities with Sambia: prepubertal homosexual practices; "ingestion" of semen; a conviction that this semen masculinizes boys; and an outcome of relatively exclusive adult heterosexuality. Other points could be added, but this one is essential: prolonged homosexual contacts are more than a ceremony, they constitute powerful personal experiences that inculcate masculinity. Without these experiences, maleness and manliness lag behind.

The correlation between initiation, ritual beliefs, and institutionalized homosexual practices in these societies indicates that comparable psychosocial problems have found similar solutions in this symbolic complex. This developmental focus seems to distinguish Melanesian initiation from that of other areas, since the emphasis is on masculinization. As Hogbin (1970:103) noted of Wogeo Island (off the northern coast of New Guinea), compared to Africa: "Wogeo is different. The purpose of the rites here is to make certain that the boy will grow into a man, and the elders direct all their endeavors to this end." Once more we need to speculate. Is the existence of ritualized homosexuality a manifestation of the unfinished process of male separation-individuation in such societies? Present findings suggest that it is: early initiation,[13] radical maternal detachment, masculine secrecy, homosexual contacts, and female avoidance all point in that direction.

Adult Erotic Behavior

Just as Sambia initiations begin before puberty, so do they extend after it, pushing youths from adolescence into adulthood. Allen (1967:22) has noted that the Whiting et al. (1958) paper ignored subsequent postinitiation developmental experiences in understanding male identity or behavior. I agree; and what could be added is that present research is hampered

---

13. See Van Baal (1966:478, 351, 480, 494) who persuasively documented how early initiation was manifestly related to ritual homosexuality among the Marind-Anim.

by a lack of usable, believable data on an essential part of later development: adult erotic behavior.

Viewed in developmental perspective, the final outcome of Sambia successive initiations is a particular kind of stilted adult masculinity. That character structure is both stoic and fiery, a combination perfectly suited to warriors on whom small hamlets relied. Its roots are planted at first initiation, in late childhood. Warfare, hunting, peer ties, ritual, and other social activities follow in its wake. Erotic impulses may be directed only toward other males, even though females are always tantalizingly nearby. Still other initiations follow puberty. Bachelorhood then cements a rigid, effortful interaction between the sexes; but meanwhile, youths have the run of the men's house and an easy homosexual outlet. Marriage changes this life; heterosexual contacts sooner or later follow the wife's menarche; and homosexual practices should cease with marital cohabitation or fatherhood. We still do not understand the details of this eroticism. But male idioms portray it as difficult and tenuous, with men both misogynous and possessive about women. What should be obvious is that this developmental line was established years before.

Masculinity represents a delicate balance between formative childhood experiences and later ritualized manly comportment. The two layers of socialization have countervailing subjectivities; Whiting and his colleagues labeled them primary and secondary identification. This schema was fine in its day, but we still lack observations with which to demonstrate its relevance or utility, the difference between the two hypothetical stages, or their chasms and compromises. What idioms reveal is that the tension between the subjectivities of core gender-identity experience and ritual masculinization provides a dynamic, driving force behind ritual symbols, secrecy, and erotic activities. The levels of male identity are thus drawn on, made profitable, merged or separated over and again, in ritual behavior that may create ritual triumph out of old traumas. The meaning men attach to their rituals and their masculinity belongs to that symbolic complex of worthy customs and personal disguises.

Once again, Read's (1951, 1952) early writings drew attention to this masculine dialectic. He indicated the dissimilarity between what men say they possess at birth and what they acquire and maintain through secret rituals. Those rites had various consequences, of course, like the building of male solidarity within local political groupings. But that provides only part of the dynamics of ritual behavior. In his own way, and in spite of his Durkheimian perspective, Read also saw that New Guinea male cults were, on the surface, a one-sided species of Durkheim's religion: society worshiped only males (compare Rosaldo 1974:30). Masculine ritual comes down on the side of maleness, since its creation is not easy, unproblematic, or "natural." Read, like Bateson (1958:130–141) before him, then, came close to stating what initiations were also about: the manufacturing of a certain phallic sense of maleness and masculine cultural identity. This last point is not the least but rather the most of what Sambia initiation is about: prescribing experiences whose consequences, I think, are a particular kind of developmental experience for males, who need a capacity to act and feel contextually competent in ways not at all "natural" but still required for masculine adulthood. Initiation is the means for stimulating these propensities within individual gender identity.

The problem, to reiterate, is not one of males being masculine or feminine, but rather of the creation of an intense, phallic masculinity defending one against any possibility of ever turning quiet or soft. Whiting and Whiting (1975) have persuasively made this point. To build that strident subjectivity and the gender behavior that it commands must be reckoned as Sambia masculine society's greatest imperative. For war remained constant, enemies abounded, and they feasted on the slightest signs of weakness. Yet, as we have seen, societal and psychological forces that would pull boys in an opposite direction are also impressive. This may be why masculine culture is constructed around barriers that rigidly channel gender identity and behavior, after initiation, into the warrior's mold, admitting of no alternative masculinities (see also LeVine 1979:311–316). (Excepting, in only limited ways, the shaman; Sambia would have had no use for poets or artists.) It also helps explain why gender idioms depict boys as having so little, while girls possess so much, of the biological anlagen that stimulates reproductive maturity. We thus see redundantly coded, in perceptions of the natural and human worlds, men's unbearable envy of the female's fast-growing reproductive competence (see Bettelheim 1955). Ritualized homosexuality likewise reinforces the rigidity of the masculine ethic; it allows of no exceptions in the race for acquiring maleness—semen—even at the expense of the donor's vitality; and its ambience as latter-day male breast-feeding must harden one's resolve in facing the future by remaking the past. And it is, finally, the consuming need for those homosexual experiences that comes as a sign: that a Sambia boy's sense of maleness is too soft and malleable, that it must be filled up—as if at age six a door had been left ajar that could have been slammed shut. Initiation supervises that task, inculcating the defensive masculinity —fear of women—that can be placed in the service of the male cult. The only threat to this design is that it may succeed too well.

The constitution of Melanesian societies hinges on an expectable ordered morality regulated by politics. Firm rules govern this social contract (even if they are sometimes bypassed or broken). Who can do what to whom, why that is so, and its price—this give and take is carefully measured by the social exchange ceremonies so common throughout other parts of the area (Forge 1972). More than anything else, however, sex poses a threat to this order. As distinct from war, and unlike famines or flash floods, sexual behavior can be legislated right in one's neighborhood, through taboos. This control is necessary: internal conflict is a disaster for a small community whose enemies await any divisive calamities. Squabbles over women, wife-stealing, or adultery hastened such disasters, a fact that Sambia men never forget. Once again the male cult's edicts provide that control. The youths who feel their growing strength and want to test their power are regulated by a ritual hierarchy: elders and war leaders on top, youths and boys underneath, and women safely apart at the bottom. All sexual contact is regulated, even casual glances between the sexes; ritualized homosexual contacts cordon bachelors, directing their erotic impulses; after marriage, men are still obliged to be faithful to their wives, not promiscuous. Contained within this control is an implication that Sambia men's heterosexuality is deep and powerful, despite years of dormancy: so strong, in fact, that its eventual manifestations also require ritualized constraints (a point to be taken up elsewhere).

Unlike Bettelheim (1955), Reik (1946), Stephens (1962), or Whiting et al. (1958), I have avoided discussing the role of Oedipal factors in Sambia gender identity, and this omission deserves a note. No one could deny the presence of Oedipal factors in the Sambia material, since the myth of parthenogenesis manifestly mentions it. But what are we to make of that element? Instead of Oedipal conflict, Bettelheim (1955:104–123) would have argued that the myth expresses men's envy of women's bodies and procreative powers. The problem is one of a lack of data. Sambia readily discuss maternal bonding and its effects; in my experience, however, mention of incest (even obliquely) was rare. (This we should expect if the psychoanalytic argument about the repression of Oedipal conflict and its unconscious consequences is correct.) Without reference to systematic observations of ritual and individual behavior, then, the myth is much too skimpy a piece of evidence to warrant speculation. Anthropologists (see Allen 1967:22; Langness 1974:204; A. J. Strathern 1970) have generally disputed Oedipal factors (but see Layard 1959:113–114) in the New Guinea situation; I would not preclude the significance of Oedipal conflict, but there is little to be added here. By contrast, contemporary shifts in Oedipal theory (Stoller 1975) suggest that before the Oedipal phase there is something as fundamental: the question of sensing one's existence in terms of maleness or femaleness (see especially Lidz and Lidz 1977). This is what men's idioms underline in the more generalized difficulty of the infant's separation-individuation from its mother.

One of the emphases in this book has been on the ethnographic need for more detailed observations of individual behavior. Anthropology's chief strength has been its holistic, contextual approach: we prefer studies of naturalistic behavior. In the investigation of intimate communications

324 Guardians of the Flutes

this approach is even more vital. And fine-grained ethnography demands not only more of the native's presence but more of the researcher's, too. Nowhere is this as true as in the description of eroticism, for of all human experiences it is perhaps the most private, and it is maddeningly tough to document. We know virtually nothing about it because we never needed to before. But without reports, there are no data; without data, there is no cause for consternation about the problem-solving phase of theory and method formulation (B. Whiting 1979). The various phases of gender-identity formation require that information; no one except the field-worker can obtain it in tribal societies. Such data will not only clarify what is obscure; they will also help alter the impression that gender ideology and identity—masculinity and femininity—do not change in the course of individual development. Later experiences surely influence earlier identity constructs; and especially in the personal meanings, not just the stereo-typed patterns, of adult erotic behavior, will this become apparent (LeVine 1979). This is what I tried to show in my analysis of the myth.

That parthenogenetic myth, to reemphasize, holds the several keys for understanding Sambia adult eroticism.[14] Its functions and disguised scripts are similar to an erotic daydream, for, as Stoller (1976:904) has argued, a daydream's capacity to evoke excitement reveals how "frustration and trauma are converted into triumph." The secret myth recreates old scenarios, summoning up uncanny resonances of personal history. Its experience, then as later, helps preserve the core sense of self, "of existing as a male or female," by restoring an imagined balance of power between the "child and attacker," allowing fantasied revenge (Stoller 1979:14). Such interchanges of hostility we saw in the myth and its context: secrecy and mystery; gender confusion, differentiation, and finally transformation; risks—such as worrisome identification with the ancestral pseudoherma-phrodite or with the father who avoids disaster by instituting fraternal homosexual practices; and pseudorisks—guards stationed against the threat that women or boys may penetrate. In such ways the myth falsifies an individual's past, with its baggage of so much trauma, changing a "bad" ending into a "happy" one. In this way, too, parthenogenesis becomes a "vital lie" (*Lebensluge:* Simmel 1950:310) in a double sense: it conceals from others men's sense that maleness comes not from within but from older men who humiliated one; and its falsification disguises the original early childhood experiences from oneself. The myth experience works to shift erotic behavior subjectively. It confirms the need for surrendering homosexual contacts at a time when heterosexuality is blocked by the

---

14. For comparative data on New Guinea, see Van Baal (1966:230–231, 268, 273) and Williams (1936b:387–389); see also Dundes (1976:234), Lindenbaum (1976:60), and Wagner (1972:17–32).

postpartum taboo. Lastly, it reinforces the demands for heterosexual distance, threatening gender confusion and chaos again if a man succumbs to the sensual symbiosis his wife provides the baby.

A striking implication of this study concerns the "sexual antagonism" that anthropologists have long observed to pervade Melanesian societies. Langness (1967) believed that such cultural patterns were a response to the warring conditions of New Guinea communities: men had to deny their dependence on, and desire for, women. Others have discussed this suggestion (see Brown and Buchbinder 1976; A. J. Strathern 1969; Tuzin 1972, 1977). Bateson (1958) long ago showed that the character of Iatmul masculine pride was such that it resisted equality in relationships with others, requiring dominance in relationships with women and children. The psychological distancing mechanisms (e.g., female avoidance, ritualized homosexuality, secrecy) present in Sambia ritual and myth imply something more about maleness and masculine subjectivity. In all facets of one's existence the differences between maleness and femaleness are constantly exaggerated and blown up. In the case of idioms this exaggeration amounts to a denial of men's suspicion that femaleness is more primary than maleness. In the instance of erotics, however, it suggests that homosexual experiences, distance, and dehumanization of women are often needed to create *enough* hostility to allow the sexual excitement necessary for culturally appropriate heterosexuality and the "reproduction" of society. Men need this sexual polarity and hostility to maintain their personal boundaries in love, marriage, and sex.

Yet if that is true, how are we to explain the choice of Sambia ritual imagery? For example, the use of traumatic nose-bleeding rites whose personal affects and cultural significance derive precisely from a conscious comparison with female menstruation? The answer must come from more detailed individual case studies.

Now, instead of normative surface descriptions of such phenomena, we want to know more about their observed details. Instead of a spectator's testimony, we need insiders' observations of subjective experience. Instead of only collective representations, we require a theory of symbolic meaning. And in place of dry typologies of ritual, we urgently need a theory of ritual excitement.

All of these things we need for understanding the meaning of this prolonged pattern of ritualized homosexual behavior and why anthropologists have for so long ignored it. But that must derive from behavioral observations of Sambia initiation, the subject of our next investigation.

APPENDIX A *"Tali Says"*

On the Problem of Symbolic Meaning
and Its Relationship to Field Conditions
among the Sambia

When I state, as I have innumerable times in the above text, that Tali "says this," or "means that," what conditions governed the related communications and my interpretation of them? Rephrased in analytic terms, how shall we think about native statements concerning ritual matters or secular knowledge? Our answers concern the assignment of meaning to complex human behaviors and the corresponding hermeneutics of contemporary anthropology's interest in symbolism. In this note, I wish to explore these questions within the outlines of the fieldwork situation through which my research was conducted.

It is well known that anthropological achievements in studying ritual behavior and symbolism followed the work of Robertson Smith (1927), Van Gennep (1960), and Durkheim's classic study, *The Elementary Structures of the Religious Life* (1965). Durkheim (1966) wanted to establish the autonomy of "social facts" as proper determinants of human behavior. To create a new discipline, he advised that "the first and most fundamental rule is: *consider social facts as things*" (Durkheim 1966:14, original emphasis). The study of "social facts" in Western societies became modern sociology; studies of "social facts" in tribal societies became social anthropology. "Religion is something eminently social," Durkheim (1965: 22) believed, and by this he meant that its embodiment in collective institutions transcended cultural systems or individual experience. And the "structure" of a tribal society was based on its religion, which was, in turn, reducible to its rituals (see Evans-Pritchard 1965:53). Durkheim was thus led to conceptualize symbolic meaning—the "logic of collective representations"—as only a phenomenon of group ritual tradition. This positivist paradigm has been well studied, and it is not my aim, here, to undertake another critique of that *terre familier* (see Evans-Pritchard

1965, 1970; Firth 1973; Geertz 1966a; Leach 1961, 1976; Lévi-Strauss 1963:59ff., 96ff.; Parsons 1968; Tuzin 1976). Rather, I wish to examine its contribution to the anthropological treatment of symbolic meaning in relation to individual behavior and ritual.

Insofar as studies of ritual symbolism have succeeded, they have done so by assuming too much about the homogeneity of meaning in tribal societies, while excluding too much about the conditions under which data are collected to support interpretations of related symbolic behavior. These two points are crystallized in what I shall call the doctrine of experiential unity: the philosophy that individual members of a tribal society share identically in a structure of beliefs, rules, and meanings. (We know this stance in ethnographic statements like: "Members of the X tribe believe that . . . ": Leach [1969:40], cited in Needham [1973:5].) This perspective biases the normatively focused ethnographic report to exclude observations of individual acts, or intersubjective communications. It takes too little cognizance of the feedback effect of individual experience on symbolic systems, or vice versa, assuming that humans are the passive recipients of cultural traditions. Unfortunately, these suppositions still pervade sociocultural anthropology, much as they did Durkheim's writings. Not until we dispel the illusion that they are not the givens of nature, but rather were research strategies taken up in the formation of our scientific paradigms (Kuhn 1970), shall we be able to construct a more productive approach in studying the significance of ritual symbolism and its meaning.

Since Victor Turner's (1962, 1964, 1967, 1968a) work, social anthropologists have come explicitly to recognize verbal statements—exegesis, as Turner has it—in interpreting the meaning of ritual symbols. This development was critical for our research paradigm in two ways. First, it accorded theoretical significance to native commentaries or meanings attached to ritual symbols. Second, and following Turner's (1964:50–51) own explication of the matter, it meant that field-workers could no longer dismiss native verbal behavior out of hand, without understanding that they were choosing to exclude systematically one dimension of information from their ethnographic reports. Turner was admittedly cautious about the psychological interpretations of ritual symbols, or their significance for the "structure and property of psyches." But by accepting native statements as one component of the system of ritual symbolism, Turner had, willy-nilly, opened up that Pandora's box, the mind. This in itself was laudable and a major achievement whose theoretical implications are still not fully appreciated (see Turner 1978). The thrust of these implications represents a challenge to the Durkheimian doctrine of experiential unity.

Turner's choice of the concept "exegesis," as a cover term for the parameters of native verbal meaning phenomena, was felicitous in circumventing various problems with which his critics have been concerned. First, Turner's definition of "meaning" itself remains ambiguous, as Sperber (1975:13) has noted. Moreover, exegesis, in its liturgical sense of being an "official" textual opinion, one held up to speak for a community (e.g., of worshipers, a "church") of believers, relied on the convenient assumption of uniform meanings represented within an entire population (see Sperber 1975:19–20). One has the feeling (see Griaule 1965, for instance) that in some African states, exegesis is an appropriate concept for describing certain institutionalized narrative systems (see also Barth 1975:226; Gell 1975:211–212) in certain cultural contexts. In New Guinea societies, however, this concept is much more problematical, given that some groups entirely lack exegetic traditions (Barth 1975:226; Gell 1975:213). Even among Sambia, who institutionalize verbal meanings and interpretations in relation to ritual, particularly in ritual initiation teachings and some mundane (e.g., dream) events, the question of whether such narrative contexts or behaviors should be termed "exegesis," in its proper sense, seems debatable. Many other problems could be raised, for example: the internal validation or consistency of native interpretations (Geertz 1973:17–18; Gell 1975:212–213); the logical or analogical character of the meanings corresponding to ritual symbols (Barth 1975: 226–227); the degree to which natives are conscious of (or can bring into consciousness) the experiential connotations of symbols (Geertz 1968: 107–114; Gell 1975:213; Keesing 1979); or the stress placed on "affective" rituals versus the cognitive structures of myths (Lévi-Strauss 1971:597, cited in Turner 1975:149). We cannot do justice to either Turner or his critics here, since that would require extended arguments and a review of the literature. What needs emphasis, however, is the point that regardless of whether a tribal society possesses an elaborate interpretational system of its own, the ethnographer can still investigate the meaning of ritual symbols, beliefs, or pragmatic knowledge and experience among its individual members. This procedure, of course, raises many of its own conceptual problems, as noted above, and I shall enumerate some of them shortly. But first it is important to define my own use of the term "meaning," since it differs from that of other workers (see Geertz 1973:3–30; Schneider 1968:1–18; Wagner 1972:3–13).

I take the view that meanings are constructed from experiences beginning in the first days of life and gradually enriched with subsequent learning and training. The handling, feeding, and responsiveness to an infant convey fundamental feelings and attitudes about how he or she is desired, regarded, and ought to behave. The finest nuances of facial gestures, body motion, voice pitch, intonation, and syntax convey essential information to the child. From such stuff meaning is created and transformed. Meaning implies information, but it is more than that. Information, in its simple representations, conveys a "choice" of consciousness (Shannon and Weaver 1949; Neisser 1967), a "difference that makes a difference," in Bateson's (1972) terms. Meaning is an act of intention, especially in speech. A pattern of recognizable information that an individual assigns to an entity or an experience I call a meaning. When conscious, a meaning is therefore an intentional choice which assigns informational patterns to an aspect of consciousness (see Colby 1978; Fodor 1975; Harré and Secord 1972). Some meanings no doubt arise from one's earliest socialization and are not conscious, or fully conscious (Stoller 1979). The emotions are probably a class of fundamental experiences containing deeply embedded meanings. On the other hand, encyclopedic knowledge—about the forest and persons and the names of things—probably draws less on infantile developmental experience, following language acquisition; and hence, its meanings more fully reflect cognitive antecedents (Piaget 1954).

Since experience shapes meaning, it is likely that each of us comes to hold somewhat different meanings, about all manner of things. Unless individuals share identical developmental patterns, it is difficult to understand how their experiences could be identical. And we cannot neglect "temperament," the biology and neuropsychology, for example, of sex differences (Maccoby and Jacklin 1974; Reynolds 1976), which create unique internal impulses and feelings undoubtedly affecting development. Styles of mothering intervene too, as does the presence and availability of a father figure; and gender ideologies are of course essential (see Chapter 9). Each of these factors potentially contributes to the manner in which an individual experiences caretakers, family, himself, and eventually the world. Each difference in the contribution of any of these factors probably precipitates varying qualitative and quantitative outcomes in awareness and behavior. These experiential differences suggest that the mind and CNS information processing are affected, as is the choice of meanings arising from them. This approach leads to developmental questions about behavior and meaning: what experiences lead individuals to subscribe to their own private symbols, and the meanings attached to them? And, for the purposes of this study, what is the relationship of sex, and gender constructs, to collective ritual symbols in tribal societies?

This viewpoint forces us to rethink ritual symbolism in the developmental context of the individual's experience and meaning. We shall necessarily turn to the description of group collective rites, and individual experience, as separable but complementary descriptive levels. Cultural context will assume a fundamental place in our analyses. For it is not only symbols that are introduced by ritual, but also a context for recognizing and orienting symbols and behavior.

In New Guinea societies, I believe that there is a gender divergence of meaning based on the disjunctive character of early socialization and later ritual initiations. Male ritual drastically separates the sexes, imposing radical discontinuities—cognitive, affective, sociological—on initiates. Bateson (1958:198–203) insightfully and persuasively argued as much in his analysis of the *naven* ceremony years ago: initiation precipitates contrary psychological frames, among the sexes, for interpreting the meaning of social behavior and personal experience. These symbolic systems shatter and remake an individual's sense of meaningfulness. A model of symbolic meaning as homogeneous makes even less sense, therefore, in these disjunctive cultures than elsewhere in the world. In other words, New Guinea systems suggest a different perspective based on the existence of quite distinct subcultures: the masculine and the feminine. Consequently, Sambia children grow up experiencing their mothers (bodies, companionship, occupations), and their mothers' cultural and personal meanings, far more than those of their fathers or other men. These conditions of socialization definitely bear on a boy's sense of himself and his maleness, directing gender role development along certain lines, albeit ritualized, following initiation. These problems are examined more closely in the text. My interest, in what follows, is to show how I went about studying individual meaning, given the constraints of fieldwork conditions among Sambia.

Let me start with several forewarnings. This book is limited, and therefore distorted, in three ways: by my choice of ethnographic content, ontogenetic perspective, and informants. Although my goal is to describe the knowledge surrounding selected idioms, this is not an encyclopedia, or even a partial lexicon, of Sambia idioms. I have arbitrarily restricted my choice of ethnographic content by examining only certain domains of natural species, human femininity and masculinity, that I judge to be of importance in understanding the collective initiation rituals. It is, moreover, patently clear that one researcher, in even a handful of books, could not possibly communicate all the relevant knowledge available to hundreds of Sambia tribesmen. (See Chapter 9 for some implications of this idea.) It is not possible to even present all my own data in this book; that would become confusing and inconsistent, would require too much space, and still worse, no one would read the excessive product. I have, then, only sampled my observations of masculine behavior and idioms. But this random sampling creates a potential distortion in the presentation of the data and of their significance.

Four criteria have therefore guided my selection of Sambia domains and their idioms. First priority is given to the key idioms that eventually find their way into men's collective rituals. Second, I also emphasize those idioms that are recurrently familiar in everyday usage to most men (whether in public or in secret). Third, most of the idioms pertaining to natural species also touch on desirable natural resources, such as cassowaries and pandanus nuts. Finally, the designata of many such idioms are thought to be endowed with relative amounts of "strength" (*jerungdu*) or "power," and are correlated with beliefs about maleness and femaleness in humans (compare Wagner 1967:47–48, 60). Other ethnographic domains would no doubt raise somewhat different issues.[1] Arbitrary choices of content like these are unavoidable in presenting ethnographic material, but we are still obliged somehow to explicate them. By this admission I am simply underlining an enduring truth about the qualitative "clinical" data of all ethnographic reports: that we rely on the anthropologist to communicate observations honestly, weighing for readers their relative weaknesses and strengths, without known errors or omissions, as far as possible. We still have reason to be cautious about the final product, though: as Evans-Pritchard (1962:176) once remarked, ethnographic reports are taken "far too much on trust." Let me, then, more closely examine the potential biases in my own presentation.

First, this material has a gender bias: it represents, almost exclusively, an adult man's perspective. Not only do I write and investigate as a male American, viewing things through my own cultural and personal interests and experiences, but my informants were mostly men. There are several reasons for this lopsidedness, factors that arise from the conditions of field research in many New Guinea societies. The four most important are: (1) male ritual secrecy, (2) "sexual antagonism" and the status of women, (3) language difficulties, and (4) my personal status. These conditions contribute to the masculine bias in my writing that I now illustrate in summary form.

Sambia life depends on a balance of uneven forces not easily observable by an outsider. The reason is simple: their society is built on secrecy and cultural disjunction of an extraordinarily deep order. This rift finds expression in developmental experience, cultural knowledge, and the eloquently complex subterfuge of daily communicative acts and ritual alike. I first visited my hamlet in late afternoon and was awe-struck by its apparent harmony and untainted beauty. As daylight died, the hamlet awakened as people returned from their gardens; children ran freely, women gossiped over cooking fires, and men shared the day's events. In the cool evening men gathered round the hearth of their clubhouse and started a songfest.

---

1. The ethnographer's role in editing data raises a different issue, too, namely the conviction that the internal consistency of an ethnographic report is an indicator of the truth value of its interpretation (see Gell 1975:209f.). While there is something to be said for this methodological dictum, we should not substitute it for the provision of actual observations, even when they are not always consistent (see also Geertz 1973:16ff.).

Elsewhere people assembled for a shamanistic healing ceremony. Others chatted with neighbors. These things I came to know and cherish in the pattern of Sambia life. Yet there is another side of their existence: harsher, more opaque, but as much a part of men as their war weapons, rituals, and the values they hold. One first senses this in the elders' watchful eyes of reproach, and the silent movements of boys' avoidance, which seem so much a part of the compunctions directing a shame culture like that of Sambia. This face of men's doings belongs to their clubhouse, an institution rooted in mysteries of masculine pride and female duplicity, mixed with powerful restraining emotions like respect and anger; and a self-conception that leads men to ever greater assertions of mastery and dominance.

In such circumstances, ritualized secrecy pervades every sphere of social life and existence. Women are kept as downtrodden as possible, as ignorant as necessary, to sustain men's secrets. Children are generally treated the way women are. That is because all children are close to their mothers and boys cannot be entrusted with secrets; and also because children are potentially polluting, since they can unwittingly transfer their mother's contaminating fluids to men. Furthermore, the strict division of labor ensures that women have more general knowledge of planting garden crops and tending them, and that they know far less than men about the forest world—man's domain. Nor may women approach the clubhouse, especially after dark; and likewise, men do not approach the women's menstrual hut. This separation is absolute and unfailing: no man has ever entered the menstrual hut, no woman has ever been inside the men's clubhouse or ritual cult houses. When men discuss secret matters, they first check to remove women from the immediate area. In sustained discussions, a man is posted to guard against the intrusions of women (see Chapter 8). This exclusion applies equally and at all times to children, and also to younger initiates regarding conversations centered on adult ritual matters forbidden to them.

Cultural knowledge is, therefore, funneled and classified on two planes: horizontally, as a division separating men from women and children; and vertically, as a hierarchical division within the category of males depending on one's ritual status, e.g., first-stage initiate or adult man. To confound these ritual categories is to disrupt the right order of things. To penetrate secrets willfully is so dangerous that it is sanctioned by death; and such sanctions have, in fact, been tragically exercised in the past.

Such were the conditions of my fieldwork, then, that it became nearly impossible to work closely with women and still have the men trust me. Though I was allowed to observe all the men's rituals and gained entrance into their secret life, this entry came about only slowly, with many difficulties, and at times it created grave interpersonal problems. It is true that

I intermittently used several female informants, but like others I have not, as Langness (1976:100) notes of a general criticism by Faithorn (1976: 86), "carefully researched the female domain" as experienced by women.

Language was another problem with women. By way of male chauvinism, and by their design for keeping women ignorant as far as possible and thereby in "their place," Sambia men have actively hindered women from learning Neo-Melanesian as a second language. (Neo-Melanesian is now preferred as a substitute name for Pidgin English.) In 1976, only two out of a total of 292 women in the vicinity of my hamlet spoke any Pidgin at all, and these women seldom did, at least not publicly. Faithorn's (1976:86) comments are instructive on this point, for the Highlands at large. Our "reliance on Pidgin English as a field language . . . has led to direct communication primarily with men," since they have usually experienced "the most contact with Europeans through contract labor" and their fluency is greater. Faithorn adds: "Women, except in the few urban areas, have remained fairly isolated in their rural communities, and consequently have not become fluent Pidgin speakers. Thus ethnographers have relied on male informants and translators in collecting data involving both sexes." (See S. Ardener [1978] on this problem more generally.)

I, too, had to communicate primarily with men. And my data on women reflect this inadequacy. Working with Sambia women was as tantalizing as it was frustrating. Men were nearly always threateningly present; women were often hesitant, and sometimes visibly tense, in responding; and I could never control the language or my translators well enough to ensure a fair measure of the data. Whether a female anthropologist might have surmounted these difficulties remains doubtful. Nonetheless, she would surely have pursued somewhat different interests and obtained richer material on Sambia women, their subjectivities and subculture. I am also convinced, likewise, that she would have learned little if anything about the men's cult, their secret rites, and especially homosexual activities. (This male bias still remains; and I shall take up its implications for the subject of women, and male and female relationships, elsewhere.) The ethnographic material presented in this book thus pertains expressly to men and their view of Sambia ritual and existence.

Second, besides delimiting my description to the cultural knowledge of males, there is another constraint contained within this one. That pertains to one's choice of ontogenetic perspective in presenting cultural materials. The most significant factor for Sambia, in this respect, is ritual teachings. Here I take an adult man's point of view of the ritual system. Much of the richness of Sambia ritual behavior stems from its elaborate instructive system, which is an extensive native interpretational system, as I shall describe elsewhere. Sambia men not only subject boys involuntarily to initiation rites, they also feel compelled to "explain" their significance to them. Novices are taught a body of knowledge, and while some facets of this information appear "esoteric" (see Barth 1971, 1975), ritual teachings in the main concern matters thought to be pragmatic and fundamental to masculine life. The Sambia initiatory system is, moreover, age graded; pieces of ritual knowledge are revealed step by step as one is ritually promoted. The meanings of a certain rite, such as nose-bleeding, that is performed successively in later initiations, are transformed and enriched as one approaches full manhood. This means that we cannot afford to take a static, synchronic view of ritual knowledge and meaning. In this book, my aim is to communicate ontogenetic aspects of the whole ritual ideology, as an introduction to the collective ritual behavior of first-, second-, and third-stage initiations.

There are, furthermore, three additional reasons for taking this adult male slant on ritual knowledge. The first one is prompted by the teleological character of the native instructional system. It is apparent that boys, seven to ten years old, are pulled into the male cult purposely to transform their behavior, including what they say in speech, and how they sense themselves and conform to their elders' expectations. The ritual knowledge they receive is largely secret and must remain so. Various rituals have different beliefs and subjective implications taught in them, leading, as it were, teleologically to the knowledge and behavior of the idealized adult warrior. It is that ultimate state of being, then, that ought to guide us in understanding what men communicate through their use of idioms about the natural world, masculinity, and femininity. The second reason is merely procedural. I wish simply to orient the reader to the aspirations and ritual experiences that color most men's everyday verbal behavior. (This orientation will also provide a secular background for the use of similar idioms in ritual behavior.) My last reason is that this treatment of cultural knowledge will provide methodological advantages for studying the material on focused studies of individual boys and men presented elsewhere. By observing all stages of initiation and working with all types of male informants—initiates, bachelors, and elders—I have come to develop an appreciation of the overall cognitive system of Sambia men. In short, this "composite" product is my own observer's model of the cultural knowledge underlying rituals that I believe informs much of everyday speech and action. (I shall draw on that view, subsequently, in describing the context of clinical studies of what males do, say, and think as whole persons; and I shall also need to show the correlation between ritual knowledge and experience, and what particular individuals and others of their ritual status do, say, and think; as well as how this subjectivity changes from childhood onward, with each passing initiation, into adulthood, among a cross-sectional sample of men.)

Third, and especially important, is my choice of informants. This raises the related question, too, of how my own personality intervened in the field research. One of the potential sources of distortion in our research is our selection (or ad hoc choice) of collaborators. Sometimes circumstances dictate this choice (see Edgerton and Langness 1974:35). Mostly, however, it is our style of operating and our research goals that affect our selection of informants, through whose eyes and ears we come to interpret things (see Geertz 1973:20). So besides the ethnographer's biases there are those that filter through our informants. This is not to deny that researchers differ in their capacity to correct this distortion. The extent to which an ethnographer monitors and reflects on the collection of data depends on all the factors mentioned earlier: language, one's capacity to work with men and women, and the restrictions placed on the privileged communications of secret or personal matters. Langness (1976:106*n.*) mentions a related one: "The investigator's own cultural background may affect his or her choice of informants." This issue has aroused little serious interest (see, for example, Pelto 1970:95–98; Edgerton and Langness 1974:33–36). I suggest that the primary reason for this lack of interest is the absence of attention paid to the related factor of the ethnographer's personality. Along with language, the design of the culture, and the like, personality must also rank as a key variable influencing the conduct of research, one's theoretical perspectives and methods, and the resulting data and their manner of presentation (see Devereux 1967, 1978).

These factors influence how we select and come to rely on particular informants and collaborators. Some may dismiss this question out of hand as trivial, or, sadder yet, as the product of tawdry methodologism. But this little-pondered issue no doubt harbors some of the greatest problems in anthropological research. So far we have mostly swept them under the rug, and so far field research is more an art than a science. Anthropology rests on doing fieldwork, and, classically, this task meant total submersion in an exotic (see Frellich 1977) way of life. This submersion is our rite of passage, akin to the psychoanalyst's experience of being analyzed (Lévi-Strauss 1969:62–63). Freud taught this, but who analyzed Freud? Malinowski (1922) instructed his students in the procedures of fieldwork, but who trained Malinowski? Why have we so adhered to the Malinowskian mode of doing fieldwork, and why did it so upset us to discover, belatedly, that Malinowski's diary (1967) conveys personal biases never conveyed in his seminars or books? Why is this dimension of fieldwork—the ethnographer's personality and his or her influence on, and presence in, the data—still ignored? The answers to such questions have far-reaching implications.

All these heuristic factors are outstanding, for they have impinged on the ethnographic data I have presented and my "style" of presenting them, and they are essential constraints in the description of focused individual behavior. It is impossible to convey their complexities in a few pages. But the importance of the interpersonal situation in which the data were collected is such that I need to describe a piece of it—if only in anecdotal form—so that readers may better understand my criticisms of the above anthropological perspectives on symbolic meaning, and how my data reflect a different approach. Social anthropology's great reluctance to confront individual behavior and experience is tied to these factors (see above on V. Turner's mode of "exegetic" analysis, and see also I. M. Lewis 1971:178–205); for example, in the nature of the "observer's effect" on behavior that may distort it, or in the representativeness of native statements (e.g., sample size, contextual constraints, control samples) for a population as a whole. There is good reason for this concern: without a methodology that takes account of elicitation procedures, psychological involvement, and the nature of elicitation contexts, there *must* be genuine concern about the degree of an investigator's influence on his or her informants. The ethnographer's data are embedded in those interpersonal relationships; the meaning of those relationships is a part of the data.[2] This is my research stance and it is epitomized in my references to Tali.

Tali's comments may have had various audiences—himself, his peers, women, or myself—but when I was present, our own relationship was usually in the air. Tali's remarks belong to that complexity; there is no reason to reduce it (unless for particular analytic purposes) to anything less. When "Tali says" this or that, his views are commentaries, not "exegesis." (In subsequent writings we shall see how his rhetorical teaching, in ritual contexts, has more of a flavor of true exegesis.) This holds for others as well, especially Moondi and Weiyu, who were "youngsters" in the ritual system, and in Tali's eyes. Nilutwo's adult status was similar to Tali's, but his remarks meant less to his peers, except on the subject of cassowaries.

Tali is, nonetheless, special, and not just because I came to know him well. For not only was he frequently cited by others as a ritual specialist (*mokei-mutnyi,* he who "sings" out for the collective initiations), but he

---

2. Verbal statements about ritual matters dig precisely at this sensitive spot, since the Durkheimian legacy has always held ritual as a part of the collective consciousness par excellence in tribal societies. Thus to collect one or another individual's views (about ideas, actions, or affects) was unnecessary, even absurd. Furthermore, the natives were not believed able to provide analytic insights about their customs; and if one sought meanings "deeper" than those visibly apparent to the observer—there being no anthropological techniques for doing so—the resulting data were either "psychological" or "philosophical" (not ethnographic), and they were dismissed as contrived, contaminated, or both, by virtue of the researcher's techniques or motives.

saw himself in this role; and he was self-conscious about his ritual knowledge. For example, on half a dozen occasions he and others made it clear that he had, of his own personal interest, sought mythological and ritual information from a knowledgeable paternal uncle and from a distant kinsman. This was unusual; in my sample of informants, no one else had done this; and in all of my contacts, I knew of only four or five other men (out of hundreds) who had done so. Tali, and his idiomatic remarks, represent that personal interest in the ritual traditions of his own community.

Tali was in his early thirties when I first knew him. Even by then he had already distinguished himself as a knowledgeable ritual leader. He knew more magical spells than most men; he knew the ones that counted—like the one needed for the *kwolyi-mutnyi* object (see Chapter 7). Tali was respected: by 1975 he had become a hearer of local courts—and this despite his lack of Pidgin (which he never spoke) and outside experience (he had never been out of the Mountain District), or much desire for it. (Tali did look enviously at the men who had been to the coast, but he always tended to dismiss them as minor actors on the local scene.) Tali was married; he married late (allegedly not by his own choice); he married a strong woman, who has given him two children thus far; and in 1978 he married again (much against his first wife's protests). Tali, unlike Weiyu, was not an unabashed womanizer; he was no friend of women, nor of his wife; yet he enjoyed coitus much as he had (in his own words) enjoyed homosexual contacts for years. (He does not now engage in homosexual practices, nor do I think he has any desire to do so.) Tali has fought in some battles; he was not known as a war leader, but he had done his duty as a good warrior, people said.

He was, furthermore, a traditionalist; he lamented the falling away of ritual customs, saying dolefully, or with anger, that youths and initiates were beginning to regard taboos and ritual purification as "rubbish." But in saying this he sometimes added (with a gleam in his eye) that he knew they would one day pay the price in weakness and short life. Their women would outlive them.

My relationship with Tali and older men has always been psychologically simpler for me than my relationship with other informants, especially youths and initiates. This was, as usual, much of my own making. For a long time I largely ignored Tali, something I could not do with the initiates. Having come to investigate the psychological experience of undergoing ritual initiation, I felt it a duty to attend first to that much neglected topic before others, and before it was too late (after the cult had dramatically changed following Westernization). Working alone, classed as a bachelor, I was more identified with bachelors and had to overcome, as much as possible, the tensions, turmoils, and one-sided dominance of that social position in my dealings with initiates. (With some of them I never succeeded; I remained either too threatening, or too much a "rich" white European, to achieve empathic trust.) With the bachelors, like Weiyu (who married shortly after my arrival), the pressures were different, since I was perceived more as a peer (a colleague, a competitor). With women I remained a relatively distant curiosity; benign, congenial, and eligible, but much too roped off by the men to be very personally involved with them. With elders I was (at least with my sponsors) adopted affectionately, cared for, and mutually exploited (e.g., I gave them canned fish and small gifts), but was still regarded as immature, and below them. Tali never got entangled much in these early scenarios; he was simply there, going about his hunting (he is an avid hunter and a successful one) and saying, from time to time, that he had a lot to teach me.

Two things changed our relationship in 1975. The first was my work on ritual. Following the performance of collective initiations that year, I started working on myth and ritual. The previous time was spent on social organization, and then interview work with initiates. For over two months I conducted standardized interviews with some forty initiates as a means of collecting relatively comparable data on their experiences. (That material is presented elsewhere.) Moondi, my best interpreter, served as the chief collaborator in that work. Eventually, though, I needed to interpret the texts gained from ritual observations. The men all said that Tali was the one to ask. But, because of the stratification of ritual knowledge, I had then to acquire another interpreter—Weiyu—who, as a married man, could discuss such matters secretly with Tali and me, while the initiates, and Moondi, were kept well removed at such times. Likewise, for fear of their embarrassment or shame, I had always to take care in arranging work with Moondi and other initiates, especially on topics like dreams and sex, when the adults were gone. (I needn't belabor the obvious: that this presented countless logistical problems, much conflict in interpersonal ties, and did, after some months, definitely change my identity to one of being more like a middleman accomplice with initiates who trusted me, on the neutral territory of my house. My acquisition of ritual secrets was not complicated, though, by any more involvement with women, since I remained a spectator in relation to them.)

In these circumstances, Tali took to working with me frequently, communicating secrets about ritual and his opinions regarding them. He would, in addition, often visit my house in the evening, accompanied by his three-year-old son. I would offer him tea, or a cigarette, and a few disjointed pieces of Sambia conversation; but because of my lack of language proficiency at that period, we usually said little, and he stayed only briefly.[3] But something else, an accident, then changed our relationship.

Late in 1975, I returned from the Mountain Patrol Station to Nilangu, hiking through the mountains with some Sambia, including Tali. We arrived in the hamlet the day after his house had burnt to the ground. (This is not altogether rare, since grass huts are totally consumed in a few minutes, once they catch fire.) Tali was devastated: all his worldly possessions, including his ritual items and money, were lost. He was furious at his wife (whom he blamed). As usual, though, he handled this event with a brief flurry of emotion, followed by sullenness, and then quiet depression. After a day or so of detachment, feeling sympathy for him and trying to bolster his spirits, I gave him a pair of my walking shorts (he had lost all his garments too), some tobacco, and a little money. (He could use the money to help him feel better; for instance, he would have to barter or buy all of his ritual ornaments again, and he did so.) He accepted the gifts with thanks, was obviously moved, but otherwise said nothing.

Over the next year, those two events—our ritual work and those gifts at the time of his misfortune—came back upon me in unexpected ways. More than once, Tali harked back to his misfortune, and my kindness, when I least expected it. When I was once in need of a favor, he did it without my asking; later he said that I had also helped him out. On patrol (1976) among the neighboring Yana tribe, Tali also helped me in a special way: he went among his cronies, found a bilingual Sambia, and they sent word to a Yana man of a distant hamlet known to hold many myths. The man arrived near midnight the next evening, to my complete surprise; there and then, Tali led us in setting about to collect as many myths as possible (acquiring them for his own repertoire too), till the wee hours of the morning. In ways like that he made me a friend.

But what impressed me more than anything else occurred one evening in late 1976, after a day of working with Tali and Weiyu on ritual matters. It was near the end of my fieldwork; men knew I would leave in a few weeks. And even though I told them I would return, and even though they wanted to believe this, life is filled with uncertainties, as they also know. Late, around 8 P.M., Tali walked into my house with his son, and we began to chat. (I could speak more Sambia now, and felt more comfortable mixing my Pidgin with Sambia, to talk with him; he could always "hear" my Pidgin; I could always "hear" his Sambia; our problem was in convers-

---

3. Some Sambia refer to my house as a "hotel," since I invited people to come and go freely, and usually had residing, aside from my old sponsor, Kanteilo, one or two initiates like Moondi, plus an initiate who did chores for me, sleeping in one of the back rooms of my house. (In time, men spoke of my house as a clubhouse.) This distance between Tali and me I experienced without much hostility, being content to work alone in a room, writing, after I had greeted him and had been hospitable. (Nonetheless, I often felt disturbed that I lacked any real privacy, a feeling I communicated in various ways despite myself.)

ing directly.) Weiyu also arrived. After some tea and little jokes, Tali said he had thought about the *tingu* again, and that he wanted to say something else he had neglected during that morning. This surprised me, for it had happened only once before. (That is, after some elicited work, Tali returned later wanting to discuss a specific point.) After he shared his thoughts, I thanked him, obviously communicating my surprise. Then he added: "You really want to know about our ways. We thought you came just to learn about the *mokeiyu* [ritual] customs. [Serious.] But you want to understand [*koontu-tuv,* think about] us, don't you? That's why I thought about this and told you."

That is what Tali said: my data are wrapped up in this complex interpersonal relationship. Obviously I affected his actions; obviously he affected mine. Plus ça change, plus c'est la même chose.

This sketch is not meant to be exhaustive; it is a preliminary note, biographical and autobiographical, and elsewhere I hope to detail more of this medium—methodology—within which Tali's and other men's behavior is suspended. For the reader who feels more comfortable in assessing the present report, I hope that that promise suffices. For the skeptical reader, who wishes that I had stayed more removed from Sambia, had kept that distance some label "objectivity" and had disguised my presence throughout the text, I can only add that to have done so would have been dishonest; it is not my personal style; it was not my fieldwork approach; and I would have needed to resort to deception endlessly, to disguise the true situation and its resultant data. Because of this style, my data are different from those of another worker who might have adopted a different stance. But until such time as anthropology (and the other behavioral sciences) has discovered a more precise procedure for describing intimate communications, this seems to me our most objective route.

APPENDIX B *Nilutwo's Dreams*

For a period of about sixteen months, on and off, Nilutwo related his dreams to me.[1] My research with him simply began, appropriately enough, with his cassowary-hunting activities. No sooner had we started, however, than Nilutwo began relating the dreams that led to his decision to set a trap or check one. Communicating dreams like this is common among Sambia (see Herdt 1977), and Nilutwo often shared his own dreams with others. Still, there were, after a few weeks, some private aspects that compelled me to assure Nilutwo of the confidentiality of his communications; we then began to work more and more in private; and he responded in kind by sharing more of his thoughts, which in time focused on dreams and the meanings he associated with them.

I fear that much of the tape-recorded (and transcribed) data that follow will scarcely be intelligible to a general reader, even with this cursory introduction. A special problem endemic to Sambia dream experience still plagues me: it is sometimes difficult to know when Nilutwo is only recounting his dream and when he is going further and also associating to it: the two experiences tend to merge unself-consciously. Even after getting detailed biographical data, many different dreams, and investigating Nilutwo's thoughts about his dreams, I had difficulty in contextually distinguishing dreams from associations when Nilutwo was talking quickly.[2]

---

1. During 1974–1976. I estimate that we had some 200 sessions during this period, most lasting about an hour. I did follow-up work, more intensively, in 1979.

2. This tendency only increases the problem of translating Sambia dreams into another language, something that Freud (1953:121–132 *n.* 2) long ago doubted could be done. Since Nilutwo was a steady "dreamer," other Sambia sometimes consulted him, along with the shamans (though Nilutwo was not one of the latter), in interpreting their dreams; and our

Did he trust me? Here our methodological problem becomes one of defining trust, and defining how Sambia think of it. Nilutwo trusted me enough, after a year, to begin recounting a long-standing daydream he had harbored since childhood (and had never explicitly shared with others); he trusted enough to share his most troublesome dream (at least known to me, and as defined by him): the wet dream whose (erotic) dream figure was often his brother's wife. Then finally came a dream in which I was a key figure, and then more such dreams: a clinical sign of Nilutwo's trust on a deeper level.[3]

Despite over two years of extensive work, I still feel that much about Nilutwo remains obscure and undiscovered; and his dream style is still not clearly describable. Only the surface has been scratched.

First Dream

Several days out on a patrol to a neighboring hostile group (May, 1976), Nilutwo is accompanying me, and he reports the following nightmare.

> I went down along a place, a bad place, a stone place [associated with ghosts and spirits] and there was a woman [of another tribe]. This garden, a new garden, what kind is it? A new garden of reeds, and she was cleaning the reeds, weeding. She stood up. She pulled up some sweet potatoes. I stood up close to her. She didn't talk. I thought to myself, not good that her man would come along here [see us flirting] and kill me. He could come and kill me. So then I left her.
>
> I went into the forest and I saw a small steam. And I thought, not good that this is a stamping ground of the cassowary [meaning, I think this would be a good place for finding cassowaries]. And so I looked to find tracks of the cassowary. I located and followed some. I went into the forest. I thought I would go into the forest and I find one [cassowary]. But there were W and K [an older man and his son; the son is somewhat younger than N].[4] The two of them, the father and his son, belonged here. [It was their forest land.] The two of them were chopping down a huge tree. The two of them cut it, and I stood up nearby them. I stood up—but I didn't stand up too close to them. . . . [Then] I stood up a long way away; a little bit farther away I thought, not good that this kills us [unclear whether he means it kills me, or it kills all of us, if the tree falls over]. And so I shout to them, "Not good that this tree, it kills all of us!" And [although] I said this, W, he said that to us [not to Nilutwo but to his son]; K

---

work also centered on relating Nilutwo's dreams to the standard dream-interpretation "code" that forms one part of their overall meaning (see Tuzin 1975).

3. What psychoanalysts refer to as the transference.
4. W, the father, is about fifty years old; Nilutwo has never liked him much.

replied: "We want to cut down this tree" [hostile, emphatic]. So I felt, not good that he kills all of us. . . . And so I left them behind and I went to another place.

So I followed the nearby stream. It had no stones [fast moving]. It had no stones inside it. I followed it and I went on top [some branches], following a tree. I followed the pathway of some possums. And as I climbed up that tree, stood up along a branch of the tree . . . I stood up and it broke [anxious]. I fell down into the water. . . . And I floated along in the water.[5] I went and I went . . . the water carried me. I went, and I held onto a small stone, inside the water. And I felt, not good that this stream kills me. And this time I woke up afraid, very scared [tight-mouthed, nervous]. I got up and I felt this was very bad. I was afraid. . . .

Then Nilutwo began to talk more about the dream with me, alone inside the small native house where I was then camped.

Why did I go on top that tree, following the possum? And I fell down, the water it carried me. I saw the huge footprints of the possum. And that woman, I felt in the dream, her man he made the fence around the garden. Not good that that man should come back and see me and cross me. But I didn't even touch the woman. [GH: Did you think of copulating with the woman?] No, I didn't think about that. I thought of her man: not good that he should kill me. [A proverbial fantasy—temptation—among men is to find and ravish a woman willing and alone in an isolated garden.] I was afraid. So I went to another place. This garden, it was a new garden. It was below an old garden. The fence was new. And I thought that the limb of that tree [that I stood on], it was strong, but it broke. The water it was deep. It was up to my head. Only my head, it stood out of the water. When I woke up, I thought: my thinking—it was mixed up [meaning, I was thinking crazy]. Why should I go up there? Why should I have this dream that was so bad . . . ? [This led Nilutwo into other material that is described elsewhere.]

Second Dream

This dream Nilutwo reported in June, 1976. It occurred in the following context: the day before there had been a local government election in a neighboring village. N had gone there the day before and was in the village with several of his cronies. That night, after the election, sitting around with some other people, he decided to spend the night in the house of S, an older man. (S is a former fight leader. He is a very stiff, quiet man, who is prone to violence.) The two men, N and S, ate some food; then they decided to go to sleep. Both these men are married adults. And N said that the two of them "slept together" under S's blanket. He

5. Nilutwo, like other Sambia, does not swim, and is never afloat in streams like this, since people are terrified of drowning.

said, "He covered the two of us up," smiling as he said this. This behavior is somewhat inappropriate for two adult men, and it is somewhat unusual that N would take to sleeping with S, who is not a close friend of his.[6] So N came to me late the next afternoon, as he usually did, and began to recount his related dream. We went into my office, closed the door, and he sat down in a chair opposite me. I had paper and notebook in hand, and he began to recount the dream immediately. (This was unusual.) Without stalling, he simply said, "Here's what I dreamt." (Our dream sessions had now been going on for almost sixteen months.)

This woman [a Yana tribesman], she came up close to me in the forest. I reprimanded her. "You have come from what place that you come here and find me?" And then she started collecting wild pandanus leaves. She put these inside her string bag. They weren't dry. They were new leaves. [As a woman she couldn't do this without a man's help in climbing a tree.] And I asked her, "You're fetching these from where?" And she said, "I've gotten them from the place where you were patrolling before." [This is a reference to the above-mentioned summer patrol in 1976 when N accompanied me to the enemy tribe. This woman, then, is associated with that tribe.] Then I started to butter her up, *really* butter her up. And I said, "All the time, you are big-headed toward me. Now, you and I, we must work it good" [copulate]. She responded like this, "It's not good that you and I fornicate here and all of them [people] see the two of us."

Then the two of us went into the nearby bush. We two really fornicated. [N smiles.] But the semen, it didn't come outside. I worked [thrust] it—her . . . I went and went, but no water [semen] came out. [Perplexed, serious.] Now, that thing of hers [vagina], it wasn't *hot* [emphasis] either . . . [it was cold]. So I asked her, "Have you got something down there that's blocking up inside of you? It's [vagina] just like water" [cold, slippery, not exciting]. And so she said back to me, "No, you yet" [meaning, it's your problem]. Then, now, I worked her and worked her [thrusting] and I was, I became hot, really hot. She wasn't easy for me [I was sweating profusely]. [GH: (interrupts) Why was that?] I worked her and I went on and on but my water [semen], it didn't come. So then I wanted to leave her. I said to her, "Let me eat [chew some] betel nut first, and then later, I think then my water it can come outside." So then I got the betel.

The betel [in my mouth], it didn't turn *red* [emphatic], the betel it didn't turn red[7] [worried]. It didn't come up red. [GH: What color was it?] White. And that something that belonged to the woman [vagina], it was red, completely. [Fast talking; this implies the woman was menstruating.] And she didn't have

---

6. S was, years ago, an occasional fellated partner of Nilutwo's. Nonetheless, there was not, in Nilutwo's expressions, any conscious hint of what would be deviant sex contact between them.

7. Ripe, chewable betel nut is creamy white inside its green shell, but it turns bright red after being mixed with lime compound and chewed.

any pubic hair [her vagina was red and she had no pubic hair]! And I looked
at her face. And her hand, her leg, she was very nice [excited]. But that
something [vagina], it was cold. So then I worked her [fornicated] again. But
this time I got up and I crossed her. I really crossed her [some anger in voice].
I crossed her because she [vagina] was cold. And I said to her, "You mustn't
go back to your own place. You must stay here. I'll go to my own place [hamlet]
and later you can come and follow me. You can leave me now. I can find my
own way back to him [reference to GH], and I can find him [GH] and I can
court you. I can find my white man and I can court you." [N is saying that out
of vengeance, out of being humiliated by this woman, because he couldn't
ejaculate, he is threatening her with finding me, GH, and then using the native
court system to fine her for his humiliation. This he reports as a thought that
he says he felt at that moment in the dream.] I looked at her breasts and they
were *swollen* [emphasis], they were big![8] I had held them [breasts] before. And
I thought that seeing them, it [semen] would come out quickly . . . [but it didn't
occur].

And then S, he woke me up by breaking firewood; and I got up. And I was
angry . . . at him for awakening me.[9]

Comment

Nilutwo made no tangential associations at all after the dream as he usually
did. In recounting the dream, he became visibly excited by the sensation
of finding a beautiful woman awaiting him in the forest, a woman he says
he had seen while touring the enemy tribe; having this woman there,
copulating with her (vaginally), and thinking that because of her voluptu-
ousness, it would be easy for him to ejaculate. And yet he remarked, over
and over, about the coldness of her vagina and about how it was not
exciting enough for him. He scolded the woman because of this coldness,
slipperiness, and redness, and then too because of his mood of anxiety in
the dream: that is, the experience of copulating with a woman without
being able to ejaculate. He was angered by what he saw as inadequacy in
the condition of her vagina. But she turned it back on him. They then
returned to fornicating, and he again got up—saying he would chew a
betel nut and thinking that perhaps that would somehow help restore him.
But when he broke open the shell and chewed the nut, instead of its
becoming the blood-red color that it should have been, it remained white.
And at the same time, he noticed that the woman's vagina was blood
colored, and furthermore, that she had no pubic hair. That disturbed him.
He went back and penetrated her again, and even though they copulated
again, he never ejaculated. This disturbed him, but he did not wake up

---

8. Implicit reference that the woman was lactating.

9. N is always getting mildly angry at whoever awakens him from a dream like this.

frightened and shaking, as he usually does when he has a nightmare. Somehow, this outcome was linked to his last thought: that he would, in the dream, find me (GH) and use me (defend himself by) trying the woman and humiliating her, too, out of revenge (a manifest theme that has recurred in Nilutwo's dreams over the years).

The Myth of Cassowary

This myth was one of several collected among the Eastern Sambia and their neighbors, the Yana tribe. Unlike the other myths recorded in this book, it is not indigenous to the Sambia River Valley groups, although Tali knew of it. Indeed, it was, to a large extent, Tali's contacts, on patrols through those borderland hamlets in 1976, that enabled me to collect this story and related ones. (See my notes on that experience in Appendix A.) The myth was told by a large group of elders and married men (who excluded younger men and initiates) to Tali, Nilutwo, Weiyu, and me, along with some other Sambia adult men. The myth (for reasons still unclear) is secret, and to ensure that secrecy, our hosts posted guards outside the hut we sat in. The following text is a verbatim transcription of a tape recording made of the myth-telling, together with a few explanatory comments later added by Tali.

A father and his son were cooking salt. They were making salt bars and they thought: "What can we contain the salt in?" Then the father, an older man, said to his boy: "A long time has passed since your mother went to the river [to collect leaves with which to contain the vegetal salt]. You go search for her."

So the boy went to look for his mother. He searched, and then he spied her doing something different than before. He thought to himself, "I'll stand here, hide, and watch her." Now this woman [his mother] was sitting on the river bank removing the bone of her own thigh [femur bone]. She sharpened it down; it looked like a bamboo knife.[1]

The child left and walked back to his father and said: "Mother removed her

---

1. Sambia use cassowary femur-bone awls to open pandanus fruits, whereas their neighbors use bamboo knives for this purpose.

thigh bone and I've come back." [The boy expressed puzzlement.] And his father wondered, "Is the boy telling the truth or is he lying? I'll go watch her." So the man went down to the river but his woman wasn't there. She had already gone and so he followed her. He carried a bamboo torch and followed the footprints of the woman who belonged to him.

The footprints led to a place where the earth had broken and slid away [i.e., a landslide]. He saw a piece of a torch but his woman wasn't there. The father and son wondered: "Did the woman fall down there where the earth broke?" Then they saw a bright torch off in the distance. At that place the torch turned into yellow-green bamboo trees and the great pine tree. (The name of this place we know as Kwonukono.) The men went to Kwonukono and searched: a torch appeared afar at Kokona.[2] So then they went there, inside that village. They found a man asleep. They didn't put out their torches; they wanted to see who he was. So they awakened him and he griped. They thus called him Leichi [*eluchi* or *eruki*, dawn].

Then Illuchi took up a torch and continued to follow the footprints. He came upon a place called *ikoonai-lolu* [pandanus forest/thunder]. And at this place he got red ocher and painted a great stone [red]. That stone is still there. Now the woman from earlier who'd escaped, one man, only he found her. Now he cut her hand [in punishment]. So this woman changed and turned into a cassowary. Because of this, the cassowary has no "hands," it's wingless. And now we cut off its legs, the big toe [for necklace decorations].

Now the father and his boy removed their bark-cape buttock covers and left them at Kokona. The buttock covers turned into a stone [pillar]. This stone became just like a man. If they hadn't put a buttock cover on it, it would have turned into only a round stone [not a tall pillar].[3]

Then they removed their buttock covers to dam up some water. This place is called Yalta—it still exists. At another place they made a round pool of water [*boongu*]—that place is called Kooneru. Next, another man said to them: "Sorry, our [sweet potato and greens] gardens, the sun has cooked them, they are dried up." Now they thought: "Let's dam up [some more] *water*." So they dammed up a stream, and hence, in the morning, small drops of dew appeared. This dew made the gardens very nice always after. The sun cooks gardens, and they dry. If they hadn't made a round water pool, only the sun would be here; it would block the rain, only the sun would be.

Then they went to another place and they broke off some of their own head hair. And at that place you can see great pine trees growing abundantly.

They traveled on and finally reached a final place. The father made a hole atop a great stone. The boy asked him: "Father, what are you doing?" The father then urinated in the hole, and this became a round pool. This still remains; it's a big pool atop a large boulder. And now we men can look into this pool, we see ourselves. But we hide it from all the women, because it came

2. The legendary home of Sambia; see Chapter 1.
3. A basalt pillar that informants describe (and I have seen) as having features resembling a man's head, hat, arms, and a stone club.

from the urine of the men. And it would not be good that women saw their own faces and said to us [men]: "You're all ugly. Why should we marry you?" So because of that, only we men can see our reflections.

On the Origins of Warfare and Initiation

This little semipublic myth told by Kanteilo and Tali, a mere fragment in any discourse, is typical of Sambia myths, which for the most part are thin, matter-of-fact, and rather unimpressive. Nonetheless, it still does its job: to reaffirm the essential and natural order of things for men.

Numboolyu's wife, Chenchi, killed her first male child. Why? That pregnancy was very painful. She griped [*cheruntu*]; then she took a stick from the *beruptu* tree and she hit the infant; she killed it.

Because she killed the first male child, we [men] now fight—war. Because she killed that child, we now have initiations and we ceremonially beat our male children. Like in the *kwat'nbagu* [first-stage initiation stretching rite], where we do what Chenchi did—hit boys with sticks [of the *beruptu* tree].

The male children gave the women [sic] labor pains for four days. On the fifth day the child was born. This was because the child had no pathway [birth canal]. It [vulva] had to be cut out with a bamboo knife. Numboolyu did this. For that reason [prolonged labor], babies aren't born quickly.

And therefore men fight. Men hold initiations. And women do not fight; they have no weapons.

The Myth of Gandei

I first heard a reference to this little Amazon tale made by Kanteilo, my elder sponsor, a few months after arriving in Nilangu. He mentioned it in passing—matter-of-factly inserting it into a discussion on women and sex. But when questioned further, he turned sheepish, grinned, and changed the subject. (I did not pursue the story further then.) A few months later, Konu mentioned it again among a group of elders and men in my house. Spurred on by Konu, the men told me the following version of the story, taking care to send the initiates out of doors, and leaving Weiyu and Nilutwo to translate. Nevertheless, Gandei, unlike the myth of parthenogenesis, is not a great secret, though it is private "men's talk," and is, as far as I know, not told to women. The reasons are those of prudishness and the men's restrictions on matters of heterosexuality vis-à-vis initiates, not rituals or their taboos directly. Gandei is the closest thing, in Sambia myth, that I could uncover that might be called a kind of Sambia men's "pornography"—in the sense that it is a bawdy, exciting fantasy capable of arousing erotic feelings, as in the case of Konu, below. My tape recording of that storytelling is here presented verbatim.

Gandei is a place near Menyamya. This place it has only women. It has no men. If women have any male children they kill them. Some men of other places have heard about Gandei. One time some men, strangers, came to the edge of the rocks overlooking where the women lived [the women inhabited a deep canyon enshrouded with trees and overgrowth]. The men realized that there were only women there. Then the men attempted to slide down vines [called *oolyegu*, which serve as the only means of transport into and out of that barricaded valley; Tali called it a cavernous place, a bad place]. The vine is very big and thick, like a house post. The women cannot cut the vine, otherwise they'd have no way of leaving their valley. [GH: On the other hand, this leaves them vulnerable to attack.] Whenever men do attempt to slide down the vine, women chase them back up with very large sticks called *gandu* [hence *gandei,* wooden war clubs] from which the women take their names.

The Gandei women do not wear grass skirts. They all go about naked. [After Konu said this he interpolated, "When I first heard the big men tell me this story, I was only an initiate, and my penis it grew very, very hard."] The women don't wear grass skirts. "Why should they?" the men asked, "They don't have any husbands."

But the "man belonging to these women" is a big old *yaandu* tree. The tree stands tall and straight in a small, round pool of water [*boongu*].[1] The women live and they sleep beside this pool near the tree. The tree fruit of the *yaandu* tree looks like the glans penis [*nungdeiyu;* this tree fruit is actually used as a toy spinning top by initiates, who jokingly refer to it as the glans penis]. This fruit it falls into the round water. Eventually, some of the pool water is splashed up onto the women's vulvas and, hence, the women become pregnant. But when male babies are born they are killed. [Here Nilutwo excitedly interpolated: "If I saw this tree, I'd cut it down. Then I'd *take* a woman for *myself!*"]

The Gandei women they always chase away intruding men because they already have a huge man [the *yaandu* tree] belonging to them [Weiyu reflected: "Perhaps that is why they are afraid that real men will cut down their tree." And then, thoughtfully, Nilutwo said, "*Yaandu* fruit has its own nose belonging to it!" Here nose refers to the glans penis; Nilutwo is joking about the tree being a penis.]

Then I asked, "Why do the women kill their male children?" To which Weiyu replied: "Women think, 'If we have boys and let them grow up they can kill us . . .[2] Oh—they could kill the tree, cut it down.' And so all the women think it bad that boys would cut down the tree."

And now Nilutwo and Weiyu both added, "Suppose we were there, we would cut that tree down and then *we'd* be able to *take food* for our 'child,' for us only [a convoluted metaphoric statement meaning "our penises— our children—would then have women to fornicate"; "being able to fornicate women" is likened to "penis food"]. Our food [sex], it wouldn't ever finish. We'd have plenty and more, and later, one woman, if she wasn't any good or if she was big-headed or lazy, we would simply get rid of her and get a new one." Then Konu reasserted, "When I first heard that story, my penis grew very erect, just like half a stick—when I first heard that story."

---

1. Here again (and see also Appendix C) we encounter the image of the *boongu* (see Chapter 6), this time as a round pool with a large tree growing from within it.

2. Weiyu made a verbal slip when he said, "If we have boys and let them grow up they can kill *us*"; he meant to say that the boys could "kill the *tree,* cut it down," substituting "us" (men) for the tree.

References

Ainsworth, M. D. S. 1972. "Attachment and dependency," in *Attachment and Dependency*. Edited by L. Jacob and J. Gewertz, pp. 97–137. Washington, D.C.: Winston.

Allen, M. R. 1967. *Male Cults and Secret Initiations in Melanesia*. Melbourne: Melbourne University Press.

Ardener, E. 1975. "Belief and the problem of women," [and] "The 'problem' revisited," in *Perceiving Women*. Edited by S. Ardener, pp. 1–27. London: Dent/Malaby.

Ardener, S. 1978. "Introduction: The nature of women in society," in *Defining Females: The Nature of Women in Society*. Edited by S. Ardener, pp. 9–48. New York: Wiley.

Bandura, A., and R. H. Walters. 1963. *Social Learning and Personality Development*. New York: Holt, Rinehart & Winston.

Barry, H., III, M. K. Bacon, and I. L. Child. 1957. A cross-cultural survey of sex differences in socialization. *Journal of Abnormal and Social Psychology* 55:327–332.

Barth, F. 1971. Tribes and intertribal relations in the Fly headwaters. *Oceania* 41:171–191.

———. 1975. *Ritual and Knowledge among the Baktaman of New Guinea*. New Haven: Yale University Press.

Basso, K. H. 1976. " 'Wise words' of the Western Apache: Metaphor and semantic theory," in *Meaning in Anthropology*. Edited by K. H. Basso and H. A. Selby, pp. 93–121. Albuquerque: School for American Research and University of New Mexico Press.

Bateson, G. 1949. "Bali: The value system of a steady state," in *Social Structure: Studies Presented to A. R. Radcliffe-Brown*. Edited by M. Fortes, pp. 35–53. Oxford: Clarendon Press.

———. 1958 (1936). *Naven*. Second edition. Stanford: Stanford University Press.

———. 1972. *Steps to an Ecology of Mind*. New York: Ballantine Books.

Becker, E. 1971. *The Lost Science of Man*. New York: George Braziller.

Beidelman, T. O. 1964. Pig (*Guluwe*): An essay on Ngulu sexual symbolism and ceremony. *Southwestern Journal of Anthropology* 20:359–392.

———. 1966a. The ox and Nuer sacrifice: Some Freudian hypotheses about Nuer symbolism. *Man* 1:453–467.

———. 1966b. Swazi royal ritual. *Africa* 36:373–405.

Benedict, R. 1938. Continuities and discontinuities in cultural conditioning. *Psychiatry* 1:161–167.

————. 1946. *The Chrysanthemum and the Sword*. Boston: Houghton Mifflin.

Berndt, R. M. 1962. *Excess and Restraint*. Chicago: University of Chicago Press.

————. 1965. "The Kamo, Usurufa, Jate and Fore of the Eastern Highlands," in *Gods, Ghosts and Men in Melanesia*. Edited by P. Lawrence and M. J. Meggitt, pp. 78–104. Melbourne: Melbourne University Press.

Bettelheim, B. 1955. *Symbolic Wounds, Puberty Rites and the Envious Male*. New York: Collier Books.

Biller, H. B. 1970. Father absence and personality development of the male child. *Developmental Psychology* 2:181–270.

Blackwood, B. 1939a. Life on the Upper Watut, New Guinea. *Geographical Journal* 94:11–28.

————. 1939b. "Use of plants among the Kukukuku of Southeast-Central New Guinea," in *Proceedings of the Sixth Pacific Science Congress*, vol. 4, pp. 111–126. Berkeley, Cal.

————. 1950. *The Technology of a Modern Stone Age People in New Guinea*. Occasional Paper on Technology 3, Oxford: Pitt Rivers Museum.

Bowers, N. 1965. Permanent bachelorhood in the Upper Kaugel Valley of Highland New Guinea. *Oceania* 36:27–37.

Bowlby, J. 1958. The nature of the child's tie to his mother. *International Journal of Psycho-Analysis* 39:350–373.

————. 1969. *Attachment and Loss*. Vol. 1. *Attachment*. New York: Basic Books.

————. 1973. *Attachment and Loss*. Vol. 2. *Separation*. New York: Basic Books.

Brookfield, H. 1964. "The ecology of Highlands settlement: Some suggestions," in New Guinea: The Central Highlands. Edited by J. B. Watson, pp. 20–38. *American Anthropologist* 66(Part 2).

Brookfield, H., and D. Hart. 1971. *Melanesia: A Geographic Interpretation of an Island World*. London: Methuen.

Brown, J. K. 1963. A cross-cultural study of female intitiation rites. *American Anthropologist* 65:837–853.

Brown, P. 1978. *Highland Peoples of New Guinea*. New York: Cambridge University Press.

Brown, P., and G. Buchbinder. 1976. "Introduction," in *Man and Woman in the New Guinea Highlands*. Edited by P. Brown and G. Buchbinder, pp. 1–12. Washington, D.C.: American Anthropological Association.

Buchbinder, G. 1973. Maring microadaptation: A study of demographic, nutritional, genetic and phenotypic variation in a Highland New Guinea population. Unpublished Ph.D. dissertation, Columbia University.

Buchbinder, G., and R. A. Rappaport. 1976. "Fertility and death among the Maring," in *Man and Woman in the New Guinea Highlands*. Edited by P. Brown and G. Buchbinder, pp. 13–35. Washington, D.C.: American Anthropological Association.

Bulmer, R. N. H. 1967. Why is the cassowary not a bird? *Man* 2:5–25.

————. 1971. "Traditional forms of family limitation in New Guinea," in *Population Growth and Socio-Economic Change*, pp. 137–162. Research Bulletin No. 42. Canberra: A.N.U. Press.

————. 1974. Folk biology in the New Guinea Highlands. *Social Science Information* 13:9–28.

Burridge, K. O. 1969. *Tangu Traditions*. Oxford: Clarendon Press.

Burton, R. V., and J. W. M. Whiting. 1961. The absent father and cross-sex identity. *Merrill-Palmer Quarterly of Behavior and Development* 7:85–95.

Cassirer, E. 1970 (1944). *An Essay on Man*. Toronto: Bantam.

Chinnery, E. W. P. 1934. The central ranges of the mandated territory of New Guinea from Mount Chapman to Mount Hagen. *Geographical Journal* 84:398–412.

Chodorow, N. 1974. "Family structure and feminine personality," in *Woman, Culture, and Society.* Edited by M. Z. Rosaldo and L. Lamphere, pp. 43–66. Stanford: Stanford University Press.

Clarke, W. 1971. *People and Place.* Berkeley: University of California Press.

Clay, B. 1975. *Pinikindu.* Chicago: University of Chicago Press.

Cohen, Y. A. 1964a. The establishment of identity in a social nexus: The special case of initiation ceremonies and their relation to value and legal systems. *American Anthropologist* 66(Part 1):529–552.

———. 1964b. *The Transition from Childhood to Adolescence.* Chicago: Aldine.

Colby, K. M. 1978. Mind models: An overview of current work. *Mathematical Biosciences,* 39:159–185.

———. 1979. "Appendix A: Some enigmas of pronouns in explanations of human behavior," in *Sexual Excitement.* By R. J. Stoller, pp. 231–234. New York: Pantheon.

Cole, M. 1975. "An ethnographic psychology of cognition," in *Cross-Cultural Perspectives on Learning.* Edited by R. W. Brislin et al., pp. 157–175. New York: Wiley.

Cook, E. A. 1969. "Marriage among the Manga," in *Pigs, Pearlshells, and Women.* Edited by R. M. Glasse and M. J. Meggitt, pp. 96–116. Englewood Cliffs, N.J.: Prentice-Hall.

Crapanzano, V. 1973. *The Hamadsha: A Study in Moroccan Ethnopsychiatry.* Berkeley: University of California Press.

Crome, F. H. J. 1975. Some observations on the biology of the cassowary in Northern Queensland. *Emu* 76:8–14.

D'Andrade, R. G. 1973. Father absence, identification, and identity. *Ethos* 1:440–455.

Davis, A. J. 1969. *Report on Sexual Assaults in the Prison System and Sheriff's Vans.* Philadelphia: District Attorney's Office and Police Department.

Deacon, A. B. 1934. *Malekula: A Vanishing People in the New Hebrides.* London: George Routledge.

Devereux, G. 1967. *From Anxiety to Method in the Behavioral Sciences.* The Hague: Mouton.

———. 1975. Fantasy as a reflection of reality. Unpublished manuscript.

———. 1978. "The works of George Devereux," in *The Making of Psychological Anthropology.* Edited by G. D. Spindler, pp. 364–406. Berkeley: University of California Press.

De Vos, G. 1975. The dangers of pure theory in anthropology. *Ethos* 3:77–91.

Diamond, M. 1968. "Genetic-endocrine interactions and human sexuality," in *Perspectives in Reproduction and Sexual Behavior.* Edited by M. Diamond, pp. 417–443. Bloomington: University of Indiana Press.

Douglas, M. 1966. *Purity and Danger.* London: Routledge & Kegan Paul.

———. 1970. *Natural Symbols.* London: Cresset Press.

———. 1975. *Implicit Meanings.* London: Routledge & Kegan Paul.

Dundes, A. 1976. A psychoanalytic study of the bullroarer. *Man* 11:220–238.

Durkheim, E. 1965. (1915) *The Elementary Forms of the Religious Life.* Translated by J. W. Swain. New York: Free Press.

———. 1966 (1938). *The Rules of the Sociological Method.* Eighth edition. Edited by G. E. G. Catlin. Translated by S. A. Solovay and J. H. Mueller. New York: Free Press.

Edgerton, R. B., and L. L. Langness. 1974. *Methods and Styles in the Study of Culture.* San Francisco: Chandler & Sharp.

Erikson, E. H. 1968. *Identity: Youth and Crisis.* New York: Norton.

Evans-Pritchard, E. E. 1937. *Witchcraft, Oracles and Magic among the Azande.* Oxford: Oxford University Press.

———. 1962. *Social Anthropology and Other Essays.* New York: Free Press.

———. 1965. *Theories of Primitive Religion.* London: Oxford University Press.

———. 1970. *The Sociology of Comte: An Appreciation.* Manchester: Manchester University Press.

Faithorn, E. 1976. "Women as persons: Aspects of female life and male-female relations among the Kafe," in *Man and Woman in the New Guinea Highlands.* Edited by P. Brown and G. Buchbinder, pp. 86–95. Washington, D.C.: American Anthropological Association.

Fernandez, J. W. 1965. Symbolic consensus in a Fang reformative cult. *American Anthropologist* 15:902–929.

———. 1974. The mission of metaphor in expressive culture. *Current Anthropology* 15:119–145.

Firth, R. 1967. *The Work of the Gods in Tikopia.* Second edition. London: Humanities Press.

———. 1973. *Symbols: Public and Private.* Ithaca: Cornell University Press.

Fodor, J. A. 1975. *The Language of Thought.* New York: Thomas Y. Crowell.

Forge, A. 1972. The golden fleece. *Man* 7:527–540.

———. 1973. "Style and meaning in Sepik art," in *Primitive Art and Society.* Edited by A. Forge, pp. 169–192. London: Oxford University Press.

Frake, C. O. 1969. "Notes and queries in ethnography," in *Cognitive Anthropology.* Edited by S. A. Tyler, pp. 123–137. New York: Holt, Rinehart & Winston.

Frazer, J. G. 1911 (-1915). *The Golden Bough: A Study in Magic and Religion.* Third edition. 12 volumes. London: Macmillan.

Freeman, J. D. 1970. "Human nature and culture," in *Man and the New Biology.* Edited by D. Slayer, pp. 50–75. Canberra: A.N.U. Press.

———. 1977. Towards an anthropology both scientific and humanistic. Unpublished manuscript. Department of Anthropology, Research School of Pacific Studies, Australian National University.

Frellich, M. 1977. *Marginal Natives at Work.* New York: Halsted Press.

Freud, A. 1963. The concept of developmental lines. *Psychoanalytic Study of the Child* 18:245–265.

Freud, S. 1953 (1900). "The interpretation of dreams," in *The Standard Edition of the Complete Psychological Works of Sigmund Freud.* Edited and translated by J. Strachey, vols. 4–5. London: Hogarth.

———. 1955a (1913). "Totem and taboo," in *The Standard Edition of the Complete Psychological Works of Sigmund Freud.* Edited and translated by J. Strachey, vol. 13, pp. 1–164. London: Hogarth.

———. 1955b (1919). "The 'uncanny,' " in *The Standard Edition of the Complete Psychological Works of Sigmund Freud.* Edited and translated by J. Strachey, vol. 17, pp. 219–252. London: Hogarth.

———. 1960 (1905). "Jokes and their relation to the unconscious," in *The Standard Edition of the Complete Psychological Works of Sigmund Freud.* Edited and translated by J. Strachey, vol. 8. London: Hogarth.

———. 1961 (1927). "The future of an illusion," in *The Standard Edition of the Complete Psychological Works of Sigmund Freud.* Edited and translated by J. Strachey, vol. 21, pp. 3–57. London: Hogarth.

———. 1963 (1916–1917). "Introductory lectures on psycho-analysis," in *The Standard Edition of the Complete Psychological Works of Sigmund Freud.* Edited and translated by J. Strachey, vols. 15–16. London: Hogarth.

Gajdusek, D. C., and V. Zigas. 1961. Studies on kuru. I: The ethnologic setting of kuru. *American Journal of Tropical Medicine and Hygiene* 10:80–91.

Geertz, C. 1964. "Ideology as a cultural system," in *Ideology and Discontent.* Edited by D. Apter, pp. 47–56. Glencoe, Ill.: Free Press.

———. 1966a. "Religion as a cultural system," in *Anthropological Approaches to the Study of Religion.* Edited by M. Bantam, pp. 1–46. London: Tavistock Publications.

———. 1966b. *Person, Time and Conduct in Bali: An Essay in Cultural Analysis.* Yale Southeast Asia Program, Cultural Report No. 14. New Haven: Yale University Press.

———. 1967. The cerebral savage: On the work of Claude Lévi-Strauss. *Encounter* 28:25–32.

———. 1968. *Islam Observed.* New Haven: Yale University Press.

———. 1973. "Thick description: Toward an interpretative theory of culture," in *The Interpretation of Cultures: Selected Essays by C. Geertz,* pp. 3–30. New York: Basic Books.

———. 1976. "From the native's point of view: On the nature of anthropological understanding," in *Meaning in Anthropology.* Edited by K. Basso and H. Selby, pp. 221–237. Albuquerque: School for American Research and University of New Mexico Press.

Gell, A. 1975. *Metamorphosis of the Cassowaries.* London: Athlone.

Gilberttson, G. 1964. *Encyclopedia of Cybernetics.* Manchester: Manchester University Press.

Gilliard, E. 1953. New Guinea's rare birds and stone age men. *National Geographic* 104:421–488.

Glick, L. B. 1964. "Categories and relations in Gimi natural science," in New Guinea: The Central Highlands. Edited by J. B. Watson, pp. 273–280. *American Anthropologist* 66(Part 2).

Gluckman, M. 1967. "Introduction," in *The Craft of Social Anthropology.* Edited by A. L. Epstein, pp. xi–xx. London: Tavistock Publications.

———. 1969 (1956). "The license in ritual," in *Custom and Conflict in Africa.* pp. 109–136. New York: Barnes & Noble.

Godelier, M. 1969. Land tenure among the Baruya of New Guinea. *Journal of the Papua New Guinea Society* 3:17–23.

———. 1971. " 'Salt currency' and the circulation of commodities among the Baruya of New Guinea," in *Studies in Economic Anthropology,* pp. 53–73. Washington, D.C.: American Anthropological Association.

———. 1976. "Le sexe comme fondement ultime de l'ordre social et cosmique chez les Baruya de Nouvelle-Guinée," in *Sexualite et Pouvoir.* Edited by A. Verdiglione, pp. 268–306. Paris: Traces Payot.

Gourlay, K. A. 1975. *Sound-Producing Instruments in a Traditional Society: A Study of Esoteric Instruments and Their Role in Male-Female Relationships.* New Guinea Research Bulletin No. 60. Port Moresby: A.N.U. Press.

Green, R. 1974. *Sexual Identity Conflict in Children and Adults.* New York: Basic Books.

———. 1978. "Sexuality and aggressivity: Development in the human primate," in *Recent Advances in Primatology.* Vol. 1. Edited by D. J. Chivers and J. Herbert, pp. 515–528. New York: Academic.

Greenson, R. 1968. Dis-identifying from mother. *International Journal of Psycho-Analysis* 49:370–374.

Griaule, M. 1965. *Conversations with Ogotemmeli: An Introduction to Dogon Religious Ideas.* London: Oxford University Press.

Guthrie, G. M. 1975. "A behavioral analysis of cultural learning," in *Cross-Cultural Perspectives on Learning.* Edited by R. W. Brislin et al., pp. 95–115. New York: Wiley.

Hallowell, A. I. 1967. *Culture and Experience.* New York: Schocken Books.

Harré, R., and P. F. Secord. 1972. *The Explanation of Social Behaviour.* Oxford: Blackwell.

Harrington, C. 1968. Sexual differentiation in socialization and some male genital mutilations. *American Anthropologist* 70:952–956.

Harrington, C., and J. W. M. Whiting. 1972. "Socialization process and personality," in *Psychological Anthropology*. Edited by F. L. K. Hsu, pp. 469–507. Cambridge, Mass.: Schenkman.

Harris, M. 1968. *The Rise of Anthropological Theory*. New York: Thomas Y. Crowell.

Hau'ofa, E. 1975. Mekeo: A study of a Papua New Guinea society. Unpublished Ph.D. dissertation, Australian National University.

Hays, T. E. 1979. Plant classification and nomenclature in Ndumba, Papua New Guinea Highlands. *Ethnology* 18:253–270.

Heider, K. 1976. Dani sexuality: A low energy system. *Man* 11:188–201.

Herdt, G. H. 1977. "The shaman's 'calling' among the Sambia of New Guinea," in Madness, Possession and Shamanism in New Guinea. Edited by B. Juillerat, pp. 153–167. *Journal de la Société des Océanistes* 33(Special edition).

Hiatt, L. R. 1971. "Secret pseudo-procreative rites among Australian aborigines," in *Anthropology in Oceania: Essays Presented to Ian Hogbin*. Edited by L. R. Hiatt and C. Jayawardena, pp. 77–88. Sydney: Angus & Robertson.

Hogbin, I. 1970. *The Island of Menstruating Men*. Scranton, Pa.: Chandler Publishing Co.

Hogbin, I., and C. Wedgwood. 1953. Local grouping in Melanesia. *Oceania* 23:241–276; 24:58–76.

Honigmann, J. J. 1978. "The personal approach in culture and personality research," in *The Making of Psychological Anthropology*. Edited by G. D. Spindler, pp. 302–329. Berkeley: University of California Press.

Horton, R. 1967. African traditional thought and Western science. *Africa* 37:50–71, 159–187.

———. 1968. Neo-Tylorianism: Sound sense or sinister prejudice? *Man* 3:625–634.

Hoyle, F. 1966. *Man in the Universe*. New York: Columbia University Press.

Johnson, C. K., M. D. Gilbert, and G. H. Herdt. 1979. Implications for adult roles from differentiated styles of mother-infant bonding: An ethological study. *Journal of Nervous and Mental Disease* 167:29–37.

Jolly, A. 1972. *The Evolution of Primate Behavior*. New York: Macmillan.

Kallmar, F. J. 1952. Twin and sibship study of overt homosexuality. *American Journal of Human Genetics* 4:136–146.

Kardiner, A. 1939. *The Individual and His Society*. New York: Columbia University Press.

Katchadourian, H. A. 1979. "The terminology of sex and gender," in *Human Sexuality: A Comparative and Developmental Perspective*. Edited by H. A. Katchadourian, pp. 8–34. Berkeley: University of California Press.

Keesing, R. M. 1972. Paradigms lost: The new ethnology and the new linguistics. *Southwestern Journal of Anthropology* 28:299–332.

———. 1976. *Cultural Anthropology: A Contemporary Perspective*. New York: Holt, Rinehart & Winston.

———. 1979. Linguistic knowledge and cultural knowledge: Some doubts and speculations. *American Anthropologist* 81:14–36.

Kelly, R. 1968. Demographic pressure and descent group structure in the New Guinea Highlands. *Oceania* 39:36–63.

———. 1976. "Witchcraft and sexual relations: An exploration in the social and semantic implications of a structure of belief," in *Man and Woman in the New Guinea Highlands*. Edited by P. Brown and G. Buchbinder, pp. 36–53. Washington, D.C.: American Anthropological Association.

———. 1977. *Etero Social Structure.* Ann Arbor: University of Michigan Press.

Klaus, M. H., and J. H. Kennell. 1976. *Maternal-Infant Bonding.* St. Louis: Mosby.

Koch, K. F. 1974a. Sociogenic and psychogenic models in anthropology: The functions of Jalé initiation. *Man* 9:397–422.

———. 1974b. *War and Peace in Jalémo.* Cambridge, Mass.: Harvard University Press.

Kolodny, R. C., et al. 1971. Plasma testosterone and serum analysis in male homosexuals. *New England Journal of Medicine* 285:1170–1174.

Kracke, W. H. 1979. Review of G. Roheim, *Children of the Desert* (1974). *Journal of the American Psychoanalytic Association* 27:223–231.

Kuhn, T. S. 1970 (1962). *The Structure of Scientific Revolutions.* Second edition. Chicago: University of Chicago Press.

La Barre, W. 1970. *The Ghost Dance: The Origins of Religion.* New York: Doubleday.

Lamb, M. 1976. *The Role of the Father in Child Development.* New York: Wiley.

Lambert, W. W., L. Triandis, and M. Wolf. 1959. Some correlates of beliefs in the malevolence and benevolence of supernatural beings: A cross-cultural study. *Journal of Abnormal and Social Psychology* 58:162–169.

Landtman, G. 1927. *The Kiwai Papuans of British New Guinea.* London: Macmillan.

Langness, L. L. 1965. Hysterical psychosis in the New Guinea Highlands: A Bena Bena example. *Psychiatry* 28:258–277.

———. 1967. Sexual antagonism in the New Guinea Highlands: A Bena Bena example. *Oceania* 37:161–177.

———. 1972. "Political organization," in *Encyclopedia of Papua New Guinea,* pp. 922–935. Melbourne: Melbourne University Press.

———. 1974. Ritual power and male domination in the New Guinea Highlands. *Ethos* 2:189–212.

———. 1976. "Discussion," in *Man and Woman in the New Guinea Highlands.* Edited by P. Brown and G. Buchbinder, pp. 96–106. Washington, D.C.: American Anthropological Association.

Lawrence, P. 1965–1966. The Garia of the Madang district. *Anthropological Forum* 1:371–392.

———. 1971. "Introduction," in *Politics in New Guinea.* Edited by R. M. Berndt and P. Lawrence, pp. 1–34. Seattle: University of Washington Press.

Lawrence, P., and M. J. Meggitt. 1965. *Gods, Ghosts and Men in Melanesia.* Melbourne: Melbourne University Press.

Layard, J. 1959. Homo-eroticism in primitive society as a function of the self. *Journal of Analytical Psychology* 4:101–115.

Leach, E. R. 1961. *Pul Eliya: A Village in Ceylon.* Cambridge: Cambridge University Press.

———. 1964a. "Animal categories and verbal abuse," in *New Directions in the Study of Language.* Edited by E. H. Lenneberg, pp. 23–63. Cambridge, Mass.: M.I.T. Press.

———. 1964b (1954). *Political Systems of Highland Burma.* Boston: Beacon Press.

———. 1969. *Genesis as Myth and Other Essays.* London: Cape.

———. 1973. "Levels of communication and of taboo in the appreciation of primitive art," in *Primitive Art and Society.* Edited by A. Forge, pp. 221–234. London: Oxford University Press.

———. 1976. *Culture and Communication.* Cambridge: Cambridge University Press.

Leites, N. 1970. *The New Ego.* New York: Science House.

LeVine, R. A. 1973. *Culture, Behavior, and Personality.* Chicago: Aldine.

———. 1979. "Anthropology and sex: Developmental aspects," in *Human Sexuality: A*

Comparative and Developmental Perspective. Edited by H. A. Katchadourian, pp. 309–319. Berkeley: University of California Press.

Lévi-Strauss, C. 1963 (1961). *Totemism.* Translated by R. Needham. Boston: Beacon Press.

——. 1966 (1962). *The Savage Mind.* Chicago: University of Chicago Press.

——. 1967 (1958). *Structural Anthropology.* Translated by C. Jacobson and B. G. Schoepf. Garden City, N.Y.: Anchor Books.

——. 1968. "The concept of primitiveness," in *Man the Hunter.* Edited by R. Lee and I. De Vore, pp. 349–352. New York: Aldine and The Wenner-Gren Foundation for Anthropological Research.

——. 1969 (1955). *Tristes Tropiques.* Translated by J. Russell. New York: Atheneum.

——. 1971. *L'Homme Nu.* Paris: Plon.

Levy, R. I. 1973. *The Tahitians: Mind and Experience in the Society Islands.* Chicago: University of Chicago Press.

Lewin, K. 1949. *Field Theory in Social Science.* London: Tavistock Publications.

Lewis, G. 1975. *Knowledge and Illness in a Sepik Society.* London: Athlone.

Lewis, I. M. 1971. *Ecstatic Religion: An Anthropological Study of Spirit Possession and Shamanism.* Middlesex, England: Penguin Books.

Lichtenstein, H. 1961. Identity and sexuality. *Journal of the American Psychoanalytic Association* 9:179–260.

Lidz, R. W., and T. Lidz. 1977. Male menstruation: A ritual alternative to the Oedipal transition. *International Journal of Psycho-Analysis* 58:17–31.

Lindenbaum, S. 1972. Sorcerers, ghosts, and polluting women: An analysis of religious belief and population control. *Ethnology* 11:241–253.

——. 1976. "A wife is the hand of man," in *Man and Woman in the New Guinea Highlands.* Edited by P. Brown and G. Buchbinder, pp. 54–62. Washington, D.C.: American Anthropological Association.

Lloyd, R. G. 1973. "The Angan language family," in *The Linguistic Situation in the Gulf District and Adjacent Areas, Papua New Guinea.* Edited by K. Franklin, pp. 31–111. Pacific Linguistics, Series C, No. 26. Canberra: Linguistic Circle of Canberra.

——. 1974. "Baruya kith and kin," in *Kinship Studies in Papua New Guinea.* Edited by R. D. Shaw, pp. 97–114. Ukarumpa, Papua New Guinea: S.I.L. Press.

Longabaugh, R. 1973. Mother behavior as a variable modifying the effects of father absence. *Ethos* 1:456–465.

Luria, Z. 1979. "Psychosocial determinants of gender identity, role and orientation," in *Human Sexuality: A Comparative and Developmental Perspective.* Edited by H. A. Katchadourian, pp. 163–193. Berkeley: University of California Press.

Maccoby, E. E. 1979. "Gender identity and sex-role adoption," in *Human Sexuality: A Comparative and Developmental Perspective.* Edited by H. A. Katchadourian, pp. 194–203. Berkeley: University of California Press.

Maccoby, E. E., and C. N. Jacklin. 1974. *The Psychology of Sex Differences.* Stanford: Stanford University Press.

Mahler, M. 1968. *On Human Symbiosis and the Vicissitudes of Individuation.* New York: International Universities Press.

Malcolm, L. A. 1966. The age of puberty in the Bundi peoples. *Papua New Guinea Medical Journal* 9:16–20.

——. 1970. Growth, malnutrition and mortality of the infant and toddler in the Asai Valley of the New Guinea Highlands. *American Journal of Clinical Nutrition* 23:1090–1095.

Malinowski, B. 1922. *Argonauts of the Western Pacific.* New York: Dutton.

————. 1929. *The Sexual Life of Savages in North-Western Melanesia.* New York: Harcourt, Brace.

————. 1954 (1948). *Magic, Science and Religion and Other Essays.* Garden City, N.Y.: Anchor Books.

————. 1967. *A Diary in the Strict Sense of the Term.* Translated by N. Guterman. New York: Harcourt, Brace & World.

Mauss, M. 1967. *The Gift.* Translated by I. Cunnison. New York: Norton.

Mead, M. 1928. *Coming of Age in Samoa.* New York: Morrow.

————. 1940. The Mountain Arapesh: Supernaturalism. American Museum of Natural History, *Anthropological Papers* 37:319–451.

————. 1949. *Male and Female: A Study of the Sexes in a Changing World.* New York: Morrow.

————. 1962. "Retrospects and prospects," in *Anthropology and Human Behavior,* pp. 115–149. Washington, D.C.: Anthropological Society of Washington.

————. 1968 (1935). *Sex and Temperament in Three Primitive Societies.* New York: Dell.

Meggitt, M. 1964. "Male-female relationships in the Highlands of Australian New Guinea," in New Guinea: The Central Highlands. Edited by J. B. Watson, pp. 204–224. *American Anthropologist* 66 (Part 2).

————. 1969. "Introduction," in *Pigs, Pearlshells, and Women.* Edited by R. M. Glasse and M. J. Meggitt, pp. 1–15. Englewood Cliffs, N.J.: Prentice-Hall.

Meigs, A. 1976. Male pregnancy and the reduction of sexual opposition in a New Guinea Highlands society. *Ethnology* 25:393–407.

————. 1978. A Papuan perspective on pollution. *Man* 13:204–318.

Money, J., and A. Ehrhardt. 1972. *Man, Woman, Boy, Girl.* Baltimore: John Hopkins University Press.

Moore, S. F., and B. G. Myerhoff. 1977. *Secular Ritual.* Edited by S. F. Moore and B. G. Myerhoff. Essen: Van Gorcum.

Munn, N. 1973. *Walbiri Iconography: Graphic Representation and Cultural Symbolism in a Central Australian Society.* Ithaca: Cornell University Press.

Munroe, R. L., and R. H. Munroe. 1971. Male pregnancy symptoms and cross-sex identity in three societies. *Journal of Social Psychology* 84:11–25.

————. 1973. Psychological interpretation of male initiation rites: The case of male pregnancy symptoms. *Ethos* 1:490–498.

Munroe, R. L., R. H. Munroe, and J. W. Whiting. 1973. The couvade: A psychological analysis. *Ethos* 1:30–74.

Murphy, R. F. 1959. Social structure and sex antagonism. *Southwestern Journal of Anthropology* 15:89–98.

Murray, J. H. P. 1912. *Papua or British New Guinea.* London: T. Fisher Unwin.

Needham, R. 1962. *Structure and Sentiment.* Chicago: University of Chicago Press.

————. 1973. *Belief, Language, and Experience.* Chicago: University of Chicago Press.

Neisser, U. 1967. *Cognitive Psychology.* New York: Appleton-Century-Crofts.

Nelson, H. 1972. *Papua New Guinea: Black Unity or Black Chaos?* Middlesex, England: Penguin Books.

Newman, P. 1962. Supernaturalism and ritual among the Gururumba. Unpublished Ph.D. dissertation, University of Washington.

————. 1964. "Religious belief and ritual in a New Guinea Society," in New Guinea: The Central Highlands. Edited by J. B. Watson, pp. 257–272. *American Anthropologist* 66(Part 2).

————. 1965. *Knowing the Gururumba.* New York: Holt, Rinehart & Winston.

Norbeck, E., D. E. Walker, and M. Cohen. 1962. The interpretation of data: Puberty rites. *American Anthropologist* 64:463–485.

Nutini, H. G. 1965. Some considerations on the nature of social structure and model building: A critique of Claude Lévi-Strauss and Edmund Leach. *American Anthropologist* 67:707–731.

Oliver, D. 1955. *A Soloman Island Society.* Cambridge, Mass.: Harvard University Press.

Paijmans, K. 1976. *New Guinea Vegetation.* Edited by K. Paijmans. Canberra: A.N.U. Press.

Parsons, A. 1969. *Belief, Magic and Anomie: Essays in Psychological Anthropology.* New York: Free Press.

Parsons, T. 1968 (1937). *The Structure of Social Action.* Vol. 1. *Marshall, Pareto, Durkheim.* New York: Free Press.

Peckover, W. S., and L. W. C. Filewood. 1976. *Birds of New Guinea and Tropical Australia.* Sydney: Reed.

Pelto, P. J. 1970. *Anthropological Research: The Structure of Inquiry.* New York: Harper & Row.

Pelto, P. J., and G. H. Pelto. 1975. Intra-cultural diversity: Some theoretical issues. *American Ethnologist* 2:1–18.

Piaget, J. 1954 (1937). *The Construction of Reality in the Child.* Translated by M. Cook. New York: Basic Book.

————. 1971 (1968). *Structuralism.* Translated and edited by C. Maschler. New York: Harper Torchbooks.

Pierson, E. C., and W. V. D'Antonio. 1974. *Female and Male: Dimensions of Human Sexuality.* Philadelphia: Lippincott.

Polanyi, M. 1966. *The Tacit Dimension.* Garden City, N.Y.: Anchor Books.

Poole, F. J. P. 1980. "Transforming 'natural' woman: Female ritual leaders and gender ideology among Binin-Kuskusmin," in *Sexual Meanings.* Edited by S. B. Ortner and H. Whitehead, pp. 1–93. (In preparation.)

Popper, K., and J. Eccles. 1977. *The Self and Its Brain.* New York: Springer International.

Powers, W. T. 1973. *Behavior: The Control of Perception.* Chicago: Aldine.

Precourt, W. E. 1975. "Initiation ceremonies and secret societies as educational institutions," in *Cross-Cultural Perspectives on Learning.* Edited by R. W. Brislin et al., pp. 231–250. New York: Wiley.

Price-Williams, D. 1975. *Explorations in Cross-Cultural Psychology.* San Francisco: Chandler & Sharp.

Radcliffe-Brown, A. R. 1922. *The Andaman Islanders.* Cambridge: Cambridge University Press.

————. 1952. *Structure and Function in Primitive Society.* London: Oxford University Press.

Rank, O. 1952 (1909). *The Myth of the Birth of the Hero: A Psychological Interpretation of Mythology.* Translated by F. Robbins and S. Jelliffe. New York: R. Brunner.

Rappaport, R. 1968. *Pigs for the Ancestors.* New Haven: Yale University Press.

————. 1971. Ritual, sanctity, and cybernetics. *American Anthropologist* 73:59–76.

Read, K. E. 1951. The Gahuku-Gama of the Central Highlands. *South Pacific* 5:154–164.

————. 1952. Nama cult of the Central Highlands, New Guinea. *Oceania* 23:1–25.

————. 1954. Cultures of the Central Highlands. *Southwestern Journal of Anthropology* 10:1–43.

————. 1955. Morality and the concept of the person among the Gahuku-Gama. *Oceania* 25:233–282.

————. 1959. Leadership and consensus in a New Guinea society. *American Anthropologist* 61:425–436.

————. 1965. *The High Valley.* London: Allen & Unwin.

Reay, M. 1959. *The Kuma.* Melbourne: Melbourne University Press.

————. 1966. "Women in traditional society," in *New Guinea on the Threshold.* Edited by E. K. Fisk, pp. 166–184. Canberra: A.N.U. Press.

Reik, T. 1946. *Ritual: Four Psycho-Analytic Studies.* New York: Grove Press.

Reynolds, V. 1976. *The Biology of Human Action.* Reading & San Francisco: Freeman.

Richards, A. I. 1956. *Chisungu: A Girl's Initiation Ceremony among the Bemba of Northern Rhodesia.* London: Faber & Faber.

Robbins, R. G. 1961. The vegetation of New Guinea. *Australia Territoria* 1:21–32.

Roheim, G. 1974. *Children of the Desert.* Edited by W. Muensterberger. New York: Basic Books.

Rosaldo, M. Z. 1974. "Woman, culture, and society: A theoretical overview," in *Woman, Culture, and Society.* Edited by M. Z. Rosaldo and L. Lamphere, pp. 17–42. Stanford: Stanford University Press.

Rosaldo, M. Z., and L. Lamphere. 1974. "Introduction," in *Woman, Culture, and Society.* Edited by M. Z. Rosaldo and L. Lamphere, pp. 1–15. Stanford: Stanford University Press.

Rossman, P. 1973. The Pederasts. *Society* 10:28–35.

Rowley, C. D. 1970. *The Destruction of Aboriginal Society.* Canberra: A.N.U. Press.

Sackett, G. P. 1972. Exploratory behavior of rhesus monkeys as a function of rearing experiences and sex. *Developmental Psychology* 6:260–270.

Sahlins, M. 1963. Poor man, rich man, big man, chief. *Comparative Studies in Society and History* 5:285–303.

Salisbury, R. F. 1956. Unilineal descent groups in the New Guinea Highlands. *Man* 56:2–7.

————. 1962. *From Stone to Steel.* Melbourne: Melbourne University Press.

————. 1965. "The Siane of the Eastern Highlands," in *Gods, Ghosts and Men in Melanesia.* Edited by P. Lawrence and M. Meggitt, pp. 50–77. Melbourne: Melbourne University Press.

————. 1966. "Politics and shell-money finance in New Britain," in *Political Anthropology.* Edited by M. Swartz, V. Turner, and A. Tuden, pp. 113–128. Chicago: Aldine.

Sapir, E. 1949. *Selected Writings of Edward Sapir in Language, Culture and Personality.* Edited by D. G. Mandelbaum. Berkeley: University of California Press.

Sartre, J.-P. 1956 (1943). *Being and Nothingness: An Essay on Phenomenological Ontology.* Translated by H. E. Barnes. New York: Philosophical Library.

Schieffelin. E. L. 1976. *The Sorrow of the Lonely and the Burning of the Dancers.* New York: St. Martin's.

————. 1977. "The unseen influence: Tranced mediums as historical innovators," in Madness, Possession and Shamanism in New Guinea. Edited by B. Juillerat, pp. 169–178. *Journal de la Société des Océanistes* 33(Special edition).

Schneider, D. 1968. *American Kinship: A Cultural Account.* Englewood Cliffs, N.J.: Prentice-Hall.

Schwartz, T. 1973. Cult and context: The paranoid ethos in Melanesia. *Ethos* 1:153–174.

————. 1978. "Where is the culture? Personality as the distributive locus of culture," in *The Making of Psychological Anthropology.* Edited by G. D. Spindler, pp. 419–441. Berkeley: University of California.

Schwimmer, E. Editor. 1977. "Introduction: F. E. Williams as ancestor and rain-maker," in *The Vailala Madness and Other Essays.* By F. E. Williams, pp. 11–47. Honolulu: University Press of Hawaii.

Sears, R. R. 1965. "Development of gender role," in *Sex and Behavior*. Edited by F. A. Beach, pp. 133–163. New York: Wiley.

Sears, R. R., E. E. Maccoby, and H. Levin. 1957. *Patterns of Child Rearing*. Evanston, Ill.: Row, Peterson.

Shannon, C. E., and W. Weaver. 1949. *The Mathematical Theory of Communication*. Urbana: University of Illinois Press.

Shapiro, J. 1979. "Cross-cultural perspectives on sexual differentiation," in *Human Sexuality: A Comparative and Developmental Perspective*. Edited by H. A. Katchadourian, pp. 269–308. Berkeley: University of California Press.

Simmel, G. 1950. *The Sociology of Georg Simmel*. Edited by K. Wolff. Glencoe, Ill.: Free Press.

Simpson, C. 1953. *Adam with Arrows*. Sydney: Angus & Robertson.

Sinclair, J. P. 1966. *Behind the Ranges*. Melbourne: Melbourne University Press.

Skorupski, J. 1976. *Symbol and Theory*. Cambridge: Cambridge University Press.

Smith, W. R. 1927 (1889). *The Religion of the Semites*. Third edition. New York: Appleton.

Sontag, S. 1966. *Against Interpretation*. New York: Farrar, Straus & Giroux.

Sperber, D. 1975. *Rethinking Symbolism*. Translated by A. L. Morton. Cambridge: Cambridge University Press.

Spiro, M. E. 1964. "Religion and the irrational," in *Symposium on New Approaches to the Study of Religion*. Edited by J. Helm, pp. 102–115. Seattle: American Ethnological Society and University of Washington Press.

————. 1965. "Religious systems as culturally constituted defense mechanisms," in *Context and Meaning in Cultural Anthropology*. Edited by M. E. Spiro, pp. 100–115. New York: Free Press.

————. 1966. "Religion: Problems of definition and explanation," in *Anthropological Approaches to the Study of Religion*. Edited by M. Banton, pp. 85–126. London: Tavistock Publications.

————. 1968a. *Burmese Supernaturalism*. Englewood Cliffs, N.J.: Prentice-Hall.

————. 1968b. "Culture and personality," in *International Encyclopedia of the Social Sciences*. Edited by D. Sills, vol. 3, pp. 558–563. New York: Macmillan.

————. 1969. "Discussion," in *Forms of Symbolic Action*. Edited by R. F. Spencer, pp. 208–214. Seattle: University of Washington Press.

————. 1979. Whatever happened to the id? *American Anthropologist* 81:5–13.

Stephens, W. N. 1962. *The Oedipus Complex: Cross-Cultural Evidence*. New York: Free Press.

Stocking, G. 1968. *Race, Culture, and Evolution: Essays in the History of Anthropology*. New York: Free Press.

Stoller, R. J. 1968. *Sex and Gender*. Vol. 1. *On the Development of Masculinity and Femininity*. New York: Science House.

————. 1973. *Splitting: A Case of Female Masculinity*. New York: Quadrangle.

————. 1975. *Sex and Gender*. Vol. 2. *The Transsexual Experiment*. New York: Jason Aronson.

————. 1976. Sexual excitement. *Archives of General Psychiatry* 33:899–909.

————. 1977. *Perversion: The Erotic Form of Hatred*. London: Quartet Books.

————. 1979. *Sexual Excitement: Dynamics of Erotic Life*. New York: Pantheon.

Strathern, A. J. 1969. Descent and alliance in the New Guinea Highlands: Some problems of comparison. *Proceedings of the Royal Anthropological Institute of Great Britain and Northern Ireland for 1968*, pp. 37–52.

———. 1970. Male initiation in the New Guinea Highland societies. *Ethnology* 9:373–379.

———. 1971. *The Rope of Moku.* Cambridge: Cambridge University Press.

———. 1972. *One Father, One Blood.* Canberra: A.N.U. Press.

Strathern, A. J., and M. Strathern. 1968. "Marsupials and magic: A study of spell symbolism among the Mbowamb," in *Dialectic in Practical Religion.* Edited by E. R. Leach, pp. 179–207. Cambridge: Cambridge University Press.

Strathern, M. 1972a. *Official and Unofficial Courts.* New Guinea Research Bulletin No. 48. Canberra: A.N.U. Press.

———. 1972b. *Women in Between.* London: Seminar Press.

———. 1978. "The achievement of sex: Paradoxes in Hagen gender-thinking," in *The Yearbook of Symbolic Anthropology I.* Edited by E. G. Schwimmer, pp. 171–202. London: C. Hurst.

Tambiah, S. J. 1973. "Form and meaning of magical acts: A point of view," in *Modes of Thought.* Edited by R. Horton and R. Finnegan, pp. 230–248. London: Faber & Faber.

Tart, C. T. 1975. *States of Consciousness.* New York: Dutton.

Taylor, M. 1971. Interpretation and the sciences of man. *Review of Metaphysics* 25:1–51.

Tiger, L. 1970. *Men in Groups.* New York: Vintage Books.

Turner, V. 1957. *Schism and Continuity in an African Society.* Manchester: Manchester University Press.

———. 1962. *Chihamba: The White Spirit.* Rhodes-Livingston Paper No. 33. Manchester: Manchester University Press.

———. 1964. "Symbols in Ndembu ritual," in *Closed Systems and Open Minds: The Limits of Naivety in Social Anthropology.* Edited by M. Gluckman, pp. 20–51. Chicago: Aldine.

———. 1967. *The Forest of Symbols.* Ithaca: Cornell University Press.

———. 1968a. *The Drums of Affliction.* Oxford: Clarendon Press.

———. 1968b. "Myth and symbol," in *International Encyclopedia of the Social Sciences.* Edited by D. Sills, vol. 10, pp. 576–582. New York: Macmillan.

———. 1975. "Symbolic studies," in *Annual Review of Anthropology.* Edited by B. J. Siegel, pp. 145–161. Palo Alto: Annual Reviews.

———. 1978. "Encounter with Freud: The making of a comparative symbologist," in *The Making of Psychological Anthropology.* Edited by G. D. Spindler, pp. 558–583. Berkeley: University of California Press.

Tuzin, D. F. 1972. Yam symbolism in the Sepik: An interpretive account. *Southwestern Journal of Anthropology* 28:230–254.

———. 1975. The breath of a ghost: Dreams and the fear of the dead. *Ethos* 3:555–578.

———. 1976. *The Ilahita Arapesh: Dimensions of Duality.* Berkeley: University of California Press.

———. 1977. Reflections of being in Arapesh water symbolism. *Ethos* 5:195–223.

———. 1980. *The Voice of the Tambaran: Truth and Illusion in Ilahita Arapesh Religion.* Berkeley: University of California Press.

Tyler, S. A. 1978. *The Said and the Unsaid: Mind, Meaning, and Culture.* New York: Academic.

Tylor, E. B. 1873. *Primitive Culture: Researches into the Development of Mythology, Philosophy, Religion, Language, Art, and Custom.* Second edition. 2 volumes. London: John Murray.

Van Baal, J. 1966. *Dema.* The Hague: Martinus Nijoff.

Van Gennep, A. 1960 (1909). *The Rites of Passage.* Translated by M. K. Vizedom and G. L. Gaffee. Chicago: University of Chicago Press.

Vanggaard, T. 1972. *Phallos.* New York: International Universities Press.

Waddell, E. 1972. *The Mound Builders.* Seattle: University of Washington Press.

Wagner, R. 1967. *The Curse of Souw: Principles of Daribi Clan Definition and Alliance.* Chicago: University of Chicago Press.

———. 1972. *Habu: The Innovation of Meaning in Daribi Religion.* Chicago: University of Chicago Press.

———. 1975. *The Invention of Culture.* Englewood Cliffs, N.J.: Prentice-Hall.

———. 1978. *Lethal Speech: Daribi Myth as Symbolic Obviation.* Ithaca: Cornell University Press.

Wallace, A. 1969. *Culture and Personality.* Second edition. New York: Random House.

Watson, J. B. 1964. "Anthropology in the New Guinea Highlands," in *New Guinea: The Central Highlands.* Edited by J. B. Watson, pp. 1–19. *American Anthropologist* 66(Part 2).

———. 1967. Horticultural traditions of the Eastern New Guinea Highlands. *Oceania* 38:81–98.

———. 1970. Society as organized flow: The Tairora case. *Soutwestern Journal of Anthropology* 26:107–124.

———. 1973. "Tairora: The politics of despotism in a small society," in *Politics in New Guinea.* Edited by R. M. Berndt and P. Lawrence, pp. 224–275. Seattle: University of Washington Press.

———. 1977. Pigs, fodder, and the Jones effect in postipomoean New Guinea. *Ethnology* 26:57–70.

Whiting, B. 1965. Sex identity conflict and physical violence: A comparative study. *American Anthropologist* 67(Part 2)123–140.

———. 1979. "Identity, gender role, and sexual behavior," in *Human Sexuality: A Comparative and Developmental Perspective.* Edited by H. A. Katchadourian, pp. 320–331. Berkeley: University of California Press.

Whiting, J. W. M. 1941. *Becoming a Kwoma: Teaching and Learning in a New Guinea Tribe.* New Haven: Yale University Press.

———. 1961. "Socialization process and personality," in *Psychological Anthropology: Approaches to Culture and Personality.* Edited by F. L. K. Hsu, pp. 355–399. Homewood, Ill.: Dorsey.

Whiting, J. W. M., and B. B. Whiting. 1975. Aloofness and intimacy of husbands and wives: A cross-cultural study. *Ethos* 3:183–207.

Whiting, J. W. M., R. Kluckhohn, and A. Anthony. 1958. "The function of male initiation ceremonies at puberty," in *Readings in Social Psychology.* Edited by E. E. Maccoby, T. M. Newcomb, and E. L. Hartley, pp. 359–370. New York: Holt.

Williams, F. E. 1936a. *Bull Roarers of the Papuan Gulf.* (Territory of Papua, Anthropology Report No. 17.) Port Moresby: Walter A. Bock.

———. 1936b. *Papuans of the Trans-Fly.* Oxford: Clarendon Press.

Wilson, M. 1957. *Rituals of Kinship among The Nyakyusa.* London: Oxford University Press.

Young, F. W. 1965. *Initiation Ceremonies: A Cross-Cultural Study of Status Dramatization.* Indianapolis: Bobbs-Merrill.

Young, M. W. 1971. *Fighting with Food.* Canberra: A.N.U. Press.

———. 1977. Bursting with laughter: Obscenity, values, and sexual control in a Massim society. *Canberra Anthropology* 1:75–87.

Name Index

Subject Index

Adultery, 167, 207n.
  boys lectured on, 104
Adulthood *(aatmwunu)* concept, 54, 200
Affects:
  and communication, 298–299
  unacceptable, 300
Affines, terminology for, 35
Age distinctions between spouses, 175
Age-mates:
  cassowaries and women, 145, 146
  in myth, 256, 270–272
  trees as, 103, 105, 227, 240
Akovanyu (purificatory ceremony), 105, 114–116,
    240, 270
Amazon myth, 294, 352–353
Animals *(see* Cassowaries; Possum; *Yaamwi)*
Anthropology:
  Durkheimian model for, 4–7, 327
  history of, 5–6, 296
  methodology, 4, 6–11, 58, 67–68, 127–129,
    336–337
  psychoanalysis versus, 8–9
  theories about magical beliefs, 155, 156
  (See also Symbolism, anthropological concept of)
Anus of cassowary, 146, 147, 151
  and birth, 151, 154–155
Armbands, pandanus-frond, 105, 112–113
Attachment behavior, Bowlby's theory of, 309–
    310

Bachelor fellateds, 56, 233n., 234, 236, 242
  erotic outlet for, 271, 275n., 282, 284, 287–
    288, 319
  semen "replacement" by, 111, 251
Bachelor(s):
  author as, 338–339
  impersonating behavior of, 284n.
  permanent, 176n.
  as ritual assistants, 56, 242
  (See also Moondi)

Barren woman *(kwoliku)*, 170, 193–194
Baruya (tribe), 23, 48, 49
Behavioral approach:
  in anthropology, 6, 12, 156
  to homosexual development, 8
Belief systems:
  and cultural knowledge, 64
  definition of, 14
"Big men":
  concept of, 46
  souls of, beliefs about, 86
Birds, 90–94
  feathers, 92–94, 125, 126, 147–149
  (See also Cassowaries)
Birth, 197–200, 206
  anal, 151, 154–155
  ceremony, 41, 54, 201, 258n., 293n.
  in myth, 257, 272, 273, 285
Birth house, 197
  in initiation ceremony, 231–232
Blood:
  dreams of, 170
  as life-supporting substance, 101, 191–
    192
  maturation, role in, 226
  menstrual, 206, 246–248
    (See also Menstruation: Pollution, female;
    Tingu)
  procreative function, 192, 195–196, 206,
    217–218
  "tree blood," 100, 101, 201
  (See also Cane-swallowing; Nose-bleeding)
Body painting *(see* Painting, body)
Boongu (pool):
  in myth, 349, 353
  in pandanus, 117
  in women, 169–171, 191, 192
Breast-feeding, 209, 213
  homosexual fellatio as, 234–235
  men's avoidance of, 210–211
Breast milk *(see* Mother's milk)